Terror, Culture, Politics

TERROR, CULTURE, POLITICS
is Volume 1 in the series

21st Century Studies
Center for 21st Century Studies
University of Wisconsin–Milwaukee

Daniel J. Sherman
General Editor

DANIEL J. SHERMAN AND
TERRY NARDIN, EDITORS

Terror, Culture, Politics

RETHINKING 9/11

INDIANA UNIVERSITY PRESS

Bloomington and Indianapolis

This book is a publication of

Indiana University Press
601 North Morton Street
Bloomington, IN 47404-3797 USA

http://iupress.indiana.edu

Telephone orders   800-842-6796
Fax orders   812-855-7931
Orders by e-mail   iuporder@indiana.edu

The paper used in this publication meets the minimum requirements of American National Standard for Information Sciences—Permanence of Paper for Printed Library Materials, ANSI Z39.48-1984.

Manufactured in the United States of America

Library of Congress Cataloging-in-Publication Data

Terror, culture, politics : rethinking 9/11 / Daniel J. Sherman and Terry Nardin, editors.
    p. cm. — (21st Century studies ; v. 1)
    Originated in a conference held at the Center for 21st Century Studies, University of Wisconsin-Milwaukee, Oct. 2002.
Includes bibliographical references and index.
    ISBN 0-253-34672-X (cloth : alk. paper) — ISBN 0-253-21812-8 (pbk. : alk. paper)
    1. September 11 Terrorist Attacks, 2001—Social aspects. 2. September 11 Terrorist Attacks, 2001—Psychological aspects. 3. Civil defense—United States—Management—History—21st century. 4. September 11 Terrorist Attacks, 2001—Causes. 5. United States—Civilization—1970-6. Civil rights—United States. 7. War on Terrorism, 2001—Political aspects. 8. United States—Foreign relations—2001- I. Sherman, Daniel J. II. Nardin, Terry, date III. Series.
    HV6432.7.T445 2005
    303.6'25'0973—dc22

                                                                        2005014173

1 2 3 4 5   11 10 09 08 07 06

Contents

Acknowledgments

This book originated in a conference, "9/11: Reconstructions," held at the Center for 21st Century Studies, University of Wisconsin-Milwaukee, in October 2002. We would like to thank the conference coordinator, the Center's then executive director Carol Tennessen, for her work putting the conference together, and the Center's business manager, Maria Liesegang, and 2002–2004 graduate assistants Claire Hicks and Briana Smith for all their efforts both at the conference and as we moved toward publication. We are also grateful for a grant from the Carnegie Council on Ethics and International Affairs that helped fund the conference. Organized as a series of round-tables, the conference provided a stimulating forum for reflection that marked the real starting point of this book; we appreciate the contributions of participants whose work could not be included in this volume. Thanks also to the two anonymous readers at Indiana University Press for their many helpful suggestions.

The Center's successive assistant directors/editors, William B. Turner (2002–2003) and Rutger (Ruud) van Dijk (since 2003), have served as manuscript editors for the project; without their help, the project might have taken considerably longer. We are particularly grateful to Ruud for preparing the index and for his efforts to secure photographs and permission to publish them, to standardize the manuscripts, and to keep everything straight. Graduate assistants Matthew Cook and Amity McGinnis were also very helpful in the final stages of preparing the manuscript in 2004–2005. We would also like to express our thanks to our patient and professional colleagues at Indiana University Press, notably Michael Lundell and Elisabeth Marsh. Although this volume marks the inauguration of a new series title, "21st Century Studies," the Center is now moving into its third decade of productive association with the Press, with pride and excitement.

Finally, the editors would like to express their thanks to each other: we couldn't have done it without you.

Terror, Culture, Politics

Introduction

In the weeks and months following 9/11, observers scanned the cultural landscape for signs of some fundamental shift. It seemed inconceivable that an attack as sudden, as murderous, and as apparently unprecedented as that of 9/11 could have left no trace in the cultural domain. The search, however, had only meager results. The acclaimed NBC drama *The West Wing* rushed to air a special episode, isolated from its normal story arc, in which characters debate freedom and security during a lock-down of the White House occasioned by concerns (eventually found to be unwarranted) about a terrorist attack. Regular viewers found it less than compelling. Studios delayed the release of some movies, chiefly those relating to terrorism or in some way critical of the American military or of American foreign policy—even an episode as remote as the one presented in *The Quiet American.* Purveyors of nostalgia like Restoration Hardware continued to expand their businesses, but this expansion began long before 9/11. The only trend that could be discerned across the whole culture, the so-called "death of irony," never went uncontested, and lasted barely as long as its inventors took to describe it. Within a year, the attacks were turning up as plot elements in familiar places, such as the long-running police series *Law and Order*. In 2003, after two years of self-restraint, Halloween retailers were able to report a return to horror as usual.

It is still too soon to judge whether the events of 9/11 and their aftermath will have any lasting effect on American culture, even if we understand that term in its conventional sense, as a realm of creative expression, rather than in the more general anthropological sense common in the academy. Around the second anniversary of the attacks in 2003, the Bush administration undertook a major campaign both to justify and to expand the USA Patriot Act, which conservatives as well as liberals had begun to condemn as an assault on civil liberties, notably the right to privacy. In the course of this campaign, the attorney general, John Ashcroft, noted that the act had never been used to gather information on Americans' private reading or viewing habits. But even the potential for such surveillance can have a chilling effect, just as the mere possibility of censorship can lead to a self-censorship that is even more disturbing because the contours of repression remain vague. The overall picture so far is mixed: if an American leftist as well-known and pugnacious as Noam Chomsky could achieve surprising success with an anti-American polemic equating American foreign policy with terrorism, a work of art that dared only to be ambiguous, Eric Fischl's *Tumbling Woman,* had quickly to be removed from view. Events like the 2004 release of Michael Moore's film *Fahrenheit 9/11* might signal that American culture is recovering from the repression and sentimentality of the past few years, but, as the Disney Corporation's refusal to distribute the film indicates, it would be foolish to mistake this recovery for immunity to the dynamic of terrorism and repression.

Expressive culture, in any case, has a somewhat paradoxical place in common wisdom, by which we mean, broadly speaking, the truisms that zeitgeist commentators draw on, often unthinkingly, in newspaper editorials, magazine articles, and on-line chat rooms. On the one hand, culture—or, in its more sententious usage, "the arts"—tells us about ourselves, expresses who and where we are. On the other hand, "art"—in a more general if rarely reflected upon sense—has the capacity to change us, whether through the consolations of beauty or the provocations of unfamiliar or uncomfortable truths. These two usages are not, of course, incompatible, for one of the ways art exercises its transformative capacity is by unleashing some presumptively universal creative force, thus again, though in an admittedly new way, telling people something about themselves. Certainly differences in culture—language, costume, music, or other forms of self-expression—have long seemed more bridgeable than economic, religious, or ethnic differences, though these usually have cultural dimensions if not cultural roots. But it is precisely at the intersection of these significations that American culture after 9/11 most cries out for critical scrutiny.

A chief aim of this book, then, is to explore the connections between the narrower and broader senses of culture, between the creative arts and the arts of living together, between culture as image and memory and as the ethical and political frame within which we live together. The essays in the "Image/Memory" section, although they employ different approaches, share a broad general topic, the place of 9/11 in our imaginative culture, and a common spirit of critique. The authors not only gauge the effects of 9/11 on the phenomena they consider but also examine the possibilities for a critical cultural practice today. Respecting the autonomous norms and transformative potential of the media they study, from photography to sculpture, comic books to landscape architecture, the contributors also understand them, through the structures of their production, ownership, distribution, and reception, if not in their explicit content, as having a politics. In the first instance, it is a politics of constraint and admonition, haunted by images and framed by, indeed virtually constituted as, memory.

From the memory palaces of the Greek poet Simonides to those of the Jesuit missionary Matteo Ricci, from Henri Bergson's concept of memory images to the central place of dreams in the work of Sigmund Freud, the association of memory with visual imagery has a long pedigree. But memory, whether understood in individual or socio-cultural terms, is not only a repertoire but also a set of practices: it comprises both images and methods for storing, sorting, and retrieving them. Patricia Morton's survey of the imaging of the World Trade Center both before and after 9/11 makes clear that modern societies have a wide range of images from which to choose; the process of memory retrieval is always partial and selective, moves on multiple tracks at once, and never remains fixed for long. A number of the essays in this volume look closely at this complex process, which often goes by the name of commemoration. But by associating "image" and "memory," we also call attention to the ways that the pre-existing structures of image circulation prefigure the terms in which a given society remembers its past. In the rating system of the Motion Picture Association of America, for example, explicit depictions of sex involving nudity are far more likely to be proscribed than the graphic portrayal of even extreme violence. What we see in the movies and on television provides a context and prior set of meanings within and with which we interpret events like the 9/11 attacks. It is not simply that we find images of destruction familiar; they come to us as part of a system of fixed meanings. When we see buildings destroyed, we think of movies in which foreigners are responsible, and we know that retribution will follow. In this way our cultural image bank provides a template for subsequent patterns of memory; as a society we are far more likely to remember a moment of violence that comes, as it were, precategorized than we are to attend to the ongoing brutality of, for example, domestic violence or sexual exploitation.

Without either assuming or denying that 9/11 has transformed cultural politics in any decisive or lasting way, the new terrain of self-examination it opened affords us the opportunity to ask not only where our culture is right now, but where it might be headed, what it might yet do. Whether in the form of the alternative comics that Henry Jenkins studies, the critical reading Susan Lurie both urges and practices, the unconventional urban configurations offered by Laura Kurgan and Patricia Morton, or the break with commemorative pieties that Kirk Savage and Daniel Sherman call for, the transformative power of art requires a sophisticated understanding of our existing cultural politics. To the extent that it works against the dominant discourses of those politics, moreover, critical scholarship may play some modest role in altering or subverting them and offer a different way of remembering.

A spirit of critique is also evident in the essays in the section explicitly concerned with "Ethics/Politics." We shift in these essays to culture in the broader or anthropological sense, to cultural premises reflected not only in the imaginative arts but also in laws and policies, in moral claims and public attitudes. Here we encounter what Stephen Toope identifies as a Manichean "culture of security" that emerges whenever a civil order appears to be threatened by external or internal enemies, a way of conceiving and responding to danger that itself threatens the rights and liberties—the constraints and safeguards—that constitute the civil order. Here another meaning of the word "political" comes into focus, one that has its roots in the ancient Greek idea of the *polis* as an association of equals, in contrast to the Persian model in which subjects are ruled, and in fact owned, by a despot. It is an association of citizens with one another, not of servants with their master. Only the former is truly "political" in this sense of the term, truly "civil" in the parallel Latin sense of *civitas*. By a civil order, then, we may understand one constituted by laws, within whose limits individuals pursue their own self-chosen purposes. In such an order, government respects individual freedom and basic human rights. It worries about the material and social conditions of authentic citizenship. And it treasures the rule of law, understood, at a minimum, as a constraint on the exercise of governmental power. It is this understanding of civil association that Elaine Scarry and William Scheuerman bring to bear in criticizing the claim that, in an age of speed, only a centrally coordinated response, which implies an executive and military power freed from the constraints of legislative oversight or democratic accountability, can deal with the threat of global terrorism. Like Toope, they challenge the indefinite expansion of executive power and the erosion of civil freedom it entails. Sohail Hashmi and miriam cooke reveal parallel tensions in Islamic moral and political discourse, undercutting attempts to map the struggle between civility and terrorism onto a distinction between the West and the rest. All the contributors challenge the binaries of good and evil invoked by defenders of extraordinary acts and powers, whether terrorist or antiterrorist.

Some of the ethical and political questions raised by 9/11 are immediately practical: How should we (Americans) respond to terrorism? Are the policies our government has chosen likely to be effective? Are they legally and morally defensible? Other questions go deeper: What assumptions undergird the moral and political debate about terrorism and appropriate ways of responding to it, and what conclusions emerge from examining them critically? These assumptions include the claim that with the emergence of al-Qaida the United States and liberal democracies face unprecedented threats that call for a response appropriate to the gravity of that situation. They include the identification of terrorism and counterterrorism as "war" and the consequent reliance on ideas of emergency and necessity, with their corrosive implications for moral restraint in the conduct of that war, for informed public discussion of national policy, for the rule of law both at home and in foreign relations, for political and artistic freedom.

Consider the now threadbare assertion that "9/11 changed everything." That formula, which several of our contributors interrogate, expresses the immediate shock of the attack, the destruction it wrought, and the vulnerability it exposed. The destruction of the World Trade Center brought home to many Americans the terrifying, and therefore understandably repressed, truth that we live in dark times—an expression Hannah Arendt and others had popularized in discussing an earlier and, for those who experienced it, far more appalling period of war and depression, terror and oppression. Who are the "we" over whose lives 9/11 has cast a shadow? As Toope suggests, the insecurity Americans felt in the days after the attack is a constant of everyday life in many parts of the world. To speak in these terms, then, is to confirm that our situation is not necessarily worse than that of many other people. If we abandon the suppressed premise that emerges when we ask "changed for whom?" it is clear that the claim that 9/11 changed everything expresses the belated discovery by members of one particularly privileged community that they are not invulnerable.

It seems clear, moreover, that 9/11 has in an important sense simply accentuated pre-existing anxieties in American society, as well as a long-standing tendency to blame them on poorly understood foreign enemies. The economic restructuring known, in one of its guises, as globalization has had a disproportionate effect on occupations long dominated by white, working-class males. Yet there is a market for popular novels and movies that channel white male anger and frustration away from its direct causes and toward an imaginary enemy that is "evil" because it opposes American ideals of individualism, devotion to family, patriotism, and self-sacrifice. Besides leading to a dramatic expansion of the security industry, which has offered a limited outlet to the aggrieved unemployed, 9/11 has seen only a marginal, if possibly fateful, shift in the cultural politics of anxiety. The mobilization of "Western Civilization" on behalf of those left behind by global economic restructuring has had ramifications well beyond the cultural sphere. Indeed, the fixation on a temporal identifier, 9/11, has allowed the United States unparalleled latitude in recasting fundamental spatial relationships at home and what used to be called abroad—both now in the sights of a greater American imperium. The Bush administration's new doctrine of preventive war, to take just one example, enfolds any potentially threatening country or region within the coercive jurisdiction of American power.

If we want to achieve a less parochial understanding of the events of 9/11 and of our own response to those events, we would do well to avoid the hyperbole that turns sober reflection into a quasi-theological engagement with evil. Every community has its enemies, its "evildoers," who are not just its enemies but enemies of all that is good in the world; by resisting those evildoers, a community's actual or would-be leaders claim world-historical significance. Osama bin Laden and other Islamic militants use precisely this kind of hyperbole when they claim that it is their duty to save the world and especially the Islamic world from Satanic corruption. It is just such hyperbole that George W. Bush and others who would save the world and especially the American world from Satanic terrorism echo. And because they so uncritically embrace a dichotomy between good and evil, aligned with the dichotomy between self and other, war becomes the central metaphor both for terrorists and antiterrorists. But that metaphor has some possibly crippling implications. In a war one is not dealing with an endemic problem but fighting an enemy who can be beaten and made to acknowledge its defeat. Because this enemy is bad, those who make war on it are good, no matter what they do. If the enemy is "evil," that war is a holy war not subject to the constraints of ordinary combat. Since such an enemy violates all rules to achieve its ends, we must also violate the rules, whether they are our own laws and principles or those that govern our relations with others. Far from moving us into a world in which everything is changed, then, this view of 9/11 puts us right back in an all-too-familiar world in which barbarism emerges inside the community that sees itself as defending civilization. As Patricia Morton's essay reminds us, the relationship between civilization and barbarism is best understood as a dialectic susceptible to, and constantly in need of, criticism.

If society in normal times is a civil order within whose frame people look after their own affairs, in war it becomes an enterprise that subordinates these affairs to the common task. A society at war must be organized for defense against its enemies. Citizens cannot be allowed to please themselves but are mobilized for the common effort. Private concerns must give way to an asserted public interest, individual rights to the needs of the threatened community. In this sense, then, war is the enemy of a civil order, corroding its rights and liberties from within as it is remade to serve the imperatives of defense. When those imperatives escalate to the level of national survival and the defense of civilization, the damage to civil life is correspondingly magnified.

Not surprisingly, then, both sides—terrorist and antiterrorist—rely on similar arguments when they embrace the vocabulary and logic of war. Terrorists invoke commonly recognized moral principles, interpreting them in ways that appear to justify their violence. More often than not religiously inspired, terrorism today is rationalized within a culture of violence whose basic tropes—judgment, punishment, self-sacrifice, purity, utopia—are disturbingly mimicked in the security culture that has emerged to defeat it. In the internal logic of religious violence, terrorism has symbolic significance. A terrorist act is a religious performance, a re-enactment of the cosmic war between the forces of good and evil. But so, for some, is the response to terrorism, which easily moves from the pragmatic realm of maintaining a particular civil order to the religious realm of punishing and then permanently suppressing the "evil" of terrorism. Christian activists who defend the murder of abortionists believe that such killing is justified by the moral duty, undeniably important in Christian ethics, to defend the innocent from violence. Muslim suicide bombers justify their acts as fulfilling the moral duty of *jihad*, forgetting that there are also moral constraints on *jihad*, as on the pursuit of any purpose, however noble. But the misuse of moral arguments is equally apparent on the other side, as when a war to depose Saddam Hussein is portrayed as self-defense and criticism of that war attacked as subversive. 9/11 is a pivotal event in American culture because it has given us villains on whom to focus a wide range of anxieties. In the moral narrative we have constructed, we are entitled to take revenge on those who are responsible (even if we can't see exactly how) for what has gone wrong in the world and for whatever frustrations we have encountered in our individual lives. In this frame, the crossover of the "Terminator" from movies to politics seems especially fitting.

If revenge drives terrorism and counterterrorism by exploiting their symbolic resonance, so also does the dialectic of fear and safety that Susan Lurie identifies in her exploration of the photographic inheritance of 9/11—the images that, assembled and preserved, help to define the event in our cultural memory and to mobilize the nation for war. Those images suggest that the total destruction of the World Trade Center (which, culturally speaking, overshadows the damage suffered by the Pentagon, a "military target") moved the American public from spectator to participant in the terrorist drama. That event enacted a narrative in which the terror spectacle widened to embrace its audience—a point tellingly illustrated in the video of a man sitting outdoors near a smoldering World Trade Center tower listening to a radio for news of the first attack as, in the background, a second plane appears and plows into the other tower. As the man looks up and then rushes from the frame, we grasp first his sudden awareness of vulnerability, then his actual vulnerability, and finally our own potential vulnerability as no longer safe spectators of terrorist violence.

Images like this play a part in mobilizing the nation for war, but that is not their only significance. In a poignant passage in his *History of the Peloponnesian War*, Thucydides tells how the Athenians, failing in their foolish and doomed effort to conquer Sicily, attempt to break the naval blockade that has trapped them in the harbor of Syracuse. Athenian soldiers on the shore watch the sea battle on which their survival depends and we watch them watching, their safety as spectators fragile and (as we know) temporary. With no photo to accompany them, Thucydides's words nonetheless conjure up a visual image photographic in its clarity. Yet this image is emotionally compelling not because *we* are affected by the outcome but simply because we can identify with the doomed Athenians. Thucydides did not write his history to mobilize anyone for war—on the contrary, its tragic ironies move one to pity and fear, to contemplation and not to action. Art, as art, has a significance that transcends the practical and that exceeds the limits of the economic and political structures in which it is embedded. And this conclusion in turn reinforces a political conclusion: that an authentic civil order protects ways of thinking and being that are contemplative, not merely practical.

In recent years, art's claims on society, at least in the United States, have increasingly been mediated through discourses of memory. Kirk Savage's essay focuses on the now prevalent idea that an object or site conceived, in aesthetic terms, as a place of reflection can provide solace to those who have suffered traumatic loss. Today, memorials often grow out of multi-stage competitions involving, to varying degrees, victims and their families, community members, and design professionals. Both the idea of the redeeming power of art and society's interest in official remembrance justify such elaborate and expensive processes, but at the same time, as Savage and Daniel Sherman both argue, they make commemoration particularly susceptible to political appropriation. Sherman, indeed, takes commemoration, even when cast in the therapeutic mode so prevalent today, as always already political, in the sense that any collective affirmation of shared values is political. The difficulty comes when commemorative structures and rituals claim some sort of universality, failing to recognize the partiality, the situated assumptions, and the exclusions that inevitably undergird them. Unfortunately, the post-9/11 situation in the United States, which the administration presents as a simplistic and all-encompassing "war against terror," with fronts both domestic and international, has made such recognition especially difficult.

If terrorism and counterterrorism have such diverse and complicated meanings, it is not surprising that both sides look for ways to select and simplify those meanings and to communicate their preferred interpretations to those they want to influence or by whom they want to be noticed. This is why the media are so important for both terrorists and governments fighting terrorism. Terrorism propagates its message by acts of violence, and terrorists today are able to exploit the media's, and especially television's, interest in violent spectacle. Governments cannot fight terrorism without public support, and they need the media to secure that support. In a crisis, the media are likely to follow the public in supporting government, becoming partisans in the war between terrorism and counterterrorism. And the media's interest in violent spectacle in turn supports a military response. Not only the blatantly partisan Fox News Network but that would-be guardian of journalistic integrity, *The New York Times,* are guilty here. The media thus invite and amplify violence on both sides. They are not necessarily to be faulted for this, for it is their responsibility to report important news. But when reporting spills over into entertainment, when the profits of the media industry, not the requirements of democratic politics, determine what is covered and how, or when editors trim to avoid the wrath of the powers that be, we can condemn the media for failing in their responsibility to help the public understand the issues raised by terrorism and responses to it.

Two of the contributions to this volume offer glimpses of alternative strategies through which the media can provide information and promote reflection. Both Henry Jenkins and Laura Kurgan are known professionally for their work on and in digital media, but "Captain America Sheds His Mighty Tears" and "Around Ground Zero" embrace genres long rooted in print: comic books and maps. Jenkins's study certainly found the expected instances of jingoism, xenophobia, and warmongering in post-9/11 comics, mostly those produced by mainstream corporate publishers. But in the alternative comics, which Jenkins likens to the R&D branch of the industry, both characters and plot lines challenge readers to think carefully about reflexive violence and the inclination to blame foreigners for insecurity. He discusses a particularly striking illustrative pane in a series about United Airlines Flight 93, hijacked and crashed in Pennsylvania on the morning of 9/11. What has become the standard narrative of this crash pictures the passengers rising up to thwart the hijackers. Reading or telling that story places the reader or narrator in the position of a passenger, perhaps getting up and rushing the terrorists in the front of the plane, or else watching from the (merely relative) safety of a seat. But in this pane, we get a terrorist's-eye view of angry passengers running toward him. The artist seeks not to validate the terrorist's position but to imagine it—surely a necessary step toward understanding and then dealing with terrorism. We have seen where demonizing the people who are terrorists and where the complicated situations and motives that generate terrorism can lead us—we have only to think of the economic, human, and diplomatic costs of the war in Iraq, or the moral situation of countries divided by religious or ethnic hatred. Of course the artists who create these comics have a constituency whose basic sympathy they can take for granted. But alternative comics may nonetheless offer a model for those dissatisfied with mainstream media.

Laura Kurgan's effort to provide basic information in the aftermath of 9/11 was, in contrast, directed not at a familiar constituency but at the quintessential unknowns of contemporary society: tourists. Her map of Ground Zero, produced by a small group of students and designers without any assistance from public agencies, seeks simply to orient people whose presence at the site many at first regarded as at best an unavoidable nuisance, at worst something like sacrilege. Although careful not to equate seeing with understanding, Kurgan wanted to facilitate visits to the site as a way of reintegrating it into a damaged but recovering, and thus ever-changing, city. The *polis,* in her work, can only exist as a combination of real and imagined spaces, activated by ordinary people. The information "Around Ground Zero" provides visitors is basic, but without it, Kurgan argues, deeper understanding is impossible. In a similar way her piece "Four Days Later," based on satellite imagery freely available to the public, presents the digital realm as a possible source of more complex combinations of art, politics, and individual meanings. In this work, Kurgan uses a satellite photo of Manhattan in which a plume of smoke rising miles above the World Trade Center site is all too clearly visible. The image is the size of a living-room rug and is displayed on the floor so that you can walk on it and peer down, in a satellite's-eye view, on the destruction below—which, of course, from this altitude you can hardly see. Like the comic book hijacker's-eye view of insurgent passengers, this image shifts the frame that art always puts around experience, provoking us to see that experience in a new way. This is not political art in the sense that it has a specific message to convey, like conventional images of evil terrorists or brave firemen. Instead, it invites contemplation. It invites *thought,* and when we think, we do not necessarily go where the artist might have us go. Less an artistic "response" to 9/11 than an engagement, both practical and critical, with it, Kurgan's two pieces occupy precisely the intersection between the two senses of culture, as self-expression and as social glue, that this book seeks to explore.

Central to the public understanding of terrorism and responses to terrorism that the media help to shape is its recognition, or rejection, of two propositions. First, terrorist violence, by any group for any end, however glamorous or warranted it may seem, involves murdering some to influence others. It deliberately targets ordinary people, going about their everyday lives, as an end in itself or as a means to an end. Such people are "innocent" because they are bystanders, noncombatants, not engaged in harming anyone, and to harm them is criminal, unless that harm is accidental and unavoidable. But for terrorists, such harm is intentional; it sends the message that no one is safe. Terrorists, and also governments engaged in counterterrorism, sometimes rationalize the deaths of ordinary citizens by implying that those who died were not innocent, not bystanders, not noncombatants. But to make this claim is to acknowledge the convention that war occurs between identifiable combatants, and this obscures what is distinctive of terrorism: that it is violence aimed at some to frighten others. This is why when governments in war attack civilians on purpose we call it "terror bombing," and it is why the system of nuclear deterrence between the United States and the Soviet Union during the Cold War was called "the balance of terror." Terrorism, in short, is by its very nature unjust. It offends against fundamental moral distinctions and against a civil order based on human rights.

Second, the terrorists win if we fight terrorism with torture, assassination, bombing, and humiliation. Terrorism violates that civil order, but so does the unthinking impulse to fight back by suspending laws, procedures, and moral constraints that appear as obstacles to suppressing terrorism but also protect the innocent. That response, too, violates the rights and liberties that constitute the civil order. That order is threatened, then, not only by terrorism but also by the way its custodians respond to terrorism, unless that response is carefully deliberated and carried out in a way that recognizes the fragility of civil order. As William Scheuerman observes, the physical metaphor of "the body politic" is often invoked to rationalize an immediate and physical—military—response to perceived threats. But the metaphor has other uses. Here, we may say that the body politic, like the human body, can repair itself when it has been damaged. It can even repair self-inflicted abuse. But repair is not automatic, recovery not guaranteed.

Elaine Scarry, aware of this fragility, asks how we can fight terrorism while "operating in a civil frame." In a piece that has already become a classic of post-9/11 writing, and which we reprint as such, Scarry identifies two ways of responding to the 9/11 attacks, one directed by government, the other distributed among citizens, and she suggests that the country can be defended in ways that are decentralized or democratic and at the same time consistent with our Constitution and laws. But as this way of stating the issue makes clear, democracy and law are not necessarily compatible. Citizen activism, especially if it is spontaneous and unconstrained by normal procedures, can easily violate the civil liberties those procedures are intended to protect. Authentic democracy presupposes a body of law that defines the community whose members are to make collective decisions and on whom these decisions are binding. It presupposes a defined membership, a way of distinguishing citizens from noncitizens and of identifying those who may participate, directly or indirectly, in making the laws by which the community is governed. Democracy without law means deliberation without a civil framework of rules to guide that deliberation or be altered by it. For a full and probing discussion of the relationship between democracy and law in the context of responses to 9/11, the reader need only turn to the essays by William Scheuerman and Stephen Toope.

Scarry is concerned with citizen participation in defense decision making from the standpoint not only of law and rights but also of combating terrorism, and she rightly challenges the presumption that centralized governmental action is necessarily more effective. She is not the first to consider citizen action as an alternative way of dealing with defense. A few strategists, for example, argued during the Cold War for nonviolent civilian resistance in case of a Soviet invasion of Western Europe, seeking to apply the lessons of Gandhi's movement to the nuclear age. Scarry echoes the pacifist observation that people are inclined to presume the effectiveness of military force when in fact it often fails to achieve its goals. One might say that force must fail at least half the time, for matching every military victory is a military defeat on the other side. "At least" because this ignores the frequent catastrophes in which each side punishes the other without achieving its own aims, situations in which war ceases to be an instrument and takes on a life of its own, humbling and destroying those who thought they could control it. But Scarry is not a pacifist. The particular citizen action she investigates is a collective act of violence against hijackers designed to thwart their terrorist mission even at the cost of death. Hers is not a model of nonviolent resistance or of negotiation or dialogue; it does not challenge the premise that war is sometimes necessary to defend a nation. Instead, it challenges the premise that war is best left to the executive branch on grounds of either principle or expediency. Her essay on *The 9/11 Commission Report*, written especially for this volume, provides additional and compelling evidence of how our national security apparatus failed and will surely fail again in future crises. But citizens, too, are responsible insofar as they abdicate from politics. Scarry's model of engaged citizenship challenges what Scheuerman identifies as an atavistic yearning for a king-like leader to assuage the anxieties of a threatened community.

Monarchy stands for many things, but those things have to do with unity, and unity often means the suppression of difference. But it doesn't have to mean that. Diversity can flourish within a unified framework of laws carefully designed and maintained to preserve it. Call it civil diversity. Terrorism, unfortunately, drives society toward a different kind of unity. When *jihad* as a struggle for moral perfection becomes an armed *jihad* to realize that perfection through war, when that war becomes a war against an entire society with the suicide bomber as its emblem, when dealing with terrorism becomes a war on terrorists employing its own extreme expedients, there is little room for disagreement, for difference, for individuality. When a society is at war, its various parts—its popular arts and memorial practices, its moral justifications and legal codes, its journalistic standards and standards of administrative accountability—are pressed together in a new, factitious, unity shaped to the perceived demands of the struggle and imposed in part to quell ordinary political debate. Whether we focus on terrorism or counterterrorism, we see the same narrowing of imaginative and ethical possibilities, the same repression of cultural and political differences, the same fear and hatred of individuality.

Fortunately, some people always go their own way, escaping the oppressive weight of a normative social consensus and challenging the new acknowledged truths. Fortunately, too, these thoughtful people often disagree with one another. Our aim in this volume is to capture some of this thoughtful diversity in rethinking the cultural and political significance of 9/11. The differences among our contributors, which in any case are more a matter of emphasis and method than of substance, are part of the book's strength, for they invite the reader to join an ongoing conversation from different disciplines about a subject that defies neat conclusions and disciplinary boundaries. In conversation, as in art and politics, alternative viewpoints challenge but do not destroy one another. Terrorists are fanatics, convinced that their beliefs negate all others. One of the marks of a civilized response to terrorism is its refusal to share that conviction.

PART 1   *Image/Memory*

1 "Document of Civilization and Document of Barbarism": The World Trade Center Near and Far

Patricia A. Morton

In an early note for his Arcades Project, Walter Benjamin designated architecture as "the most important witness of the latent 'mythology'" of historical progress.[1] Part of architecture's importance as historical material to Benjamin consisted in its static temporal status, since he posited a historical method of "blasting" a work out of the apparent continuity of history.[2] According to Benjamin, architecture makes visible the transience of "the new" and the illusoriness of progress in commodity culture by physically embodying outmoded styles and functions beyond their moment of fashion. Precisely because of the lag between the generation of new modes of consumption and the production of architectural forms, architecture serves as a gauge for the "progress" of fashion under capitalism. The intractable nature of architecture's physicality was the measure of its value to Benjamin's struggle against the myth of progress. Architectural artifacts, rather than the intentions of architects, were his "witnesses." The World Trade Center, however, no longer stands as a physical witness to postwar culture, having been obliterated in the name of resistance to American domination.

Buildings and cities have long been destroyed in the guise of saving civilization from the power of the barbarians who constructed them. These demolitions reverberate with the horror Benjamin recounted in the "Theses on the Philosophy of History": "There is no document of civilization which is not at the same time a document of barbarism."[3] Benjamin's statement is complemented by the current discourse on architecture as a means of repression and domination. Benjamin encapsulated this discourse in his "Theses" when he evoked the "triumphal procession" of rulers who display their spoils, the "cultural treasures" of the vanquished.[4] If, for Benjamin, architecture serves as a witness to the mythology of progress, it also provides a means for control, discipline, and the expression of power. Michel Foucault's extrapolation of the Panopticon as a modern system of discipline, the Venice School of Marxist ideological architecture criticism, and certain feminist theories of architecture, for example, tend to treat architecture as a weapon for representing and enforcing power.[5]

Georges Bataille, the French philosopher and writer, presented a radical version of this view when he defined architecture as monumental productions that "now truly dominate the whole earth, grouping the servile multitudes under their shadow, imposing admiration and wonder, order and constraint."[6] For Bataille, architecture is inextricable from authority and official culture: "it is in the form of cathedrals and palaces that Church and State speak to and impose silence upon the crowds. . . . Indeed monuments obviously inspire good social behavior and often even genuine fear." The spectacular architecture of monuments operates as the representation and repressive arm of authority and, according to Bataille, it provokes popular hostility and attacks on monuments that are "veritable masters," such as the Bastille, destroyed during the 1789 French Revolution.[7]

In recent history, individual buildings as well as entire cities have been attacked and destroyed. Civil wars destroyed the city of Beirut (1975–1992), the Mostar Bridge in the former Yugoslavia (1993), and the city of Cuito, Angola (1993–94), and terrorist attacks destroyed the Babri Mosque in Ayodhya, India (1992), the Alfred P. Murrah building in Oklahoma City (1995), and the city center of Manchester, UK (1996).[8] Why did the World Trade Center join this list? Why were buildings of such banality the target of two terrorist attacks when they seemed to have so little potential for symbolic weight compared with the Mostar Bridge or Babri Mosque (fig. 1.1)? The Trade Center had more in common with the Murrah Building. Each was an undistinguished example of late-Modernist design, a style that has accumulated associations with the American political and economic system despite its international range.[9] While the skyscraper has become an ubiquitous element of globalizing culture and a symbol of advanced economic development, few tall buildings have achieved such iconic status as the World Trade Center.[10] Over its lifespan, the Center metamorphosed from yet another tall corporate skyscraper (such as the Sears Tower in Chicago) into an icon worthy of destruction.

The World Trade Center, therefore, illustrates well Benjamin's dialectic between civilization and barbarism.[11] The compound meanings, readings, and signification of the World Trade Center have dissipated in favor of a unified expression of horror at its loss. Yet the ambivalence with which the Trade Center was regarded during its history can perhaps be recovered by using Benjamin's schema, examining it as a document of both civilization and barbarism and recording some of the voices that have interpreted its construction and destruction. This reading will be largely American, with a few documents from other parts of the world. Until 9/11, we might have labeled that perspective unambiguously "victorious," in Benjamin's terms, but the attacks have called into question our assumption that we can distinguish easily between victor and vanquished.

Benjamin provides a template for organizing these voices in his description of the play between near and far views of a building, landscape, or city:

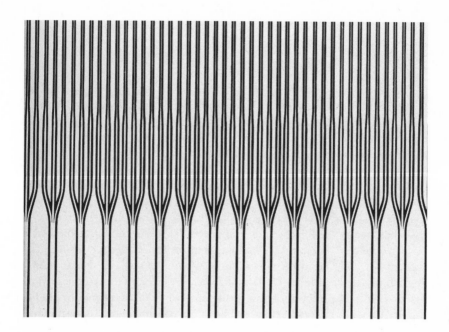

Figure 1.1. Flyleaf of Minoru Yamasaki, *A Life in Architecture* (New York: Weather-hill, 1979).
By permission of Yamasaki Associates, Inc.

> What makes the very first glimpse of a village, a town, in the landscape so incomparable and irretrievable is the rigorous connection between foreground and distance. Habit has not yet done its work. As soon as we find our bearings, the landscape vanishes at a stroke like the facade of a house as we enter it. . . . Once we begin to find our way about, that earliest picture can never be restored.[12]

The distant view is imbued with mystery and allure, whereas the close-up obliterates the surrounding landscape and the individual building alike. Habit takes the distinct object out of consciousness and substitutes distraction instead. As Benjamin pointed out in "The Work of Art in the Age of Mechanical Reproduction," architecture is perceived through use and habit rather than contemplation.[13] Habit eliminates the distancing of "aura," a quality that Benjamin allied with the traditional, unique work of art. By means of habit and familiarity, the World Trade Center was absorbed into lower Manhattan despite its colossal size and disjunction from neighboring buildings. Seen up close, out of habit, the towers virtually disappeared from view, leaving their raised platform as primary presence at ground level. Manhattan's dense urban fabric obscured a middle view and reinforced the dichotomy of perspective between close-up and long shot. From afar, the Trade Center represented the most laudable or the most despicable qualities of American culture and economy, depending on the ideological position of the viewer. It was this view from afar that made icons out of the Twin Towers, but it was the near view that made them integral components of New York.

Near

The Trade Center was simultaneously the landmark anchoring the southern edge of Manhattan's skyline and a devastating instrument of real estate manipulation wielded by New York's power elite; it was workplace for thousands of "bridge and tunnel people" who commuted there daily and a despised symbol of American economic and cultural imperialism. New Yorkers were famously ambivalent about the Trade Center, and architecture critics tended to be brutal when condemning its fussy details and insipid conception. *New York Times* critic Ada Louise Huxtable, enthusiastic when Yamasaki's Trade Center design was first publicized in 1964, became critical of its "dainty" details and muted historical references. "These are big buildings but they are not great architecture. The grill-like metal façade stripes are curiously without scale. . . . The Port Authority has built the ultimate Disneyland fairytale blockbuster. It is General Motors Gothic."[14] The disparity between the massive, undifferentiated blocks as seen from afar and the ornamental detailing at its base produced this dismissive attitude.

Eric Darton began his portrait of the World Trade Center with a conceptual exercise in making the Towers disappear from sight, a trick he noted did not require one to be a "terrorist, a demolition expert, or a photo retoucher." He directed the reader to go to the Plaza level, stand very close to a beveled corner on either the north or south tower, and look straight up. The tower, "four million square feet of office space stacked a quarter mile into New York's skyline," would disappear into a thin gray line. "With a subtle shift in perspective, you have caused one of the most massive buildings of the modern era to perform its built-in vanishing act."[15] This uncanny anticipation of the Center's disappearance can be contextualized further within its everyday dissolution into lower Manhattan's urban fabric.

Up close, the World Trade Center was difficult to perceive clearly. At the ground, the tallness and grayness of the Towers reduced their overpowering scale to an indistinct background; they were too high to be seen as a whole amidst the congestion of lower Manhattan skyscrapers. When approached from the north or east, the Towers were lost to view as other, lesser towers blocked the view. At closest proximity, the podium containing a shopping mall and transportation hub was visible, but without a strong representational presence. The Gothic details and narrow rhythm of the steel bays were legible, yet they were not the right scale (too small and uniform) to create a monumental aura at street level. For the people who worked there daily, the Towers had little direct presence, since many entered from below ground and traveled to upper floors by elevator. They experienced the World Trade Center as a series of dislocated spaces detached from the whole by habit (fig. 1.2). Jane Ellen Rubin, who worked

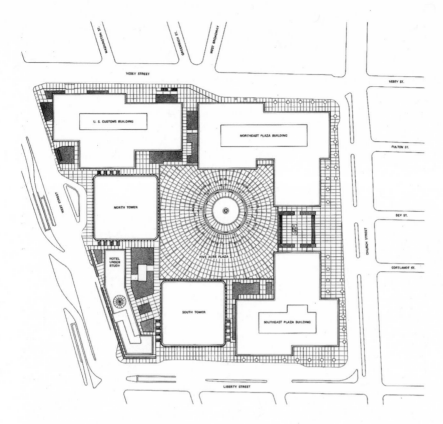

Figure 1.2. Site plan of the World Trade Center, Minoru Yamasaki, *A Life in Architecture* (New York: Weatherhill, 1979), 119.
By permission of Yamasaki Associates, Inc.

on the seventy-second floor of Two World Trade Center for the New York State Department of Labor, described the Trade Center of her experience:

> There were jazz concerts at lunchtime on the plaza and after-work drinks at Windows On The World, because it was someone's birthday, or just because. If we wanted to stay "in" we could eat lunch at the State Employees cafeteria on the 43rd floor or the Custom House cafeteria in Building 5 or the Restaurant on the 44th floor in Building One. Or go out to Popeye's Chicken out the "back door" or walk a few blocks to Rosie O'Grady's or the Japanese dumpling place. It was our place of work and it was our playground.[16]

The subway and PATH station, the Plaza, the mall, the offices, Windows on the World restaurant, and the observation deck each had a different clientele; together they constructed disparate World Trade Centers.

Architect Minoru Yamasaki focused less on the World Trade Center's quotidian life and more on the utopian role of its architecture. From the nearness of his experience creating the Center, Yamasaki projected a global vision:

> As I learned to understand the purpose of the project, it became clear that the Trade Center, with its location facing the entry to New York harbor, could symbolize the importance of world trade to this country and its major metropolis and become a physical expression of the universal effort of men to seek and achieve world peace.[17]

Yamasaki's now infamous statement has been eulogized and ridiculed in equal measure, but it is almost always taken literally. In an essay written in response to 9/11, architectural theorist Mark Wigley asks the following questions: "Did we really think that the emergent forces of globalization were so innocent, and that architecture could embody that innocence? Did we really think that buildings could be in any way neutral? Or did we just agree to pretend?"[18] I doubt that Yamasaki was so naïve as to believe that buildings can be neutral or that architecture is not implicated in regimes of power. In fact, Yamasaki's autobiography, *A Life in Architecture*, and interviews he gave about the World Trade Center indicate otherwise: that he understood architecture's capacity to represent power and ideology and, as a humanist, sought the means to ameliorate its brutal tendencies. Another interview with Yamasaki demonstrates more precisely how he came to equate world trade and peace and to rely on architecture to represent their equivalence. "World trade means world peace and consequently the World Trade Center buildings in New York . . . had a bigger purpose than just to provide room for tenants. The World Trade Center is a living symbol of man's dedication to world peace . . . beyond the compelling need to make this a monument to world peace, the World Trade Center should, because of its importance, become a representation of man's belief in humanity, his need for individual dignity, his beliefs in the cooperation of men, and through cooperation, his ability to find greatness."[19] The conflation of world trade and world peace, and the faith that commerce could bring people together, is the central fallacy of Yamasaki's premise, but this was a common misconception of American Cold War ideology.[20]

The Twin Towers transmuted according to the observer's viewpoint and often became more beautiful or more hideous retrospectively. This chameleon quality was more pronounced in reporting immediately after 9/11. A fractured if earnest story by *National Geographic* reporter Bijal Trivedi identified both the World Trade Center and the Pentagon as "revered symbols around which the psyche of the country is tightly wrapped." The Trade Center was targeted by terrorists because the "sophisticated structure of the slender, crystalline twin towers made them especially inviting symbols of America's achievement—glass and steel pillars reaching into the clouds, their ethereal surfaces reflecting the changing moods of New York City. The World Trade Center represented the elite and the powerful; its tenants were household names. It was the financial hub of the country, and even, some would argue, the world."[21] In this story,

Figure 1.3. View of the tow-
ers from lower Manhattan,
Balthazar Korab.
Courtesy of Balthazar Korab
Ltd. Photography.

Trivedi draws on several associations. He links monumental architecture with power, light, high towers with a heavenly or spiritual aspiration, as in medieval religious architecture in the West, where the Gothic cathedral evokes Heavenly Jerusalem.

For Marshall Berman, New York resident and passionate advocate of metro-politan culture, the World Trade Center was a brutal and brutalizing complex without redeeming qualities that destroyed lower Manhattan, and it could not and should not be loved. "They were the most hated buildings in town. They were brutal and overbearing . . . expressions of an urbanism that disdained the city and its people. They loomed over Downtown and blotted out the sky."[22] (fig. 1.3) The Twin Towers were a tool of domination over ordinary New Yorkers, wielded by real estate and financial elites. Berman articulates the New Yorker's ambivalence toward the Towers; they were interlopers in Manhattan's fabric, an unwelcome reminder of finance capital's supremacy in the New York economy, and a bastion of state bureaucracy. David Harvey sees the Twin Towers as mark-ers in glass and steel of the "moment of transition from Fordism to flexible ac-cumulation led by financialization of everything."[23] Poet Meg Feeley gives an extreme vision of the World Trade Center as a malevolent presence in Manhat-tan. She sees the Towers as toxic containers of ordinary but lethal chemicals that were benign as long as the buildings were intact, but were deadly when released after the collapse: "Now my vision of the Towers is of two huge upright milk containers, filled with inert toxic gasses and particulate. . . . With the astound-ing amount of office space housed within, the complex may have been the larg-est single collection of routine, normal, toxic materials from partitions to desks to computers to the glass in the windows, anywhere."[24] For Berman, Harvey, and Feeley, the Towers had no transcendent, saving grace that eradicated their instrumentality for dominant power regimes.

Far

Roland Barthes's essay on the Eiffel Tower describes the operation of the Tower as an almost empty sign, an icon, and as part of modern semiotic "mythologies," the things and experiences that make meaning in everyday life. For Barthes, the Eiffel Tower is powerful because it is ubiquitous (you can see it everywhere in Paris and it appears around the globe), it is elemental (it has a simple, primary shape), and it is a pure, empty sign (it means whatever the viewer imagines rather than having a fixed meaning). It fulfills more than one function (in fact, it was built without any use) because it appeals to the human imagination. According to Barthes, "architecture is always dream and function, expression of a utopia and instrument of convenience."[25] The World Trade Center took on mythological functions for New York. It appeared on more postcards than any other Manhattan building, it was visible from outlying areas, and it had a simple, elemental form. It also evinced the oscillation between dream and function typical of the mythological, as in Yamasaki's dream of an architecture signifying and promoting world peace. Adam Gopnik summed up its twin legacy as landmark and dreary office building: "The World Trade Center existed both as a thrilling double exclamation point at the end of the island and as a rotten place to have to go and get your card stamped, your registration renewed."[26] The Towers provided lower Manhattan with a terminus, and, viewed from a distance, their banality became iconic simplicity.

In *The Practice of Everyday Life,* French philosopher Michel de Certeau identified another view: looking down at the city from the Twin Towers. De Certeau dissected the "erotics of knowledge," the pleasure of "seeing the whole" and totalizing the city, available at the summit of the World Trade Center. At the top floor, one's body was no longer clasped by the streets below, according to de Certeau. Instead of dissolving into Manhattan's dense fabric as viewed from the street, the Trade Center disappeared under one's feet from the observation platform, and gave the illusion of optical omnipotence, effacing everyday street life. One could became a voyeur distanced from the mass and a practitioner of the "atopia-utopia of optical knowledge" capable of reading the "bewitching world" beneath.[27] At the edge of Manhattan, a view of the entire New York/New Jersey region was available to the spectator, a unique perspective of the whole not possible from other skyscrapers that were set in the New York grid. This bodiless and masterful perspective and the will to dominate it predated the Towers, de Certeau notes, but the World Trade Center was "the most monumental figure of Western urban development" and exemplary in its capacity to make the city seem simple and comprehensible. The simultaneous obliteration of the Trade Center from the New York skyline and the demise of the legibility of the city from its observation deck effaced this function and the possibility of that particular distant view.

By contrast with Yamasaki's humanism, architect Rem Koolhaas fabricated a history of what he called "Manhattanism" and the theory of a "Culture of Congestion," a fluid, chaotic condition of density and overstimulation that he extrapolated onto Manhattan retrospectively in *Delirious New York* (1978). Koolhaas identified a tradition of building and projects dating from the 1850s to the 1930s (marked by the two world's fairs of 1853 and 1939) that produced Manhattanism's shameless architecture, inspiring an ecstasy about architecture proportional to the degree that it went too far.[28] Koolhaas likened the proliferation of eclectic pre–World War II skyscrapers to a costume ball, the skyscrapers' true function as fantasy concealed by the "alibi" of business. "Only in New York has architecture become the design of costumes that do not reveal the true nature of repetitive interiors, but slip smoothly into the subconscious to perform their roles as symbols." The Manhattan grid provided the framework within which the skyscraper could mutate indefinitely.[29]

Koolhaas does not discuss the World Trade Center, but it clearly belonged to the postwar era in which he believes Manhattanism was "unlearned." Its closest cousins were not the Chrysler and Empire State Buildings, but the portions of Rockefeller Center, begun in the 1930s, completed after World War II along Sixth Avenue, where "the Skyscraper has come full circle; once again, it is a simple extrusion of the site that stops somewhere arbitrarily."[30] Instead of Manhattanism's "mosaic of episodes . . . that contest each other . . . ordered and fluid, a metropolis of rigid chaos," the Trade Center participated in the corporate world of normalization and univalence exemplified by the new Rockefeller Center.[31] This world emerged when architects forgot Manhattanism and its Culture of Congestion and became susceptible to European idealism, revealed in Yamasaki's utopian vision of the Trade Center as a symbol of world peace.

For Jean Baudrillard, the association between the Twin Towers and commerce had a historic connotation. The Twin Towers are examples of what Baudrillard calls "the simulacrum," the system of contemporary representation in which there are no originals, only simulations that reverse the traditional relationship between origin and representation. For example, the map is conventionally considered the record of an originary territory. In contemporary culture, for Baudrillard, the map precedes the territory it depicts, so that it is impossible to determine what is "real." This system of representation is the product of current conditions of economic and cultural production. By contrast with the surrounding panorama of Manhattan skyscrapers that represented earlier, competitive phases of capitalism, the double World Trade Center towers were a pure sign of monopoly and compatibility: "The fact that there are two of them signifies the end of all competition, the end of all original reference."[32] (fig. 1.4) They were like the digital 0/1 binary system that creates difference with only two variables. The skyscrapers of Manhattan "competed" with each other, according to Baudrillard, whereas the World Trade Center towers mirrored each other like Andy Warhol's multiple replicas of Marilyn Monroe's face, which demonstrate "the death of the original and the end of representation."[33] After their destruction, Baudrillard went so far as to declare that the Twin Towers were a party to their own destruction by inspiring ambivalent feelings of attraction and repulsion and a "secret desire to see them disappear."[34] "They, which

Figure 1.4. Distant view of the towers, Balthazar Korab.
Courtesy of Balthazar Korab Ltd. Photography.

were the symbol of omnipotence, have become by their absence, the symbol of the possible disappearance of that omnipotence."[35] Yet their demolition has left behind an intense awareness of their former presence, a perfect example of Baudrillard's simulacrum. Their absence, in other words, makes what they simulated more "real" than their former physical presence.

In its demise, the World Trade Center has acquired a surreal "martyrdom" that has generated outpourings of sentimental affection for these previously reviled structures. The World Trade Center was transformed from banal work-place (for some), soaring inspiration (for a few), and despised capitalist mon-strosity (for others) into a character in a classic tragedy (its very size and the hubris of its builders led to its destruction) and an awkward but cherished icon (the ubiquitous landmark that defined Manhattan's lower boundary).[36] The rhetoric about the World Trade Center's destruction is filled with references to barbarism and the destruction of civilization. Nearing the first anniversary of the attacks, conservative *National Review* columnist Deroy Murdock declared, "The eleven months that have passed since barbarians demolished the Twin Towers have not diminished the sense of amputation one feels when absorb-ing lower Manhattan's skyline."[37] On the other end of the political spectrum, critic Slavoj Žižek read the attacks themselves through the discourse on the civilized Inside versus the barbaric Outside. "The safe Sphere in which Ameri-cans live is experienced as under threat from the Outside of terrorist attackers who are ruthlessly self-sacrificing AND cowards, cunningly intelligent AND primitive barbarians. Whenever we encounter such a purely evil Outside, we should gather the courage to endorse the Hegelian lesson: in this pure Outside, we should recognize the distilled version of our own essence."[38] The Trade Cen-ter occupied a site between the "civilized" Inside of American culture and the barbaric Other of global culture. It sat on the edge of Manhattan, a suspect milieu of cosmopolitanism and heterogeneity that cannot be easily accommo-dated in America's Inside, despite recent attempts to refashion New York into America's hometown.

Bigness

Another discourse on the World Trade Center focuses less on its am-biguous image than on its enormous size. Architecture critic Paul Goldberger saw a direct link between the terrorist attacks and the sheer magnitude of the Trade Center: "The towers were not beautiful buildings. They were gargantuan and banal, blandness blown up to a gigantic size. But size was the point, and the people who stood in line to visit the hundred-and-seventh floor observation deck . . . understood this, just as real-estate developers did, and as the terrorists who rammed their planes into the towers last week did."[39]

Most studies of the World Trade Center recited a set of gigantic facts about the complex. The two towers were 110 stories each, 1368 feet and 1362 feet tall, and contained 9,000,000 square feet of rentable space, an acre of rentable space on each floor of each tower. Together they had 50,000 occupants and 80,000 daily visitors. The site is sixteen acres in area, bounded by Vesey Street on the north, Church Street on the east, Liberty Street on the south, and West Street on the west. The World Trade Center was built, owned, and operated by the Port Authority of New York and New Jersey, one of the largest public agencies in the United States. Construction began in August 1966 and a ribbon-cutting cere-mony was held in April 1973, but the entire complex was not finished until 1977, at a cost of $1.5 billion. It was for a short time the world's tallest building, exceeding the Empire State Building (1931, 102 stories), but was soon surpassed by the Sears Tower in Chicago (1973, 1450 feet and 110 stories). At the forty-fourth and seventy-eighth floors, skylobbies allowed elevator transfer to upper stories, served by ninety-five express and local elevators. The complex contained seven underground levels including services, shopping, and a subway station. The two nine-story Plaza Buildings, with roughly L-shaped plans, flanked the main entrance to the complex from Church Street, with WTC 4 on the south and WTC 5 on the north.[40]

As the world's tallest building, if only for a few months, the World Trade Center was emblematic of American engineering, capital, and puissance. As Yamasaki put it, "There are a few very influential architects who sincerely believe that all buildings must be 'strong'. The word 'strong' in this context seems to connote 'powerful'—that is, each building should be a monument to the virility of our society."[41] The Center was a marvel of large-scale planning, political maneuvering, and construction technology, and its overwhelming scale was an essential part of its symbolic value for American commentators like Deroy Murdock: "There was something sickeningly second grade about the World Trade Center's demise. The fanatic Muslim attackers seemed to say: 'We're too pathetic to design our own Twin Towers. So, you can't have yours, either.' Should buildings of only 60 or 70 stories grow at Ground Zero, we will fulfill their perverse wish."[42] For Murdock, the Towers were a sign of U.S. competence and justifiable confidence. Jealousy of the expertise and vision that created them motivated their barbaric destruction. Murdock called for "soldiers, spies and diplomats" to obviate future threats to this American dream of glory and prevent these "cruel, backward Middle Easterners" and "Islamists" from destroying the Towers again.

New York Times reporters James Glanz and Eric Lipton, authors of a book on the Twin Towers, extended the metaphor of scale to an epic tale of hubris. "From its inception, the World Trade Center was sustained by the mysterious but undeniable power of bigness."[43] For them, the World Trade Center was actually doomed by its size and prominence as a feat of American engineering, which generated its inherent vulnerability. "They were the biggest and brashest icons that New York has ever produced—physically magnificent, intimately familiar structures. Their builders were possessed of a determination that sometimes crossed the line into hubris: they refused to admit defeat before any problem that natural forces, economics, or politics could throw in their way."[44] The combination of political and formal ingenuity that enabled the Trade Center's erection simultaneously made it too powerfully symbolic and generated the structural vulnerabilities that permitted its destruction. Glanz and Lipton characterize the World Trade Center's history in terms of a Greek tragedy with an outcome foretold by the actions of the protagonists: "When they determined the enormous size for the trade center, they shaped it into an icon of international financial prowess and—most important—when they drew the blueprints for its construction, they had unwittingly helped write the script for its eventual destruction."[45] The reporters treat Ada Louise Huxtable as a prophet of doom, who questioned the wisdom of "gigantism" and "the gamble of triumph or tragedy at this scale."

They recite the now familiar story of the Trade Center's conception by the Rockefellers, its innovative if "untested" design and construction, and the resistance that it provoked among Radio Row businesspeople, residents, and urban activists. Even the resistance, according to Glanz and Lipton, centered on the Trade Center's dangerous bigness. Ultimately, the Twin Towers were doomed by their structural originality, the consequences of the highly touted engineering consisting of a lightweight tube with considerable flexibility, which allowed them to reach vast heights at relatively economical cost. The Towers' ephemeral attributes, celebrated by Bijal Trivedi, were mirrored in the structure's lightness, yet they contained the seeds of their demise because fireproofing the structure was sacrificed in favor of less heavy materials, the Towers' "Achilles heel." In a variation on the Tower of Babel fable, the aspiration to go too high undid the World Trade Center.[46] This view reduces the Trade Center's bigness and structural innovation to a metaphor for capitalist greed and corporate self-interest, effacing both its power as a symbol for New Yorkers and its similarity to other tall buildings.

Koolhaas's theory of Bigness in contemporary urbanism seems more accommodating to the World Trade Center and its ambiguous reception. "In spite of its dumb name, Bigness is a theoretical domain at this fin de siècle: in a landscape of disarray, disassembly, dissociation, disclamation, the attraction of Bigness is its potential to reconstruct the Whole, resurrect the Real, reinvent the collective, reclaim maximum possibility."[47] Koolhaas viewed Bigness as "the one architecture that could survive, even exploit, the now-global condition of the tabula rasa." He took Manhattan out of Manhattanism; like the skyscraper, these new megastructures would house various programs, and they would not be limited by the grid. They became urbanism not out of programmatic concerns or a unified theory of the city, but by default, due to their bigness and their wholeness. In contexts as diverse as Shanghai and lower Manhattan, Koolhaas believes the Big Building takes over most of the functions of chaotic urban centers and provides new, seemingly unified forms. "Beyond a certain critical mass, a building becomes a Big Building. Such a mass can no longer be controlled by a single architectural gesture."[48] The World Trade Center was similarly a Big Building beyond the control of Yamasaki's attempts to mediate aesthetically the discrepancy between its massing and street facades. As art historian Hal Foster notes, however, "the Modernist dream of free movement through cosmopolitan space" was perverted by the attack on the World Trade Center and "much damage was done to this great vision of skyscraper and city—and to New York as the capital of this dream."[49]

In rebuilding the World Trade Center site, some of the outrageousness of Rem Koolhaas's Manhattanism might be revived, if not the Big Building itself. Daniel Libeskind's Master Plan reinstates the "lust for optical knowledge" without retaining any of the unstable utopia or subconscious drives of Manhattanism. Previously, Libeskind's work opposed systematically Cartesian geometry and the grid in favor of antirationalism and non-objective space. His successful entry for the World Trade Center site, however, constructs a facile symbolism of "Democracy" consisting of Miss Liberty's torch, the empty bedrock foundations of the Twin Towers, and a Big Building, the Freedom Tower, that substitutes for the iconic Towers on the Manhattan skyline. Koolhaas described Manhattan as a grid not only covered with "architectural mutations (Central Park, The Skyscraper), utopian fragments (Rockefeller Center, the UN Building) and irrational phenomena (Radio City Music Hall)" but also bearing the traces of "phantom architecture in the form of past occupancies, aborted projects and popular fantasies that provide alternative images to the New York that exists."[50] Libeskind and the other architects engaged with rebuilding at Ground Zero might take clues from the phantom architecture of the site. Nineteenth-century Radio Row buildings, the Trade Center's Plaza, and the hidden subterranean world of shopping mall, transportation hub, and service spaces might be recreated rather than its Bigness alone, the most simplistic aspect of the complex.[51]

Georges Bataille's theory of architecture offers a counter to the reductive stories of the World Trade Center and its fall as a classic narrative of hubris or an instance of cultural envy. Bataille echoes Yamasaki's insight into architecture's implication with power and finds architecture inextricable from authority and official culture, although he would have resolutely rejected any humanistic mission for architecture. In Bataille's terms, one might say that the World Trade Center's ambiguous notoriety as an icon of American empire, capitalism, and technology made it a prime target of those who resist "architecture" and other weapons of domination. In his virulent antihumanism, Bataille viewed architecture as a mechanism for the repression of the masses and the suppression of anything exceeding the norm. According to Bataille, "an attack on architecture, whose monumental productions now dominate the earth . . . is necessarily, as it were, an attack on man."[52] In their introduction to an anthology of critical essays on 9/11, social scientists Eric Hershberg and Kevin W. Moore voiced a weak echo of Bataille's declaration: "The World Trade Center and the Pentagon represented more than *American* economic and military dominance. They also symbolized the global economic, military, and cultural ascendancy of the West, and the comparative marginalization of much of the rest of the world. As the terrorists of September 11 knew and many others have since learned, to attack the symbols is to strike at the heart of power."[53]

Yet the World Trade Center was not and is not an unambiguous symbol of American ingenuity, global hegemony, or world peace, whether viewed from near or far. It was the celebrated terminus of the Manhattan skyline and a poorly designed monstrosity. It was part of lower Manhattan everyday life and an overbearing presence above it. It destroyed a historic neighborhood and provided a viewpoint from which the entire city became legible. It was the quintessential Big Building, a maze of shopping, mass transit, offices, invisible service spaces, and high-end restaurants. Its very banality allowed it to evolve into an icon onto which observers could project diverse meanings. The attacks of September 11, 2001, perhaps join the legacy of the storming of the Bastille, which Bataille attributes to the hostility of those dominated by the monuments of authority.

These monuments are witnesses of the split heritage of any cultural treasure, simultaneously documents of civilization and barbarism decipherable in multivalent ways depending on perspective. Viewed through Benjamin's ambivalent dialectic of civilization and barbarism, the Twin Towers and cultural monuments destroyed at other sites provoke a critical practice that must account for the contingency of political and cultural meaning. Looking from near and far allows us to dissect some of those multiple layers of civilization and barbarism that adhered to the World Trade Center.

Notes

I would like to thank Daniel Sherman and Terry Nardin for their sensitive criticism of this essay and great editorial patience with its author.

1. Walter Benjamin, *Das Passagen-Werk* (Frankfurt am Main: Suhrkamp Verlag, 1982), 1002 (Do, 7).

2. Walter Benjamin, "Theses on the Philosophy of History," in *Illuminations,* trans. Harry Zohn (New York: Schocken Books, 1969), 262–263.

3. Ibid., 256.

4. "Whoever has emerged victorious participates to this day in the triumphal procession in which the present rulers step over those who are lying prostrate. According to traditional practice, the spoils are carried along in this procession. They are called cultural treasures and a historical materialist views them with cautious detachment. For without exception the cultural treasures he surveys have an origin which he cannot contemplate without horror. They owe their existence not only to the efforts of the great minds and talents who have created them, but also to the anonymous toil of their contemporaries." Ibid.

5. Michel Foucault, "The Power of the Eye," in *Power/Knowledge: Selected Interviews and Other Writings, 1972–1977,* ed. Colin Gordon (New York: Pantheon, 1980), 146–165; Manfredo Tafuri, *Architecture and Utopia: Design and Capitalist Development,* trans. Barbara Luigia La Penta (Cambridge, Mass.: MIT Press, 1976); Diana Agrest, *Architecture from Without: Theoretical Framings for a Critical Practice* (Cambridge, Mass.: MIT Press, 1991). Many of the essays in Michael Sorkin and Sharon Zukin's collection, *After the World Trade Center: Rethinking New York City* (New York: Routledge, 2002), presume that architecture is integral to hegemonic power systems.

6. Georges Bataille, "Architecture," in *Encyclopaedia Acephalica,* ed. Robert Lebel and Isabelle Waldberg (London: Atlas Press, 1995), 36.

7. Ibid., 35. See Denis Hollier, *Against Architecture: The Writings of Georges Bataille* (Cambridge, Mass.: MIT Press, 1989).

8. On recent city rebuilding efforts, see Raymond W. Gastil and Zoë Ryan, *Information Exchange: How Cities Renew, Rebuild, and Remember* (New York: Van Alen Institute, 2002).

9. For example, see Lawrence Vale, *Architecture, Power, and National Identity* (New Haven, Conn.: Yale University Press, 1992).

10. Carol Willis, *Form Follows Finance: Skyscrapers and Skylines in New York and Chicago* (New York: Princeton Architectural Press, 1995); Anthony D. King, "Worlds in the City: Manhattan Transfer and the Ascendance of Spectacular Space," *Planning Perspectives* 11 (1996): 97–114.

11. By contrast with the other 9/11 target, the Pentagon, the World Trade Center never had a single, unambiguous meaning. The Pentagon, little discussed in the aftermath of the attacks, is metonymic for the American military and its imperial apparatus, but the building's form is rarely featured in media images because of security concerns.

12. Walter Benjamin, "One Way Street," in *One Way Street and Other Writings,* trans. Edmund Jephcott and Kingsley Shorter (London: New Left Books, 1979), 78.

13. Walter Benjamin. "The Work of Art in the Age of Mechanical Reproduction," in *Illuminations.*

14. Ada Louise Huxtable, "Big but Not So Bold," *New York Times,* April 5, 1973, quoted in Angus K. Gillespie, *Twin Towers: The Life of New York City's World Trade Center* (New Brunswick, N.J.: Rutgers University Press, 1999), 176.

15. Eric Darton, *Divided We Stand: A Biography of New York's World Trade Center* (New York: Basic Books, 1999), 4. Darton maintains a valuable web site that contains first-person accounts from people who built and occupied the Trade Center, a significant archive of New Yorkers' attachment to the Twin Towers. Eric Darton, New York's World Trade Center: A Living Archive, http://ericdarton.net/.

16. Jane Ellen Rubin, "The Towers Stand," New York's World Trade Center: A Living Archive, http://ericdarton.net/afterwords/recollections.html.

17. Minoru Yamasaki, *A Life in Architecture* (New York and Tokyo: Weatherhill, 1979), 112.

18. Mark Wigley, "Insecurity by Design," in Sorkin and Zukin, *After the World Trade Center,* 84.

19. Minoru Yamasaki, quoted in Paul Heyer, *Architects on Architecture: New Directions in America* (New York: Walker, 1966), 186.

20. This equation between world peace and world trade persists. Guy Tozzoli, one of the World Trade Center's creators and now president of the World Trade Centers Association, has been nominated for the Nobel Peace Prize on the strength of his conviction "that the surest way to achieve peace is through healthy commerce." World Trade Center Association, "Guy Tozzoli, WTCA president, nominated for Nobel Peace Prize," http://www.wtc-corps.org/news/articles/nobelnom021401.htm.

21. Bijal P. Trivedi, "Why Symbols Become Targets," *National Geographic Today,* September 13, 2001, http://news.nationalgeographic.com/news/2001/09/0913_TVsymbol.html.

22. Marshall Berman, "When Bad Buildings Happen to Good People," in Sorkin and Zukin, *After the World Trade Center,* 6–7.

23. David Harvey, "Cracks in the Edifice of the Empire State," in Sorkin and Zukin, *After the World Trade Center,* 58.

24. Meg Feeley, "The Towers: The Seen and the Obscene," at Eric Darton, New York's World Trade Center: A Living Archive, http://ericdarton.net/afterwords/fireandair.html.

25.   Roland Barthes, *The Eiffel Tower, and Other Mythologies,* trans. Richard Howard (New York: Hill and Wang, 1979), 6.

26.   Adam Gopnik, "The City and the Pillars," *The New Yorker,* September 24, 2001, 36 and 38.

27.   Michel de Certeau, *The Practice of Everyday Life,* trans. Steven Rendall (Berkeley: University of California Press, 1984), 92–93.

28.   Rem Koolhaas, *Delirious New York: A Retrospective Manifesto for Manhattan* (New York: Oxford University Press, 1978), 7.

29.   Ibid., 13.

30.   Ibid., 240.

31.   Ibid.

32.   "New York is the world's only city therefore that retraces all along its history, and with a prodigious fidelity and in all its scope, the actual form of the capitalistic system—it changes instantly in function of the latter. No European city does so." Jean Baudrillard, *Simulations,* trans. Paul Foss, Paul Patton, and Phil Beitchman (New York: Semiotext[e], 1983), 136.

33.   Ibid.

34.   Jean Baudrillard, *The Spirit of Terrorism and Other Essays* (London: Verso, 2003), 46.

35.   Ibid., 52.

36.   "it hurts to see the city there without them. and i don't know anything but that i'm wishing for the mayor to come on the radio, and swear to build them again, and higher, and better, and occupied by all the things that we do that are most worthy of pride." ozi, Brooklyn, 12 Sep 2001 15:19:24 -0700(PDT) at Eric Darton, New York's World Trade Center: A Living Archive, http://ericdarton.net/afterwords/.

37.   Deroy Murdock, "Rebuild the Towers," *National Review Online,* August 16, 2002, http://www.nationalreview.com/murdock/murdock081602.asp.

38.   Slavoj Žižek, *Welcome to the Desert of the Real!: Five Essays on September 11 and Related Dates* (New York and London: Verso, 2002).

39.   Paul Goldberger, "Building Plans: What the World Trade Center Meant," *The New Yorker* September 24, 2001, 76.

40.   Leonard I. Ruchelman, *The World Trade Center: Politics and Policies of Skyscraper Development* (Syracuse: Syracuse University Press, 1977), 11–12.

41.   "These architects look with derision upon attempts to build a friendly, more gentle kind of building. The basis for their belief is that our culture is derived primarily from Europe, and that most of the important traditional examples of European architecture are monumental, reflecting the need of the state, church, or the feudal families—the primary patrons of these buildings—to awe and impress the masses. This is incongruous today. Although it is inevitable for architects who admire these great monumental buildings of Europe to strive for the quality most evident in them—grandeur, the elements of mysticism and power, basic to cathedrals and palaces, are also incongruous today, because the buildings we build for our times are for a totally different purpose." Yamasaki in Heyer, *Architects on Architecture,* 186.

42.   Murdock, "Rebuild the Towers."

43.   James Glanz and Eric Lipton, "The Height of Ambition: In the epic story of how the World Trade Towers rose, their fall was foretold," *New York Times*

Magazine September 8, 2002, 34. This article has been expanded into a book, James Glanz and Eric Lipton, *City In The Sky: The Rise and Fall of the World Trade Center* (New York: Times Books, 2003).

44. Ibid.

45. Ibid.

46. Mark Wigley spins another tale of flawed or fatal faith, in his case the deeply ingrained belief that architecture can produce and sustain stability and security. Wigley attempts to account for the shocked, disbelieving response to the Center's collapse. Mark Wigley, "Insecurity by Design" in Sorkin and Zukin, *After the World Trade Center.*

47. Rem Koolhaas, "Bigness or the Problem of Large," in *Small, Medium, Large, Extra-Large* (New York: Monacelli Press, 1995), 510.

48. Ibid., 499.

49. Hal Foster, "Bigness," *London Review of Books* 23:23 (November 29, 2001).

50. Koolhaas, *Delirious New York,* 6.

51. For an astute analysis of the entries in the competition for the Ground Zero master plan, see Lauren Kogod with Michael Osman, "Girding the Grid: Abstraction and Figuration at Ground Zero," *Grey Room* 13 (Fall 2003): 108–121.

52. Bataille, "Architecture," 36.

53. Eric Hershberg and Kevin W. Moore, eds. *Critical Views of September 11: Analyses from Around the World* (New York, New Press, 2002).

2 Two Projects with Commentary: "Around Ground Zero" (Map) and "New York, September 11, 2001—Four Days Later" (Satellite Photographs)

Laura Kurgan

"Around Ground Zero"

"Around Ground Zero" was designed as a pocket-sized, fold-out map to orient viewers to the former site of the World Trade Center during the winter of 2001-2002. It sought to enable both pedestrian and intellectual access to the area in the immediate aftermath of the September 11 attacks. Two versions of the map were produced, the first in December 2001 and a second in March 2002. The versions were dated and updated to indicate changes to the area.

The map was produced as both a practical guide to the site and as a memorial document. It addressed the multitude of people who were going to the site to see it for themselves, people who were simply looking or who were seeking to add something of their own to the many spontaneous memorials that had proliferated there. The aim of the map was to help people make sense of what they were seeing, or, if that was asking too much, at least to measure their disorientation in the face of the unimaginable. The site around the World Trade Center was manifestly disorienting, but the map sought to address that confusion and allow visitors to begin to take stock of what had happened.

It served as a document of a place that was changing, of a line in the city that would soon disappear as the debris was removed. The map documented the site, and, specifically, its condition as a mass grave in the process of being disassembled and removed. This temporary condition was soon sanitized—erased—in a complex political and economic debate over different proposals for rebuilding and memorializing. The map exposes the most troubling aspect of the site, the mass grave, as the one most properly deserving of witness and memory.

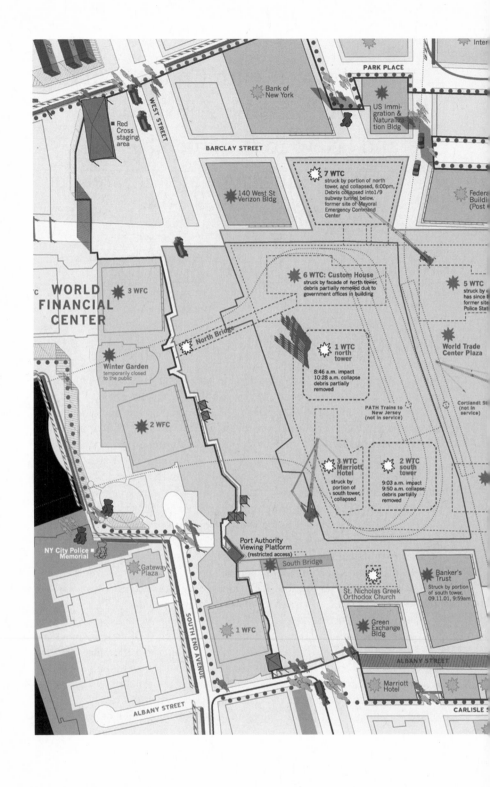

PARK PLACE

Bank of
New York

US Immi-
gration &
Naturaliza-
tion Bldg

Inter

Red
Cross
staging
area

BARCLAY STREET

7 WTC
struck by portion of north
tower, and collapsed, 6:00pm,
Debris collapsed into1/9
subway tunnel below.
former site of Mayoral
Emergency Command
Center

Federa
Buildi
(Post

140 West St
Verizon Bldg

6 WTC: Custom House
struck by facade of north tower,
debris partially removed due to
government offices in building

5 WTC
struck by
has since
former site
Police Stat

WORLD
FINANCIAL
CENTER

3 WFC

World Trade
Center Plaza

North Bridge

1 WTC
north
tower

8:46 a.m. impact
10:28 a.m. collapse
debris partially
removed

Winter Garden
temporarily closed
to the public

Cortlandt St
(not in
service)

2 WFC

PATH Trains to
New Jersey
(not in service)

3 WTC
Marriott
Hotel

struck by
portion of
south tower,
collapsed

2 WTC
south
tower

9:03 a.m. impact
9:50 a.m. collapse
debris partially
removed

Port Authority
Viewing Platform
(restricted access)

NY City Police
Memorial

South Bridge

Gateway
Plaza

St. Nicholas Greek
Orthodox Church

Banker's
Trust
Struck by portion
of south tower,
09.11.01, 9:59am

Green
Exchange
Bldg

1 WFC

ALBANY STREET

Marriott
Hotel

ALBANY STREET

CARLISLE S

WEST STREET

SOUTH END AVENUE

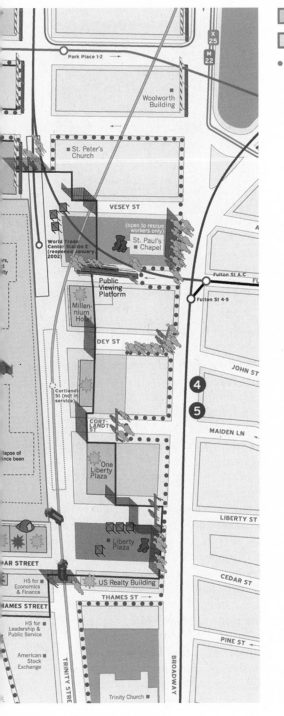

GROUND ZERO

RESTRICTED ACCESS

• • • • SUGGESTED PATH

OPEN VIEW

VIEWING PLATFORM

FENCE

TEMPORARY MEMORIAL

CURTAINED GLASS

POLICE

POLICE STATION

FIREHOUSE

CRANE

TRUCK

BARGE

HIGH VOLTAGE LINE

COLLAPSE

PARTIAL COLLAPSE

MAJOR DAMAGE

MODERATE DAMAGE

M 22 MTA BUS

5 MTA SUBWAY

FERRY/CRUISE

"New York, September 11, 2001 —Four Days Later"

. . . as seen by the IKONOS satellite, a high-resolution snapshot from outer space of a city in a state of emergency. The satellite monitors the earth's surface, collecting data. On Saturday morning at 11:54 A.M., in between the satellite and the bodies of some 3,000 people, a cloud of smoke slowly drifts away from the disaster.

There is a lot to see in this picture, too much in fact. The density of its detail demands that it be viewed close up. But there is no single thing to look for, and no particular piece of evidence which tells the decisive story. In the gallery the entire image is enlarged, too large to see all at once. The zoom offers no revelation, though, no instant of enlightenment and no sublime incomprehension either. It tells many stories. What has happened?

Figure 2.1. A visitor looks at the installation "New York, September 11, 2001—Four Days Later," by artist Laura Kurgan, at the ZKM Center for Art and Media in Karlsruhe, Germany, on October 12, 2001. Uli Deck/dpa/Landov.

This image should not exist, nor should the event it has captured. Although the crime is not, in fact, unrepresentable—here you see it—it is unacceptable. The image makes us witnesses; it is imperative that we look at it.

The satellite's sensors capture a mass grave, what remains of a crime or an act of war. Nothing can justify or rationalize what happened here. Unfortunately, or fortunately, the image itself offers no instructions about how to understand or respond to what it has recorded in memory.

One-meter resolution satellite images of the aftermath of the event: detailed pictures of a disaster.

Figures 2.2. and 2.3. These images can be downloaded from http://www.spaceimaging.com. Copyright Space Imaging LLC.

The image on the left was collected at 11:43 A.M. EDT on Sept. 12, 2001, the one on the right at 11:54 A.M. EDT on Sept. 15, 2001, by Space Imaging's IKONOS, the world's first high-resolution commercial earth imaging satellite. It travels 661 kilometers above the earth's surface at a speed of seven kilometers per second, orbiting the planet once every ninety-eight minutes.

The image on the left was downloaded as a 25-megabyte file from Space Imaging's website. The image on the right was purchased, at a cost of several thousand dollars, in the form

Figure 2.4. IKONOS Satellite Data. September 15, 2001. By Space Imaging. 1 pixel = 1 meter. Detail. Actual scale of pixels as displayed in the gallery. Emergency vehicles on the West Side Highway at West 12th Street.

of a 323-megabyte data file from Space Imaging, and forms the basis of the images in this installation.

According to the company, "one-meter resolution" means that "objects that are 1-meter in size on the ground can be distinguished, provided those objects are well removed from other objects and have separate and distinct visual characteristics. One-meter imagery cannot 'see' individual people."

Image analyst John Pike says, more simply, "generally you need one pixel to detect, about four lines of pixels to recognize, and about six lines of pixels to identify a target."

As democratic norms spread, as civil society grows stronger and more effective in its demands for information around the world, as globalization gives people an ever greater stake in knowing more about what is going on in other parts of the

Within the image:

Northeast Long/Lat:73°59'25.11"W/40°45'29.98"N | Northwest Long/Lat:74°01'08.26"W/40°45'29.98"N East 14th St & Broadway | Scale: 1 pixel = 1 meter   Scene ID: 2000010901500THC   Canal St

6 meters

9km | 8km | 7km | 6km | 5k

Figure 2.5. IKONOS Satellite Data. September 15, 2001. By Space Imaging. 1 pixel = 1 meter. Full image as installed
the gallery.

world, and as technology makes such knowledge easier to attain, transparency
would appear to be the ineluctable wave of the future.

The legitimacy of remote sensing satellites is part of this global trend toward
transparency. Imagery from high-resolution satellites is becoming available now
not only because technology has advanced to the point of making the imagery a
potential source of substantial profits, but because governmental policies permit,
and indeed encourage, such satellites to be operated. Yet as is always the case with
increases in transparency, not everyone benefits and not all uses of the resulting
information are benign. (Carnegie Endowment for International Peace, "No More
Secrets?" June 1999)

CNN reported in January 2000 that "the sort of spy-in-the-sky images previously available only to intelligence agencies and defense departments are
now within reach of almost all the rest of us." The *Los Angeles Times* wrote in

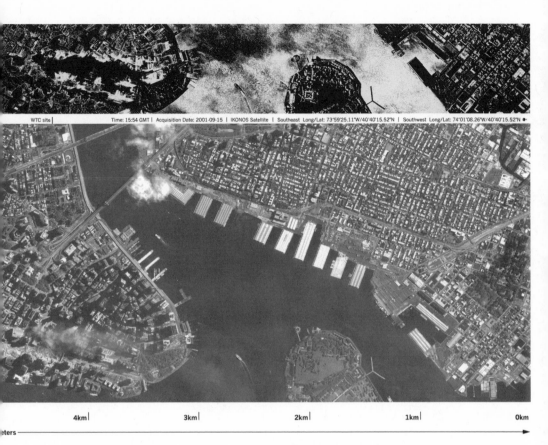

June 2001 that these images "make everyone an eyewitness in a world in which anyone—not just Big Brother—can be watching."

High-resolution satellite images are one of our most powerful metaphors for a supposed transition from an age of surveillance to one of transparency: an all-seeing image, potentially of any point on earth, available to almost anyone, rich in data that can be used for purposes we cannot even predict. But what is this image? It wants to represent the incomprehensible magnitude of the event; with the sublimity proper to a catastrophe, it offers the view from above, from "overhead," in which the city is seen in the midst of an emergency. It tries to see everything at once, everything that cannot usually be seen with the human eye.

The buildings are missing, disintegrated into a vast zone of ruin. The city is quiet, except for intensive activity around the site. There are trucks along ominously empty highways removing the debris. New York City's rigorous urban

Figure 2.6. IKONOS Satellite Data. September 15, 2001. By Space Imaging. 1 pixel = 1 meter. Detail, Ground Zero.

grids are broken up by the shadows of the buildings which remain, but also by the dust and smoke and the rubble of the very large buildings which have collapsed. At 11:54 in the morning, four days later, the image says, this is what it all looked like.

But the image offers only a certain kind of evidence. When the pixels finally reveal themselves as simply the pixels that make up the image, they are as silent as what they are picturing. This evidence reveals little, and is of little use forensically. But the pixels will stay, here on this image, even as the debris is removed, day by day, from the site. At least we will always be able to locate the rubble here.

So if in fact transparency is trivial, and nothing new is discovered about the event, we must rather say: here it is, the event is encoded right here, by the light that has traveled from the ground to the satellite, captured in an instant as the memory of this event. As data. Mutable, yes, but no less a memory all the same.

* * *

What is missing from this image is what is missing now from the city or the world, and it is always missing at the limits of one-meter resolution, for all its detail. What is missing are the missing, more than 5,000 people now presumed

40 *Laura Kurgan*

dead. Beneath or beyond the limits of visibility, of data, are the dead. And yet they remain in the image, in the ruin of the image, and they ask something of us.

The ruin is still on fire.

Smoke hovers nearby, displaced from the site by the wind. It does not cast a shadow the way a cloud further to the south obscures the area near the rubble of the World Trade Center. During the weeks following September 11, one could not always register directly what had happened in the city—until the wind changed direction and one could smell the smoke.

It is hard to isolate anything on this image. When one tries to isolate the disaster site by selecting similar pixels, the image processing software tends to equate rubble with buildings. But it can isolate the smoke, and what remains hazily below the smoke. So choose a pixel in the middle of the disaster site—it has a longitude and a latitude and a spectral signature. The software can then associate this pixel with similar pixels, and the area can grow to define the most changeable part of the site: the cloud of smoke that bears witness to the crime. Displaced, caught in motion, it records a particular moment of September 11, four days later.

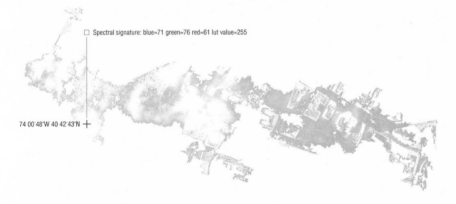

Figure 2.7. IKONOS Satellite Data. September 15, 2001. By Space Imaging, 1 pixel = 1 meter. Cloud detail.

Postscript

The text above was written just a few days after September 11, 2001. Many of the initial reports about the event, particularly the estimates of the number who died, were wrong. As it turns out, 2,801 people were killed during the collapse of the buildings. But something else might have been wrong with the picture too, or with the fact that I had been given the chance to purchase that image from September 15th.

On October 7th, twenty-two days after the IKONOS image appeared in the Space Imaging archive, ready for purchase, the U.S. began "Operation Enduring Freedom" in Afghanistan. Imagery of the war in Afghanistan was not as easy to obtain. There was something asymmetrical going on, especially in terms of images. As a CNN anchor said a few weeks into it, "this is not a television war." It was also not a transparent war. The U.S. government, which had the power to prohibit the sale of satellite imagery in wartime, chose not to exercise it. Instead, they simply purchased exclusive access to the IKONOS imagery for a period of two months. When I sought to purchase an image from over Afghanistan, my request was denied. What became significant was the lack of imagery—and the resolve of the Pentagon to insist on the lack.

We are still in the present tense of the consequences of the event pictured here. And its aftermath is unfolding in real time. There are many questions to be asked. Are we looking at the end of the post–Cold War embedded in these pixels? Should we rather be looking elsewhere, or at other images—the humanitarian crisis that unfolded on the border with Pakistan, surely visible by this same satellite? Or should we be focusing on other forms of surveillance—at the trail of evidence being collected by the U.S. intelligence agencies and their future plans for keeping the world "safe"? The danger in this image is that it sometimes closes down these other questions, and more, when it ought to open them up.

Notes:

"Around Ground Zero" emerged out of discussions in a subcommittee of the Temporary Memorials Committee of New York New Visions, a group of architects and designers who met informally in the months following the events of September 11 to imagine responses on an urban scale. The first map, dated December 2001, had a print run of 50,000 copies, the bulk of which were distributed at and around the site. 100,000 copies of the second map were printed in March 2002. The maps were distributed by volunteers around the city, and especially around Ground Zero, again for free. The back of the map included photography of the areas around Ground Zero by Margaret Morton and high-resolution aerial photographs of the then-inaccessible inner zone from the National Oceanographic and Atmospheric Administration, the Federal Emergency Management Administration, and the Mitre Corporation.

Concept and Design: Laura Kurgan

Project team: Janette Kim and Bethia Liu with Rivka Mazar and Donald Shillingburg

Photography: Margaret Morton

Support from the following organizations and corporations is gratefully acknowledged: American Institute of Architects, New York Chapter; Con Edison; The New York Community Trust; The New York Foundation for the Arts; The Open Society Institute; Princeton University; TWBA/Chiat/Day; The Van Alen Institute; and two anonymous donors.

For further information: http://www.aroundgroundzero.net

Web Design: Razorfish

Web Hosting: Logicworks

The installation "New York, September 11—Four Days Later" was first exhibited at the Zentrum für Kunst und Medientechnologie, Karlsruhe, Germany, in October 2001 as part of CTRL [Space].

3   Falling Persons and National Embodiment: The Reconstruction of Safe Spectatorship in the Photographic Record of 9/11

Susan Lurie

This project began for me with my response to an image of a man falling from the north tower of the World Trade Center that appeared in the *New York Times* on September 12, 2001 (see fig. 3.1).[1] I was riveted by this picture of a man falling upside-down toward certain death. My horror upon looking at this un-stoppable fall in a terrifyingly helpless bodily position was inflected as well by a helplessness such a photograph evoked: though the image freezes the descent at the split second of its taking, what we see is a fall that could not be stopped. Contemplating this image, one wishes that the camera's ability to freeze the moment might have made a magical intervention in the fall itself.

At the same time, the responses of horrified identification and the wish that seeing could translate into saving are inextricable from the difference the image registers between the spectator and the falling man, the difference between safety and mortal danger. Both the framing of the image and its caption enlarge this distance by presenting the doomed man as an anonymous body caught in the fatal throes of forces (gravity, terrorists) that U.S. citizens, at least prior to 9/11, usually felt were under control. Because the image both emphasizes a visual rhyme between the man's body and the building's girders (they share similarities in width and in tones of white, gray, and black) and represents the man's world as shrunk to the context of the doomed tower (the background is made up entirely of the buildings), it seems to objectify the falling man, to rep-resent him as like the building whose fate determines his own. This sense of objectification owes something as well to the anonymity of the man, which is underscored by the caption: "A person falls head first after jumping from the north tower of the World Trade Center. It was a horrific sight that was repeated in the moments after the planes struck the towers." Indeed, in the caption, ano-nymity segues into displacement. Not only is the falling man an unidentifiable "person," the image is described as referencing not his horror but that of the spectators: the picture shows us a "horrific sight that was repeated."[2]

Figure 3.1. A man falling from the north tower.
Richard Drew, AP/Wide World Photos.

On the one hand, then, the image elicits an empathic identification with the man; we wish to save him, to replace anonymity with the dignity of human identity. On the other, the image is a "horrifying sight" that refers more to the spectator's horror, which the man's anonymity and objectification can help to assuage. Such tension between identification with and repudiation of 9/11's most horrifying sights—those of the trapped and falling people—I will argue, is central to reconstructions of secure national identity after 9/11. Whether nostalgic for or critical of U.S. power, such reconstructions negotiate these contradictory impulses, ones that take their peculiar force from the unprecedented aspect of the traumatic events: the vulnerability of thousands on U.S. soil to enemy attack. Images of these people compel identification because they are like us both in our everyday assumption of immunity from such attacks and in our new vulnerability to them. But for the same reasons, it is compelling to see the falling and the imagined dead in ways that assure us both of our difference from them and of safety restored. Indeed, "seeing" itself, I will further argue, is centrally at issue in restoring a sense of safety. Because U.S. spectators customarily view the atrocities of warlike attacks from a safe distance and because the relentless succession of horrifying events on 9/11 repeatedly made the return to safe seeing impossible, sights of heretofore unimaginable dangers on U.S. soil instigate what we might call a trauma of spectatorship.

In the following pages, I will explore how this trauma of spectatorship fuels the mainstream photographic record of 9/11—images that appeared prolifically in major newspapers and later in commemorative volumes and are arguably iconic ones in the 9/11 record.[3] Almost all the photos I discuss have multiple analogs published in newspapers, magazines, and other volumes.[4] Together they contribute to an identifiable photographic lexicon dedicated to recovering a sense of secure national identity, of feeling safe because we live in the U.S. and are protected by national power, by restoring a sense of safe spectatorship in a particular form: the transformation of the horrifying sight of falling people, which compels intertwined empathic and threatening identifications, into reassuring sights. While these photos simultaneously attempt to produce counter-images of a resilient body and to renew the fit between a sense of photographic mastery over what is seen and the safety of U.S. spectators, they also necessarily keep visible or are haunted by the very sights they seek to transform. As a result, this photographic lexicon allows for the emergence of images that ask spectators to reformulate critically the relation between the recalled sight of falling people and the meaning of "safety" itself.

Other critics have called attention to the importance of both spectatorship and photography to the processing of 9/11's previously unimaginable horrors. Marianne Hirsch points to the role of delayed understanding in photography's emergence "as the most evocative medium in our attempts to deal with the aftermath of September 11." Because of the time lag between shooting and contemplating the developed image, she suggests, "deferral connects photography to trauma, which is characterized by a delayed understanding."[5] Similarly, Barbie Zelizer looks to the relation between photography and the processing of trauma to explain why "the popular press was dominated by photographs for days—of the attacks themselves, shattered buildings and streets, people running or grieving, sites of mourning—and they appeared repeatedly."[6] For Zelizer, though, these photos contribute to a processing of trauma that also helps recruit consent to war and, moreover, does so by reference to a well-known photographic lexicon from the past. The emphasis in the 9/11 photos on spectators per se, ones bearing witness to awful sights we cannot see, constitutes a "near-full repeat of the Holocaust aesthetic" of spectators looking at unshown Nazi atrocities.[7] In calling to mind these 1945 images, the 9/11 photos likewise galvanize "support for political and military actions" in the present.[8] Both Hirsch's and Zelizer's accounts are compatible with my emphasis on the role of photographs in processing a trauma of spectatorship; one emphasizes deferred encounters with sights initially too horrible to see, and the other posits displacements of the horrible sights with images that recall past atrocities elsewhere.

The centrality of the horrifying sights themselves to the reconstruction of safe spectatorship, however, may seem counterintuitive, especially as after several days these images all but disappeared from the photographic record. As Zelizer points out, although numerous other images were repeated for weeks and months beyond the point of their newsworthiness, "by the weekend, [the images of falling people] basically disappeared from view, appearing in a few news magazines, and remained out of view in much of the commemorative literature over the following months."[9] Certainly, restraint dictated by respect and appeals to good taste are motivations for this disappearance; the sheer horror of the images is another. Perhaps because such explanations seem so obvious, critics have tended neither to interrogate further the exclusion of these images nor to consider their possible contribution to the meaning of the photos that we did see again and again. Indeed, Zelizer's argument seems to require the invisibility in the photo record of the falling and the dead; for her the 1945 photographic lexicon can emerge with such ideological force precisely because the 9/11 casualties are nowhere to be seen: "There was, in effect, no need 'to see' the bodies in the later event, for the structural similarities in presentation called to memory the corpses of earlier times."[10]

In contrast, I argue that post-9/11 safe spectatorship cannot be achieved without paying attention to the peculiar horror of seeing Americans threatened on U.S. soil. Images that solicit an identification with previous U.S. spectators of atrocities elsewhere demonstrate, alternatively, a nostalgia for a spectatorship made safe, in Susan Sontag's terms, by "regarding the pain of others." As Sontag points out in the book of the same title, we in the U.S. are accustomed to feeling compassion for atrocities by looking at "the grievously injured bodies shown in published photographs . . . from Asia or Africa" and from "remote and exotic" places generally.[11] Though her first reference to 9/11 is itself a detailed description of photos that depict the gruesome killing of a Taliban soldier by one from the Northern Alliance, it is also the occasion to emphasize that such images should press us to ask, "what pictures, whose cruelties, whose deaths are *not* being shown."[12] Similarly, she explicitly criticizes the "judgments about 'good taste'—always a repressive standard when invoked by institutions" that censor the publication of horrific photos taken on 9/11.[13]

Thus, for Sontag as for Zelizer, the 9/11 photographic record represses intolerably horrific sights of our fellow citizens as it reinstates our habits of seeing atrocities only in the suffering of others. To an extent, this is true. But seeing only this mode of repression and treating it as the most important response to the photo record keeps us from considering that old habits of safe seeing may not be as persuasive for U.S. spectators after 9/11.[14] On that day we saw those who live in the U.S. unprotected from foreign attack and suffering extremely terrifying deaths. Unable to "confirm that this is the sort of thing that happens in that [benighted, backward, distant] place,"[15] these sights make it impossible to restore safe spectatorship by simply eliminating the trapped and falling people from the photo record, or by displacing them with seeing old or new atrocities in other lands, or by mobilizing them to inspire support for war. Instead, the 9/11 photos that solicit a patriotic faith in restored national power make safe spectatorship a matter of seeing the transformation of horrifying sights into reassuring ones. Much of the iconography of this transformation follows the drama of the 9/11 survivors' escapes, in which representations of and visual allusions to the falling people signify the survival and repudiation of a terrifying identification with them. Eventually, however, articulations of dissent to the dangers of war respond to the patriotic photo record by bringing back the horrifying sight. Deployed as signifiers of dissent to policies that keep us vulnerable, these images look to an empathic identification with the falling people as a condition for counterintuitive ways of seeing what constitutes safe national identity.

The Horrifying Sight

The image of the man falling head first accompanied the lead article in the *New York Times* on September 12, at the center of the continuation of the front-page story on an inside page.[16] Though tastefully embedded, for the largest part of the article the image is insistently present, making it impossible to forget the falling people as the story unfolds and putting that image at the story's center. Indeed, the centrality of this image to this early account is indicative of how the horrifying sight of falling people functions in the national memory of 9/11, specifically through the photographic record. The article, both here and as revised in *A Nation Challenged*, gives us clues not only to how the framing and description of the few photos of trapped and falling people responds to the traumas of 9/11's successive events, but also to how the images that proliferated are in visual dialogue with the horrifying sights that disappeared from the record.

Although the article begins by focusing on eyewitness sightings of falling people, its narrative quickly becomes a story about the escape of survivors in which the image of the falling man comes to stand in for a relentlessly repeated threat that the survivors ultimately escape. Indeed, while the caption to the photo refers to repeated horrific sights of those who fell, the most riveting repetition in the story is the dramatic oscillation between safety and danger experienced by those who escape both the tower and its collapse. And with this oscillation, the meaning of the falling people changes. Whereas the sightings after the first attack inspire sympathetic horror as well as the fear of lethal falling objects, with the second attack and the successive collapses of the towers, the difference between the spectators and the victims cannot be so easily assumed, and identification with those who fell comes to mean a fear of being turned into them. As a result, the dramatic story of escape unfolds also as the escape from that identification. In the end, moreover, the safe survivor emerges explicitly as a spectator, who both displaces the sight of the falling man with a safer image of devastation and turns it into a metaphor for his own safety: a dislocation of self in relation to the former towers that is unsettling but not lethal.

Even from the first sightings, horrified sympathy involves an objectifying of and opposition to the falling people. "Dark spots fell from the sides of the buildings, and at first it wasn't clear what they were," says one spectator. "[People high in the north tower] seemed like tiny figurines," says another. When the story shifts to the people inside the building, we learn about the close escapes of those who got out, whose sightings of falling and fallen bodies seem to signify both the fate they escaped and even the escape itself. One survivor connects his safe emergence from the tower with having access to the horrifying sight: "we got out. We started to see people jumping from the top of the World Trade Center."[17] The revised version in the *Times*'s photo volume demonstrates how a safety measured by a difference from the sight of people jumping is difficult to maintain: "The unreal yielded to the unimaginable. Specks appeared fluttering from the highest floors of the building; they had to be birds but astonishingly they were people leaping to their deaths, dresses and pants fluttering in the air currents, some of the jumpers with clasped hands in the swift descent. A fire fighter died when a falling man landed on him. Bystanders gasped. Some retched."[18] From inanimate specks to birds to fluttering clothing, those who leap from the tower come into view as human subjects only for a fleeting moment when a spectator makes out the held hands. A second later empathy proves fatal as the leapers become deadly objects for dedicated rescuers.

If in this passage objectifying the falling people initially reflects a distance that allows for empathy, eliminating that distance turns the falling into lethal objects for those who care the most. With the surprise of the second attack, however, the survivors' *conceptual* as well as actual distance from the falling people collapses, and identification with them comes to describe threats to those who flee the scene: "People in the street panicked and ran. Some tripped, fell, got knocked down, were pulled up. People lost their keys, their phones, their handbags, their shoes." Earlier in the *Times* article, those who make it out of the north tower see "endless . . . unmatched shoes," presumably belonging to those who fell; now losing one's shoes signifies the escape efforts of the those on the ground. Likewise, falling becomes what endangers *them*. But then a calm sets in, we are told, and people begin inching back downtown, apparently to get a better view of the disaster. However, this safety, marked by a return to safe spectatorship, is short-lived, and when the first tower falls, the renewal of life-threatening terror leads again to literal threats of being turned into the falling people. The collapse, we are told, knocked one person "over onto other people. Bodies fell on top of him—not all of them, he thought, alive."[19] The speaker, who is alive, marks his survival both as a difference and as an escape from the falling bodies.

For the many who flee the scene, the collapsed buildings themselves become a version of a lethal falling body: "People began running, chased by the smoke. The air rained white ash and plaster dust, coating people until they looked ghostlike." Rendered ghostlike because they cannot escape the building's debris, a representation that recalls, perhaps to pay tribute to, the horror felt by those who died in the attacks, the people who flee the collapse are horrified as well by a fear *of* the dead, already turned to ash. "'Don't breathe the air,' people shouted. 'It could be toxic.'"[20] Thus imagining the pulverized bodies as part of the building's debris inspires both remembrance and fear of the dead. A more seamless articulation of this conceptualization comes from Andrew Sullivan, who can always be relied on to give us insights into the contradictions that support dominant national subjectivity. In condemning the attack, he states, "It was a crime—the filling of the air of a great and free city with the irradiated dust of innocent human lives."[21] For Sullivan, the crime of murdering innocents seems also to be a crime of air pollution in which the human dust threatens, one imagines, those who still live and breathe in the great city.

The *Times* article, we should note, renders the fear of being turned into the dead and the falling in explicitly visual terms. The drama of outrunning the smoke involves moving through, first, a visual identification with the dead (coated with ash, those who flee are "ghostlike"), then an immediate repudiation of them, to reach a safe place. Significantly, this safe arrival is marked by nostalgic spectatorship. When they outrun the smoke, we are told, people look back downtown where "an unthinkable sight presented itself: empty space where a 110-story tower had been." The "unthinkable" sight of the empty space now replaces the "unimaginable" images of the falling people. When the south tower falls, the trajectory repeats itself: people outrun the smoke and then look back mournfully at a second empty space. The final words of the article come from a spectator who explicitly mourns the loss of the towers as a loss of location in relation to them. "You always know where you are when you see those two buildings. And now, they're gone."[22] In shaking off the dust of the collapsed towers, the escaping subject seems also to escape an identification with the falling people. In the end, the article produces the escaping subject as safe by transforming him into a spectator of the ruined buildings, nostalgic for the once secure sense of self that the towers conveyed.[23] In the context of the survivor's quote, moreover, the image of the falling man itself becomes a safer sight: the photo now references the dislocation of the survivor, the unmooring of a self from a crucial, supportive connection to the buildings. Not so far-fetched in light of how this same story ends in the photo volume: "Once the smoke had lifted, as people brushed the dust off their clothes and out of their hair, there was this void." People "did not know where to go or what to say, how to be themselves. Their frame of reality had cracked."[24]

If the safe spectator's reality has cracked, however, it, like the collapsed towers, can be replaced. Certainly, the article deliberately seeks to elicit empathic identifications between survivors and those who fell with or from the building. Yet it also, less wittingly, records and enacts the repudiation that such identifications generate. As the displacement of the sight of the falling man with the sight of ruined buildings demonstrates, such repudiation sets the stage for reconstructing a familiar, secure world by replacing 9/11's "unimaginable" sights with more tolerable ones. At the same time, much of the iconic 9/11 photographic record references and recalls the horrifying sights. These photos, which link safe spectatorship to the sight of figures surviving a visual likeness to the falling people, predicate embodied national strength on difference from rather than vengeful identification with the intolerably vulnerable, trapped, and falling figures.

Photography and Post-9/11 Safe Spectatorship

While the *Times* article illustrates the story of escape with the one photograph of the falling man, the photo volumes give visual shape to 9/11 events in multiple images: of horrified spectators, the damaged north tower, the second attack, people fleeing for their lives to a point of safety—images that occurred repeatedly in the mainstream press for weeks and months after 9/11. In these images, we can see how a visual lexicon emerges for turning the horrifying sights into safer ones and, in so doing, restoring the safe spectatorship associated for those in the U.S. with viewing photographs of wartime atrocities. Beginning with the framing of the images of the falling themselves, this lexicon extends beyond the survivors' escapes to the photographic reconstruction of a resilient body, often symbolic of national strength restored.

At the same time, photography allows for ways of seeing that can illuminate as well as pursue this quest for safe spectatorship. Consider, for example, the widely circulated video (broadcast to millions on 9/11) shot by Evan Fairbanks, which makes a strong connection between the surprise of the second attack and an assault on spectatorship itself. The stills reproduced in this essay are taken from a large sequence published in *One Nation* (see figs. 3.2, 3.3, and 3.4).[25] Working on a video project for nearby Trinity Church, Fairbanks heard an explosion, grabbed his camera, ran outside, and shot the sequence. At the beginning of the sequence, we see not the unobstructed view of the injured north tower, which Fairbanks wanted to record, but one both inhabited by a human subject and blocked by the undamaged south tower. The man in the picture compels our attention and identification; he appears to be listening to a radio for news of the first attack, just as many of us were glued to the news of what we thought was the only attack. His sense of relative safety, derived perhaps from participating in the national community addressed by the newscast, is underscored by the presence of the bright, high south tower that intervenes between him and the smoking north tower. But with the entrance of United Flight 175 into the frame (see fig. 3.2), the buildings are implicated in obscuring the view from the ground and intensifying the surprise of the second attack.

Thus, the sequence emphasizes the traumatic shock of witnessing the unanticipated second attack that the ubiquitous wide-angle, mainstream photographs of it help to efface. Indeed, it is tempting to pose the authenticity of the documentary camera against the more empowering vantage point and intentional framing of the TV news cameras that were able to record the approach of the second plane only because they were already trained on the burning north tower. Fairbanks seems to offer the more accurate view of the attack, showing us the terrifying surprise, seen from a limited perspective and underscored by the presence and perspective of a vulnerable human subject. All of this is true, but in the rush to see this sequence as getting closer to truth, we may miss its demonstration of the impulse to get rid of the very vulnerability it reveals. And here intolerable vulnerability takes a specific form: traumatized spectatorship.

Top to bottom: Figures 3.2, 3.3, 3.4. Stills from Evan Fairbanks's documentary video of the second attack. Evan Fairbanks, Magnum Photos.

If in showing Flight 175 emerging into view just before impact, the sequence reminds its spectators of their own vulnerability to terrifying visual surprises, that vulnerability intensifies in the man who, unlike the spectator of the video, becomes a spectator of the attack only because the sound of the impact and/or its description on the radio make him look up (see fig. 3.3). Thus, his visual capacities are even more limited than the camera's and our own. We see the plane before he does, and he sees it only when the sound of the attack compels his gaze. That is, the video shows us, from a safer viewing position, the second attack as one that brings into being a shocked and horrified spectator. When, however, the man runs away from what he sees and out of the frame, Fairbanks points his camera higher, focusing on the damaged buildings, the only remaining object of vulnerability (see fig. 3.4). For the spectator *of* the video, then, identifying with the physically endangered, terrified spectator *in* the video is replaced by seeing only the effects of the attack on the damaged building. Thus, the sequence both thematizes the second attack as producing a trauma of spectatorship and shows us that the terrified spectator (in the video) can be replaced by a safe(r) spectator (of the video), one whose look both sees the attack coming and ultimately focuses on damaged but replaceable buildings.

Indeed, the wide appeal of the Fairbanks sequence may indicate a post-9/11 need to assure ourselves that photographic images that record but cannot stop the shocking trajectories of planes and human bodies on 9/11 can be displaced by photos of more tolerable, safer sights. The Fairbanks stills record this displacement as change in the course of the frame-by-frame sequence, but the still photographic record of 9/11 and its aftermath does so in terms of a symbolic visual vocabulary. We will recall that Marianne Hirsch points to the importance of photographs in processing the traumatic events of 9/11 because of the way they defer viewing and understanding. One important consequence of such deferral, according to Hirsch, is the possibility of "what Walter Benjamin called the camera's 'optical unconscious'—the technologies of sight reveal more than we can see through the eye, but the realization of that revelation is deferred."[26] Significantly for my argument, Hirsch offers the actual example of a lab technician who informs a photographer that his image makes visible what he, in fact, had not seen as he shot the exploding towers: "a person holding on to a piece of the falling building."[27] Her point is that what we do not want to see can show up in the image anyway, and the deferred revelation can help us process the trauma. While I will continue to emphasize the impulse to repress such images, we can see that repression not only in their speedy disappearance from the photographic record or in their appearance at the margins in the photos that are meant to record something else. We can also see efforts to repress the most traumatic sights both in the few images that deliberately record the trapped and falling bodies themselves and in the many that refer back to and transform them in reassuring ways. The deferred understanding through sustained contemplation that these photographs enable involves not only the capacity to see more than the photographer intended. It involves as well the construction of a visual lexicon in which images of 9/11and its aftermath take their meaning from other such images.

If the disappearance of the photographs of falling people points to their repression, the reappearance of these images in the photo volumes, usually as one or two iconic images presented in the first few pages, helps us to see how they provide a visual template for many of the volumes' subsequent photos, often ones we saw repeatedly in the weeks and months after 9/11. The image of the falling man at the center of the *Times* article, which appears as a full-page image in *A Nation Challenged* (see fig. 3.1), is typical of the distinctive features of these photos; the horrifying image of trapped and falling people also stresses the visual similarity between the human body and the width, the verticality, and the hues of the buildings' girders. The sympathetic horror a spectator feels upon looking at this image can be mitigated by this formal dimension, which, as I observed earlier, seems to objectify the falling man—to suggest to the spectator that he is somehow part of, just like, and conceptually bound to the doomed building that constitutes his entire landscape. Whatever the photographer or editor intended, this formal dimension helps to shift the image from being about the man's terror to being about the safer framing of this horrifying sight.[28] For the post-9/11 spectator, having survived in one morning successive terrifying events and having followed the dramatic story of the survivors' escapes, the image allows for a retreat from an intolerable, recurring identification with the trapped and falling people. Seeing the falling man as anonymous and visually like the building helps both to articulate a difference from his plight and to bury a recollection of intolerable vulnerability in the lost but replaceable buildings.

Like this photo, others of trapped and falling people preserved in the photo volumes show us doomed figures whose body widths fit those of the building's vertical girders and whose clothes, when black, gray, or white, have the effect of making it hard to visually separate the figures from the building. In contrast to the iconic photo's closer-in shot of a single, relatively large figure against an isolated and intact part of the building, however, the other images show the burning building from a greater distance. Figure 3.5 is typical of images that emphasize the fatal height of the towers and show the trapped people as tiny figurines leaning and climbing out of windows.[29] Even the most distinct of these figures seem doomed to fall with or from the building. But we can make out many of the figures, embedded in the shadows of the window recesses between girders and obscured by smoke and debris, only through an intensive search for them. In another such image, published in *One Nation,* a small figure of a man, dressed in a white shirt and gray trousers, completely outside the building and vertical, seems to blend visually into the recess between the white and grey vertical girders.[30] It's as if this visual fit signifies the jump we know is coming as a symbolic merging with the building. Others in the image who will fall from or with the building, whose bodies are partially out of the windows, are even harder to distinguish from the building. At the same time, however, at the lower right portion of the two-page image, a person is falling, horizontal with arms spread out, both quite distinct from the building and suggesting a posture of flight. Perhaps here

Figure 3.5. People trapped high in the north tower and leaning out of windows.
Thomas Dallal, All rights reserved.

at the bottom of the photo, we have an instance of the camera seeing more, in Benjamin's sense, than what the photographer wanted to record.

The impulse to see the trapped and falling people as part of the doomed buildings has perhaps its most literal representation in a series of two photographs from *A Nation Challenged*. The first of these, whose caption reads, "a woman (near bottom, left of center) looks out from the north tower after it was hit," shows another instance of the trapped person whose body is barely distinguishable from the building (see fig. 3.6).[31] Even though we are given clues about where to look, the tones of white and gray the woman shares with the damaged structure make it hard to find in this picture the woman to whom the caption refers. We see far more distinctly and at the center of the frame the remnants of the plane that has lodged in the building. Once discovered, however, the woman appears to be waving toward the camera and calling for help, rather than merely looking out; indeed, the woman's appeal for recognition would seem to work against her assimilation to the iconography that produces the safe spectator. But, if anything, she is even more lost in the building than those in similar photos; by the time we make out her image, her relation to the building has become entangled with that of the far more apparent plane, welded to the gap in which the woman stands as well. Perhaps most tellingly, this same image appears in a smaller version several pages later, as a representation of the *building* only, with no mention of the woman, whom we now can locate right away (see fig. 3.7).[32] In this picture, arrows and lines overlay the image, indicating the structural components near the damaged area that might be improved in new buildings. With this image, the picture of the trapped woman literally is resignified as a picture of the damaged building as an object that can be rebuilt.

In the pictures that record the escape of those on the ground, the visual trope of assimilating trapped or doomed people to the damaged buildings applies to those who are threatened by the towers' collapse but who make it out alive. Multiple photos of the flight from Ground Zero record it as a desperate escape from the debris that coats bodies, faces, and hair, rendering the fleeing figures, as many a caption points out, ghostlike. Echoing the *Times* story, then, the photos show us this flight both as the occasion to identify with those who could not escape the damaged and collapsed buildings and the occasion for emerging safely from that identification. We see the cloud of debris pursuing those who run (imagined in the story, we will recall, as the animated building containing the dust of the dead), and we see people emerge from almost invisibility in the cloud to a visibility made more emphatic because their foregrounded bodies, in stark contrast to those trapped in or falling from the towers, occupy the entire frame.

In this same vein, a remarkable photograph from the Magnum collection shows a statue of a businessman, seated on a long bench at a distance from the fallen towers and holding a briefcase that is coated with the dust of the collapsed buildings. We learn from the caption that this sight of the dust-coated statue, "frozen in place," struck the photographer as a fitting memorial for the 9/11 dead.[33] Yet it is an image that, in the contexts both of media narratives and of the photographic record of the escape, represents more accurately a climactic moment in the story of the *survivors'* dramatic flight from being frozen in place by the falling debris: the terrifying identification, rendered as those on the ground being covered by ash and dust, with those who fell. Thus, it seems that a sincere desire to pay tribute to the dead finds its expression unwittingly in an image that memorializes the dreaded but transcended identification. This image, and the photographer's description of it, point to how the production of safe spectatorship involves remembering the sight of the falling and the doomed by seeing the sight of a threatened identification that survivors have escaped.

The repudiation of this identification extends beyond the images of the escape and into the photographic record of 9/11's aftermath. In the multitude of photos depicting the search and rescue activities at Ground Zero, the specific visual lexicon associated with the photos of the trapped and falling people becomes the visual vocabulary for reassembling the safe national self. The documentation of the early rescue effort, of course, returns live figures to the ruins of the building, and in this image from *A Nation Challenged*, as in many similar ones, several of the workers are almost indistinguishable from the wreckage (see fig. 3.8).[34] Especially, the tiny figures in the background, dispersed among fallen rows of the buildings' girders, recall images of those trapped in the still-standing buildings. Yet even some of the larger figures in the foreground, including a row of uniformed rescuers at the base of the fallen girders, visually

Figure 3.6. A trapped woman, near the bottom and left of center, is very hard to distinguish in this photo.
Brian Manning/The New York Times.

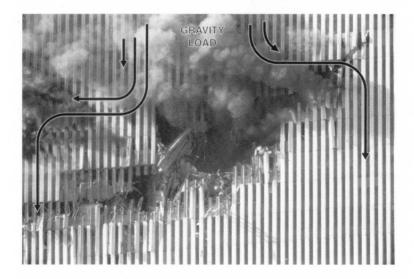

Figure 3.7. Lines and arrows drawn over the same photo of the trapped woman for the purpose of analyzing why the building fell.
Brian Manning/The New York Times.

Figure 3.8. Rescue workers among the towers' wreckage.
Ruth Fremson/The New York Times.

blend into the whites and grays of the debris. We might see here an effort to record in the debris a memorial trace of the bodies that have now in fact disappeared in it. Yet by recalling the photographic iconography of the trapped and falling bodies as hard to distinguish from the buildings, the image gestures toward remembering the dead within the very visual lexicon that objectifies and repudiates an identification with the falling people. Even as the image recalls the dead, then, the live workers—many in official rescue uniforms and many larger and more distinct in the foreground—are well-situated to help the spectator see a new national body emerge from the threatening ones. Those who were trapped or fell have now, without a doubt, disappeared in the building's wreckage.

Not surprisingly, photos like this one prefigure those in which the bodies of the rescue workers grow ever larger, rising above the wreckage that still surrounds them. A dramatic photo from the Magnum collection shifts to a focus on a single figure, a fireman climbing up a ladder through the towers' debris but framed by the broken window of an adjacent building.[35] Seen through the jagged edges of the wide window frame, the image of an official rescue worker climbing out of the debris shows us how the fall of the towers signifies that reality, linked to the built environment, has cracked for survivors. But if in the *Times* essay the survivors' cracked reality becomes the referent for the image of the falling man at the center of the text, here the image that conveys the rupturing of the survivors' location in relation to the built environment is one of climbing, not falling. In the context of the photo record, this climbing is almost a resurrection from a visual identification with those who were trapped in or fell with and from the towers.

By necessity, of course, all images focused closely on Ground Zero have as their context the empty space where the towers once stood. While numerous photos show us relatively small figures of official workers rising larger in this space, as if they were growing up and out of their visual likeness to the trapped and falling people, other images fill up that empty space with large, foregrounded figures of firemen, soldiers, policemen, and public officials—that is, those associated with the official power to rescue and protect. The largest of these official figures are presented without any environmental context at all, as if designed to reconstruct the safe self as a body supported by national or official power, not by the built structures that failed the falling people. Not surprisingly, it is photographic technology that makes it possible to see the true dimensions of this fantasy. A whole section of *One Nation* is dedicated to presenting a series of full-page images of 9/11 heroes, shot with a special camera that transforms them into giants.[36] These larger-than-life figures are presented with no other context than the background of the white page on which they appear. Endowed by photographic technology with superhuman bodies, these figures are indeed sights for the sore eyes that endured the threatening sight of people unmoored from the support of high buildings. Some of these, however, are more convincing than others. Some seem properly imposing; others, like one of Rudy Giuliani, overweight with hunched shoulders and striving to look impressive, expose the limits of such Herculean national embodiment.[37]

If these high-tech images can trace their lineage to the small, trapped figures from which they seem to rise in the 9/11 photo volumes, a variation on the fantasy of invincible national embodiment comes ready-made in the pre-9/11 photos of the Statue of Liberty, juxtaposed against the still-standing towers. These appear in almost all the volumes and seem to have the shared goal of posing this most weighty of symbolic figures against the buildings. As images of a body whose background is the towers, these photos invoke the falling bodies in order to replace them with the sight of a symbolic national body, immune not only to the vulnerability of actual bodies but also to that of the now-destroyed buildings. If the distinguishing component of the photos of trapped and falling people is the visual assimilation of their bodies to the buildings, here we have the reverse visual effect. Because we know that the statue is still standing and the buildings are not, these images insist that the towers take their ultimate significance from, as they live on in, this massive, indestructible, symbolic national body. We can see this impulse perhaps most clearly in an image that constitutes the first full-page photo in *One Nation,* whose subtitle is "*America Remembers September 11, 2001.*"[38] As the foregrounded statue looms larger than the buildings, they seem almost small in comparison, as if to gesture toward a rebuilding overseen by this indestructible national body. Certainly the image aims to reassure us that national power and security have survived the loss of the towers. Yet, positioned facing the title page of the photo volume, this image appeals to the reader to "remember September 11, 2001" in the context of a specific photographic lexicon it here initiates and which will continue to unfold in the pages that follow: one dedicated to transforming 9/11's most horrifying sights into reassuring ones.

Images of Falling People as Icons of Dissent

As the photo volumes indicate, the post-9/11 belief in a safety conferred by U.S. national identity requires seeing that U.S. survivors both are different from and have survived an identification with the falling people. Yet the photographic construction of the spectator's difference from the victims is also haunted by these figures, testimony to their power to elicit not only an irrepressible horror but also an insistent identification. I turn now to images that actually "bring back" the sight of falling people in the name of empathy with those who are just like us, including the return of the photo of the falling man with which I began. Certainly the restoration of these images to wide public view owes much to the special dignity afforded to U.S. victims by U.S. spectators. And the mere passage of time without subsequent attacks on our shores may also make it possible to contemplate formerly intolerable sights. Yet, I think we can best understand the return of the censored images as responses and contributions to the photographic record that seeks to reconstruct safe spectatorship after 9/11. If the exclusion and reformulation of the horrifying sights is central to the record I have been tracing, these sights return in the service of protesting the censorship that is integral to dangerous post-9/11 U.S. national policies. Presented as icons of a truth that is obfuscated by dangerous official narratives, these images also help to formulate new possibilities for what safety might look like.

An early and quickly censored effort to restore an image of a falling person is Eric Fischl's *Tumbling Woman*. A bronze rendering of a naked female figure in free fall, the sculpture was meant to commemorate those who jumped or fell to their deaths. Upon being displayed at Rockefeller Center, however, it instigated a public outcry that led first to the draping of the sculpture and then to its removal after only a few days. But although it was removed from Rockefeller Center, images of *Tumbling Woman* survived in the photos that accompanied newspaper and Internet debates about its fate.[39] While some complained about the removal, they often appealed, in language reminiscent of Holocaust discourse, to the need to keep the memory of horror alive, to "never forget."[40] Such rhetoric is clearly compatible with the invocation of the World War II photographic template that, as Zelizer argues, is mobilized in place of the actual 9/11 dead to generate support for war; defenses of the sculpture that are framed by this rhetoric may well be symptomatic of the continued need to link the horrifying sights, recalling Sontag's phrase, to "the pain of others." In contrast, Eric Fischl's response to his critics stressed the national specificity of his sculpture as well as his desire to generate feelings of vulnerability rather than revenge: "The sculpture was not meant to hurt anybody. It was a sincere expression of deepest sympathy for the vulnerability of the human condition. Both specifically towards the victims of 9/11 and towards humanity in general."[41] The sculpture is meant to inspire a sense of shared subjectivity between the spectator and the tumbling woman, rather than to inspire vengeance and/or repudiation.

Nonetheless, repudiation proves hard to displace. Indeed, a reporter from the *Times* shows how sustaining repudiation is bound up with sustaining a censorship authorized by the 9/11 photo record. He suggests to Fischl that those offended "might have interpreted this body in freefall as a piece of grim, plastic photojournalism." Here the rationale for censoring the sculpture requires seeing in it not the falling people but the photos of them, whose disappearance, the reporter implies, reflects the good taste that the photo record rightly exhibits. Fischl offers an alternate way of seeing: "The thing is that if you look at the piece itself, it feels like a dream in which somebody is floating. There's no weight there that is sending this crushing, rippling current back through the body as it hits a solid mass. It feels more like a tumbleweed, even though it's a massive sculpture. So, somebody looking at it might say, 'God, it reminds me of falling in a dream right before I wake up.' Both of those are probably correct."[42]

Tumbling, Fischl suggests, can provide a sense of freedom as well as generate fear, and remembering our own experiences in dreams right before we "wake up" may make it possible to imagine terrifying vulnerability without feeling as though we are trapped irrevocably in nightmarish identifications. Appealing to the reporter to look at "the thing itself," rather than to see the sculpture in context of the photo record, Fischl emphasizes a difference sculpture can make in the representation of falling: "there's no weight there" he says, as the sculpture makes contact with the ground. Rather, the massiveness of the sculpture paradoxically preserves precisely this tumbling, floating, dreamlike quality. Putting weight on the side of weightlessness, the artist marshals a classic sculptural technique to make the sight of extreme vulnerability tolerable, and, implicitly, he poses this generic difference against the hegemony of the photo record.

Moreover, the censoring of efforts to change the way spectators remember the falling people is, according to Fischl, directly related to the censorship of criticism of national policy. "No one can criticize the president because we're in a very vulnerable time, even though he's doing some things that are terrible. You can't express your personal horror and trauma at something that we all experienced."[43] Censorship of criticizing the president's policies is intimately connected to the censorship of "offensive" representations of trauma and horror. Recruiting consent to national agendas—war, retaliation, draconian homeland security initiatives—Fischl seems to imply, may require that unimaginable trauma be processed only in particular ways.

Recent evidence suggests that images of the falling, including the iconic image of the falling man, are surfacing to play a new role in a process heretofore dedicated to repudiating and excluding an identification with such horrifying sights. In an article by Tom Junod in *Esquire,* accompanied by a full-page image of the falling man as well as by the outtake footage that records several moments of his fall, that role explicitly is to make visible the censorship in the photo record. Junod decries the disappearance of such images and the relegation of the falling to a "lemminglike class" of sights we cannot bear to see;[44] in contrast, he offers Fischl, who "did not go away . . . turn away, or avert his eyes," and suggests that *Tumbling Woman* is "perhaps *the* redemptive image of 9/11."[45] Moreover, Junod calls attention not only to the disappearance of the image he recovers but also to what the image itself excludes: the outtakes in which the man, like the woman in Fischl's sculpture, is tumbling. The photo, whose framing gives us "a study of doomed verticality . . . with a human being slivered at the center," shows that even censored "photographs lie."[46] Like my own, Junod's argument implicates the formal elements of the image, which liken the man to the building's vertical girders, in modulating the terror of seeing the fall. Yet, despite this opposition between the published but censored photo that lies and the previously unpublished outtakes of tumbling that do not, and despite his failed effort to replace the man's anonymity with knowledge of his identity, in the end Junod returns to the importance of both the iconic image and its anonymity. He asks us to focus once more on this image, this time seeing the man as "buried inside [the photo's] frame— . . . the Unknown Soldier in a war whose end we have not yet seen" and "a measure of what we know of ourselves."[47] It is not clear whether this means we should identify with the falling man as subject to a "burial" that also affects the self-knowledge of survivors or whether our recognition of the man as the "Unknown Soldier" requires the aesthetic framing that buries him in order to elevate him from "lemminglike" to hero in the context of post-9/11 wars.

No such ambiguity informs Frank Rich's enthusiastic appropriation of Junod's recovery of the iconic photo to illustrate a *Times* article on how the public has been denied crucial knowledge about 9/11 and its aftermath. In the article, accompanied by the photo, Rich explicitly links the censorship in the photo record that Junod emphasizes to official obfuscations that seek to recruit consent to unprincipled wars. What we need, according to Rich, are artistic responses to 9/11 that "stri[p] away all the layers of government propaganda and cultural kitsch that have obscured and neutered the raw edges of 9/11 itself."[48] Such art would exhibit the "courage and imagination to challenge a government of brilliant fabulists" who mislead us about the reasons for and the scope of retaliatory wars. Junod receives high praise for bringing back the image of the falling man, and, following him, Rich goes on also to protest the disappearance of Fischl's sculpture.

Remarkably, however, Rich sees the sculpture as "employing iconography similar" to the photo.[49] Whether Rich forgets Junod's insistence on the difference between the photo and its outtakes, and thus between the photo and the sculpture, or whether he deems it insignificant, for him the photo neither represses nor modulates the tumbling fall represented by the sculpture; rather, the photo and the sculpture show us the same thing. Thus, whereas the reporter who interviewed Fischl saw the 9/11 photos of the falling people in the sculpture (by way of invoking the good taste that has censored the photos), Rich sees the sculpture in the iconic photo of the falling man (by way of suggesting that all images of the falling signify an official censorship that should be undone). The first way of seeing, I have argued, is involved in constructing safe spectatorship and recruiting consent to war; the second links the restoration of 9/11's censored images to the truth covered over by "government propaganda" that keeps us unsafe precisely by recruiting consent to war. By linking the censored images to a truth censored by official narratives, Rich points to the importance of the photographic record in shaping what constitutes safety after 9/11.

In the shift of context for the photo of the falling man from the early *Times* article that narrates the 9/11 survivors' escapes to the one, two years later, that advocates an escape from dangerous official lies, the photo's formal elements become, for Rich, insignificant to its new status as the return of what the iconic photo record doesn't show. Yet for the project of reformulating the content of safe spectatorship in terms that take into account the efficacy of the 9/11 photo record, it may be better to engage with rather than to dismiss the iconography that makes the likeness between bodies and buildings a fundamental component of seeing safely. Because that iconography points to the ease with which empathic identification with the trapped and falling people slips to a terrified repudiation of them, neglecting it runs the risk that the return of the censored images may mean the continuation of their ability to "bury" identifications with the kinds of dangers that Rich wants them to bring to light. Moreover, analyzing the way the photo record constructs safe spectatorship makes it possible both to reformulate and to see the reformulation of meanings for the dominant visual tropes circulated in the photo record. Within a context where national protections are revealed as dangerous to those in the U.S., for example, paying attention to the importance of the fit between body and building in the image of the falling man might allow us to see how the disappearance of all context except the tower may gesture toward the risks of taking identity, the sense of where and who you are, from nationally symbolic buildings that confer literal and figurative support.

Such a critical reading of the relation between upside-down bodies and a prominent building seems to inform my final example, which shows a protest against a company that has "interests in several military contractors," "ties to elite circles in Washington," and headquarters in San Francisco's Transamerica Building. The caption reads, "Police keep an eye on demonstrators Monday during a protest against the Carlyle Group" (see fig. 3.9).[50] These riot police recall the uniformed official figures that rise from Ground Zero to enormous heights as part of a visual lexicon meant to produce safe and nostalgic national spectators. Not surprisingly, as official spectators themselves, they "keep an eye on" protesters against the war in Iraq. Yet the photographer encourages another perspective, one that, following the strategy of the activists, places a figure recalling the photo of the upside-down falling man front, center, and looming over the police. The similarity to the iconic photo extends as well to the emphasis on the rhyme between the body and the building. Standing on their heads, the protesters use their bodies to mimic the pyramidal shape of the building, perhaps suggesting and creating a photo opportunity for suggesting new ways of thinking about the similarity between the vulnerably positioned body and landmark buildings: If buildings indeed convey identity, if those who occupy them are

Figure 3.9. Antiwar demonstrators standing on their heads outside the building which houses the Carlyle Group. Fred Larson/San Francisco Chronicle.

implicated in the shape of the business that goes on there, then buildings can put people in dangerous positions.

But this image suggests another reading as well. Here, a position that recalls intolerable 9/11 vulnerability also literally stands out as suggesting a new referent: the exceptional skill it takes to support the body in unfamiliar, counterintuitive ways. An image that permits a sustained contemplation of the upside-down body against the context of a tall building also makes that position a condition for contemplating alternative ways of seeing the body supported safely. Perhaps the protestors meant to suggest a connection between their criticism of the Carlyle Group, housed in the building, and the freedom of an upside-down body from the building's support. In this sense, this image of antiwar protest, which deliberately seeks to transform the post-9/11 iconography that Rich ignores, also shares important features with *Tumbling Woman*. Like the sculpture, this image gestures toward magical and/or counterintuitive modes of providing support for the falling, upside-down body. As they seem to respond to the desire to really stop the fall that the photo freezes, both representations link identification with the falling not only to horror but also to freedom, the agency of dissent, and to new ways of imagining national safety.

Thus, the photographic lexicon I have traced may substantiate Fischl's intuition of a connection between the policing of the representation that processes this most unimaginable of national traumas and the censoring of dissent. Because, as I have argued, post-9/11 safety is also a matter of restoring safe spectatorship, of restoring a link between the photographic mastery of the seen and safe spectatorship, much of the iconic photo record secures this connection by showing us heretofore unthinkable vulnerability banished and strength restored. Yet this record can itself inspire images in which sustaining an identification with the falling people emerges, much as Fischl seems to suggest it might, as a condition for sustaining the capacity to critique national policy, despite and finally because of our national vulnerability. While I have argued that the photographic record works to create a safe spectator precisely by repressing and reformulating that identification, this record's preoccupation with framing and transforming the horrifying sight also keeps its memory alive. However relentlessly the impulse to repudiate overwhelms the impulse to identify with those who fell, the latter survives, becoming available for counterrepresentations of what constitutes danger and what constitutes safety. It appears, then, that the very process of sustained contemplation of photographs that produces the safe spectator of repudiated horror can lead not only to the return of what it seeks to repress but also to a critique of the ideological aims that fuel such repression. Emerging in the recovery of the iconic images themselves or in new images that make reference to them, sights of the falling people return to contest the photographic terms that, after 9/11, link the production of safe spectatorship to an uncritical embrace of national protection.

Notes

1. N. R. Kleinfield, "A Creeping Horror," *New York Times*, sec A, September 12, 2001. The image is reprinted in *A Nation Challenged: A Visual History of 9/11 and Its Aftermath*, photographs ed. Nancy Lee and Lonnie Schlein, text ed. Mitchell Levitas (New York: Callaway, 2002), 23. The image published with this essay is reprinted from *A Nation Challenged*.

2. Kleinfield, "A Creeping Horror."

3. Most of the images that accompany this essay appear in three such volumes: *A Nation Challenged*, which published photos that appeared in the *New York Times*; *One Nation: America Remembers September 11, 2001* (Boston, New York, and London: Little, Brown, and Company, 2001), whose images appeared in *Life* magazine; and Steve McCurry, Magnum Photo, *New York September 11* (New York: Powerhouse Books, 2002), a volume published by a well-known group of New York City photographers. Others are drawn from newspapers and the Internet.

4. See especially Michael Feldschuh, ed., *The September 11 Photo Project* (New York: Regan Books, 2002), a volume of images drawn from an "open forum for display of photos and words in response to the terrorist attacks," over four thousand of which were exhibited in a New York City gallery (vii). See also *Portraits: 9/11/01* (New York: Henry Holt, & Co., 2002), which collects the snapshot and narrative "portraits of grief" that ran in the months after 9/11 in the *New York Times*. The former volume shows how the iconic images I discuss—of the damaged towers, the collapse, the flight from Ground Zero, human figures among the debris—occur repeatedly in lay as well as news photography. The latter volume, with its focus on memorial snapshots of the dead and on memorial rituals, I would argue, makes a unique contribution to the visual lexicon that at one time pays (here very substantial and moving) tribute to the dead and presents safer ways of seeing them. Moreover, in the large photos that accompany the snapshots, there are a number of images of the figure that, as I will argue, plays an important role in this lexicon: the large, official, protective body, which stands free of and replaces the built environment.

5. Marianne Hirsch, "The Day Time Stopped," *Chronicle of Higher Education,* January 25, 2002, sec. B, p. 11.

6. Barbie Zelizer, "Photography, Journalism, and Trauma," in *Journalism after September 11,* ed. Barbie Zelizer and Stuart Allan (New York: Routledge, 2002), 50.

7. Ibid., 54.

8. Ibid., 49.

9. Ibid., 65.

10. Ibid.

11. Susan Sontag, *Regarding the Pain of Others* (New York: Farrar, Strauss, and Giroux, 2003), 72, 70.

12. Ibid., 14.

13. Ibid., 68.

14. In a claim for the persistence and importance of nationally empowered spectatorship to postattack U.S. citizens, Frank Lentricchia and Jody Mcauliffe argue that the rise of tourism at Ground Zero reflects that Americans feel entitled to a proprietary "right to look. Democracy gives them the right to look, to take back the view that was stolen from them." See their "Groundzeroland," *South Atlantic Quarterly* 101: 2 (Spring 2002): 359. However, I argue that after 9/11 such habits of empowered spectatorship are neither sufficient to restoring a sense of safe spectatorship nor easy to sustain.

15. Sontag, *Regarding the Pain of Others,* 71.

16. Kleinfield, "A Creeping Horror."

17. Ibid.

18. N. R. Kleinfield, "The Unimaginable," in *A Nation Challenged,* 13.

19. Kleinfield, "A Creeping Horror."

20. Ibid.

21. Andrew Sullivan, "Yes, America Has Changed," *Time,* September 9, 2002, 46.

22. Kleinfield, "A Creeping Horror."

23. Zelizer observes a similar displacement of bodies by lost and damaged buildings in the course of the U.S. media coverage of 9/11. After a few days the images of trapped and falling people disappeared, and, "What remained instead

was the reigning image of the burning towers. . . . The towers, then, displaced the bodies that might have been visualized instead." Zelizer, "Photography, Journalism, and Trauma," 65.

24. Kleinfield, "The Unimaginable," 13.

25. *One Nation*, 30–31. A sequence from the video appears prominently in the introduction to the *Magnum Photographers* (4–5).

26. Hirsch, "The Day Time Stopped." Benjamin claims that "a different nature opens itself to the camera than opens to the naked eye—if only because an unconsciously penetrated space is substituted for a space consciously explored by man." Thus, "the camera introduces us to unconscious optics as does psychoanalysis to unconscious impulses." See Walter Benjamin "The Work of Art in the Age of Mechanical Reproduction," in his *Illuminations* (New York: Schocken, 1969), 236–37, 237.

27. Hirsch, "The Day Time Stopped."

28. Jane Gallop has suggested in conversation that this formal dimension situates the image within a tradition of photographic modernism, in which subject matter and the aesthetic aspects of an image are inextricable. Thus, this aesthetic context may play a role in the way the photo of the falling man is made safe for spectatorship. For a discussion of such photographic modernism and images of the human form, see Gallop, *Living with His Camera* (Durham: Duke University Press, 2003), 139–40. See also Sontag on the tensions between the aesthetic and documentary dimensions of photographs that depict horrible events (*Regarding the Pain of Others*, 77).

29. *A Nation Challenged*, 22.

30. *One Nation*, 38–39.

31. *A Nation Challenged*, 19.

32. Ibid., 33.

33. The caption quotes the photographer, Susan Meiselas: "Late in the afternoon of that first terrible day, I came across this sculpture near the World Trade Center. Frozen in place, it seemed to stand for all those who were gone" (*Magnum Photographers*, 30–31).

34. *A Nation Challenged*, 64–65.

35. *Magnum Photographers*, 17.

36. *One Nation*, 142–167.

37. Ibid., 162.

38. Ibid., 5.

39. For example, see Russ Kick, "The Memory Hole: The 9/11 Artwork the Public Isn't Allowed to See," http://www.thememoryhole.org/911/911-art.htm.

40. See Nick Monteleone, "Rock Center's Disservice to Art," *New York Daily News: Ideas and Opinions*, http://www.nydailynews.com/news/ideas—opinions/story/20296p-1925c.html. See also William W. Lewis, "Remember," *Philadelphia City Paper*, September 26–October 2, 2002. http://www.citypaper.net/articles/2002-09-26/slant.shtml.

41. Quoted in Katherine Roth, "Statue of Falling Woman Censored," *Associated Press*, September 19, 2003. http://www.msnbc.com/news/810019.asp?1=1.

42. David Rakoff, "Questions for Eric Fischl: Post 9/11 Modernism," *New York Times Magazine*, October 27, 2002, 15.

43. Ibid.

44. Tom Junod, "The Falling Man," *Esquire*, September 2003, 177–81, 198–99.

45. Ibid., 179.
46. Ibid., 180.
47. Ibid., 199.
48. Frank Rich, "Where's Larry Kramer When We Need Him?" *New York Times,* October 5, 2003, sec. 2.
49. Ibid.
50. *San Francisco Chronicle,* March 27, 2003, Business sec. I am grateful to Elizabeth Abel for calling my attention to this image.

4 Captain America Sheds His Mighty Tears: Comics and September 11

Henry Jenkins

Consider two images. In a widely reproduced news photograph, a mother and son have gathered to lay flowers on an American flag outside the United States consulate in Sydney. The weeping boy is wearing Batman pajamas. No doubt the photographer wanted to show how the global circulation of American popular culture had extended the imaginary national community to encompass many who had never stepped foot within our geographic borders. In an image from *Heroes,* a poster book created by Marvel to raise money for the relief efforts (see fig. 4.1), Captain America towers over the Manhattan skyline, his massive legs replacing the Twin Towers. He covers his face and cries for his country. Marvel uses Captain America here as a national symbol, more or less equivalent to Uncle Sam, who also had his own superhero comic book series for a brief period during World War II.[1]

These two pictures of grieving superheroes suggest some of the ways that the language and iconography of comics have been deployed in helping the world make sense of September 11. Slower and more reflective than CNN (or for that matter the *Daily Planet*), quicker in their turnaround than television drama or Hollywood movies, comic books offered a useful testing ground for strategies by which popular culture could respond to this tragedy. Comics offered, as *Time* reports, "The first national-scale artistic interpretation of this twenty-first-century international crisis."[2] As this chapter will suggest, studying comics allows us not only to map the immediate response but also to measure the long-term impact of these events on American popular culture.[3] At the same time, the distinctive position of comics as a niche medium produced by a mainstream industry allowed something unique to happen—the emergence of a popular progressive discourse about suffering and loss, the heroism of everyday people and the power of grassroots organizations, multiculturalism and globalization, and the need to stop or slow down the cycle of hatred and violence.

I want to discuss comics as a site of vernacular theory and grassroots activism. Editorialists described George W. Bush's tendency to reduce the war on ter-

Figure 4.1. Captain America Sheds His Mighty Tears: Mike Deodato Jr. with Dennis Calero, *Heroes*.
Captain America ™© 2004 Marvel Characters, Inc. Used with permission.

rorism to a conflict between the "Axis of Evil" and the "Forces of Freedom" as "comic bookish." Yet this seems grossly unfair—to comic books. For the most part, comic creators did a better job in articulating a critical perspective on 9/11 than did cultural critics like Noam Chomsky or Edward Said, who often seemed to retreat into theoretical abstractions and polemical language ghoulishly out of touch with the emotional state of their publics. The intellectuals mostly said what we expected them to say. These comic artists and writers often broke with institutional modes and professional practices, acknowledged their own emotional stakes, rethought their existing vocabulary, and took ethical responsibility for the consequences of their work. Too often, critical theorists have portrayed popular culture as only endlessly reproducing dominant ideologies or as if resistance can only come by refusing to accept its messages. In the process, we have given up hope that popular culture can be a meaningful site for political intervention. This is a study of what happens when committed artists seek to communicate their messages through the language of popular entertainment.

September 11 brought comics back to their roots in what Michael Denning has described as the Cultural Front. Denning documents the political and economic forces which came together in the 1930s and 1940s to create a new style of cultural politics, one which gave aesthetic form to the struggle against fascism at home and abroad. During this period, artists (both elite and popular) came to see the political importance of cultural work and sought to couple ideological critique with raw emotion. Denning summarized the key themes of the Cultural Front: "A social democratic laborism based on a militant industrial unionism; an anti-racist ethnic pluralism imagining the United States as a 'nation of nations'; and an anti-fascist politics of international solidarity."[4] The leftists working in Hollywood or on Broadway or in mass-market magazines in the 1930s saw themselves as doing important "culture work," inserting progressive ideas into popular forms where they would reach out beyond those already converted to their cause. What gave their work its vitality and emotional resonance was the urgency they felt as they sought ways to craft immediate but meaningful responses to current events. The Cultural Front brought together people with fundamentally different ideological stances, a temporary tactical alliance between Marxists and liberal Democrats, which produced some of the most compelling art of the era.

The comic book superheroes took shape during this same period and were, in some largely unprocessed, rarely self-conscious way, the most popular embodiment of the Cultural Front.[5] Michael Chabon's *The Amazing Adventures of Kavalier & Clay* reminds us of the ways the earliest superhero comics were shaped by the experiences of their young, often Jewish, predominantly urban creators, many of whom saw their narratives as striking a blow against fascism.[6] Thomas Andrae described those early stories: "Superman saves an innocent woman from being electrocuted, stops a wife-beating, and halts corrupt politicians and an avaricious munitions manufacturer from fomenting an international war for their personal gain. Other early issues deal with the rights of accused persons to fair and impartial justice, with crooked unions and corrupt municipal officials, and with prison brutality, slum conditions, and other pressing social issues. In these early issues Superman was clearly the champion of the underdog, displaying a sense of class consciousness virtually absent from his later comic book stories."[7] It's right there on the page—Superman vows not to fight for truth, justice, and the American way, but rather to defend and protect the "oppressed." Captain America's shield and Wonder Woman's star-spangled costume date back to a time when Aaron Copland was composing a fanfare for common men or Woody Guthrie was singing "This Land Is My Land." Comic books were, to use one of the most offensive terms of the McCarthy era, "prematurely anti-fascist." The men in capes were punching Hitler in the snout and kicking Tojo in the butt long before Pearl Harbor, and when the nation caught up with where they had been all along, they loved the superguys all the more. Their images had been painted on the sides of battleships and fighter planes during World War II; GIs carried battered comics in their knapsacks. Their creators were cross-examined before Congress in the 1950s when reformers worried that they were a negative influence on American youth. These anti-comics crusades pushed the medium to the right, clamping down on any critique of American culture and making Superman and his kith establishment figures. By the 1960s, radical politics surfaced not in the mainstream comics industry but from the fringes. The underground comics aligned themselves with the counterculture and the anti-war movement and circulated alongside drug paraphernalia, underground newspapers, and Day-Glo posters.[8] Some mainstream comics—see, for example, Dennis O'Neil's *Green Arrow* stories which pit a latter-day Robin Hood against corporate greed and small-town bigotry[9]—struggled to preserve those radical roots, but for the most part, readers forgot what the superheroes originally stood for. September 11 brought them back to their core and renewed the themes and iconography of the Cultural Front for a new generation.

If the original Cultural Front glorified factory workers and farm laborers, the new comics celebrated firefighters, cops, and emergency workers. If the old Cultural Front aligned itself with labor unions and the Communist Party, the comics embraced the anti-globalization and environmental movements. If the original Cultural Front questioned capitalist greed, the new books depicted sensationalistic corporate media and greedy insurance companies as feeding off the suffering.[10] If the old Cultural Front repurposed American folk culture, the new books tapped into the iconography of the superheroes. If the Cultural Front urged our engagement in a war against fascism, the new comics urged caution as we entered a new war against terrorism. In some ways, the political context was profoundly different; in some ways, the themes and images remained the same.

The Context

Once mainstream, comics are increasingly a fringe (even an *avant garde*) medium, one which appeals predominantly to college students or college-educated professionals. More than twenty times the number of people went to see the Spiderman movies on their opening days than had read a Spiderman comic the previous year. As comics struggle to maintain their hardcore readership and to expand outward to new publics, they have entered a period of experimentation, testing new themes, adopting diverse styles, and expanding their genre vocabulary. And because the cost of production and thus the price of experimentation is much lower than in any other medium, the film and television industries monitor trends in comics, searching for material that can be brought from the fringes into the mainstream. Comics now function, as DC editor Dennis O'Neil has commented, as "The R&D Division" for the rest of the entertainment industry.[11] Comics may no longer be mass culture, in the sense that they attract a niche rather than a broadly constituted audience. They remain popular culture in that they draw heavily on genre formulas and are published primarily for entertainment purposes. The split between mainstream and alternative comics sometimes parallels the high/low splits that separate popular culture from *avant garde* art, yet the borders between the two are more porous than elsewhere in the art world. The marginal status of comics is paradoxical: because they are fringe media, they have more space for experimentation than most mainstream products; but because they are a feeder system for the rest of the entertainment world, those experiments are closely monitored and may have enormous influence.

Since the 1960s, two comic book companies—DC and Marvel—have dominated the American comic book industry. DC, owned by Time Warner Communications, is the home of Superman, Batman, Wonder Woman, Green Arrow, Green Lantern, The Flash, The Justice League of America, and a stable of other characters, many of whom date back to the 1930s and 1940s. Marvel, owned by Marvel Entertainment Group, launched a new generation of superhero characters in the early 1960s which included Spiderman, The Fantastic Four, The Incredible Hulk, The X-Men, and Daredevil, and it revamped some earlier figures, such as Captain America, The Submariner, and The Human Torch. In 2002, Marvel published 40 percent of all comics sold, DC 30 percent. Their next closest competitor, Image, published only seven percent.[12] Newer companies—CrossGen, Dark Horse, Image, Oni, Top Shelf, and Milestone, among others—operate on the borderline between mainstream and indie, offering their artists much greater creative control over their work. Their works fall loosely within popular genres, such as superhero, fantasy, crime, romance, and adventure comics, though they publish a broader range of material than DC or Marvel and attempt to attract niche readers. Both DC and Marvel have established boutique labels, Vertigo and Max respectively, which function not unlike Miramax, Dreamworks, or Touchstone within Hollywood, allowing the mainstream companies to tap alternative markets. Independent or *avant garde* comics tend to be self-published, though several companies, most notably Fantagraphics and Drawn and Quarterly, have sought to establish reliable distribution channels for more experimental or politically subversive titles. Historically, mainstream artists signed long-term contracts with DC or Marvel, which operated much like the old studio system in Hollywood. These companies told them what to draw and they drew it, getting little recognition beyond comics fandom and holding little control over their work. Over the past several decades, a creator's rights movement within the comics industry has altered the contractual relationships between writers, artists, and publishers. The result has been a much more fluid movement of talent between commercial and alternative comics and, in the process, a greater range of formal and thematic experimentation within the commercial mainstream.

September 11 brought about some remarkable collaborations between mainstream and alternative publishers, possible only because the artists, writers, and publishers knew each other, had worked together in the past, and had discovered compelling reasons to pool their efforts. Artists who had spent their lifetimes producing superhero stories found themselves, for the first time in some cases, exploring autobiographical or real-world themes, much as alternative comics creators were introducing new themes into the superhero genre.

We really cannot understand how American media responded to September 11 from an institutional perspective alone. This was deeply personal. Manhattan has historically been the base of operations for the mainstream publishers. The corporate headquarters of DC and Marvel are within a few miles of Ground Zero. Some of their employees lost friends and family. Some found themselves, for whatever reason, in the general vicinity of the World Trade Center (WTC) as the towers collapsed. Marvel felt especially implicated since its stories had always been set in New York City, not some imaginary Metropolis. Captain America, Spiderman, Daredevil, The Fantastic Four, live in brownstones or sky-rise apartments; they take the subway; they watch games at Yankee Stadium; they swing past the World Trade Center (or at least, they used to do so); they used to help out Mayor Giuliani.[13]

These companies saw publishing comic books to raise money for the relief effort as "our way of lifting bricks and mortar"—using their skills and labor to make a difference.[14] Marvel published a series of September 11–themed books, including *Heroes,* which billed itself "The World's Greatest Superhero Creators Honor the World's Greatest Heroes," and *Moment of Silence,* which featured more or less wordless stories depicting the real-life experiences of people who gave their lives or miraculously survived the events of September 11. DC joined forces with Dark Horse, Image, Chaos!, Oni, Top Shelf, and several other smaller presses to produce two volumes, *9-11: The World's Finest Comic Book Writers & Artists Tell Stories to Remember* and the more modestly titled *9-11: Artists Respond.* Many of the alternative or independent comic artists also lived in or around Manhattan, participating in the New York underground arts scene. The Small Press Expo, one of the major showcases for alternative comics and a central source of their income, was being held in Bethesda and thus got caught up in the panic that hit Washington, DC, following the Pentagon attack. Jeff Mason, publisher of Alternative Comics, organized a benefit project, *9-11: Emergency Relief,* which brought together some of the top independent and underground comics artists. In all these projects, the artists donated their time and labor, the printers donated ink and paper, the distributors waived their usual fees, and the publisher contributed their proceeds to groups like the Red Cross. Many comic shops and patrons saw purchasing these books as their way of showing their support. Several New York galleries displayed and sold artwork from these projects. These projects drew tremendous interest from readers. On the 2002 chart of best-selling graphic novels, the *9-11* tribute books held first and second place, *Emergency Relief* held twentieth position, and Marvel's *Moment of Silence* ranked fifteenth in the list of top-selling single issues for the year.[15]

Comparing the goals editors set for these various projects suggests the very different ideological climates shaping mainstream and alternative comics. Alternative Comics publisher Jeff Mason declared, "I am really shocked and dismayed by some of the rhetoric and behavior I've seen from some in the guise of patriotism, and I think that a book that promotes an alternative to xenophobia and antagonism would be a good thing."[16] In contrast, DC Publisher Paul Levitz stated, "We aspire to use comics to reach people; to tell tales of heroism and the ability of the human spirit to triumph over adversity; to extol the unique virtues of the American dream, and its inclusive way of life; to recall that the price of liberty is high."[17] To some degree, those different political agendas are reflected in the books themselves, but less than one might imagine, since mainstream and alternative creators contributed to both projects and since most of the contents could be loosely described as progressive. A few of the submitted pieces *are* out-and-out reactionary (see figs. 4.2 and 4.3): one of the *Heroes* posters depicts the Hulk, his green muscles bulging, waving an American flag as fighter jets fly overhead, bound for Afghanistan, with the slogan, "Strongest One There Is." Adopting a similar theme, Beau Smith imagines the thoughts of a reservist helping emergency workers today, off to fight tomorrow: "This isn't my grandfather's war. This is a war of rats. There's only one way to hunt rats that bite and then scurry off into dark holes. You send rat terriers into those holes after them, and they don't come out until all of the rats are dead. We are those rat terriers."[18] Yet these militaristic images might exist, side by side, with something like Pat Moriarity's caricature of Uncle Sam, praying on bent knee, "Dear God, Allah, supreme spaceman, great pumpkin, whoever you are—please stop the cycle of hatred!"[19] One would be hard-pressed to see such ideological diversity anywhere else in an increasingly polarized and partisan American media.

Superhero comics are carefully managed to insure no contradictions in the well-established continuity of each narrative. Developments have to be coordinated across books since DC or Marvel set their stories in a coherent narrative universe extending across all of their franchises; shifts in one book can impact all the others. But the short turnaround on these projects, with deadlines a few days or at most a few weeks after the events, made it difficult to coordinate the messages. The presses allowed the writers and artists unprecedented control over their work. There were some restrictions—both from the publishers and the American Red Cross, which demanded changes in some of the stories before it would allow itself to be listed as the books' beneficiary.[20] Yet for the most part, the artists were speaking from their hearts with few institutional barriers—a

Figure 4.2. Jingoistic imagery: Neal Adam's Superman. Reprinted with permission from DC Comics.

theme vividly expressed in Eric Drooker's cover for *9-11: Artists Respond* (see fig. 4.4) depicting an individual artist, perched on top of a New York skyscraper, with the ruins of the towers in the background.[21] The comic artists draw heavily on their own experiences and situate themselves squarely within the stories they tell.[22]

Steve Duncombe has written about the politics of authenticity that has shaped the alternative culture of zines over the past few decades. For Duncombe, what made zines radical was that they took seriously the thoughts and experiences of everyday people of all walks of life whose stories were not being told within mainstream media.[23] The alternative comics tradition had similarly been drawn toward an autobiographical mode with artists like Jessica Abel or Harvey Pekar more apt to see themselves as consumers rather than producers of mass culture.

Figure 4.3. Jingoistic imagery: Dale Keown's Hulk. The Hulk ™© 2004 Marvel Characters, Inc. Used with permission.

Duncombe describes how the mainstream media began to imitate and appropriate the style of zine culture for their own commercial purposes.

This concern with cooptation surfaced as the comics community debated the value of these publication efforts. In a scathing review, *The Comics Journal*'s R. Fiore asked whether "[t]he best response to the situation was to throw comics at it." Fiore reduced their messages to a list of well-meaning clichés, some suggesting the pomposity of mainstream comics ("Superman thinks police and firemen are the real heroes"), others the self-indulgence of alternative comics ("Having 3000 people crushed to death not far from where you are really gets on your nerves.").[24] Some artists refused to participate, questioning whether the publishers were seeing the tragedy as just another branding opportunity. *Too Much Coffee Man*'s Shannon Wheeler, an alternative comic creator noted for his satires of corporate media, contributed a single page to *Emergency Relief* showing entertainment executives debating how they might profit from the events: "How about a poster of a superhero with a tear on his cheek?"[25] No doubt, some amount of cooptation was taking place as Marvel and DC tried to get "street cred" by aligning themselves with underground artists, but something else was

Figure 4.4. The artist confronts a changed world: Eric Drooker, *9–11: Artists Respond.* Cover art © Eric Drooker. Reprinted with permission from Dark Horse Comics.

also occurring—activists were using the power of corporate media to bring countercultural messages to a new audience.

This Looks Like a Job for Superman!

Superman and Spiderman often circulate as brand icons with little or no narrative context, deployed in cross-promotions with fast food restaurants, amusement parks, soft drinks, and breakfast cereals. *Time*'s Andrew D. Arnold summarized concerns that dogged the various post-9/11 projects: "For some this will come across as a gross commodification and trivialization of an awesome, unspeakable tragedy. These characters are arguably more corporate icons than meaningful characters—like seeing Ronald McDonald and the Keebler Elves giving succor to victim's families."[26] For those only peripherally aware of comics, this may be all superheroes are. Yet for regular readers, these characters have greater depth and resonance than almost any other figures in American popular culture. The most successful comic book franchises have been in more or less continuous publication since the 1930s and 1940s; their protagonists have become both vivid personalities with complex histories and powerful symbols with heavily encrusted meanings. For some, superhero comics hark back to simpler times and get consumed as comfort food. Yet several decades of revisionist comics have questioned and rethought the superhero myth and its underlying assumptions.[27] Shortly after 9/11, Silver Age artist Jim Steranko offered a blistering rebuke of revisionist superhero creators, calling them "cultural terrorists" who had chipped away at national monuments until nothing of substance was left.[28] The result was a flame war that almost ripped the comics community apart. Nobody ever made that same kind of emotional investment in the Keebler Elves.

As comic book artists and writers re-examined these familiar characters in the wake of September 11, the characters became powerful vehicles for pondering America's place in the world. When, for example, Frank Miller depicts Captain America's shattered shield, which we once naively believed to be indestructible, he provides a powerful image of the ways the attacks had demolished America's sense of invincibility.[29] When J. Michael Straczynski and John Romita Jr. depict Spiderman clutching a young boy who has just seen his father's body carried away from the WTC wreckage, they evoke Spiderman's own beginnings (his unresolved guilt over the murder of his Uncle Ben motivates his endless war against crime).[30] But the image does more than that. It seems to be one of the great unwritten rules of comics that superheroes are orphans and that the moment of truth that makes or breaks them is the moment when their innocence is first violated. Most comic characters—good guys and villains—go through a crucible of pain and suffering; what matters is what they make of themselves in the face of adversity. Read through these genre conventions, the suffering child embodies the choices the nation must make as it works through its grief process and defines its mission for the future.[31] When Straczynski and Romita depict Doc Octopus, Doctor Doom, or the Kingpin lending their resources to the relief effort, they evoke real-world political realignments and moral reawakenings: "Even those we thought our enemies are here because some things surpass rivalries and borders." When Straczynski and Romita depict a perplexed Spiderman looking upon the pain-stricken Captain America (see fig. 4.5), they connect the events of September 11 with a much larger history of struggles against fascism and terror. The two characters embody the perspectives of two different generations—Captain America the product of the Second World War, Spiderman a product of the early 1960s (though portrayed here as a contemporary teen and thus made to embody the current generation of youth).

Comic book artists rejected fisticuffs or vigilante justice in favor of depicting the superheroes as nurturers and healers. They are more likely to be standing tall against domestic racial violence than punching out terrorists.[32] In a *Static Shock* story, Dwayne McDuffie depicts the African American superhero and his girlfriend sitting in a coffee shop, discussing when and where military response

Figure 4.5. "He's Been Here Before": John Romita Jr., *The Amazing Spiderman,* 36. Spiderman ™© 2004 Marvel Characters, Inc. Used with permission.

to the attacks might be justifiable.[33] If he knew who was responsible, Static Shock says, he might use his superpowers to "take the bastards out myself," but should one attack a nation for the actions of a few individuals? Using criminal mastermind Lex Luthor as an example, he asks, "What if to get Luthor I had to kill some of his family? Or some of the people who live nearby? Or not so near? There's a line there. I'm not sure where to draw it." Virgil, Static Shock's alter ego, doesn't trust himself to do the right thing and he trusts the government even less. The philosophical debate gets disrupted by flag-waving, baseball-bat-wielding youths who smash through the shop's window and threaten its Arab-American owner (see fig. 4.6): "Pearl Harbor yesterday Kristallnacht today." In a rhetorical move that mirrors the Cultural Front's attempts to link fascism abroad with struggles against segregation in the states, Static Shock learns that his fight isn't overseas but in his own community.

Geoff John's "A Burning Hate" uses superhero comics to defuse the tensions between native-born and immigrant school kids, reminding readers that DC's Justice League of America is full of "foreigners"—Superman from Metropolis, the Martian Manhunter, Wonder Woman from Paradise Island, and Aquaman

Figure 4.6. "Pearl Harbor Yesterday, Kristallnacht Today": Denys Cowan's and Prentis Rollins' "Static Shock: 'Wednesday Afternoon.'"
Reprinted with permission from DC Comics.

from Atlantis.[34] The superhero mythos was defined, in large part, by the sons of immigrants working through conflicting investments in assimilation and ethnic pride. DC superheroes almost always come from elsewhere but they have chosen to be defenders of the American dream; sometimes they blend in, trying to pass as mild-mannered reporters, sometimes they stand out, wearing their colors on their chest.[35]

9/11 forced a reconsideration of what Susan Sontag has called the "imagination of disaster"—popular culture's fascination with mass destruction.[36] Such stories, Sontag suggests, can help us to explore moral questions by breaking down everyday routines and disrupting established social roles. Comic book artists, from Jack Kirby to Todd McFarland, love to draw splash-pages or whole books full of nothing but bone-crushing, muscle-stretching, building-shattering, fist-flying action. Troubled by that legacy, *Superman: Day of Doom* returns to one of the most controversial chapters in the genre's history—the much-hyped death and resurrection of Superman following a world-shattering battle with Doomsday.[37] In November 1992, DC had announced the death of Superman, only to bring him back from the dead some months later. Following September 11, DC asked its original author, Dan Jurgens, to revisit this landmark event in the Superman franchise. In the earlier story, the civilian populations had been simply extras in an epic battle between two superpowers. The post-9/11 *Day of Doom* made their loss, fear, and suffering its focal point. Paralleling Jurgens's own reassessment of the earlier series, *Daily Planet* reporter Ty Duffy is assigned the task of writing a report re-examining those traumatic events some years later. Publisher Perry White evokes the widespread assertion that September 11 took away the perception of America's indestructibility as he summarizes what Superman's death meant to Metropolis: "Superman had done so much. Conquered so many dangers . . . that we took him for granted. So long as he was around, I think we considered ourselves invincible. When he died, we all lost something precious . . . If a superman could die, how could any of us feel safe?"

As the story continues, Duffy shifts his investigation away from the Man of Steel and onto the civilians who got caught in the crossfire. Clark Kent scans through old microfilm with tears in his eyes, realizing for the first time how many people died when Superman wasn't there. Yet Kent is sobered by a new threat that is terrorizing Metropolis—the "Remnant." A kind of crazed victims-rights advocate or perhaps an embodiment of Kent's survivor guilt, the Remnant challenges Superman to justify his own existence when so many others have died: "I am the memory of what you did. A ghost of tragedies past. A remnant of the chaos you heaped upon the world. . . . The drifting wind that hears the moans of the forgotten. I do this for them." Superman, like his readers, must confront the consequences of mass destruction and wrestle with the complex range of emotion it provokes.

Perhaps most powerfully, reworking the superheroes meant rethinking the "American way" in a post–Cold War universe. In Alex Ross and Paul Dini's graphic novel *Wonder Woman: Spirit of Truth,* Wonder Woman struggles to decide which side she's on in a changing political landscape.[38] Published by DC in September 2001, this comic in some sense prefigures the questioning of America's place in the world that many experienced in the immediate aftermath of the attacks. Should Wonder Woman be taking on anti-government rebels or fascistic dictators, street criminals or environmentally irresponsible corporations? But most persistently, she asks herself what kind of face she should present to the world. As Hippolyta, her mother, asks, "Don't they logically recognize your benevolence and accept you as a guide to truth and understanding?" Wonder Woman doesn't know what to think when her assistance is rejected by a young Asian woman about to be run over by government tanks, "The girl had seen me only as an unwelcome intrusion into her world. A bizarre creature every bit as threatening as the tank that nearly killed her. Once again I was mystified at how someone's perception of me could be so wrong, and my kindly effort so completely misinterpreted."

Dini's script emphasizes Wonder Woman's self-doubts and self-justifications, giving voice to the thoughts of a superpower nation asking itself why "they" hate "us" so much. Yet Alex Ross's extraordinary images put a human face on

Figure 4.7. Shock and awe before a super-power: Alex Ross's *Wonder Woman: Spirit of Truth*. Reprinted with permission from DC Comics.

that debate. Ross is known for his photorealistic style, which owes as much to Norman Rockwell or Edward Hopper as it does to the comic book tradition. His images are so richly textured that we see the skin pores, the sheen of light, and the wrinkles in the fabric. Ross's distinctive style first emerged in Kurt Busiek's *Marvels* (1994), which shows how average citizens have to cope with the destruction of property and the disruption of their lives caused by the battles between superheroes and their rivals.[39] Ross's style manages to make the superheroes seem both more real and more removed from the realm of human affairs. As readers, we no longer share their perspective but are forced to look up at them as their battles overhead smash buildings and snarl traffic. Here, Ross uses this style to estrange us from Wonder Woman's moral and physical "perfection" and invite us to critique her from an outsider's perspective—in this case, implicitly at least, from a third-world perspective.

At a climactic moment (see fig. 4.7), Wonder Woman dons a burka to sneak into a camp of Muslim women whom an Arab dictator is cynically using as "human shields," and she rips off the burka as she defies the armed thugs guarding the captives. She imagines herself to be "a judgment upon all people who, for whatever reason or rationale, would subjugate others." Half-naked and garishly dressed, she is more a figure of moral transgression than political liberation. The look of horror and disapproval on the Muslim women's faces speaks volumes about the gap between American feminism and the everyday experience of third-world women: "In their eyes I was a brazen symbol of confrontation. I was a foreigner come to provoke them and make a hostile situation worse. Though I'm used to my traditional attire, it only made the clash of our cultures more painfully evident." These women can forge no bonds with her, suspecting her motives and distrusting her values. She is an alien presence in their world. This is a perspective rarely presented in American media—an attempt to explain why our presence in the third world is not always welcomed even when we think we are doing good.

Captain America was probably the superhero title most directly affected by 9/11. John Cassaday, the book's primary artist, was on the pier just blocks from his Upper West Side apartment when the towers fell: "The streets were gray, all covered in dust. So were the people. Gray like ghosts."[40] These impressions inspired the comic book's style and imagery (see fig. 4.8). The first pages of his post-9/11 story are sparse in text and drained of color. The opening image shows the shadow of an airplane flying across the clouds, then rows of passengers inside, and finally an extreme close-up of a box cutter blade: "It doesn't matter where you thought you were going today. You're part of the bomb now."[41] The Cap first appears several pages later, a blurry figure making his way across a colorless wasteland. Cassaday undersaturates his costume as if we were looking at it through a cloud of dust. Only in the book's final moments, when Cap resolves to take his fight to the enemy, do we see anything like his familiar red, white, and blue. Cassaday does the entire comic in shades of gray and tan.

Cassaday's collaborator, John Ney Rieber, almost pulled out of the project after September 11, wanting no part of jingoistic militarism. He agreed to continue only if he could use the book to ask some hard questions about America's culpability in bloodshed around the world: "I don't know how you could write Captain America if you weren't interested in writing about America. I feel very strongly that Cap should be about the rough questions. . . . If it weren't controversial, if it were only fulfilling people's expectations or making them comfortable—I'd feel as though I'd let Cap down. I'd be ashamed."[42] The resulting series sets up a strong contrast between its retro-style covers strongly influenced by World War II recruitment posters and the stories inside, which interrogate such patriotic rhetoric. When his commander, Nick Fury, orders Cap to head for Kandahar, he refuses, saying he has responsibilities at home helping the relief effort and battling hate crimes. Captain America was, in effect, created by the U.S. military during the Second World War. Military research developed a super serum that turned a somewhat sickly recruit into a mighty fighting machine. As Cap explains, he's "military technology." He has spent his career following orders and fighting wars. Now, he refuses to go into the trenches until he has answers to the questions that haunt him. Fury urges him to abandon his

Figure 4.8. John Cassaday's murky images in Captain America reflects his eyewitness perspective on the collapse of the World Trade Center.
Captain America ™© 2004 Marvel Characters, Inc. Used with permission.

investigation, but Cap refuses: "I'm here to protect the people and the dream, not your secrets."

By the time the series gives the Cap someone he can fight, terrorists have taken command of a small town some 200 miles into the American heartland, strewing land mines in the streets and holding hostages in a church. Centerville is far from an innocent community; the factories where the men work make land mines and cluster bombs or, as one man insists in the face of his wife's moral scrutiny, "component parts." Every attempt to draw a clear distinction between America's global mission and terrorism proves futile. When the Cap tells the terrorist leader that America doesn't make war on children, Al-Tarq points to the men under his command: "Tell our children, then, American, who sowed death in their fields and left it for the innocent to harvest? Who took their hands? Their feet?"

After recapturing Centerville, the Cap discovers that the terrorists are wearing a high-tech identification system being implemented by S.H.I.E.L.D., the American special ops force. Echoing the real-world relations between Osama bin Laden and the U.S. intelligence community, the American government may be more involved with these terrorists than it wants to admit. Clues force the Cap to retrace his own steps, returning to Dresden, where he had fought some of his first battles. As he wanders among what remains of the old section of the city, Cap ponders the firebombing that occurred here half a century earlier: "You didn't understand what we'd done here until September 11. . . . These people weren't soldiers. They huddled in the dark. Trapped. While the fire raged above them." Rieber never allows him to escape his personal responsibility and political culpability for the horrific acts his government had executed. He has been their tool and their apologist; now he must face the truth. The terrorist leader offers to turn himself in if Cap can answer a simple question: "Guerrillas gunned my father down while he was at work in the fields. With American bullets. American weapons. Where am I from? . . . My mother was interrogated and shot. Our home was burned. . . . You know your history, Captain America. Tell your monster where he's from." And it is clear from the Cap's pained expression that he recognizes that this story could be told over and over in countless parts of the world. He protests that these were the actions of a government that acted outside public knowledge and without democratic authorization. But how could he be fighting to make the world safe for democracy and defend a government that was hiding the truth from its own people? In the end, Captain America murders his antagonist in cold blood, recognizing as he does so that there is no way to wash his hands clean of his past actions.

Ordinary Heroes

Marvel and DC both actively discouraged artists and writers from using superheroes within the tribute books—though they didn't refuse to publish images or stories that included their franchised characters. As we have seen, this prohibition eventually broke down as various superhero series struggled to redefine themselves for the post-9/11 world, but in the immediate aftermath, the focus was on the real men and women who gave their lives protecting the public. Steven T. Seagle's "Unreal" starts with hyperbolic images of Superman battling evil, but as we turn the page, we realize that Superman is simply the character in a comic book that a teary-eyed young girl is reading; the real hero is the fireman who sweeps her up in his arms and carries her away from danger. Superman laments that he cannot "break free from the fictional pages," but he realizes that Earth is well-served by flesh-and-blood heroes in times of emergency.[43]

"Where were you? Why didn't you stop this?" angry New Yorkers demand. Spiderman tells them he didn't know and couldn't have imagined that such events were going to occur. Captain America says he wasn't there and leaves it at that. The superheroes couldn't have used their fantastic speed or extraordinary strength to stop what happened. They couldn't put out the fires or hold up

Figure 4.10. Passengers on the Pennsylvania flight battle the hijackers: Paul Chadwick's "Sacrifice."
Sacrifice © Paul Chadwick. Reprinted with permission from Dark Horse Comics.

their own lives rather than allow innocents to suffer, a trait that distinguishes them from the terrorists they defeat.

What Chadwick takes several pages to do, Marvel's Igor Kordey accomplishes in a single image (see fig. 4.11).[52] Kordey was born in Croatia and fought in the Balkan wars before moving to Canada with his wife and children, hoping to escape the destruction he had seen around him. Kordey was the only artist in *Heroes* who directly depicts the terrorists, and he chose to do so in a morally complex fashion. As Marvel publisher Joe Quesada explained, "He knows what it's like to live in war, and he doesn't want to sweep anything under the carpet."[53] The image is framed over the shoulders of the panic-stricken terrorists who are clustered together as passengers come storming up the aisles. It is a haunting image because Kordey invites us to see the events from the terrorists' perspectives and encourages us to dwell for a moment on their vulnerability and humanity.

Kordey also contributed one of the most compelling stories in Marvel's *Moment of Silence*: a firefighter father is playing soccer with his preteen son when he gets the call to report to the WTC.[54] For the rest of the story, we see the lad, still holding the soccer ball, waiting stoically on the front stoops juxtaposed

Figure 4.11. Croatian-born Igor Kordey shows us the events from the hijackers'
perspective.
Reprinted with permission from Igor Kordey.

with the rest of the family breaking down and hugging each other for comfort. When the mother brings the boy down to Ground Zero, he is hit by the enormity and finality of what has happened. Across a series of tight close-ups, we see his mouth scrunch together, his eyes well up, and then the tears burst like a summer rainstorm. So many of the books draw on melodramatic clichés to represent the violated innocence of the emergency worker's kids, but Kordey's "Sick Day" conveys a psychological nuance few others achieve.

The Politics of Grief

Some might argue that the media coverage of September 11 was too focused on personal grief and loss. I would disagree. Several days after the tragedy, Netscape posted a survey asking visitors to their homepage, "How do you feel about Tuesday's terrorist attacks?" Given the choices "angry," "sad," or "shocked," each respondent could choose one, and only one, to describe the intense array of feelings they were experiencing and read how others had responded. As of Sunday afternoon, 53 percent of respondents had chosen "angry," 26 percent "shocked," and 21 percent "sad."[55] The Bush administration was directing that anger against a global network of "evildoers." In *9-11: Artists Respond*, R. Sikoryak spoofs such simplified responses with a pastiche of Word Search: "Can you find the words in the puzzle below that express your feelings? Answer: Probably not."[56]

The tribute books stand out because they refuse to simplify the emotional stakes, refuse to fuel the war effort with their personal pain, refuse to equate grief with vulnerability. The alternative comics compilations are striking for the sheer range of emotional responses they depict, from the understatement of Harvey Pekar ("I bet it doesn't get any easier from here"), to Frank Miller's bombastic dismissal ("I am sick of flags. I am sick of God"), from the despair of a young mental patient to the resourcefulness of an office worker who uses the glow of his cell phone to navigate a darkened WTC stairwell.[57] Donna Barr, who contributed a story about how she couldn't stop vomiting, summarizes the philosophy behind this project: "Everybody's got a story to tell, everybody got hit differently. This way, people can look at it and say, 'oh, I'm not a weirdo because I feel that way.' You got all kinds of reactions, and they're all valid."[58]

Some depicted first-hand encounters with death and destruction; others write from a greater distance, talking about what it was like to watch the towers fall over and over on television. Dean Haspiel (see fig. 4.12) plays with our expectations, starting out his story with the character watching television news coverage, until the set goes blank, his apartment is rocked by a huge explosion, and we see the smoke from the nearby towers billowing skyward through the window behind him.[59] Henrik Rehr's self-published *Tuesday* tells the story of how he and his newborn were evacuated from the Gateway Plaza apartment complex in the shadows of the Twin Towers, how he struggled to reconnect with his wife and elder son, and how they coped with weeks of makeshift arrangements and temporary housing.[60] Rehr is a master of the telling detail: an aban-

Figure 4.12. Reality disrupts television images in Dean Haspiel's autobiographical story in *Emergency Relief.* Reprinted with permission from Alternative Comics.

doned baby carriage on the deserted esplanade, a cop's instructions to cover the baby's mouth as they run through the ash and smoke (see fig. 4.13), his older son's sudden concern about whether his toys are safe, a forgotten mural depicting the Twin Towers in the building's lobby, the half-drunk cup of coffee he finds when he is finally allowed back into his apartment. Rehr is particularly eloquent on the gap between the immediacy of personal experience and the distancing rhetoric which helps the rest of the country cope with such devastating loss: "She was putting the day in historical perspective. I had a kid missing. Peculiar thing about being the news. Your problems are suddenly somebody else's product." Rehr refuses to depict himself as a hero. He's just a father worried about his children and trying to protect his family.

"The personalization of politics," Steve Duncombe writes, "is a way that zinesters confront the distance between themselves and a mainstream political

Figure 4.13. A father flees his apartment, clutching his kid, in Henrick Rehr's *Tuesday*. Reprinted with permission from the artist.

world in which they effectively have no say. . . . The personalization of politics within zines is an attempt . . . to redraw connections between everyday 'losers' like themselves and the politics that affect them, to collapse the distance between the personal self and the political world."[61] On 9/11, we were all losers, all suddenly rendered powerless by monstrous forces beyond our control. The alternative comics ask what happens next. Many of these artists were accustomed to telling stories celebrating their alienation and now wanted to express sudden new feelings of connectivity. Some remained on the outside, embracing neither the sentimentality the events inspired in some or the cynicism in others. Some distrusted patriotism, cops, and religion, wanted no part of flag waving, yet wanted to affirm life and to be part of the imaginary national community for at least a few moments. How, they ask, do we build a political coalition around fragmented identities and diverse perspectives? How do we move from the individualized accounts represented in the tribute books toward common goals and shared commitments?

The artists who did the best job of "redrawing" connections between the personal and the political fit the 9/11 events into a larger historical or international context. "Spirit," for example, stages a debate about the nature of terror, which incorporates many different historical perspectives, juxtaposing Martin Luther King's accounts of standing firm against police with attack dogs, Chief Joseph's tales of facing down cavalry attacks on tribal villages, and Shaka Zulu's stories of the British colonization of Africa.[62] Terror takes many forms; sometimes America has been the victim, but more often it has been the victimizer, and only when we see the connection between these various horrors can we think outside the relentless cycle of violence and retaliation. Alan Moore and Melinda Gebbie's "This Is Information" starts with the image of a dust-covered hand reaching out from a bombsite, "This could be London, New York, Baghdad, Belfast, or Kabul. Or anywhere else? It's the dismal universal landscape of the bombed. Picasso's Guernica. All color gone, nothing but black and white and grey, above all grey. Likewise, the jutting hand contains little information. Dust-covered, its race, age, gender, none of these can be determined. It could be anyone."[63] It doesn't matter, he suggests, who's killing whom; all that matters is the pain and suffering being inflicted on people around the world. Peter Gross and Darick Robertson show a mother of the future taking her child to visit a monument built on the WTC footprint (see fig. 4.14) and telling how the attacks altered political consciousness. "People realized that the old ways of country against country and culture against culture could no longer apply. They accomplished what governments never could—they united the world."[64] Here, in a classic example of the utopian imagination, the artists depict what they hope will come out of the ruins of the WTC—a new commitment to international cooperation and grassroots activism. Such images stand as a challenge to the reader to resist the dominant pull of their culture and transform fear and anger into hope.

September 11 represented a brief opening for a new way of thinking about America's place in the world, for a response not so much "anti-American," as conservative critics might claim, but global. The roots of such thinking can be traced back to the complex coalitions of interests that organized the anti–World Trade Organization protests in Seattle and elsewhere. In an odd way, the struggle against corporate conceptions of globalization led to a new style of politics that cut across regional differences and transcended physical geography. Such thinking was quickly shut down by the rhetoric about an attack on America and by Bush administration unilateralism, but for a brief period, the American public was searching for new answers. The legacy of that thinking can be seen in the surprising scale of the anti-war movement that emerged as America threatened Iraq and by the significant gaps in support for that war compared to public opinion during the first Gulf War.

As they embraced globalism, comics writers moved away from the autobiographical and realist styles that dominated the alternative comics contributions

Figure 4.14. Peter Gross and Darick Robertson envision a future monument for the September 11 dead.
Reprinted with permission from DC Comics.

to the 9/11 collections and toward more metaphorical or utopian modes of expression. They want us to see not what is but what could be. Too often, critical theory has been preoccupied with what we are fighting against and has paid scant attention to what we are fighting for. Utopian rhetoric can seem, on first blush, naive, yet it establishes a set of ideals or standards against which the limits of the present moment can be mapped and a set of blueprints through which a future political culture might be constructed. In this process, the comics are perhaps little more than a relay system, communicating messages from one community to another, taking ideas out of the counterculture and transmitting them into the mainstream. We can see this process occurring in several stages, beginning with the movement of ideas from counterculture into comics-culture (itself fringe, but defined around patterns of consumption rather than political ideologies). Here, the fusion of alternative and mainstream publishers meant ideas that once circulated among the most politically committed now reach readers who would not otherwise have encountered them. As such, these comics do important cultural work, translating the abstract categories of political debate and cultural theory into vivid and emotionally compelling images. They simplify the concepts, to be sure, but at the same time they give them an urgency that academic theory lacks.

As the market responds to these ideas, they become more deeply embedded within the genres that constitute the bulk of contemporary comics publishing. Much as the Depression, the Second World War, and Vietnam left lasting imprints on the superhero genres, giving rise to new characters, plots, and themes which were mined by subsequent generations, September 11 shows signs of altering the way the genre operates. As the tribute books moved into the remainder bins at my local comics shop in the winter of 2003, every month brought new projects shaped in one way or another by the political climate of post-9/11 America. The comics industry seemed to be engaged in an extended process of self-examination, still questioning their long-standing genre traditions, pondering the nature of the heroic and of evil, reinventing their hero's missions for a new political landscape, and trying to figure out how to absorb the realism and topicality of alternative comics into mainstream entertainment. Some titles, like *Captain America,* were permanently altered. Cassaday and Rieber still circled around issues of guilt and responsibility. A new miniseries, *Truth,* used Captain America to re-examine the racism that shaped the experience of American GIs during World War II, suggesting eerie parallels between the "super soldier" serum tests that created Captain America and the experiments at Tuskegee Institute; it included the astonishing image of the American army systematically slaughtering hundreds of African Americans in order to protect their secrets.[65] Other books returned to business as usual. In *The Ultimates,* Captain America, Giant Man, Wasp Woman, and Thor smash half of Manhattan, demolishing Grand Central Station, all because Bruce Banner turns into the Hulk when he gets jealous that his girlfriend is going out with Freddie Prinze Jr.[66] One would describe the book as totally untouched by 9/11 if the artist didn't draw so heavily on what we had learned about what happens when real-world skyscrapers come crashing down. These shifts do not need to be felt uniformly across all comics to make a difference. Not all superhero comics—not even all mainstream titles—embrace the same ideologies, tell the same stories, and represent the world in the same terms. But enough creative artists from enough different sectors of the industry have been impacted by September 11 that these influences will be felt across a range of different titles for some time to come.

The long-term impact of September 11 could also be seen in the emergence of new comic book series that celebrate the heroism of average citizens. For example, Warren Ellis's *Global Frequency,* which Wildstorm, a smaller independent press, launched in fall 2002, depicted a multiracial, multinational organization of ordinary people who contribute their services on an *ad hoc* basis.[67] Ellis rejected the mighty demigods and elite groups of the superhero tradition and instead depicted the twenty-first-century equivalent of a volunteer fire department. Ellis has stated that the series grew out of his frustration with the hunger for paternalism expressed by superhero fans in the wake of September 11, his pride in the civilian resistance aboard the aircraft over Pennsylvania, and his fascination with the emerging concept of the "smart mob"—a self-organized group that uses the resources of information technology to coordinate their decentralized actions. As Ellis explains, "Global Frequency is about us saving ourselves." Each issue focuses on a different set of characters in a different location, examining what it means for Global Frequency members personally and professionally to contribute their labor to a cause larger than themselves. Once they are called into action, most of the key decisions get made on site as the volunteers act on localized knowledge. Most of the challenges come, appropriately enough, from the debris left behind by the collapse of the military-industrial complex and the end of the Cold War, "the bad mad things in the dark that the public never found out about." In other words, the citizen solders use distributed knowledge to overcome the dangers of government secrecy.

Marvel launched a new *411* series that first hit the shelves in April 2003 even as American troops were marching into Baghdad. Taking its name from an old telecommunications code for information, the series expresses a belief that it is important to inform the public about alternatives to war and violence. As Marvel president Bill Jemas explained, "*411* is about peacemakers: people who make sacrifices in the name of humanity. These are people willing to die to keep all of us—on all sides—alive. . . . But the theme of sacrifice for the sake of peace, for the sake of all of humanity, is hard for many Americans to accept right now, with the hearts and minds of the body politics rising in a patriotic furor. . . . These stories are neither anti-American nor anti-Iraqi, not anti-French, nor anti-Israeli. *411* is pro-human."[68] Opening with an essay on "Understanding the Culture of Nonviolence" written by Mohandas Gandhi's grandson, the series includes contributions by playwright Tony Kushner, longtime anti-nuclear activist Helen Caldicott, and political cartoonist David Rees. Yet, almost as remarkably, the series also includes stories by some of the most popular superhero writers, offering another chance for them to rethink the core assumptions of their genre and to engage more directly with real-world political concerns. Marvel's overt engagement with the anti-war movement is certainly rare among American corporations.

The next step is what happens if and when these changes get absorbed into the mainstream of the entertainment industry. As already noted, comics function today as a testing ground for new themes and stories for the rest of mass media. Neither Hollywood nor network television is likely to absorb the specific stories that emerged in the immediate aftermath of September 11, but insofar as those changes work their way into the underlying logic through which the comic book industry operates, and thus into the conventions of the superhero genre, they will likely have an influence on the films and television series that emerge over the next few years. One could, for example, compare this reassessment of the heroic in comics to the revision of the superhero genre which took place in the late 1980s and early 1990s, resulting in a darker, more angsty, more psychologically complex, more physically vulnerable conception of the hero. This rethinking of the superhero affected not only future comic books but can be seen at work, albeit in a somewhat watered-down form, in the big-screen adaptations of Batman, Spiderman, and Daredevil. There, the influence is apt to be more implicit than explicit, a shift in tone or the "structure of feeling" as much as or more than a shift in ideology.

Let's be clear, though, that superheroes don't have to conquer the world for the political expressions discussed here to make a difference. What happens in comics matters. Popular culture is the space of dreams, fantasies, and emotions. In that space, it matters enormously whether Captain America stands for fascism or democracy, whether Wonder Woman represents the strong arm of American cultural imperialism or whether she respects and understands third-world critiques of her mission, whether Superman is more important than the average men and women who are accidental casualties of his power struggles, or whether everyday people have the power to solve their problems without turning to superheroes for help. Popular culture is not univocal: it remains a space of contestation and debate, it often expresses messages which run counter to dominant sentiment within the culture, and it can open up space for imagining alternatives to the prevailing political realities. It is also worth remembering that people working within the culture industries exert an active agency in shaping the ideas which circulate within popular culture; on occasion, they may act out of political ideals rather than economic agendas.

Notes

1. Mike Deodata Jr. with Dennis Calero, untitled, in *Heroes: The World's Greatest Super Hero Creators Honor the World's Greatest Heroes* (New York: Marvel Comics, December 2001), 7.
2. Andrew D. Arnold, "The Most Serious Comix Ever," Time.com, January 29, 2002, http://www.time.com/time/columnist/printout/0,8816,197890,00.html.
3. A full account of the role of comics in responding to September 11 would have to include alternative editorial cartoonists like Tom Tomorrow or Ted Rall, web comics like *Secret Asian Man*, newspaper strips like *The Boondocks*, and magazine cover artists like *The New Yorker*'s Art Spiegelman, all of whom also used comics to contest dominant framings of the event and found themselves in the center of controversy within a culture where it suddenly seemed dangerous to ask too many questions. For more, see Ted Rall, ed., *Attitude: The New Subversive Political Cartoonists* (New York: Nantier, Beall, Minoustchine, 2002).
4. Michael Denning, *The Cultural Front: The Laboring of American Culture in the Twentieth Century* (London: Verso, 1996), 125.
5. For a useful account of the early history of comic books and superheroes, see Bradford W. Wright, *Comic Book Nation: The Transformation of Youth Culture in America* (Baltimore, Md.: The Johns Hopkins University Press, 2001).
6. "Most of all the pleasure that Joe derived from administering this brutal beating [a comic book image of a superhero pummeling Hitler] was intense and durable and strangely redemptive. At odd moments over the past few days, he had consoled himself with the thought that somehow a copy of this comic book might eventually make its way to Berlin and cross the desk of Hitler himself, that he would look at the painting in which Joe had channeled all his pent-up rage and rub his jaw, and check with his tongue for a missing tooth. 'We're not in a war with Germany,' Ashkenazy said, shaking his finger at Sammy. 'It's illegal to make fun of a king or a president, or somebody like

that, if you're not at war with them. We could get sued.' " Michael Chabon, *The Amazing Adventures of Kavalier & Clay* (New York: Picador, 2000), 159.

7. Thomas Andrae, "From Menace to Messiah: The History and Historicity of Superman," in Donald Lazere, ed., *American Media and Mass Culture: Left Perspectives* (Berkeley: University of California Press, 1987), 130–131.

8. See Mark James Estren, *A History of Underground Comics* (New York: Ronin, 1993).

9. On *Green Arrow*'s progressive politics, see Gerard Jones and Will Jacobs, *The Comic Book Heroes* (New York: Prima, 1996).

10. See, for example, Mike Carey, Marcello Frusin, "John Constantine, Hellblazer: Exposed," in *9-11: The World's Finest Comic Book Writers & Artists Tell Stories to Remember* (New York: DC, 2002), 85–87.

11. Dennis O'Neil, remarks at MIT, Cambridge, Mass., September 2001.

12. Jonah Weiland, "Market Share, Top 100 Comics and Graphic Novels for All of 2002," Comic Book Resources, http://www.comicbookresources.com/news/newsitem.cgi?id=1834.

13. For a discussion of the links between superheroes and urban culture, see Scott Bukatman, "The Boys in the Hoods: A Song of the Urban Superhero," forthcoming in *Matters of Gravity: Special Effects and Supermen in the Twentieth Century* (Durham, N.C.: Duke University Press, 2003).

14. "Bricks and mortar" comment comes from Marvel publisher Joe Quesada, as quoted in Hank Stuever, "Powerless Superheroes Pay Tribute to True Heroes," *Washington Post*, October 17, 2001. The information about the benefit projects contained in this paragraph, unless otherwise noted, was compiled from Michael Dean, "9/11, Benefit Comics and the Dog-Eat-Dog World of Good Samaritanism," *The Comics Journal*, October 2002, 9–17; Andrew D. Arnold, "Will Superheroes Meet Their Doom?" *Time*, October 2, 2001; Ethan Sacks, "Comic Books Imitate Life: WTC Attack Changes Myth," *New York Daily News*, October 31, 2001.

15. Weiland, "Market Share."

16. Jeff Mason, as quoted in Dean, "9/11, Benefit Comics," xx.

17. Dean, "9/11, Benefit Comics."

18. Beau Smith, Val Semeiks, and Romeo Tanghal, untitled, in *9-11: The World's Finest*, 89–94.

19. Pat Moriarity, untitled, in *9-11: Artists Respond*, Vol. One (Milwaukie, Ore.: Dark Horse Comics, January 2002), 58.

20. On publisher interference, see Mark Martin, "Free Speech in the Comics Biz," *The Comics Journal*, Special Issue, Winter 2003, 120–121. On the Red Cross's intervention, see Dean, "9/11, Benefit Comics."

21. Eric Drooker, cover, in *9-11: Artists Respond*.

22. This focus on situated knowledge demands the same from me: As someone who frequently flies from Boston to Los Angeles, I recognized the picture of the pilot on American Flight 11 as someone who had flown me just a few weeks before, and I had a ticket on this same flight for less than a week later. My son was in Washington, D.C., at George Washington University when a rumor spread that a bomb might have been set off at the State Department just a few blocks away. Our son chose to take the train home, not realizing that it would bring him within sightlines of the collapsed tower. A full account of my experiences around September 11 can be found in "Duty Calls?"

September 16, 2002, http://web.mit.edu/cms/reconstructions/expressions/ dutycalls.html. I write this chapter as a comics fan, someone who grew up on the Silver Age adventures of Batman, the Flash, and Green Lantern, who rediscovered comics through Vertigo and Scott McCloud, and who still lines up at my local comic shop every Wednesday when they put out the new issues.

23. Steve Duncombe, "'I'm a Loser Baby': Zines and the Creation of Underground Identity," in Henry Jenkins, Tara McPherson, and Jane Shattuc, eds., *Hop on Pop: The Politics and Pleasures of Popular Culture* (Durham, N.C.: Duke University Press, 2003), 227–250.

24. R. Fiore, "A Moment of Noise," *The Comics Journal*, October 2002, 46–52.

25. Shannon Wheeler, untitled, in *9-11: Emergency Relief* (Gainesville, Fla.: Alternative Comics, 2002), 178.

26. Andrew D. Arnold, "The Most Serious Comix," Time.com, February 5, 2002, http://www.time.com/time/columnist/0,8816,198966,00.html.

27. For a useful account of this process, see Geoff Klock, *How to Read Superhero Comics and Why* (New York: Continuum, 2002).

28. Jim Steranko, as quoted in Dean, "9/11, Benefit Comics," 14.

29. Frank Miller with Alex Sinclair, untitled, *Heroes*, 9.

30. J. Michael Staczynski and John Romita Jr., *The Amazing Spiderman*, 36, December 2001.

31. See, for example, Gary Engle, "What Makes Superman So Darned American?" in Sonia Maasik and Jack Solomon, eds., *Signs of Life in the USA: Readings on Popular Culture for Writers*, 3rd ed. (New York: Bedford/St. Martin's, 2000).

32. Comic books have long borne the burden of an early history of deploying extreme racial stereotypes in their representation of African Americans and other minority groups. A highly iconic medium reduced people of color to a few easily recognizable tropes. Here, the artists struggle to break with that visual language and to construct personalized portraits of people of many different races and nationalities. This is what makes these images seem like more than simply Colors of Benetton constructions of multiculturalism. They may be mawkishly sentimental or crude agitprop, but they are also struggling to find a new language for representing race in the American comic book tradition.

33. Dwayne McDuffie, "Wednesday Afternoon," in *9-11: The World's Finest*, 29–37. Static Shock is a character which emerged from Milestone Comics, a fringe publisher which specialized in the work of African American creators and targeted the African American community. For more on this effort, see Jeffrey A. Brown, *Black Superheroes, Milestone Comics and Their Fans* (Oxford: University of Mississippi Press, 2001).

34. David S. Goyer, Geoff Johns, Humberto Ramos, and Sandra Hope, "A Burning Hate," in *9-11: The World's Finest*, 189–194.

35. See Engle, "What Makes Superman So Darned American?"; Matthew J. Smith, "The Tyranny of the Melting Pot Metaphor: Wonder Woman as the Americanized Immigrant," in Matthew P. McAllister, Edward H. Sewell Jr., and Ian Gordon, eds., *Comics & Ideology* (New York: Peter Lang, 2001).

36. Susan Sontag, "The Imagination of Disaster," in *Against Interpretation and Other Essays* (New York: Picador, 2001).

37. Dan Jurgens and Bill Sienkewicz, *Superman: Day of Doom*, 1–4, January–February 2003.

38. Alex Ross and Paul Dini, *Wonder Woman: Spirit of Truth*, November 2001.

This book was almost certainly fully developed prior to September 11, though released after. I have included it here because of its use of images of Iraq and because it so clearly fits within the tradition of using the superhero characters to question America's mission. Alex Ross also provided a memorable cover of Superman looking up in awe at a massive poster showing heroic images of police, firefighters, and emergency workers for *9-11: The World's Finest.*

39.   Kurt Busiek and Alex Ross, *Marvels* (New York: Marvel, 1994).

40.   John Cassaday, as quoted in Mike Cotton, "We Will Never Forget," *Wizard,* 133, October 2002, 52.

41.   John Ney Rieber and John Cassaday, *Captain America,* Vol. 4, No.1, June 2002. The story discussed here unfolds over the next five issues. Many readers associate comic books with a limited range of mostly garish primary colors and cheap paper; this simplified color palette reflected the cheap production budgets and limited printing technologies deployed in publishing comics. Over the past several decades, there have been dramatic improvements in the diversity of colors and the quality of the paper, reflecting, perhaps, the higher purchase price and the more mature readership. The design of the color-costumed characters still tends to deploy basic and bold colors, but the worlds they inhabit have much subtler shadings; comic artists experiment more with color saturation and hue, and color is used more expressionistically to shape the tone of a particular narrative. In this case, the comic artists restrict their color range to capture some of their impressions of what it was like to be at the base of the World Trade Center on September 11.

42.   John Ney Rieber, as quoted in Cotton, "We Will Never Forget," 54.

43.   Steven T. Seagle, Duncan Rouleau, and Aaron Sowd, "Unreal," in *9-11: The World's Finest,* 15–16.

44.   Matty Ryan, as quoted in Stuever, "Powerless Superheroes," xx.

45.   Bill Pressing and Nijo Philip, untitled, in *9-11: Artists Respond,* 56–57.

46.   Others sought to broaden the range of people who might be considered heroes, depicting physical plant guys who helped fireman navigate through the WTC's maze-like structure or teachers who had to preserve a firm, supportive face for their students despite their own worries for their loved ones. Bill Jemas, Mark Bagley, and Scott Hanna, "Moment of Truth," in *Moment of Silence,* February 2002; Brian Clopper, "School Daze," in *9-11: Emergency Relief* (Gainesville, Fla.: Alternative Comics, 2002), 23–16.

47.   Frank Cho, cover, *9-11: Emergency Relief.*

48.   Some of the alternative comics sought to complicate mainstream images of cops, worried that such a glorification of police power might make crackdowns on civil liberties more palatable. Bob Harris and Gregory Ruth ask, "Which one is real? The NYPD who used racial profiling, shot Amidou Diallo 41 times, and sodomized Abner Louima with a broomstick? Or the NYPD who rushed headlong into horror to save the lives of people of all races, losing dozens of courageous men?" Bob Harris and Gregory Ruth, "Which One Is Real?" in *9-11: Artists Respond,* 94–95.

49.   Chuck Austen and Daniel Zelzej, *The Wagon,* 1, October 2002. Credits for the other *Call of Duty* titles are Bruce Jones and Tom Mandrake, *The Precinct,* and Chuck Austen, David Finch, and Art Thibert, *The Brotherhood.* DC's *Gotham Central* makes the pointlessness of being a cop in a city patrolled by superheroes a central theme. Its beat cop protagonists struggle to solve crimes before

the Caped Crusader takes over the case. The men resent Batman's interference and are infuriated when he gets all the credit for protecting the city.

50. Paul Chadwick, "Sacrifice," in *9-11: Artists Respond,* 15–18.

51. Paul Chadwick, *Concrete: Think Like a Mountain* (Milwaukie, Ore.: Dark Horse, 1996).

52. Igor Kordey with Chris Chuckery, untitled, in *Heroes,* 17.

53. Joe Quesada, as quoted in Stuever, "Powerless Superheroes," xx.

54. Joe Quesada and Igor Kordey, "Sick Day," in *A Moment of Silence,* February 2002.

55. I discuss this incident more fully in Henry Jenkins and Shari Goldin, "Media and Catastrophe," September 16, 2001, http://web.mit.edu/cms/reconstructions/interpretations/catastrophe.html.

56. R. Sikoryak, "New York Report," in *9-11: Artists Respond,* 92–93.

57. Harvey Pekar and Tony Millionaire, "News," in *9-11: Emergency Relief,* 1; Frank Miller, untitled, in *9-11: Artists Respond,* January 2002, 64; Jenny Gonzalez, "Collapse," in *9-11: Emergency Relief,* 114–118; Evan Forsch and Robert Ullman, "Down and Out," in *9-11: Emergency Relief,* 102–108.

58. Donna Barr, as quoted in Mark Rahner, "Comic Books Find Post-Sept. 11 Role," *The Seattle Times,* January 22, 2002. Donna Barr, "Watch Your Mouth," in *9-11: Emergency Relief,* 144–145.

59. Dean Haspiel, "91101," in *9-11: Emergency Relief,* 92–97.

60. Henrik Rehr, *Tuesday,* self-published, October–December 2002.

61. Duncombe, "'I'm a Loser Baby'," 238.

62. Alex Simmons and Angelo Torres, "Spirit," in *9-11: The World's Finest,* 165–168.

63. Alan Moore and Melinda Gebbie, "This Is Information," in *9-11: Artists Respond,* 185–190.

64. Peter Gross and Darick Robertson, untitled, in *9-11: The World's Finest,* 142–145.

65. Robert Morales and Kyle Baker, *Truth: Red, White, and Black* (New York: Marvel Comics, January–July 2003).

66. Mark Millar, Bryan Hitch, and Andrew Currie, "Hulk Does Manhattan," in *The Ultimates,* July 2002.

67. Quotations in this paragraph are taken from Warren Ellis, "Global Frequency: An Introduction," http://www.warrenellis.com/gf.html. For a fuller discussion of Ellis's vision of grassroots activism and smart mobs, see Henry Jenkins, "Science Fiction and Smart Mobs," *Technology Review,* January 31, 2003.

68. Bill Jemas, Foreword, *411,* April 2003.

5 Trauma, Healing, and the Therapeutic Monument

Kirk Savage

> As a suffering father, my heart is broken. Let other hearts not be broken.
>
> —Turkish resident of the Kuba neighborhood in Istanbul, recorded
> in the video installation *Kuba* by Kutlug Ataman, 2004

We begin with a question that might seem inane, or even insulting. Why erect a monument to the victims of 9/11? The answers seem self-evident: the event was one of the most traumatic in the nation's history; a monument would give recognition where recognition is due; it would help Americans, especially those most directly affected by the tragedy, heal.

Yet until relatively recently this logic would have seemed odd, or at least novel. In the nineteenth-century, when the public monument became commonplace, disaster monuments were essentially unknown. Public monuments did not commemorate victims. If victimization is a state of powerlessness, "when action is of no avail,"[1] monuments celebrated its very opposite. They reaffirmed, over and again, the beneficial presence of human (more properly, male) agency in society. They told the stories of men who had acted decisively upon their world, by transforming it for the better or saving it from peril. It goes without saying that more than a few of these men were actually victimizers—conquerors, killers, slaveowners—but typically, monumental rhetoric ignored or mystified their misdeeds.

Dedicated as they were to heroism, public monuments were not meant to be therapeutic. They were didactic, condensing the moral lesson of the hero or the event for future generations. Their message was assumed to be as permanent and unchanging as their material form. In this way monuments functioned as a concrete sign of the permanence of the nation and of the individual agency that guaranteed the nation's progress. Thus fires, mine collapses, hurricanes, yellow fever epidemics, shipwrecks, or other traumas, no matter how devastating, did not merit commemoration in monumental form.

Wars, of course, did. In the U.S., after the Civil War, soldier monuments for the first time began to appear in large numbers. It would be anachronistic, however, to think of these as disaster monuments, or even monuments to victims.

In their own time they staked their commemorative claim on moral triumph, not on trauma. The soldiers and their loved ones deserved permanent recognition in a public monument not because they had suffered so much but because they willingly risked themselves, or their loved ones, for the good of the nation, for the triumph of right over wrong. Even the monuments to Confederate soldiers, who failed to save their nation, asserted their own moral triumph, and the successful reassertion of white supremacy in the post-war South made that triumph all too credible.[2]

The early twentieth century brought some exceptions to this moralistic pattern. In New York City, the staggering loss of more than a thousand people— almost all from the same German neighborhood in lower Manhattan—aboard a steamer carrying them to a Sunday-school picnic led to a memorial fountain in Tompkins Square, then a German-speaking enclave. The so-called Slocum Memorial (1906) featured a relief panel of two children looking out over the water, and the words "They were earth's purest children, young and fair." Entrenched in a working-class neighborhood, the monument's audience and impact remained localized, despite the enormous scale and concentration of the human loss which in its own time rivaled that of 9/11.[3] By contrast, the *Titanic* shipwreck of 1912, with 500 more deaths than the *Slocum* disaster, was quickly embraced by the media as a national tragedy of epic proportions, and a campaign for a national monument in Washington, D.C., emerged almost immediately. However, both the campaign and the monument as built (on the shore of the Potomac in 1931) dedicated the memorial not to the victims *per se*, but to the noble self-sacrifice of the male passengers, "who gave their lives that women and children might be saved." The monument's sculptural rhetoric—a male body in the shape of a cross—reinforced the textual message by producing a recognizable icon of male sacrifice.[4]

After the catastrophe of World War I, soldier monuments began to acknowledge more openly the fact of mass slaughter and the grief of those who survived it. The naming of the dead, which had been a sporadic practice before World War I, now became a standard feature of war memorials, and in Europe figures of dead soldiers or grieving family members became more common. Many of these monuments, Jay Winter has written, were "the work of individuals and groups brought together not by the state but by the need to speak out and grieve."[5] This claim is overblown, however. The state was profoundly implicated in the process of war memorialization. In that process, official "top-down" memory and more localized "bottom-up" memory intertwined and overlapped. On occasion the two forces could crystallize into opposing camps, but more often their interests merged. Veterans and their families had a stake in state-sponsored didacticism, just as the state had a stake in acknowledging their loss. In the U.S., where the impact of the war was far less traumatic, the memorials conform more obviously to the traditional soldier-monument type. But even in Europe, most war memorials (and indeed most collective rituals of mourning) followed the imperative of the state and its citizen elites to impose a moral pattern on the war experience. While a few monuments, either proposed or built,

Figure 5.1. Sir Edwin Lutyens, Cenotaph, Whitehall, London, 1920.
Photograph: Freefoto.com

did emphasize victimization, the more typical monuments confirm the moral integrity of the nation and the honor of those men who died defending it. If they do not usually trumpet their righteousness as loudly as does my local World War I monument in Pittsburgh, dedicated to the "true exemplars of the spirit of America and brave defenders of Christian civilization," they make their moral stance clear. Even Lutyens's famous Cenotaph in London, one of Winter's prime examples, dedicates itself to "Our Glorious Dead," and its elevated, altar-like form unmistakably asserts the nobility of their sacrifice (see fig. 5.1).[6]

As the scale and cruelty of victimization intensified with the Second World War, commemorative initiatives struggled to find a language that could in some way speak to the new reality. The relentless slaughter of noncombatants by both Axis and Allied forces, culminating in the U.S.'s A-bomb attack on Japan, and the Nazis' genocidal campaign to exterminate European Jewry have of course reshaped the image of war and the politics of collective identity in the contemporary world.[7] Yet traditional commemorative expectations acted as a drag on innovation. One of the earliest and best-known Holocaust monuments, Nathan Rapoport's Warsaw Ghetto Monument (1948), resurrected the image of the heroic male defender. In the U.S., Holocaust memorials did not begin appearing until the mid-1980s.[8]

It was not the Holocaust but the Vietnam War that produced the first truly therapeutic monument in the U.S. By therapeutic I mean a monument whose primary goal is not to celebrate heroic service or sacrifice, as the traditional didactic monument does, but rather to heal a collective psychological injury. The first, and still most influential, example is Maya Lin's 1982 design for the Vietnam Veterans Memorial. With its two sunken black granite walls inscribed with the names of the dead, Lin's design brilliantly crystallized the competition sponsors' demand for a monument that was supposed to "make no political statement" and to "begin a healing process."[9] It is surely no coincidence that the monument campaign that led to Lin's selection began at about the same time that "post-traumatic stress disorder" entered the official psychiatric diagnostic manual.[10] The man who hatched the campaign, Jan Scruggs, was in fact a combat veteran experiencing symptoms of post-traumatic stress. Scruggs intended the walls to serve a dual healing function: for the veterans themselves who had endured not only the stress of combat but a crushing rejection from society afterward, and for the nation, which had been so bitterly divided over the justice of the cause.

Lin's design is so well-known that it hardly needs discussion. Within the setting of an open park, the memorial provides a contemplative space, hushed and removed from the world above by its gradual subterranean descent and the shelter of the dark walls. As one descends, the walls expand in height and the true scale of their list of names gradually reveals itself in the visitor's consciousness, until this perceptual and cognitive process reaches a crescendo at the center where the two walls meet. Lin's original design offered no moral explanations whatsoever to guide the visitor, not even the simple reference to glorious death that justified Lutyens's Cenotaph. Her idea was deliberately anti-didactic: the visitor herself—not the monument—was supposed to create the moral understanding of the event. The only guidance offered was in the spatial passage, meant to encourage a process of healing. Lin paid special attention to the passage's emotional conclusion. After descending to the memorial's center, the visitor exits by reascending along a path pointing either to the Washington Monument or to the Lincoln Memorial, thereby leaving the memorial's stark reminder of death and reintegrating into the national life of the Mall. We might call this journey a kind of redemption, but it would be more apt to call it a process of recovery—the religious replaced by the psychological.

Lin's brilliant text accompanying her design entry, often quoted, is worth restating here: "Brought to a sharp awareness of such a loss, it is up to each individual to resolve or come to terms with this loss. For death is in the end a personal and private matter, and the area contained within this memorial is a quiet place, meant for personal reflection and private reckoning."[11] Significantly, Lin conceived of this encounter as individual and private rather than collective and public. Her original competition drawings of the walls are eerily empty, as if inviting solitude. Of course visitors rarely experience this at the Vietnam Veterans Memorial, since it is almost always far more crowded than Lin could ever have anticipated. Indeed, the space is therapeutic in a way that Lin herself did not imagine. As many visitors have noted, the memorial offers a shared space and a shared experience, and that very collectivity gives it a power that more "private" arenas of grief do not have. Some relatives of the dead, for example, have said that they feel more in the presence of their lost loved one at Lin's wall than they do at the actual grave.[12]

For those soldiers who survived the war, the collectivity of the memorial experience is essential. The monument functions as a communal act of recognition, and indeed, restitution. It restores their dead comrades to a place of honor in the quasi-sacred landscape of the nation's monumental core. Judith Herman, in her study of trauma, identifies recognition and restitution as the collective responses "necessary to rebuild the survivor's sense of order and justice," and she thus considers Lin's memorial "probably the most significant public contribution to the healing of [Vietnam] veterans."[13]

Yet before it was built, some regarded Lin's design as dishonorable, an inversion of the traditional honorifics of public monuments (below ground rather than above, black rather than white, and so on). Under pressure from these right-wing critics, the sponsors agreed to add, away from the walls, a monument consisting of realistic statues of servicemen; such a monument, designed by Frederick Hart, was installed in 1984. But more important for my argument, the sponsors also decided to introduce—in the center of Lin's monument, where the two walls meet—a simple didactic inscription, in two parts. The first part, the "prologue": "In honor of the men and women of the armed forces of the United States who served in the Vietnam War. The names of those who gave their lives and of those who remain missing are inscribed in the order they were taken from us" (see fig. 5.2). The second part, the "epilogue": "Our nation remembers the courage, sacrifice, and devotion to duty and country of its Vietnam veterans. This memorial was built with private donations from the American people." This is precisely the sort of imposed "message" that Lin had avoided, and most scholars writing on the memorial tend to ignore it. The inscription sits uneasily on Lin's walls because its fixity is so much at odds with the experience those walls try to create. For, as we have seen, Lin's design is a spatial and emotional passage meant to activate visitors—to have them move through the space, touching the names on the wall, generating their own response. The whole phenomenon of leaving offerings at the wall is one extension of this process.[14] The inscription, on the other hand, assumes a stationary viewer, planted front and center, passively absorbing the text's lesson. One could easily argue, after the astonishing success of Lin's design, that her walls so effectively shape the experience of the monument that they render the inscription invisible and irrelevant. The prestigious location of the monument, the elegantly inscribed names, and the overall formal beauty of the work all seem to "honor" the soldiers far more than a conventional inscription can.

Figure 5.2. Maya Lin, Vietnam Veterans Memorial, Washington, D.C., 1982, detail of upper inscription.
Photograph: Stanley M. Sherman.

Yet the added inscription also points to a deeper political problem. At first glance, the inscription simply revives the traditional rhetoric of heroic sacrifice. Not only does the opening statement make the message of "honor" explicit, but the next sentence asserts that the dead "gave" their lives—a simple verb that implies an act and an actor, a choice made. Yet the end of that same sentence brings a reversal: their lives were "taken" from us. The "give and take" of the inscription points to multiple readings of these deaths, which is how Lin had wanted it all along. What the inscription avoids, despite its invocation of the standard military values of courage, sacrifice, and devotion to country, is a statement of moral purpose. To what moral end did these men did give their lives? Why did they choose to risk their lives? They served "in" the war, but what did they serve "for"? The inscription brings the soldiers to the brink of historical agency, but then pulls back, because it fails to convince us that their actions were effective or even purposeful. We find none of Lutyens's "glory" here, no fight for "freedom," no higher cause to which their deaths contributed.[15] In the end the didactic push of the inscription justifies the soldiers not as historical agents but as honorable victims.

What the inscription is attempting to do, in the end unsuccessfully, is to address the key problem inherent in the therapeutic monument. If we can erect monuments to victims rather than agents, then whose trauma deserves to be commemorated, and why? Who deserves the therapy of a public monument?

"There is no public monument for rape survivors," Herman has written.[16] Her book argues that the "private" atrocity of rape directed at women and the "public" atrocity of warfare directed at men produce the same traumatic syndrome; yet, she observes, the collective response to the one differs radically from the collective response to the other. The question of which category of victim deserves a monument is fundamentally political, and the answer depends on the meanings that society assigns to their trauma. The severity of the trauma is not the crucial factor, but rather its collective significance.

Therefore even monuments to victims cannot escape didacticism, however muted or irrelevant that didactic message may seem to be. To justify its very existence, the therapeutic monument must assign, implicitly or explicitly, a meaning to the traumatic event that makes it worthy of collective response. Lin's deliberately anti-didactic monument, even without the inscription, participates in this process of meaning production in ways that she could not have anticipated. First, and most obviously, the monument reaffirms the traditional idea that soldiers deserve collective recognition because they risk their lives in the service of the nation-state. Even if the point of that service no longer has the moral clarity assumed in earlier war memorials, the service remains honorable and worthy of recognition. The monument's very success has helped to shift the public memory of the war. In a revealing slippage, the Vietnam Veterans Memorial is often simply referred to as the Vietnam memorial, as if the equation of the two is self-evident. By focusing the memory of the war on American veterans, the monument has helped to thwart recognition of others whose lives were disrupted or indeed traumatized by the war: antiwar activists, some who were injured or killed; draft resisters, some who went into prison or exile; South Vietnamese soldiers, with whom American soldiers were allied, who died in greater numbers, and many of whose family members now live as U.S. citizens; the millions of noncombatants in Vietnam, many of them children, who were killed or disabled or orphaned by the very forces trying to "save" them. These are the groups that do not have monuments, do not have lists of names to grieve over.

The Vietnam Veterans Memorial has shaped not only American memory of the war in Vietnam, but more general patterns of commemoration ever since. Its success has relegitimated the public monument by creating a powerful model for how monuments help traumatized groups heal. It has established a design standard for the therapeutic monument, in which the monument is not a fixed moral text or image but rather a flexible, multifaceted space in which "to evoke feelings and create memorable experiences" (to quote the mission statement for the Oklahoma City National Memorial).[17] The focal point for these feelings and experiences is almost invariably a list of the names of those lost—as if the names somehow speak for themselves, as if in that one fixed set of unarguable human losses the monument finds its moral center and its justification.

Yet the names alone cannot do this didactic work. Why these names? Why not names of others who have died tragically? If we look at how the therapeutic model has been applied in the case of the Oklahoma City National Memorial—

the most direct precedent for the commemoration of 9/11—we see that the problem of self-justification inherent in the therapeutic monument becomes increasingly acute as we move further away from the war memorial prototype, For the Vietnam Veterans Memorial justifies its existence in part on the assumption that the dead exercised some measure of agency—that they "gave" their lives in the service of the U.S. armed forces. But this assumption disappears altogether for the citizen victims of an unexpected terrorist attack. One could argue with the assertion of even partial agency for the American soldiers in Vietnam, especially since the draft was in force. But the U.S. military force in Vietnam was not a conscript army, as is often maintained. Most of the Americans who served and died there were enlisted men, not draftees. And even the draftees knowingly faced a choice: possible combat in Vietnam, punishment at home, or exile abroad. Not an easy choice by any stretch of the imagination, but a choice nevertheless. The men, women, and children who spent their days at the Murrah Federal Building in Oklahoma City did not have such a choice; they did not go to the building expecting to face a lethal attack, much less to fight it. The victims of Timothy McVeigh's bomb underwent a more complete loss of agency, a more absolute victimization.

However, this did not stop some from applying the rhetoric of military sacrifice to the event. At the dedication of the national monument in Oklahoma City in 2000, then-President Clinton compared the site to Valley Forge and Gettysburg, all places "scarred by freedom's sacrifice."[18] The rhetoric brought an eloquent rejoinder from Pam Whicher, the widow of a Secret Service agent who had died in the blast; for her there was a clear difference between dying while defending the life of the president, which her husband was willing to do, and dying without even the opportunity to choose or to act. "I believe we heal better when we accept the truth," Whicher wrote later. "This was nothing more than a damn waste of lives. All the more worthy of our heartbreak, and the families, all the more worthy of our sympathy."[19] The very absence of conscious purpose to their deaths only intensified the trauma, she suggests, and made the suffering of family members and survivors even more worthy of recognition.

Whicher's own heroic effort to resist the comforting didacticism of "sacrifice" for the nation and to tell the truth about her husband's death exposes the core dilemma of the traumatic memorial. For the invocation of sacrifice and martyrdom is a time-honored way of fixing the collective significance of violent death, and if that invocation is rejected, some other explanation is needed. Whicher is absolutely right that the lack of purpose makes the Oklahoma City victims' deaths even more heartbreaking, but millions of other violent deaths are equally heartbreaking for the same reason. Throughout history, structural imbalances of power have left one group exposed to victimization by another (slaves to slaveowners, wives to husbands, children to fathers) with death just as wasteful and trauma just as intense as in Oklahoma City the day that a nobody named McVeigh, for one fleeting moment, took control of the Murrah Building.

And so, paradoxically, we are still left groping to explain how these "wasted" deaths are significant—why they should be remembered when others are not. Indeed, in the traumatic monument, the challenge is to find collective purpose when the victims' own individual purpose has been violated and destroyed. The Oklahoma City Memorial Foundation assigned itself this task when it set out to write a "mission statement" that would guide the memorial process. The statement makes the claim, throughout its six pages, that although the bombing in some way touched the whole nation, control over the commemorative form and message should rest with the families of the 168 dead and the direct survivors of the blast, the "trauma club," as some of its own members called it.[20] "Ensuring that families and survivors are involved to the greatest degree feasible in development, design, funding, construction and maintenance of the Memorial is one way to honor those who died, those who survived and those who love them."[21] But why honor *them*? Why does their suffering merit a monument, and not the suffering of all others who have "had those precious to them taken away so brutally"? The document explains that this was a "public" attack, and although localized, its losses "are shared with a community, a nation and the world." This explanation raises another problem. If the event is worthy of commemoration because of its significance beyond the "trauma club," why does that group's feelings and wishes take precedence over those of the larger collective? If the extra-local significance makes the event monumental, then should not the monument focus on that wider significance?

The mission statement continually circles around the question of the bombing's larger collective significance without ever answering it. This reticence seems to stem in part from a profound reluctance to discuss the perpetrator and his reasons for attacking the building. The word "terrorist" does not appear until near the end of the document, and only then obliquely. The statement urges the memorial to help visitors understand the victims as individuals with their own personal stories, but does not urge visitors to understand why these people were targeted. Instead, the statement calls for the inclusion of a "learning center" that "should instill an understanding of the senselessness of violence, especially as a means of effecting government change." Despite the urgency of its hope that violence of this sort never be repeated, the statement rings hollow, not only because the U.S. government endorses violence as a means of regime change (in Afghanistan, Iraq, and elsewhere) and was founded on violent regime change (the Revolutionary War), but also because McVeigh and his co-conspirators' act of violence was not "senseless" to them or other like-minded terrorists. But to acknowledge the perpetrators and their motivations simply threatened to give them a public platform, to bolster their sense of agency at the expense of those victimized. In the traumatic relationship, the perpetrator gains power and agency as the victim loses them; the last thing the survivors wanted was to reinforce the perpetrator's agency in any way. As a result, the mission statement can never actually utter the appalling truth that the bombing was a deliberate act of mass murder directed at ordinary working representatives of the U.S. government; that it might have happened anywhere, anytime, to anyone working for the federal government or doing business with it.

Figure 5.3. Hans and Torrey Butzer, Oklahoma City National Memorial, 2000, detail of bronze chair. Photograph: David Allen.

The monument and museum built in response to this mission statement—a design by Hans and Torrey Butzer chosen in an open competition—continue to focus on the 168 victims. As in the Vietnam Veterans Memorial, the victims are represented by their names, but here the names are each inscribed on an empty bronze chair in an outdoor park—a solution that would obviously be unworkable for the much larger number of names in the Vietnam Veterans Memorial (see fig. 5.3). In contrast to this uniform symbolic representation, meant to group the dead together as victims, the particularized, diversifying space of the museum offers visitors images of the individual facial features of the dead, their personal stories, and the stories of the survivors and those who helped in rescue efforts. The U.S. Holocaust Memorial Museum in Washington, D.C., dedicated in 1993, clearly served as a precedent for this element of the Oklahoma City memorial. In both cases, the museum acts to put a human face on the victims, to restore to them the humanity their killers tried to deny and negate. But there is of course a vast difference between the two. The sheer scale of death in the Holocaust is so far-reaching, both in absolute numbers and in geographical sweep, that some individuation of the victims becomes necessary just to suggest the immeasurable calamity of the event and the very incompleteness of the archive that memorializes it. At Oklahoma City, the archive is, in a sense, complete: all 168 victims are known, named, and documented. The magnitude of the event is suggested instead by the large scale of the memorial space (it covers 3.3 acres) and by its official status as a national memorial under the safekeeping of the National Park Service.

Yet the memorial as a whole gives relatively little attention to why the event radiates beyond the local circle of people traumatized by it. The process that produced this outcome, in its deference to the traumatized community, went far beyond the example of the Vietnam Veterans Memorial. In that case combat "survivors" initiated the project and guided the fundraising, but largely delegated the design process to design professionals. An architectural advisor, Paul Spreiregen, actually wrote the competition program (the closest thing to a "mission statement") and chaired the all-professional design jury. The Oklahoma City foundation also hired Spreiregen, but later fired him when he insisted on the same degree of professional control that he had exercised over the earlier memorial. While the sponsors in Oklahoma City did end up using other professional advisors, family members and survivors held a majority on the final evaluation committee.[22] This is not to claim that the Oklahoma City process was less democratic than that used for the Vietnam Veterans Memorial; in fact the Oklahoma City process was much more open and the sponsors solicited much wider input. But where the sponsors tended to see the public input mirroring the wishes of the families and survivors, a historian who has studied the process sees more divergence. And in any case, the process always returned to the core group, to its thoughts and feelings.[23]

Understandably, the sponsors believed that to make visitors feel the intensity of the trauma here required an intense personalization of the event, much more in fact than at the Vietnam Veterans Memorial. The victims in the Oklahoma City tragedy get not only the recognition of their names permanently inscribed, as they were at the Vietnam Veterans Memorial, but also a chair and museum exhibits devoted to each of them. And all this is located in the very place, the "sacred ground," where they died. Once again we come up against the paradox of the therapeutic monument: the more intense the focus on each individual victim, the less the monument justifies itself because the less there is to distinguish this particular loss from all the other traumatic losses suffered in any society. Intensifying the personal dimension of the trauma only calls into question the value system that would rank one trauma over another. In fact, singling out one trauma for special recognition can have the effect of making those people whose traumas have not been commemorated feel unrecognized and thus even further traumatized. This was one unexpected outcome of the Vietnam Veterans Memorial. Lin's walls fueled demands for the Korean War memorial (completed 1995), which in turn helped spur the drive to locate the national World War II memorial in the center of the Mall. Hart's statues of male servicemen gave rise to demands for a similar monument to women who served in the war (completed 1993). It is noteworthy that Jan Scruggs and the Vietnam Veterans Memorial Fund now want to supplement the memorial with an underground "visitor center" that would put the war in geographical and historical context and also put faces on the names of the dead. They believe that more overt explanation and personalization of the tragedy are now necessary to maintain its significance in a society further removed from the event. As fewer and fewer visitors have a personal connection to the victims, the memorial seems to lose its urgency and to require a more explicit restatement of its justification.[24]

Of course I am not advocating a return to the traditional didacticism of the public monument. Nor am I arguing that therapeutic monuments are unjustified. But therapeutic monuments are caught on the horns of a dilemma. The traditional didacticism that invokes notions of self-sacrifice to a noble cause denies the victim's real situation and therefore violates the "truth" of the traumatic experience. Yet hewing to the reality of that experience, however one understands or apprehends it, does not automatically grant it a collective significance that explains why the extraordinary recognition of a public monument is called for.

To resolve this dilemma, the therapeutic monument must invent a new kind of meaning that embraces both the reality of individual suffering and the collective significance of that suffering. There is no reason, *a priori*, why such meaning could not be articulated in any traumatic situation, whether it be a terrorist attack or sexual abuse. It is possible that the immense challenge of memorializing the events of 9/11 may lead to a solution of this problem. The enormous concentration of thought and energy on this project, from so many quarters, augurs a willingness and desire to move beyond past models.

In the more immediate aftermath of 9/11, past models proved irresistible. Traditional didacticism certainly resurfaced, especially in official observances. The term "hero" quickly came into use, with obvious justification, for all those "first responders" involved in the rescue operation—especially those who lost their lives. But the term has been stretched on occasion to encompass everyone who died, thus conflating those who deliberately risked their lives with those who were unwillingly victimized. At the first anniversary of 9/11 at the World Trade Center site, the governor of New York, following in Clinton's footsteps at Oklahoma City, read the Gettysburg Address; an official viewing fence installed at the time bore the names of all the dead displayed under the legend, "Heroes of September 11." Besides the appeal to heroism, the therapeutic model refined at Oklahoma City also loomed large. In the summer of 2002, the Families Advisory Committee (FAC) of the Lower Manhattan Development Corporation (LMDC) produced a draft mission statement for the World Trade Center memorial that was closely modeled on the Oklahoma City prototype, with its stress on the priority of the victims, survivors, and their families. The draft actually repeated much of the same language, calling, for example, for a memorial "that focuses on the victims and survivors" and for a "learning center" to help people "understand the senselessness of terrorism."[25]

Yet once the first anniversary of the event passed in the fall of 2002, the movement for a memorial took a new direction. While the high-profile design competition for rebuilding the World Trade Center site captured the headlines, the LMDC also sponsored a less publicized process to initiate a separate design competition specifically for the memorial itself. This process ultimately replaced the FAC's draft statement with a new mission statement and memorial program written by more broadly representative committees, consisting not only of family members but of community representatives and design professionals, among others. A competition jury of thirteen people was selected, with only one member from the FAC; a majority of the jury consisted of arts professionals, among them Maya Lin.

The new committees used the FAC's earlier mission statement draft "as a starting point," but changed its language and emphases considerably. The mission statement committee debated loaded terms such as "senseless," "sacrifice," and "hero"—none of which, incidentally, appear in the final draft. They also deliberately rejected "establishing any hierarchies" and settled on a very brief statement that does not appear to give precedence to one group over another; gone is the explicit "focus" on "victims and survivors," though recognition of the victims is the first of four goals articulated. The four goal statements move clearly from the idea of loss to redemption, from the injunction to remember the thousands of innocent people "murdered by terrorists" to the hope that the memorial will help "reaffirm respect for life, strengthen our resolve to preserve freedom, and inspire an end to hatred, ignorance and intolerance."[26]

The accompanying program statement, also radically condensed, deals much more explicitly with the question of the event's collective significance than did the far longer FAC draft. Of the eight guiding principles in the program statement, at least three deal directly with the question of meaning. These urge the monument to: "evoke the historical significance and worldwide impact of September 11, 2001"; "inspire and engage people to learn more about the events and impact of September 11, 2001"; and "evolve over time."[27] Neither this nor the mission statement tries to "fix" the meaning of the event; they do not even ask the monument to do so. Instead, the monument is supposed to address the question of meaning in a way that enables answers to "evolve." Moreover, the monument must do so in a setting "distinct from other memorial structures like a museum or visitor center."[28]

These principles are certainly open to multiple interpretations. Some might decide that the best way to create a memorial that "evolves" is to avoid the question of meaning altogether, to create a "neutral" memorial that asks visitors to generate their own "personal and private" interpretations of the event. But another response to these requirements would be to confront the question of meaning, not to fix it or impose it in the traditional didactic manner but to guide visitors to reflect on the problem in particular ways. Monuments can frame questions rather than answers, still leaving room for understanding to evolve. Yet how can a memorial enact the redemptive movement of the mission statement, proceeding from the recognition of "tragic loss" to inspiring "an end to hatred, ignorance and intolerance," without actively guiding visitors emotionally and intellectually? A list of names alone certainly cannot: it can just as easily inspire hate and a desire for revenge.

Indeed, the memory of 9/11 has been used by the political leadership of the

U.S. to justify a relentless campaign of violence against real or potential security threats, a campaign that has no end even in theory. However just or unjust one believes these specific actions are, this campaign has the overall effect of reproducing the trauma of 9/11 in other lands: to leave loved ones dead, children orphaned, young men tortured, communities devastated. The redemptive message of the World Trade Center memorial mission statement, like the plea in the Oklahoma City statement to grasp the "senselessness" of violence, boils down simply, in the end, to the hope that their trauma will not be revisited on others. A memorial that takes this hope seriously must wade into deeply political waters. Its significance must reverberate far beyond the "sacred ground" of the World Trade Center site and connect outward to the trauma of the innocent everywhere.

For would-be designers there is no road map. Architect Daniel Libeskind, the winner of the larger site-planning competition, envisaged leaving the slurry wall at the site exposed (the wall that held back the river water from flooding lower Manhattan) and making the memorial a pit seventy feet deep, an evocation of "Ground Zero."[29] His proposal would have created a journey of descent and reascent similar to the one pioneered by Lin at the Vietnam Veterans Memorial, yet the underlying question of the memorial's meaning would have remained submerged beneath a fixed, edifying image of resilience in the face of attack. The various local memorials to 9/11 that have sprung up all around the country often go a step further in this direction and refashion icons of the twin towers or the Pentagon, sometimes using relics salvaged from the buildings' ruins.[30] The jury for the World Trade Center memorial avoided iconic solutions such as these because their very fixity violated the core principle of the project, which was to reflect and encourage "an evolving process of memory."[31] The jury's final choice, a design dubbed "Reflecting Absence" which features two sunken pools in the tower footprints surrounded by groves of trees, is relatively minimalist, neutral, and nondirective. More "maximalist" solutions that came close to winning, such as the "Garden of Lights," were riskier but potentially more innovative. The "Garden of Lights" would have filled the tower footprints with "prairies" of wildflowers replanted each year by a different gardener chosen from around the world; its design aesthetic openly defied the modernist grid of the towers. With these gestures, this entry was one of the few that actively tried to redirect the visitor's attention toward an embrace of life beyond the enclosed world of the towers.[32]

A few blocks from the World Trade Center site sits the most recent disaster monument erected in New York City. The monument to the Irish potato famine, designed by artist Brian Tolle, was dedicated in the summer of 2002 as the work of clearing Ground Zero approached its end. Approaching from the direction of the WTC, the visitor encounters a gentle slope of fallow earth holding the ruins of a cottage brought from Ireland, a little slice of the Irish countryside unexpectedly dropped into the concrete sea of lower Manhattan (see fig. 5.4). Passing through the ruins of the house, we emerge into a totally different environment: a silver-gray wall with long, thin horizontal bars of words that seem

Figure 5.4. Brian Tolle, Irish Hunger Memorial, New York City, 2002.
Photograph: Kirk Savage.

to have no end—comments and statistics about hunger not only from the case of the Irish famine but from more recent times and places as well. There are no lists of names, no documentation to measure the magnitude of the catastrophe. The memorial does not focus on the victims of this particular tragedy, who are long gone, their personal connections to present generations now obviously attenuated. Instead the memorial is all about the reverberations of the event across time and space. The event reverberates across the Irish landscape, in an abandoned field and a crumbling house; it reverberates in the monument's view of New York harbor, where so many Irish immigrants came to flee their poverty; it reverberates in the words that link hunger to ongoing social injustice; it reverberates in the very city surrounding the monument, where extremes of wealth and deprivation persist. The monument is at once a peaceful oasis in the money-driven city and a challenge to it.

Notes

I would like to thank the editors for their insightful comments on earlier drafts of this essay.

1.   Judith Herman, *Trauma and Recovery* (New York: Basic Books, 1992), 34.

2.   Kirk Savage, *Standing Soldiers, Kneeling Slaves: Race, War, and Monument in Nineteenth-Century America* (Princeton, N.J.: Princeton University Press, 1997).

3.   David Oats, "Disaster at Hell Gate: The Sinking of the General Slocum," *Queens Courier Online* www.queenscourier.com/spclissue/slocum/slocum1.htm.

4.   Steven Biel, *Down with the Old Canoe: A Cultural History of the Titanic Disaster* (New York: Norton, 1996), 35–37.

5.   Jay Winter, "Remembrance and Redemption: A Social Interpretation of War Memorials," *Harvard Design Magazine* (Fall 1999): 71–73.

6.   I am indebted to Daniel Sherman's fine book *The Construction of Memory in Interwar France* (Chicago: University of Chicago Press, 1999), especially 274–282, and to my ensuing conversations with him.

7.   Ian Buruma, "The Joys and Perils of Victimhood," *New York Review of Books* 46:6 (April 8, 1999): 4–9.

8.   James E. Young, *The Texture of Memory: Holocaust Memorials and Meaning* (New Haven, Conn.: Yale University Press, 1993).

9.   Quoted in Jan C. Scruggs and Joel L. Swerdlow, *To Heal A Nation: The Vietnam Veterans Memorial* (New York: HarperPerennial, 1992), 53. Charles L. Griswold makes the point that the Vietnam Veterans Memorial is "therapeutic" in his "The Vietnam Veterans Memorial and the Washington Mall: Philosophical Thoughts on Political Iconography," in Harriet F. Senie and Sally Webster, eds., *Critical Issues in Public Art Content, Context, and Controversy* (Washington, D.C.: Smithsonian Institution Press, 1992), 92.

10.   Herman, *Trauma and Recovery*, 27–28.

11.   The full text of Lin's competition entry is available at http://www.nps.gov/vive/memorial/evolutionprint.htm.

12.   The best documentation of reactions to the memorial is Laura Palmer, *Shrapnel in the Heart: Letters and Remembrances from the Vietnam Veterans Memorial* (New York: Vintage Books, 1988). Lin's concept seems well-embedded in the "privatization" of grief that took place in the twentieth century. One of the fascinating results of her memorial is that, despite her original intentions, the monument has countered that trend by creating a collective space in which the process of coming to grips with death is participatory, shared, and publicly recognized.

13.   Herman, *Trauma and Recovery*, 70–71.

14.   Several writers, in different ways, have argued that these highly personal offerings are a response to the impersonality or emptiness of the names, as if visitors are trying to fill a void created by the memorial's abstraction. (See for example Karal Ann Marling and Robert Silberman, "The Statue Near the Wall: The Vietnam Veterans Memorial and the Art of Remembering," *Smithsonian Studies in American Art* [Spring 1987]: 14; Marita Sturken, *Tangled Memories: The Vietnam War, the AIDS Epidemic, and the Politics of Remembering* [Berkeley: University of California Press, 1997], 61.) I take the opposite view: that the therapeutic power of the memorial itself summons these offerings. Precisely because the memorial *does* speak to the visitors' therapeutic needs, because it encourages its viewers to engage with it, they feel that their own personal testimonials belong in the collective artifact. To claim that the me-

morial, or its list of names, is "depersonalized" is off the mark, since the therapeutic memorial personalizes the viewing experience in a new way.

15. This is precisely the point made in two of the most cogent right-wing critiques published after Lin's walls were erected: Tod Lindberg, "Of Arms, Men & Monuments," *Commentary* (October 1984): 51–56, and William Hubbard, "A Meaning for Monuments," *Public Interest* 74 (Winter 1984): 17–30. The addition of the flagpole and another inscription at its base were intended to remedy this; the inscription on the flagpole asserts that "the flag affirms the principles of freedom for which they fought and their pride in having served under difficult circumstances."

16. Herman, *Trauma and Recovery*, 73.

17. Oklahoma City Memorial Foundation, "Mission Statement," accessible on the web at www.oklahomacitynationalmemorial.org/geninfo/mission.html.

18. Edward T. Linenthal, *The Unfinished Bombing: Oklahoma City in American Memory* (New York: Oxford University Press, 2001), 234.

19. Quoted in Ibid., 235.

20. Oklahoma City Memorial Foundation, "Mission Statement." For the "trauma club" see Linenthal, *The Unfinished Bombing*, 181.

21. Oklahoma City Memorial Foundation, "Mission Statement," 5.

22. Linenthal, *The Unfinished Bombing*, 186–90, 214.

23. The sponsors solicited input in a series of local public meetings and through a survey published in newspapers and on the Internet. While the mission statement claims that "the hopes of the general public mirrored almost identically those outlined by the Families/Survivors Liaison Subcommittee," Linenthal found that the "surveys revealed strong and widely divergent feelings about who and what the memorial should honor" (183).

24. Jan Scruggs, interview with Robert Siegel, May 30, 2003, "All Things Considered," National Public Radio.

25. Lower Manhattan Development Corporation, Families Advisory Program Subcommittee, "Draft Memorial Mission Statement and Program Description," July 27, 2002. The remainder of this essay focuses on the World Trade Center site in part because the scale of loss there separates it from the Pentagon and Shanksville sites, and in part because the other two sites do not offer the same narratives of victimization. In the Shanksville case, the dead recouped a measure of historical agency by resisting the hijackers and foiling their mission; in the Pentagon case the victims were serving the national defense even if in a civilian capacity.

26. Lower Manhattan Development Corporation, "Memorial Mission Statement and Memorial Program," www.renewnyc.com/Memorial/memmission.shtml.

27. An earlier draft of this statement read, "evolve over time with our understanding of the events" (draft released January 8, 2003).

28. Lower Manhattan Development Corporation, "Memorial Mission Statement and Memorial Program."

29. Ibid.

30. I am indebted to Jon Darman of *Newsweek* magazine for sending me images and descriptions of many local 9/11 memorials, a phenomenon that deserves a study of its own. Some of these may be viewed at http://www.msnbc.com/modules/newsweek/test/911gallery.

31. This phrase is taken from the jury's statement published at http://www.wtcsitememorial.org/about_jury_txt.html. My understanding of the jury's process is also informed by James Young's preliminary account of the deliberations at the annual meeting of the Organization of American Historians, March 26, 2004. A fuller published account of the deliberations clearly is needed before any definitive analysis can be attempted.

32. For a partial description of this competition entry see http://www.wtcsitememorial.org/fin0.html.

6   Naming and the Violence of Place

Daniel J. Sherman

The events of 9/11 and their aftermath impinge on so many aspects of life that any scholarly perspective on them risks appearing insensitive, emotionless, hopelessly inadequate. Ironically, no approach incurs that risk to a greater extent than the emerging pluridisciplinary field of memory studies, which focuses on the ways the memories of individuals assume social form, physical presence, and political significance in texts and images, in memorial architecture and survivors' associations, and in the wider culture. Such an approach necessarily stands at a distance from events and their human actors, the better to concentrate on the ways those events are represented and the larger purposes memory as representation comes to serve. Yet in an age in which memorialization has become both instantaneous and a universal demand, it has arguably become harder to distinguish between event and memory. Certainly the earliest stage of commemoration, the crude photocopied pictures of the missing displayed by candlelight in Union Square, remain for many an indelible image of "the event" itself.[1] On a different plane, the political rhetoric used to justify U.S. military action first in Afghanistan and then in Iraq has from the beginning had a strong memorial element. Precisely because "remembering 9/11" can take so many forms and encompass so many different activities, understanding the workings of collective memory, the way in which images and ideas about the events take on social form, has a vital role to play in assessing those events and their consequences.

What, though, can the *history* of commemoration contribute to this discussion? To begin with, it would be a mistake to take at face value the claim that "everything changed" after 9/11; as Stephen Toope shows elsewhere in this volume, that claim belies many underlying continuities. Indeed, precisely because both memorial discourse and commemorative ritual since 9/11 have continually evoked historical precedent while at the same time claiming a situational uniqueness, we need to situate commemoration, understood as the mobilization of memorial discourses, images, and practices in the service of a larger political project, in its own historical context. For the tension between an overpowering sense of historical moment and a rejection of contextual comparison that arose after 9/11 has done much to shape American culture and behavior in the ensuing months and years, and not simply in the domain of commemoration.

In approaching the commemoration of 9/11 historically, I seek not to reduce it to a pale replica of some chimerical origin but, on the contrary, to understand its distinctness as an emergence in the Foucauldian sense. For Foucault in his study of Nietzsche, the "emergence" of new historical phenomena involves substitution, forcible displacement, and mechanisms both systematic and unpredictable because delocalized.[2] Nothing better illustrates the complexity and the stakes of this process than the ways official commemorations of 9/11 appropriate the dynamics of past commemoration without fully confronting their contradictions. In pointing out both continuity and the various attempts to ignore it, the history of commemoration presents the pieties of memorial discourse as part of a larger political project and empowers us to question that project more intensively. "If the public is content merely to remember the past," Daniel Abramson has observed, "then the powerful will be entrusted too fully with planning the future." His call for a history characterized by "critical distance and empathic engagement," history as "memory critically tested and imaginatively engaged," has special urgency in post-9/11 America.[3]

At the heart of my analysis stand two concepts, naming and place. The familiarity of both these terms should not be mistaken for simplicity, for both have played significant roles in theoretical debates in a number of fields. Naming, in the form of the inscription or recitation of the names of those being honored, has over the past two decades become perhaps the most easily identifiable element in American commemoration. Commemorative naming partakes of a broadly humanist spirit, in which the name stands for the inviolability of a person with inviolable universal rights.[4] But for theorists who challenge the humanist philosophical basis of universal rights, naming has a much more sinister function. In his commentary on Lévi-Strauss's *Tristes Tropiques,* for example, Jacques Derrida declares that "to name, to give names that it will on occasion be forbidden to pronounce, such is the originary violence of language," and thus marks the beginning of all other forms of violence.[5] Whatever its applicability to the texts of commemoration, Derrida's observation reminds us of the paradoxes and dangers involved in securing even the most apparently consensual of meanings. The very banality of the name stands for the deceptive innocence of language itself, of which the most apparently consensual manifestations, such as "united we stand," may harbor the greatest potential for violence.

If commemoration almost invariably employs language, it also has a spatial dimension, one that has expanded to the point where, in the words of the critic Herbert Muschamp, "the contemporary city has become a memorial of itself."[6] My own understanding of place owes much to Michel de Certeau, who describes places as "fragmentary and withdrawn histories, pasts others have robbed of legibility, accumulated times that can be unfolded but which are present much more as stories in waiting, remaining like rebuses."[7] Even before they become sites of commemoration, but in a way oddly akin to commemoration itself, places like the World Trade Center harbor the residues of lives, struggles, and conflicts that their own construction as places was often intended to repress. History has no more challenging task than to recover some of those hidden acts, and to elucidate the interests at play in the commemorative discourses that subsume them or even push them aside.

Naming and the creation of places of commemoration have a number of traits in common, not least their malleability and apparent resistance to political appropriation. I want to argue, however, that this commonality runs deeper, and indeed that the apparent construction of an apolitical realm of commemoration through naming and commemorative sites is an illusion. For in the commemorative realm both names and places actively, continually, and integrally appropriate the personal on behalf of the political. It is easy enough to grasp this appropriation in relation to places, where, especially when public entities are involved, it may take the form of *ex*propriation, literally a deprivation of ownership in the name of some larger collective interest. The construction of the World Trade Center offers a well-known example of such expropriation, but, as we will see, in different ways so too does the transformation of its site into a place of commemoration. Naming, in contrast, on the surface seems to privilege the personal: what could be more personal, less political, than a name? Yet commemoration appropriates names as well, making them a centerpiece of a set of ritual discourses and practices that have much more to do with the general needs of the commemorating society, and the interests of its leaders, than with the particular lives of those who once bore the names. These dynamics are not new, yet their historical roots generally go unacknowledged, and for good reason: the apparent novelty of commemoration at every historical moment it marks provides it with a legitimacy rooted in its apparent deference to personal grief. Commemoration's simultaneous use and concealment of its own past, then, embodies the greatest continuity of all, for it serves the ongoing purpose of restoring the institutionalized political project that the events commemorated at least appeared to put in jeopardy.

Restoring the historicity of commemoration therefore promises not only to expose its politics, but also to offer a different way of thinking about its future. If the commemoration of 9/11 began almost immediately after the attacks, its history can best be recounted retrospectively, beginning with the moment at which its institutionalization became most apparent, September 11, 2002. Amidst the plethora of observances, simple and grandiose, that marked that anniversary, one aspect calls for particular comment: the reluctance of public figures to speak their own words at Ground Zero, the principal focus of national attention. President Bush saved his remarks for the evening, in an event that attracted attention chiefly for the strikingly lit Statue of Liberty that formed its carefully selected backdrop.[8] Even more strikingly, the three principal political figures who appeared at Ground Zero, the governors of New York and New Jersey and the mayor of New York City, chose to give voice to the words of others: Governor George Pataki of New York recited the Gettysburg Address, Mayor Michael Bloomberg read Franklin Roosevelt's Four Freedoms speech, and Governor James McGreevey of New Jersey read excerpts from the Declaration of Independence.[9]

The ostensible political significance of these texts requires little elucidation.

All belong to the canon of documents that define the American polity in terms of its devotion to liberty or freedom as the highest political value. To be sure, the political leaders' refusal to commit themselves to words provoked some critical comment. In a "Critic's Notebook," *New York Times* cultural correspondent Michiko Kakutani wrote that the leaders "abdicated" their responsibility to speak to the hopes and fears of their constituents; more specifically, she observed that "the act of recycling treated both Lincoln's classic words and the terrible plight of those who died on 9/11 as oddly generic and interchangeable." Unlike those Lincoln honored, the victims of the terrorist attacks, as Kakutani and others noted, were not active combatants consciously giving their lives for the sake of a country whose very existence was in jeopardy.[10] They were, for the most part, people going about their daily lives, most at work, some at leisure. Invoking texts from times of much greater peril to the nation implicitly suggests a parallel between those eras and our own, casting the post-9/11 situation as a "crisis" requiring both extreme measures and, on the part of the governed, the trust that Lincoln and other heroes of the American political pantheon presumably inspired. Certainly no one who spoke at the anniversary mentioned the many restrictions on civil liberties, notably habeas corpus, that Lincoln imposed in the name of "Union."[11]

The political overtones of the 9/11 anniversary observances require further probing, but for the moment I want to call attention to an aspect of the 9/11 speeches that has attracted less notice: their enactment of a crucial dynamic of modern commemoration. "But in a larger sense," Lincoln declared at Gettysburg, "we cannot dedicate—we cannot consecrate—we cannot hallow—this ground. The brave men, living and dead, who struggled here, have consecrated it, far above our poor power to add or detract. The world will little note, nor long remember what we say here, but it can never forget what they did here."[12] This opposition between speech and action implicitly—but for Lincoln, as Garry Wills has pointed out, very consciously—invokes a tradition of classical oratory that can be traced back to ancient Greece.[13] Problematic in this instance for the reasons already noted, the trope inevitably works in paradoxical fashion, because the very deferral to deeds legitimates the words that enact it. To put it another way, only language can signify its own inefficacy in the face of human bravery, for such courage typically manifests itself in response to violence that language may unleash but can never wholly master. James Dawes has argued, indeed, that the contrast between language and violence itself plays an important part in shaping the aesthetic and cultural response to war in the modern world.[14]

The eschewal of speech, whether a rhetorical device or, as on September 11, 2002, an actual substitution, in any case calls attention to other aspects of the commemorative ritual. On the first anniversary of the 9/11 attacks, media accounts highlighted the reading of the names of the dead at Ground Zero, a process that took two and a half hours. Several television networks ran crawls on the bottom of their screens that tracked, with a few seconds' delay, the reading of the names in New York; the crawls—just the names on NBC, the names plus photographs of the dead on CBS—remained visible for the entire duration of the reading, even at moments when the networks cut away to observances at the Pentagon or in Pennsylvania.[15] The crawls fulfilled a function typical of names in a commemorative context, providing both an order and a limit to a process of commemoration that often begins with the kind of spontaneous, personal memorials that sprang up in Union Square the year before.[16] The names stand for individuals, of course, but also for the social and political order that assigns, tracks, and classifies them.

With names we find ourselves in familiar modernist territory, with a lineage extending back from Maya Lin's Vietnam Veterans Memorial, through local World War I monuments in Europe, North America, and Australia, to the Civil War memorials in courthouse squares throughout the eastern and southern United States. However broad its scope, this genealogy nonetheless has distinct contours: if the American Civil War marked the first moment of modern industrialized mass slaughter, World War I, in technological terms its logical extension, saw the emergence of a system of commemoration focused on individuals rather than commanders. Though in most of the combatant countries the aftermath of war did produce some figurative monuments, commemoration focused on the names of the dead invariably inscribed on monuments, and at ritual moments self-consciously took note of this focus. By treating the reading of names as the key moment of the rituals they had themselves devised, political figures cast post–World War I ceremonies as primarily tributes to the dead, thus seeking to naturalize the contingent political meanings they often drew from their "memories."[17]

For some scholars, the inscription of names on monuments stands for the continuity of a peculiarly "modern" cast of commemoration since World War I. Names, in this view, embody a refusal of conventional narratives justifying soldiers' deaths in terms of some overarching meaning, whether patriotic, religious, or both. The individual names themselves mattered less than their aggregation, on individual tombstones or the surfaces of monuments, which offered a physical representation of a scale of death so massive that no other meaning could be assigned to it.[18] This argument, however, may project too neatly from the common understanding of Maya Lin's Vietnam Veterans Memorial (fig. 6.1) as "healing" or therapeutic. Certainly Lin intended to create a place in which each visitor would assign his or her own meaning to the loss it inscribes. Yet the "private reckoning[s]" Lin called for still left room for considerable public rhetoric, and in the end her design had to coexist with imposed collective representations that function in a much more traditional register.[19]

My own study of interwar French commemoration, moreover, found that names often had considerable external meaning attached to them, and that they served as a kind of bridge between the individual memories of families and survivors and the larger significance attached to them by ritualized collective memory. The reading of the names of the dead in commemorative ceremonies, for example, frequently led speakers to invoke the names of martial heroes, some national, like Joan of Arc, some more localized, who would then set up

Figure 6.1. Maya Ying Lin, Vietnam Veterans Memorial, Washington, D.C., dedicated 1982: view of the apex. Photograph: Daniel Sherman, 1988.

larger historical or patriotic lessons.[20] On the first anniversary of 9/11, media coverage of the reading of names tended to emphasize their ethnic diversity, a point that flows easily into an argument about the unity that "naturally" emerges from the desire to remember.[21]

The artificial order of a list of names thus replicates, whether intentionally or not, a social order coded as "unity." On the first anniversary in 2002, the difficulty some of the readers had pronouncing names in unfamiliar languages emphasized this order, as did the occasional coincidence of a reader with the ethnicity of the names it fell on him or her to call out. The familiarity and simplicity of the alphabet serves a reassuring function: even when a person has left no physical remains, the corresponding name has a secure, recognized place in an alphabetical list and can always be "found" there. (Chronological arrangements, such as the one used at the Vietnam Veterans Memorial, require more knowledge, or at least a concordance, to navigate, but they have the same fundamental dependability.) Names may also be combined with familiar symbols that afford them an unambiguously collective meaning: for observances of the second anniversary of 9/11 in 2003, which also featured a ritualized reading of names, visitors to Ground Zero could examine the names of the dead printed on an American flag.[22]

But the calming order of the list inevitably conceals uncertainty, disorder, arbitrary classifications, and often conflict. The *New York Times* reported, for example, that the list of names read on the first anniversary included, after much discussion, those of individuals whose presence at the World Trade Center on 9/11 was entirely a matter of speculation: better to read out the name of someone still alive than to deny tribute to someone who had died.[23]

In this respect the organizers of the first anniversary observances showed themselves to be more inclusive than those in earlier situations. Yet a name read aloud, however powerful the memory image connected to it, carries much less weight than one literally carved in stone. In April 2003, more than twenty years after the completion of the Vietnam Veterans Memorial in Washington, its sponsor held a ceremony in memory of nearly 400 people who died as a result of their service in the war, for example through Agent Orange poisoning or as post-traumatic stress suicides, but who did not meet the stringent criteria for inclusion on the wall.[24] In France after World War I, the inscription of a name also attested to membership in a local community, either formal, through birth, or through recent residence; officials generally refused requests to inscribe names simply to comfort grieving relatives who had moved to a town where the dead individual had never lived.[25] But the designation "mort pour la France" that usually headed monuments' lists of names had legal connotations, entitling legitimate survivors to pensions and other benefits. As legal markers of identity, names (fig. 6.2) have more than symbolic or commemorative value: they have a direct connection to the value of the life they were attached to. The system of compensation set up by Congress after 9/11 has provoked controversy because it ignores the events of 9/11 and makes distinctions between individuals solely on the basis of earnings potential.[26] Yet such crude fiscal criteria do not lack symbolic overtones and themselves raise difficult questions about the relationship between private memories, group affiliations, and the various forms of official commemoration. Some family members, for example, have called for the inscription of the identifier "FDNY" after the names of firemen who died on 9/11, while others resist the idea of any kind of distinction among the dead.[27] This issue has continued to be, in the words of one journalist, the most "vexing" facing the builders of the World Trade Center memorial. The solution announced with the selection of the final design, to inscribe the names of all victims in a random order, but with service insignia next to the names of rescue workers, did not wholly satisfy either those who wanted police and firefighters listed separately or those who preferred the inscription of names alone.[28]

The link between the symbolic function of names and the monetary value attached to those who bore them plays out visibly in the struggle for a role in the commemorative process. In portraying itself as the outgrowth of universally shared emotions and attributes—grief, love, devotion, determination to

Figure 6.2. World War I memorial in Pont-Levoy, Loir-et-Cher department, central France. Photograph: Daniel Sherman, 1991.

remember—commemoration seeks to transcend social and political divisions and reinvigorate the group, community, or nation sponsoring it. Paradoxically, however, the process of commemoration almost invariably gives rise to such divisions, involving as it does a multiplicity of victims' or survivors' associations, expert groups, and government agencies. Thus commemoration has to mask not only the background noise of contemporary political debates but also, and even more important, the traces of its own operation from both its sites and its rituals, its spatial and temporal dimensions. If naming generally serves to legitimate larger commemorative processes, it cannot escape the controversies those processes generate even as they attempt to repress them.

The intensity and complexity of debates over commemoration derive from the competing interests in play. The process pits groups with a special claim to remembrance against those who speak for the community as a whole, from mayors and city councillors to legislators and civil servants.[29] Two groups in particular, veterans and the bereaved, have had a favored role in commemoration for at least a century; although they overlap, these groups do not invariably speak with one voice. After World War I, families' groups in both France and the United States successfully lobbied against their governments' desire to leave all their dead in grand military cemeteries near the battlefields. Only the British among the major Western powers managed to resist families' entreaties for the right to bury their loved ones in local cemeteries, but in all three countries authorities granted families considerable latitude in the construction of local monuments. Veterans too insisted on a predominant role in commemoration, and did not hesitate to disrupt the process when they did not get it.[30]

Only in the past twenty years have governments delegated the design process to veterans' or survivors' groups, for example in the case of the Oklahoma City memorial, and even in so doing they usually retain some supervisory authority. A powerful current of opinion, however, favors a more limited role for private associations. Appearing on CNN around the time of the first anniversary, the architectural critic Paul Goldberger argued that, however great its debt, society does not owe families of the victims control of the commemorative process; an art historian made a similar point with respect to rebuilding.[31] Although the various associations of victims' families set up after the 9/11 attacks do have an important voice in deliberations over commemoration and rebuilding, the process as a whole remains in the hands of government officials and design professionals. John Whitehead, chairman of the Lower Manhattan Development Corporation (LMDC), which oversees the design process for the World Trade Center memorial, declared that the architectural competition guidelines grew out of the "stewardship" of the LMDC board, the "careful deliberation among citizen volunteers," and the participation of "family members of victims of the attacks."[32] Not long after the first anniversary, families of the victims voiced anxiety that their influence over the commemorative process was waning, and the decisions of the WTC memorial jury led some to complain bitterly that their wishes had been ignored.[33] But they retained sufficient influence to bring about substantial changes in the winning design, notably greater exposure of the foundation walls or "bedrock" of the towers.[34]

Debates about the nature and purpose of commemoration often revolve around the fundamental and long controversial question of who, fundamentally, commemoration is for. A New York Times editorial on the WTC memorial finalists aptly conveys the notion that commemoration has other purposes besides consoling survivors or recognizing individual loss: "we hope that the winning design will embrace a way of remembering the dead that does not become trapped in specificity. This should be a memorial for our collective loss and not exclusively the loss suffered by the families of those who died there."[35] The mission statement of the Trade Center memorial competition in fact includes four elements, three of them imperatives: remember and honor the victims of the terrorist attacks, "respect this place made sacred through tragic loss," and recognize the courage and endurance of the survivors and rescuers. All, to some extent, focus on loss. The fourth element, however, as it encompasses the three imperatives, takes an optative form: "May the lives remembered, the deeds recognized, and the spirit reawakened be eternal beacons, which reaffirm respect for life, strengthen our resolve to preserve freedom, and inspire an end to hatred, ignorance, and intolerance." The more specific points of the "program guiding principles," which take the form of clauses completing the phrase "The memorial is to," begin with "Embody the goals and spirit of the mission statement," but also include "Evoke the historical significance and worldwide impact of September 11, 2001" and "Inspire and engage people to learn more about the events and impact of September 11, 2001 and February 26, 1993," as well as conveying the magnitude of loss, acknowledging the rescuers, encouraging reflection, enhancing the "sacred quality" of the site, and creating "an original and powerful statement of enduring and universal symbolism."[36] Perhaps aware that monuments tend to fade from public consciousness as they age, however—as Robert Musil famously observed, "The most striking feature of monuments is that you do not notice them"—the principles conclude by calling for a memorial that can "evolve over time."[37]

Several themes run through these texts: loss, recognition, sacrality, and pedagogy. Though the language carefully avoids the overloaded rhetoric of heroism or the specificity of national political discourse—the victims, after all, came from ninety-two countries—the key words "freedom" and "universal" accomplish much of the work performed in other media by American flag decals, "America Under Attack" key rings with images of the towers, and the like.[38] The notion that the memorial should "evoke" history and "inspire" learning suggests that it has an educational function extending well beyond the bereaved, notably to future generations. "Enduring" too shifts the emphasis from victims to the larger entity and purpose they have come to symbolize, and at the same time from past to future. The interim president of the LMDC uses a form of the same word in his own letter to participants in the memorial competition: "In your design, remember all those who were lost, but celebrate the values that endure, drawing inspiration from its setting in the cradle of American democracy."[39] Similarly, the brief "challenge" to entrants in the Pentagon memorial competition calls for a memorial both general and specific, and concludes, "Whether it is large or small, kinetic or static, both the sponsors and the families of the victims want the memorial to address not only the loss of those murdered at the Pentagon, but the dedication to the principles of liberty and freedom that this terrible event re-awakened in people around the world."[40]

This complex interweaving of memory and affirmation recalls Sigmund Freud's understanding of mourning as the transfer of desire from the lost to a new object, which can be either a person or "some abstraction which has taken the place of [a loved one], such as one's country, liberty, an ideal, and so on."[41] To the extent it encompasses mourning in this sense, commemoration, by the LMDC's own admission, pushes those involved in it to move on, however difficult this may be.[42] Naming plays a crucial role in this process because it places the lost individuals at the heart of commemoration both spatially (in many cases) and temporally, as the enumeration of the dead paces the rituals honoring them. Whatever the mesh between their own views and the wider political agendas of commemoration, family members and other survivors usually find a modus vivendi with monuments and ceremonies, which at least ostensibly seek to perpetuate the memory of their loved ones.

Figure 6.3. Kaseman Beckman Amsterdam Studio, winning design for Pentagon 9/11 memorial.
Courtesy of the Pentagon.

Neither the mission statement nor the guiding principles of the World Trade Center memorial competition specifically mention the victims' families, but three of the five "program elements" required of each submission pertain to them: "an area for families and loved ones of victims," a distinct zone for quiet contemplation, and "accessible space" to serve as a grave for unidentified remains from the site.[43] The program also calls, as its first element, for recognition of "each individual who was a victim of the attacks" of September 11, in Virginia and Pennsylvania as well as New York, as well as of the six killed in the 1993 attack on the World Trade Center. The Pentagon memorial competition call for submissions begins with a statement from family members that posits an indissoluble link between their loss and the larger values they wish to affirm: "The memorial should instill the ideas that patriotism is a moral duty, that freedom comes at a price, and that the victims of this attack have paid the ultimate price. Indeed, the memorial should bring an understanding that all of us have paid severely."[44] Because the statement casts its authors as "Americans and citizens of the world," the referent of the "we" hovers between the most general and more restricted senses, but it seems clear that the family members make no distinction between them.

To "recognize" an individual, as the LMDC call requires, does not necessarily mean to name him or her, yet, as Michael Kimmelman has observed and as Kirk Savage demonstrates elsewhere in this volume, the inscription of names has become something of a default for monuments to victims of war or terrorist violence.[45] Although the Pentagon memorial call for submissions did not specifically require such recognition, five of the six finalists in the competition featured 184 individual elements, including the winning design by Kaseman Beckman Amsterdam Studio of New York, a memorial park with 184 benches, each inscribed with the name of a victim (fig. 6.3).[46] All eight of the designs chosen as finalists in the World Trade Center memorial competition contained such enumerations, five through more or less conventional inscriptions, several through architectural, sculptural, or environmental elements such as altars, columns, or lighting. The critic Thomas Keenan called the projects "relentlessly numerical, devoted perhaps first of all to the project of counting, measuring, and listing."[47]

The attachment of family members to this practice derives at least in part from its function as a substitute for the individual tomb or monument, unavailable when no fragment of a body remains to be buried. At one level, the inscribed monument reconciles the characteristic modern demand for a restful place to mourn individuals in perpetuity, manifested in the eighteenth-century invention of the cemetery, with the twentieth-century's apparatuses of slaughter that make universal, localized burial impossible.[48]

Memorials can fill this substitutive function in a variety of ways and at a number of levels. Whereas the Vietnam Veterans Memorial regroups the names of the dead, dispersed in burial, for national contemplation, local war memorials offer family members a focal point for mourning and tribute even when the actual remains are buried at the front or have entirely disappeared.[49] Thus a number of communities have already dedicated their own memorials to local residents who died on 9/11, from Sudbury, Massachusetts, with three victims, to Middletown, New Jersey, which lost thirty-seven. At one entrance to Boston's Public Garden, Massachusetts is constructing its own memorial to the 197 state residents killed in the attacks; the state of New Jersey plans a monument to its nearly 700 victims in Liberty State Park.[50] The proposed World Trade Center memorial would combine these two functions, both universalizing the local and localizing the universal. The intensity of the destruction left many remains too fragmentary to be identified by current technology, and two years after the attacks nearly half of the dead had not been identified.[51] The planned burial site at the memorial thus stands in the line of the World War I memorial ossuaries that simultaneously preserve unidentified remains and offer families a place in which to mourn.[52]

But even for families who have been able to recover and bury their loved ones, and who thus already have a private place for mourning and communion with the dead, the memorial remains a crucial form of public recognition of their loss. Such recognition matters all the more because the building of any kind of memorial takes place in the context of reconstruction, which many oppose in principle.[53] The grisly ratio of victims per acre in World War I was comparable to or greater than that at the World Trade Center, but its scale made some displacement of remains and reconstruction inescapable. Nonetheless, many French veterans and relatives of the dead opposed substantial reconstruction and even the regrouping of battlefield cemeteries on the grounds that the dead should be left as close as possible to where they fell. These families claimed the right to commune with their loved ones at the site of their death.[54] The multiplicity of meanings that memorial sites and their surroundings harbor recall de Certeau's notion of places as "withdrawn histories" and "stories in waiting"; the creation of commemorative places aims to pin down and secure the stories they tell, appropriating space as the site of discourse in much the same way that commemorative naming appropriates individual life stories. To understand this dynamic, we need now to consider the specific places of commemoration of 9/11, in particular the World Trade Center.

As Brian Ladd has shown in his exemplary study *The Ghosts of Berlin,* in the aftermath of war and catastrophe urban communities typically have trouble finding a balance between reconstruction and memorialization.[55] The creation of a World Trade Center memorial has been particularly fraught precisely because it will take place as part of a complex rebuilding process. Here the Pentagon offers an instructive contrast: a speedy reconstruction, completed in under a year with only a scorched stone to differentiate the rebuilt wing from the rest of the building, and a no-nonsense memorial competition overseen by the Army Corps of Engineers with a jury that included both design experts and two former secretaries of defense.[56] Although the Pentagon arranged for the six finalists in the memorial competition to meet with families of those killed there on 9/11, its hierarchical structure of authority, as well as its undoubted control over the land it occupies, allowed memorial planners to move much more quickly than officials in New York.

The World Trade Center site, in contrast, has been the object of clashing interests virtually from the moment the planes hit the towers, and in a sense long before.[57] The multiplicity of the stakeholders in the World Trade Center epitomizes this clash of interests, although it cannot be reduced to theirs: the real estate developer Larry Silverstein, who held the lease to the Center, as well as his insurers; the owner, the Port Authority of New York and New Jersey; the states of New York and New Jersey, which jointly control the Port Authority; and even the city of New York, which has little legal authority over the site but must be involved both morally and technically in planning its future. The LMDC appears to have learned this lesson in the summer of 2002 when, after almost universal public condemnation, it quickly jettisoned the six original master plans it commissioned for the site and established a new, more consultative process that in February 2003 chose the project of German architect Daniel Libeskind.[58] Harmonizing the master plan with the vision of Silverstein's chosen architect David Childs, however, has not proved a simple matter.[59]

The program for the redevelopment of Ground Zero not only seeks to replicate the functions previously filled by the World Trade Center, which served as a transportation hub and retail center as well as providing ten million square feet of office space, it also makes room for a memorial and for a number of cultural facilities.[60] Given that Libeskind's master plan includes a 1,776-foot memorial tower or spire, a trough or pit that would leave the slurry wall of the original development visible and open to its original depth, and a "Garden of Heroes," some have wondered whether an actual memorial still had a place in the project.[61] Indeed, such questions arose at an earlier stage of the design competition, since most of the six semi-finalists incorporated prominent memorial elements in their submissions. *New York Times* critic Herbert Muschamp criticized the whole notion of separating the master plan and memorial competitions.[62] In the competition guidelines, the LMDC insisted on distinguishing between the 16-acre site and the 4.7-acre portion of it constituting the memorial site proper, itself part of a 6.5-acre "memorial and cultural complex."[63]

The idea of a memorial complex recalls a tradition, widespread in the English-speaking world although not in France, of building utilitarian civic or religious structures to honor the memory of war dead. American cities are dotted with structures built to honor the dead of the two world wars: the War Memorial Opera House in San Francisco, Soldier Field in Chicago, Memorial Church and Soldiers Field at Harvard University. Similar memorial halls, churches, auditoria, athletic facilities, hospitals, and community centers, some imposing, some quite modest in scale, exist throughout Great Britain, Australia, and New Zealand.[64] Elsewhere, monumental sculpture or structures have often served as the focal point of larger-scale urban development or redevelopment, for example the laying out of Monument Avenue in late-nineteenth-century Richmond, Virginia, around a memorial to Robert E. Lee.[65] But the idea of reconstruction as a spur to civic improvement has always provoked resistance. Survivors' groups, notably, fear that the instrumentalization of memories, which the survivors consider not only an end in themselves but sacred, will inevitably obscure the memories. To this general tendency the fraught history of the World Trade Center site, and notably of developers' and the state's disregard for the wishes of the community, has added another layer of anxiety and mistrust.

Certainly the historical background provided by the LMDC for the memorial competition guidelines leaves out a great deal. The "History and Location" section presents the Twin Towers, the tallest structures in the world on completion, as the culmination of the "skyward advance in Lower Manhattan," and notes the importance of skyscrapers to the continued presence of the financial services industry in the area.[66] It does not mention the devastating consequences the complex had on small business in the vicinity. Eric Darton, for example, has described the removal through eminent domain of 800 small businesses and an estimated 30,000 jobs in what was called Radio Row as "the legally sanctioned displacement of an entire commercial community."[67] The construction of the World Trade Center, in other words, epitomized an imperial development style heedless of the views of local occupants.

In its historical narrative, the LMDC refers to the "opening of the 60-story Chase Manhattan Bank headquarters in 1961" as a downtown precedent for the World Trade Center. But the text leaves out the name of the bank's then president, David Rockefeller, one of the prime movers, with the Port Authority chairman Austin Tobin, in launching the Trade Center project. For Rockefeller's name carries some problematic associations in this context. The contrast with Rockefeller Center, a development that offers one of New York's most beloved public spaces, the skating rink, and an elegantly conceived relationship to the street, would not favor the WTC. The comparison to Rockefeller's brother Nelson, whose Empire State complex in Albany features a sterile plaza similar to that of the Trade Center, flatters neither; as governor of New York, moreover, Nelson Rockefeller lent important support to the Trade Center project. (The

LMDC redevelopment plan, true, implicitly repudiates the raised plaza, a hall-mark of 1960s urban planning, by reopening Greenwich Street and placing the main outdoor areas at street level, although much of the memorial itself will be underground.) And simply on its own, the name of David Rockefeller is liable to raise suspicions of self-interest: Peter Marcuse charges that Rockefeller pushed a lower Manhattan location for the Center because he was "anxious to shore up the value of Chase Manhattan's real estate investment in the area."[68]

The most grievous consequences of the development style that produced the World Trade Center, however, could be measured only in retrospect. As a state agency with sovereign immunity, the Port Authority did not have to follow the municipal building code, and thus used sheetrock rather than the mandated concrete to build firewalls, as well as an untested spray-on fire retardant instead of the required sprinklers.[69] The agency's overweening ambition to build the world's tallest structures, moreover—a distinction they did not, in any case, hold for very long—made its ostensible goal of commercial viability much more chal-lenging. The chief structural innovation of the towers, moving load-bearing columns to the exterior walls, served the primary purpose of freeing up the maximum amount of rentable space; another innovation, the system of express and local elevators, facilitated the movement of office workers to the distant heights of the towers. These innovations did not succeed in making the Trade Center profitable until some years after its completion, and its overall contribu-tion to the financial health of lower Manhattan remains a matter of debate.[70] It now seems likely, however, that the lightweight external columns and lack of internal support contributed to the speed of the towers' collapse, and that the substandard fire stairways and the dual elevator system hindered both escape and rescuers' access.[71] Clearly the memorial envisioned by the LMDC screens such considerations from official memory.

If the circumstances of the towers' creation and destruction have now be-come fairly familiar, what of the nearly three decades in between? What kinds of experiences did the World Trade Center offer its occupants, its visitors, and its neighbors? What else might the commemoration of the 9/11 victims need to forget? More specifically, James Glanz and Eric Lipton have described a place "never without a current of apprehension." On a daily basis, they write, "there were constant reminders of how unnaturally high the thousands of office work-ers climbed each day—elevators went haywire, briefly going into free fall or overshooting a floor, even causing broken bones and lacerations. Some people refused to go near windows; others simply disliked the lengthy transit from their desks to the ground."[72] Writing in 1999, Eric Darton noted that "[f]rom inside the WTC, its closely spaced columns produce odd vertical window forms that feel prisonlike and chop the expected panorama into dissociative strips—hardly a fitting reward for making the labyrinthine trek from the elevator core to the perimeter."[73] Even by the low standards of modern office towers, then, the World Trade Center seems to have been an unusually oppressive place to work. The violence it did to its workers, however minor and easily shrugged off, forms part of the untold stories specific to it as a place: as Henri Lefebvre says of monumental architecture, "it replaces a brutal reality with a materially realized appearance; reality is changed into appearance."[74]

Of course the violence of place has many dimensions, including global ones that localized commemoration not only refuses to acknowledge but, in a sense, is designed to obscure. Critics of the World Trade Center believe that the uprooting of the Radio Row merchants, the authoritarian mode of development, and the outscaled buildings that resulted from it both symbolized and helped to accomplish a radical shift in the economy not only of New York but of the world. Darton argues that we need "to contemplate the building of the World Trade Center as itself a destructive act—specifically, an attack planned by the city's oligarchs and carried out with the general consent of its populace."[75] As David Harvey observes in a similar critique, if the towers were not "neutral or innocent spaces in the global or even local scheme of things, this does not mean, of course, that anyone there deserved to die."[76] But he also notes that the media's prevailing emphasis on individual stories, whether of loss, survival, heroism, or basic human decency, forestalled examination of the Trade Center's contribution to larger social problems. The discourse of "freedom," indeed, which characterized the attacks as assaults on fundamental American values, proceeded from an assumed link between political freedom and free markets, deliberately occluding such "negative freedoms" as the right to exploit workers or to degrade the environment.[77]

The LMDC guidelines for the memorial competition enact a similar elision, naturalizing the connection between lower Manhattan as "the cradle of democracy," its current role as a financial center, and the symbolism of American freedom: "On the site where Federal Hall now stands, George Washington was sworn in as the first President of the United States. In 1792, the nation's first stock exchange opened a few steps away. The Brooklyn Bridge was completed in 1883 and the Statue of Liberty was dedicated three years later in 1886. In 1892, Ellis Island opened as a gateway to the United States for immigrants from around the world." The paragraph about skyscrapers and the financial services industry follows directly.[78] The private proposal to situate a "museum of freedom" on the Ground Zero site would perpetuate this discursive maneuver in monumental form.[79] Silverstein's insistence, moreover, on retaining the World Trade Center label for the reconstructed complex caps a process in which the Twin Towers and their destruction displace all other aspects of the site's history.[80] Naming and place come together to naturalize a project of state-sponsored capitalism as the triumph of individual freedom.

Harvey's acute analysis of the connection between the media's emphasis on individuals and its lack of any critical commentary cites as a prime example the celebrated *New York Times* "Portraits of Grief." These capsule biographies of the victims took the form of tributes and eschewed the journalistic standards that the newspaper normally applies to obituaries. But the emphasis on the personal, and the appropriation of personal stories for political purposes, notably the rhetoric of American patriotism, has another precedent and indeed a longer

Figure 6.4. Michael Arad with Peter Walker, "Reflecting Absence," winning design for World Trade Center memorial: view of lower level with inscribed names.
Courtesy Lower Manhattan Development Corporation.

history. For naming as the centerpiece of commemorative practice goes back nearly a century, and recent examples, from the Vietnam Veterans Memorial to Oklahoma City, have not fundamentally changed its operation. Names continue to provide order to the untidiness of personal and group memories. As at the Pentagon memorial (see fig. 6.3), which groups the benches in clusters according to the victims' ages, against the background of a wall that rises in units of age, names continue to work with other vectors to rediscover understood or imagined truths about both the commemorated and the commemorating society or polity.[81] And yet names continue to foster the illusion that they form the basis for a commemorative practice turned away from master narratives. Many, indeed, found the eight projects selected as finalists for the World Trade Center memorial too generic and consolatory. In this view, the designs did not "create an unstated, unambiguous embodiment of what 9/11 means"; according to *New York Times* columnist Maureen Dowd, they "lack the power of narrative."[82] At the January 2004 announcement of the winning design, "Reflecting Absence," by Michael Arad with Peter Walker (fig. 6.4), with names inscribed on low walls around subterranean pools, members of the jury issued a statement pointing to the evolution of the design and expressing confidence that remaining issues including "the narrative history of that day" would be resolved.[83]

Interviewed about the Pentagon design competition, the historian John Gillis observed, "The era of collective memorialization is over. Families today insist that victims be commemorated individually. It was not enough for the names to be listed on the Vietnam Veterans Memorial. People attached pictures and personal items to the wall."[84] True enough, but the U.S. Park Service, which manages the site, routinely gathers non-perishable objects from the site, classifies them, and stores them for future exhibition. Insisting on the recognition of individuals does not make the commemoration itself any less collective, or its object anything other than the nature, present state, and future of the commemorating society. Monuments may now commemorate chiefly individuals, but they do so in a collective mode and in a single site, a place set aside for that purpose. And as an organized gesture, the very act of naming the dead confers a collective value on names that once, indeed not long ago, lacked any such quality.

By the second anniversary of 9/11, a number of survivors had decided to avoid official ceremonies; some declared that they did not wish to share their emotions with strangers, and they protested the emotional burden placed on the children tapped to recite the names of the dead. The Petrocelli family of Staten Island has chosen to build a shrine in memory of their lost son on their front lawn; it combines personal memorabilia with plantings, religious and patriotic symbols, and a small piece of steel from the World Trade Center.[85] If the American flag at the center of the Petrocelli shrine clearly links the personal and the collective, moreover, the personal predominates; it is not hard, in any case, to imagine a personal memorial of a more contestatory stripe. At the unveiling of the eight finalist designs for the World Trade Center memorial, the sister of a firefighter killed in the attacks declared that fourteen "Fire Department families were ready to remove their relatives' names from the memorial if they were listed along with civilians."[86] Suppose a few families of Pentagon victims who opposed United States military interventions abroad objected to the inclusion of benches with the names of their loved ones. Who would adjudicate? Nor should we forget the ways names link individuals to the social order, their arbitrariness, the legal procedures involved in changing them. As a conservative French veterans' association put it in 1921: "The patronymic is in no way a piece of property, but an institution of public order, even of security. To bear a name is an obligation as much as a right."[87]

In the aftermath of 9/11, commemoration has pivoted on a number of familiar dichotomies: between consolation and grand gesture, between the elemental—touching the "bedrock" of the World Trade Center—and the symbolic—rushing water, numbered lights—between the vox populi and expert judgment, between narrative and suggestion. That these represent multiple positions, shifting perspectives resistant to binarization and consensus, may be somewhat less obvious, but they give rise to a range of commemorative projects broader even than the 5,201 submissions to the WTC memorial competition. The debate over the competition finalists, with its pervasive criticism of their modernist stylistic vocabulary and carefully modulated emotions, might be taken as a watershed in America of commemorative culture, an end point to the therapeutic monument initiated by Maya Lin, even the beginning of a regression. Yet such a diagnosis is not only premature, it also misses a basic dynamic of continuity in commemoration, the negotiation between the claims of various collectivities to represent the memories of individuals. In this regard the persistent, often bitter debate over how to inscribe the names of the dead, which groups to single out, if any, what kinds of "heroism" to recognize, points to nothing so much as the continuing difficulty, which at the present moment might be called intractability, of democracy. Nothing, in other words, better exemplifies the fundamental continuity of commemorative naming than the bitter contestation to which it gives rise.

A commemoration that would break with this dynamic must first confront its past and present in a more comprehensively critical spirit. If no such commemorative renewal seems possible at the WTC and Pentagon sites, the reason may lie in the other central element of contemporary commemoration, for these memorial projects embrace highly conventional notions of space and place. In such conceptions, monumentality itself constitutes a positive good, with no concern for its costs or consequences, a position aptly summed up by a *New York Times* editorial calling for a memorial that would provide "the experience of a grand public space in the midst of grand architecture."[88] What might be called alter-commemoration, in contrast, works to destabilize not only inscription, but the idea of some elemental, intrinsic relationship between place and community; it calls for intervention, not just reflection. Such commemoration can take the form of repeated action without inscription or other representation, like the volunteer work in Boston public parks and homeless shelters carried out on the second anniversary of 9/11 by employees of Marsh Inc., the insurance company.[89] Or it might adopt the formal strategies of anti-monumentalists like Jochen Gerz and Esther Shalev-Gerz, who designed a disappearing monument "against Fascism, War, and Violence" in Harburg, a suburb of Hamburg, that over the course of seven years (1986–93) was progressively lowered into the ground.[90] More recently, the German conceptual artists Renata Stih and Frieder Schnock have proposed even more overtly political, yet still intimate, arrangements, such as a monument with surveillance cameras—a reference to post-9/11 security measures—reflecting the images of commemorating visitors back on themselves.[91] Following on the work of Laura Kurgan and others, such images could become the basis for web-based virtual memorials inviting continual reinscription by their users, much as the residents of Harburg inscribed their names and other graffiti on the disappearing monument. In such sites, meaning emerges from the individual images and desires, remaining fluid, unstable, impossible to pin down—a memory, in other words, that need speak no name.

Notes

My thanks to Eric White for his invaluable research assistance, to Ruud van Dijk and Stanley M. Sherman for their help with photographs, and to Maria Liesegang and Claire Hicks for assistance of various kinds. I also very much appreciate the thoughtful readings, criticism, and advice of Kirk Savage, Daniel Abramson, Eduardo Douglas, and my patient and supportive co-editor, Terry Nardin.

1. See Michael Kimmelman, "In a Square, A Sense of Unity," *New York Times,* September 19, 2001; Marshall Sella, "Missing: How a Grief Ritual is Born," *New York Times Magazine,* October 7, 2001, 48–51; John Kuo Wei Tchen, "Whose Downtown?!?" in *After the World Trade Center: Rethinking New York City,* ed. Michael Sorkin and Sharon Zukin (New York: Routledge, 2002), 33–36.

2. See Michel Foucault, "Nietzsche, Genealogy, History," in his *Language, Counter-Memory, Practice: Selected Essays and Interviews,* ed. Donald F. Bouchard, trans. Bouchard and Sherry Simon (Ithaca, N.Y.: Cornell University Press, 1977), 139–64; reprinted in Foucault, *Aesthetics, Method, and Epistemology,* ed. James D. Faubion, *Essential Works of Foucault 1954–1984,* vol. 2 (New York: New Press, 1998), 369–91.

3. Daniel Abramson, "Make History, Not Memory: History's Critique of Memory," *Harvard Design Magazine,* Fall 1999, 78–83.

4. James Dawes, *The Language of War: Literature and Culture in the U.S. from the Civil War through World War II* (Cambridge, Mass.: Harvard University Press, 2002), 193–94.

5. Jacques Derrida, *Of Grammatology,* trans. Gayatri Chakravorty Spivak (Baltimore, Md.: Johns Hopkins University Press, 1976), 112; for more on this contrast and its role in contemporary theory, see Dawes, *The Language of War,* 192–93.

6. H. Muschamp, "The Memorial Would Live in the Architecture," *New York Times,* December 22, 2002. This is, broadly speaking, the argument M. Christine Boyer develops in *The City of Collective Memory: Its Historical Imagery and Architectural Entertainments* (Cambridge, Mass.: MIT Press, 1994), tracing the memorial city to changes in architecture and urban planning that began in the late eighteenth and early nineteenth centuries.

7. M. de Certeau, *L'invention du quotidien,* vol. 1, *Arts de faire,* rev. ed., ed. Luce Giard, Folio Essais (Paris: Gallimard, 1990), 163; my translation differs significantly from that of Steven Rendall in *The Practice of Everyday Life* (Berkeley: University of California Press, 1984), 108.

8. See, for example, Mike Allen and Dana Milbank, "Bush Repeats Vow on Terror," *Washington Post,* September 12, 2002; Elisabeth Bumiller, "Keepers of Bush Image Lift Stagecraft to New Heights," *New York Times,* May 16, 2003.

9. Dan Barry, "A Day of Tributes, Tears, and the Litany of the Lost," *New York Times,* September 12, 2002.

10. Michiko Kakutani, "Rituals, Improvised or Traditional," *New York Times,* September 12, 2002; Michael J. Lewis, "Mourning without Meaning," *Commentary,* November 2002, 58.

11. See James M. McPherson, *Abraham Lincoln and the Second American Revolution* (New York: Oxford University Press, 1991), 56–61, and, more generally, Daniel Farber, *Lincoln's Constitution* (Chicago: University of Chicago Press, 2003).

12. Garry Wills, *Lincoln At Gettysburg: The Words that Remade America* (New York: Simon and Schuster, 1992), 263.

13. I am summarizing observations I first made in *The Construction of Memory in Interwar France* (Chicago: University of Chicago Press, 1999), 261–62.

14. Dawes, *The Language of War,* 1–23.

15. See, for example, Tom Shales, "Moving Pictures: On a Day of Remembrance,

Television Puts Itself In Our Place," *Washington Post,* September 12, 2002; Lewis, "Mourning without Meaning."

16. It is worth noting that "Union Square" itself is something of a metonym for a congeries of commemorative acts, many of which originated as something else, a search for the missing through posted flyers; see Sella, "Missing."

17. Sherman, *Construction of Memory,* 281–88.

18. See, for example, Marita Sturken, "The Wall, the Screen, and the Image: The Vietnam Veterans Memorial," *Representations* 35 (Summer 1991): 126; Thomas W. Laqueur, "Memory and Naming in the Great War," in *Commemorations: The Politics of National Identity,* ed. John R. Gillis (Princeton, N.J.: Princeton University Press, 1994), 160–63. For a thorough discussion of the critical response to the Vietnam Veterans Memorial and a persuasive alternative view, see Daniel Abramson, "Maya Lin and the 1960s: Monuments, Time Lines, and Minimalism," *Critical Inquiry* 22 (1996): 679–709.

19. One convenient source for this much-quoted passage is the National Park Service web site: http://www.nps.gov/vive/memorial/evolutionprint.htm.

20. Sherman, *Construction of Memory,* 96–97.

21. A typical account is David Von Drehle, "In Names of Victims, Volumes," *Washington Post,* September 12, 2002.

22. The *New York Times* published a photograph of the so-called "Flag of Honor" (which it referred to as the "Flag of Remembrance") on its front page on September 11, 2003. On the ceremonies, see James Barron, "Another 9/11, and the Nation Mourns Again," *New York Times,* September 12, 2003.

23. Eric Lipton, "All Names Read, Even if Some May be Alive," *New York Times,* September 12, 2002.

24. "Ceremony Honors Veterans Not on Memorial," *New York Times,* April 22, 2003.

25. Sherman, *Construction of Memory,* 91.

26. On the compensation fund set up by Congress for the victims of the 9/11 attacks and the controversy it has aroused, see Elizabeth Kolbert, "The Calculator," *New Yorker,* November 25, 2002, 42–49; Lisa Belkin, "Just Money," *New York Times Magazine,* December 8, 2002, 92–97, 122, 148–49; Diana B. Henriques, "Concern Growing as Families Bypass 9/11 Victims' Fund," *New York Times,* August 31, 2003.

27. Michael Kimmelman, "Finding Comfort in the Safety of Names," *New York Times,* August 31, 2003.

28. David W. Dunlap, "Blocks: Plans for a Random List of Names Anger Families," *New York Times,* February 19, 2004.

29. See, for example, Edward Wyatt, "Jury for Sept. 11 Memorial Is Facing Spirited Lobbying," *New York Times,* May 30, 2003.

30. See G. Kurt Piehler, "The War Dead and the Gold Star: American Commemoration of the First World War," in Gillis, ed., *Commemorations,* 168–185; Idem, *Remembering War the American Way* (Washington, D.C.: Smithsonian Institution Press, 1995), 76–77, 95–97; Laqueur, "Memory and Naming," 162; Alex King, *Memorials of the Great War in Britain: The Symbolism and Politics of Remembrance,* The Legacy of the Great War (Oxford: Berg, 1998), 90–92; Antoine Prost, *Les anciens combattants et la société française, 1914–1939,* 3 vols. (Paris: Presses de la Fondation National des Sciences Politiques, 1977), 3: 62–75; Sherman, *Construction of Memory,* 75–77; Idem, "The Nation: In What

Community? The Politics of Commemoration in Postwar France," in *Ideas and Ideals: Essays on Politics in Honor of Stanley Hoffmann,* ed. Linda Miller and Michael J. Smith (Boulder, Colo.: Westview Press, 1993), 277–95.

31. Lewis, "Mourning without Meaning," 58.

32. John C. Whitehead, "Letter from LMDC Chairman," *World Trade Center Site Memorial Competition Guidelines,* 2003, downloaded from www.wtcsitememorial.org.

33. Edward Wyatt, "Some Victims' Families Feel Influence on 9/11 Memorial Slipping Away," *New York Times,* November 16, 2002; Glenn Collins, "8 Designs Confront Many Agendas at Ground Zero," *New York Times,* November 20, 2003; see also the letter of Joan Molinaro, mother of a firefighter killed at the WTC, saying that public authorities and the jury "did not care about what the families of the victims want," *New York Times,* January 20, 2004.

34. Glenn Collins and David W. Dunlap, "Fighting for the Footprints of 9/11," *New York Times,* December 30, 2003; Collins and Dunlap, "Unveiling of the Trade Center Memorial Reveals an Abundance of New Details," *New York Times,* January 15, 2004.

35. "The Memorial Finalists," *New York Times,* November 20, 2003. Although the later selection of three finalists has led some to designate these eight projects as "semi-finalists," the narrowing to three was not an important part of the public record of the jury process. I have therefore retained the "finalist" usage with respect to the eight designs chosen in November 2003.

36. *World Trade Center Site Memorial Competition Guidelines,* 18–19; also available at www.wtcsitememorial.org/program/mission.html and www.wtcsitememorial.org/program/guiding.html respectively.

37. R. Musil, "Denkmale," in *Nachlass zu Lebzeiten* (Zurich, 1936), 87–93, cited and translated in Marina Warner, *Monuments and Maidens: The Allegory of the Female Form* (London: Weidenfeld and Nicolson, 1985), 263–70.

38. For an assortment of "Sept. 11-themed keepsakes recently on sale around Canal Street," see "Gallery: Get Your Souvenir Here," *New York Times Magazine,* August 4, 2002. The images are part of a photographic project by Robert Huber.

39. Kevin M. Rampe, "Letter from LMDC President," *World Trade Center Site Memorial Competition Guidelines.*

40. "Call for Entries: Memorial to Honor the Victims of the Attack on the Pentagon" (July 2002), 4, available at http://memorial.pentagon.mil/competition_stage/document.pdf.

41. S. Freud, "Mourning and Melancholia," in *The Standard Edition of the Complete Psychological Works of Sigmund Freud,* trans. and ed. James Strachey, 24 vols. (London: Hogarth Press, 1953–74), 14: 243.

42. An article intended for a popular audience frames what may be a growing cultural resistance to "moving on," but solely in terms of the attention society owes the bereaved individuals: Gail Sheehy, "Lessons of Two Tragedies," *Parade Magazine,* August 24, 2003, 10–11.

43. *World Trade Center Site Memorial Competition Guidelines,* 19; also available at www.wtcsitememorial.org/program.

44. "Call for Entries: Memorial to Honor the Victims of the Attack on the Pentagon," 3.

45. Kimmelman, "Finding Comfort in the Safety of Names."

46. On the six finalists, see Fred Bernstein, "At the Pentagon, Visions of 184 Pieces for the Missing," *New York Times*, December 22, 2002; for the winning design, announced in March 2003, http://memorial.pentagon.mil/description.htm.

47. See the photographs and descriptions in "Competing Designs are Shimmering Elegies in Light, Water, and Glass," *New York Times*, November 20, 2003; Thomas Keenan, "Making the Dead Count, Literally," *New York Times*, November 30, 2003.

48. On the modern invention of the cemetery, see Philippe Ariès, *The Hour of our Death* (New York: Alfred A. Knopf, 1981), Part IV; Richard Etlin, *The Architecture of Death: The Transformation of the Cemetery in Eighteenth-Century Paris* (Cambridge, Mass.: MIT Press, 1984); Thomas A. Kselman, *Death and the Afterlife in Modern France* (Princeton, N.J.: Princeton University Press, 1993), chapter 5.

49. See Sherman, "Bodies and Names: The Emergence of Commemoration in Interwar France," *American Historical Review* 103 (1998): 443–66.

50. On Sudbury, see Benjamin Gedan, "Sudbury: Sept. 11 Memorial Planned for 2d Anniversary," *Boston Globe*, April 2, 2003, and Tina Kelley, "For Some Survivors, Ground Zero is No Place for Private Day of Remembering," *New York Times*, September 7, 2003; on Middletown, see Barron, "Another 9/11." Both these memorials are gardens. On the Massachusetts memorial, see Alice Gomstyn, "Public Garden Site to Recall 9/11 Victims," *Boston Globe*, September 10, 2002, and Joanna Weiss and John Ellement, "In Somber Remembrance: Living Honor the Lost and Sanctify the Past," *Boston Globe*, September 12, 2003 (the ground-breaking). On the New Jersey state memorial, see Sarah Boxer, "New Jersey Selects its Sept. 11 Memorial," *New York Times*, July 1, 2004.

51. Michael Slackman, "Plans to Preserve Sept. 11 Remains Leaves Open Future Identification," *New York Times*, August 25, 2003.

52. Sherman, *Construction of Memory*, 91–94.

53. This is, admittedly, an opinion generally confined to the early stages of grieving and recovery; see the reference to the belief that "nothing should be built on it [Ground Zero]" in Dinitia Smith, "Hallowed Ground Zero: Competing Plans Hope to Shape a Trade Center Memorial," *New York Times*, October 25, 2001.

54. Sherman, *Construction of Memory*, 74–81.

55. Brian Ladd, *The Ghosts of Berlin: Confronting German History in the Urban Landscape* (Chicago: University of Chicago Press, 1997).

56. John Tierney, "The Pentagon Ceremony: Honoring Those Lost and Celebrating a New Symbol of Resilience," *New York Times*, September 12, 2002; Bernstein, "At the Pentagon, Visions." For a list of the eleven jury members, of whom only two were from victims' families, see http://memorial.pentagon.mil/jurors.htm.

57. According to William Langewiesche's *American Ground: Unbuilding the World Trade Center* (New York: North Point Press, 2002), 145–70, the same could be said of the recovery and cleanup of the WTC site, and not simply at notorious moments like the fistfight that broke out between firemen and police officers on November 2, 2001.

58. Edward Wyatt, "More Designers Might Be Invited to Submit Ideas on Ground Zero," *New York Times*, July 30, 2002; Idem, "Agency Seeking More Ideas In Rebuilding of Downtown," *New York Times*, August 15, 2002; Herbert

Muschamp, "Architecture for Ground Zero: Back to 6 New Drawing Boards," *New York Times,* October 1, 2002; Paul Goldberger, "Designing Downtown," *New Yorker,* January 6, 2003, 62–69; Wyatt, "Design Chosen for Rebuilding At Ground Zero," *New York Times,* February 27, 2003.

59. See Herbert Muschamp, "Critic's Notebook: Vision vs. Symbols and Politics at Ground Zero," *New York Times,* November 29, 2003, and "A Skyscaper Has a Chance to be Noble," *New York Times,* December 20, 2003.

60. The number and nature of the cultural facilities and the exact amount of space they will occupy was not determined in the master plan; the LMDC has considered a number of proposals. For interim reports, see Robin Pogrebin, "92nd St. Y Considers A Ground Zero Site," *New York Times,* August 27, 2003; Philip Nobel, "The Downtown Culture Derby Begins," *New York Times,* August 31, 2003; Robin Pogrebin, "Arts Groups Vie for a Home at Ground Zero," *New York Times,* September 16, 2003.

61. Edward Wyatt, "Designs Leave Space for 9/11 Memorial Contest," *New York Times,* February 12, 2003.

62. Muschamp, "The Memorial Would Live."

63. *World Trade Center Site Memorial Competition Guidelines,* 9 and fig. 3. By the time the LMDC announced the winning design for the memorial, the submitting architect had added a subterranean "memorial center" to house artifacts from the towers, further blurring the distinction; see David W. Dunlap and Eric Lipton, "Artifact Center Added to Revised Memorial at Ground Zero," *New York Times,* January 14, 2004.

64. On Britain, see Alan Borg, *War Memorials from Antiquity to the Present* (London: Leo Cooper, 1991), 138–42, and Derek Boorman, *At the Going Down of the Sun: British First World War Memorials* (York: William Sessions/The Ebor Press, 1988), 106–22; on Australia, where the issue provoked active debate and resulted in considerable numbers of both utilitarian and sculptural memorials after World War I, see K. S. Inglis, *Sacred Places: War Memorials in the Australian Landscape,* rev. ed. (Melbourne: The Miegunyah Press of Melbourne University Press, 1999), 138–44; on New Zealand, where the government actively promoted utilitarian memorials after World War II, see Chris Maclean and Jock Phillips, *The Sorrow and the Pride: New Zealand War Memorials* (Wellington: Historical Branch, G. B. Books, 1990), 136–55; on the U.S., see Piehler, *Remembering War,* 108–11.

65. See Kirk Savage, *Standing Soldiers, Kneeling Slaves: Race, War, and Monument in Nineteenth-Century America* (Princeton, N.J.: Princeton University Press, 1997), 148–50.

66. *World Trade Center Site Memorial Competition Guidelines,* 3.

67. Eric Darton, "The Janus Face of Architectural Terrorism: Minoru Yamasaki, Mohammed Atta, and Our World Trade Center," in *Rethinking New York,* ed. Sorkin and Zukin, 92–93; figures from Peter Marcuse, "What Kind of Planning After September 11? The Market, the Stakeholders, Consensus- or . . . ?" in *Rethinking New York,* 154–55.

68. Marcuse, "What Kind of Planning," 155.

69. Darton, "The Janus Face," 93–94.

70. See Michael Tomasky, "The World Trade Center: Before, During, and After," *The New York Review of Books* 49: 5 (March 28, 2002): 18.

71. Among the many reports, among the clearest and most comprehensive is

James Glanz and Eric Lipton, "The Height of Ambition," *New York Times Magazine,* September 8, 2002, 32–44, 59–60, 63, especially 39–42.

72. Ibid., 44. There is some additional detail in the book version of this essay, James Glanz and Eric Lipton, *City in the Sky: The Rise and Fall of the World Trade Center* (New York: Times Books, 2003), 211–15.

73. Darton, *Divided We Stand: A Biography of New York's World Trade Center* (New York: Basic Books, 1999), 129.

74. Henri Lefebvre, *The Production of Space,* trans. Donald Nicholson Smith (Oxford: Blackwell, 1991), 221.

75. Darton, "The Janus Face," 91.

76. D. Harvey, "Cracks in the Edifice of the Empire State," in *Rethinking New York,* ed. Sorkin and Zukin, 59; I have slightly modified the punctuation.

77. Ibid., 57, 60.

78. *World Trade Center Site Memorial Competition Guidelines,* 3.

79. Herbert Muschamp, "With a Dubious Idea of 'Freedom,'" *New York Times,* August 31, 2003.

80. David W. Dunlap, "World Trade Center Endures. Read the Signs," *New York Times,* September 18, 2003.

81. This is to simplify what appears to be a quite complex system: see http://memorial.pentagon.mil/description.htm. The architects emphasize that "[i]nherent tendencies—the clustering of certain age groups, the gap between the children and adults—are clearly evident and meaningful, though infinitely interpretive."

82. First citation from Letters to the Editor, *New York Times,* November 21, 2003; Maureen Dowd, "Unbearable Lightness of Memory," *New York Times,* November 30, 2003; see also Dennis Smith, "Memorials without a Memory," *New York Times,* November 26, 2003.

83. Dunlap and Lipton, "Artifact Center Added."

84. Bernstein, "At the Pentagon, Visions."

85. Kelley, "For Some Survivors"; Dan Barry, "For One 9/11 Family, Five Waves of Grief," *New York Times,* September 10, 2003.

86. Collins, "8 Designs Confront Many Agendas."

87. "Les inscriptions sur les monuments aux morts," *La voix du combattant,* December 18, 1921. The newspaper was criticizing a court decision upholding the right of a father of a dead soldier to prevent the inscription of his son's name on a monument.

88. "Toward a Final Design," *New York Times,* December 13, 2003.

89. Joanna Weiss and John Ellement, "In Somber Remembrance: Living Honor the Lost and Sanctify the Past," *Boston Globe,* September 12, 2003.

90. Stephan Schmidt-Wulffen, "The Monument Vanishes: A Conversation with Esther and Jochen Gerz," in *The Art of Memory: Holocaust Memorials in History,* ed. James E. Young (New York and Munich: The Jewish Museum/Prestel, 1994), 69–75; James E. Young, *At Memory's Edge: After-Images of the Holocaust in Contemporary Art and Architecture* (New Haven, Conn.: Yale University Press, 2000), 120–151.

91. Jane Kramer, "Dept. of Remembering: Two from Berlin," *The New Yorker,* October 27, 2003, 46.

PART 2   *Ethics/Politics*

7 9/11 and the Jihad Tradition

Sohail H. Hashmi

We're told that they were zealots fueled by religious fervor . . . religious fervor
. . . and if you live to be a thousand years old will that make any sense to you?
Will that make any goddamn sense?

—David Letterman, *Late Show with
David Letterman*, September 17, 2001

Soon after the 9/11 attacks, we learned a great deal about how the nineteen hijackers plotted, trained for, and executed their mission. We were given personal histories of many of the men: their family backgrounds, their education, their travels, the mosques they attended. But we still know relatively little about why they felt compelled to kill thousands of people and to die doing so. The clearest glimpse of their psychology comes from a handwritten note in Arabic, identical copies of which were found in the luggage of two of the hijackers and in the rubble of the World Trade Center. The note contains instructions on how to prepare mentally for the attack, instructions laced with Islamic justifications and exhortations.[1]

Many, if not all, of the nineteen hijackers were undoubtedly motivated by "religious fervor." They died because they were convinced they were waging jihad. But saying this doesn't really clarify the question of motives any more than claiming that someone died for "love of country," for "honor," for "justice"—or any other abstraction. The hijackers' religious fervor can be unpacked into a number of more tangible *potential* motivations. As the foot soldiers of al-Qaida, they may have been content to let Osama bin Laden and other al-Qaida leaders enunciate their grievances for them. Indeed, given the declarations of bin Laden and his lieutenants in the years preceding the 9/11 attack, the nineteen terrorists may have felt their cause needed no further elaboration.

Bin Laden and his supporters continually invoke the jihad tradition. They do so, I believe, not only to gain public support among Muslims, but from the fervent belief that they are authentic interpreters of jihad. By claiming to act according to the strictures of jihad, they invite a response from their opponents, not because such arguments are likely to sway the terrorists, but simply in order to show how their arguments are unrepresentative of the broad mainstream of the tradition. And indeed their many Muslim and non-Muslim opponents have vigorously disputed al-Qaida's interpretations of jihad. Too often, however, those who criticize al-Qaida's actions have settled for general denunciations such as the claims that these terrorists and other militant Muslim groups have "nothing to do with Islam," or that they have "hijacked Islam," or at the least that they distort the jihad tradition within Islam. I argue in this chapter that al-Qaida is in fact not especially radical when we confine our attention to its stated grievances or goals. But it is on the fringes of the jihad tradition when we shift our attention to the means it employs to realize its objectives. Al-Qaida, like many terrorist groups that have preceded it, seems to have embraced the idea that "the ends justify the means," and with it the logic of total war. This repudiation of limits on the means to one's ends puts al-Qaida's war outside the jihad tradition. For as in the Western just war tradition, the Islamic ethical discourse on war has historically separated two broad, related, *but morally independent* sets of questions: Under what circumstances or for what ends is war justified? And, once war has begun, how may fighting be properly conducted?

The Question of Ends

The jihad tradition emerged and began to evolve during the lifetime of the prophet Muhammad himself. For the first thirteen years of his prophetic mission (610–622 C.E.), while he was in Mecca, Muhammad refused to engage in any form of violence in response to the opposition and persecution that he and the earliest Muslims faced at the hands of the polytheist Meccans. Jihad during the Meccan period of Islam's development was an inward "struggle," as the word literally means, aimed at morally developing the character of individual Muslims. One Qurʾanic verse from this period advises Muslims to "listen not to the unbelievers, but strive [*jahada*] against them with it [the Qurʾan] with the utmost effort" (25:52). In dealing with belligerent non-Muslims, the Prophet taught nonviolent resistance.

If the Prophet had died or been killed in Mecca, Islam might have evolved along lines similar to those of early Christianity, as an otherworldly and generally pacifist sect devoid of political ambitions in this world. But the fusing of religion and politics that occurred in Christianity some three centuries after Christ occurred in Islam within the lifetime of the Prophet. In the year 622, Muhammad and most of his followers relocated from Mecca to Medina. It is in Medina that the Islamic community became a state, and where there is a state, there is sure to be, as Max Weber emphasized, violence or the threat of violence.[2]

In Medina, the jihad struggle acquired a military aspect. This development is marked in a number of Qurʾanic verses. The first verse to be revealed on this topic gives permission to Muslims to defend themselves with force if they are attacked by their enemies: "To those against whom war is made, permission is given [to fight back], because they are wronged. And surely God is most powerful in their support" (22:39). A subsequent series of verses makes such self-defense a requirement for the faithful: "Fight in the cause of God those who fight you" (2:190). The justification for the resort to violence given here is that "tumult and oppression [*fitna*] are worse than killing [*qatl*]" (2:191). Finally, after nearly eight years of warfare between the Muslims and an array of enemies, the Qur'an seems to enjoin a war of conversion against the remaining polytheist Arab tribes: "But when the forbidden months are past, then fight and slay the polytheists [*mushrikin*] wherever you find them. Seize them, besiege them, and lie in wait for them using every stratagem. But if they repent, and establish regular prayers, and practice regular charity, then open the way for them. For God is most forgiving, most merciful" (9:5). For all others, including Christians and Jews, the Qur'an seems to sanction a war of conquest aimed at political subjugation if not religious conversion: "Fight those who do not believe in God or the Last Day, nor hold forbidden that which has been forbidden by God and his Messenger, nor acknowledge the religion of truth, from among those who have been given the Book, until they pay the poll-tax [*jizya*] with willing submission, having been subdued" (9:29).

Following the Prophet's death in 632, the Islamic state spread rapidly through military conquest of the Arabian Peninsula and large parts of the Byzantine Empire and through the overthrow of the Sassanid Empire. The Islamic faith spread much more gradually through the teaching and example of missionaries and merchants. At the same time, Muslim scholars began to formulate Islamic laws of war, focusing on the Medinan notion of armed jihad while neglecting the nonviolence of the Meccan period. Thus jihad acquired a predominantly military connotation in the law books of Islam. It was left mainly to Islamic mystics, the Sufis, to emphasize the nonviolent, spiritual aspects of jihad, as in the famous tradition (*hadith*) ascribed to the Prophet, who, returning from a military engagement, told his supporters that they had left the lesser jihad only to enter the greater jihad, the one waged within one's own soul.[3]

Muslim legal theory divided wars against non-Muslims into two categories: first, defensive fighting to repulse aggression against Muslim lands (*dar al-Islam*); and second, the struggle to expand *dar al-Islam* by reducing the territory of the infidels (*dar al-harb*). Both types of struggle justified killing, although in the second type (which we may call the expansionist jihad), killing was permitted only as the final stage in a hierarchy of options to be offered the enemy: first, that they accept Islam; second, that they accept Islamic sovereignty and agree to *dhimmi* (protected) status, which accorded them a great deal of communal autonomy; and finally, that if they refused the other two options, they were to be given fair warning and fought. The goal of the Islamic state in fighting non-Muslims was to bring them under Islamic sovereignty, not to convert them, at least not through military means. Conversion to Islam, the theory assumed, would occur naturally as the conquered peoples were exposed to the principles of Islam. The theory also allowed the Muslim ruler to conclude truces with non-Muslim powers if he deemed such agreements to be in the Muslims' interests.

The legal theory of an expansionist jihad remained just that, a theory, for many centuries; indeed, the theory itself may have been formulated during the second, third, and fourth Islamic centuries (eighth to tenth centuries C.E.) to revive the spirit of Islamic expansionism that had animated the explosive growth of the first-century. The idea of expansionist jihad was resuscitated by the Ottoman Turks during the fifteenth- and sixteenth-centuries C.E., only to fade again in the seventeenth. With the advent of European imperialism in the nineteenth-century, the discourse of defensive jihad became dominant among Muslim peoples throughout Africa and Asia.

Among the vast majority of modern Muslim scholars, the only appropriate type of jihad is held to be the defensive kind. Some reject completely any expansionist aspect to jihad, arguing that the classical jurists had misinterpreted the Qur²an and the Prophet's teachings to justify it. Others hold that while it may have been historically justified in the seventh or eighth centuries C.E., the modern division of the world into nation-states that agree to abide by international law has made wars of religion obsolete and morally unjustified.

Where do Osama bin Laden and his supporters fit in this tradition? They have been characterized as extremists lurking on the fringes of Islamic thought. But in terms of the justifications for jihad, al-Qaida's statements are not radical; they are in fact quite pedestrian. Bin Laden and his supporters, like the vast majority of Islamic activists for the past two centuries, appeal to the notion of defensive jihad.

The first major statement of al-Qaida's grievances and goals came in August 1996 in a lengthy, rambling manifesto published in the London-based Arabic newspaper *al-Quds al-ᶜArabi*. The statement was later translated into English and posted on the Internet in October 1996 by the Committee for the Defense of Legitimate Rights, a Saudi dissident group with ties to bin Laden's organization. The "Ladenese Epistle: Declaration of War (Parts I–III)," as the document was dubbed, charges the "Zionist-Crusader alliance and their collaborators" with waging a war against Muslims all over the world. Muslims are being persecuted, robbed of their land and possessions, and massacred in Palestine, Kashmir, the Philippines, Eritrea, Chechnya, and other places, all while the United States and its allies, under the cover of the "iniquitous" United Nations, block means of assistance for them. "The latest and the greatest of these aggressions . . . is the occupation of the land of the two holy places—the foundation of the house of Islam, the place of the revelation, the source of the message and the place of the noble Kaᶜba, the *qibla* [direction of prayer] of all Muslims—by the armies of the American Crusaders and their allies."[4]

Much of the statement focuses on the Muslim allies of the "American Crusaders," namely, the Saudi regime that let American troops into the kingdom in 1990 during the Gulf War. King Fahd had justified his decision to allow U.S. troops on Saudi soil by promising that they would leave in a few months, as soon as the exigency under which they had arrived had passed. Yet, the statement observes, "today it is seven years since their arrival and the regime is not able to move them out of the country." Instead, the regime has rebuffed appeals from the ᶜ*ulama,* jailed religious dissidents, and continued to issue false proclamations regarding American intentions in Saudi Arabia.[5]

By doing nothing to expel the American "occupiers," the statement alleges, the current Saudi leaders continue a pattern established by the founder of the kingdom, ʿAbd al-ʿAziz, who permitted, under British urging, the loss of Palestine. Now his son, Fahd, has committed the ultimate betrayal of the Muslim community (*umma*) by calling a "Christian army to defend the regime. The crusaders were permitted to be in the land of the two holy places [i.e., Mecca and Medina]. . . . The country was widely opened from the north to the south and from the east to the west for the crusaders. The land was filled with military bases of the USA and the allies. The regime became unable to keep control without the help of these bases." When the Saudi rulers permitted the violation of the sanctity of the Arabian Peninsula, the statement charges, they had in effect renounced their Islamic identity and joined forces with the infidels (*kufr*).[6]

The 1996 statement received very little attention at the time, and even after the 9/11 attacks it was neglected in public commentary on al-Qaida's motivations. Attention after 9/11 was instead focused on a subsequent declaration, the World Islamic Front's proclamation of "Jihad against Jews and Crusaders," published in *al-Quds al-ʿArabi* on February 23, 1998. This second document was a much terser statement than the 1996 Ladenese Epistle, and it cannot be fully understood without the earlier statement. Even the 1998 statement went generally unnoticed, however, until it was resurrected on various websites after the 9/11 attacks.[7]

The proclamation of jihad lists three "crimes and sins committed by the Americans" that amount to "a clear declaration of war on God, his messenger, and Muslims." The first is the offense discussed at length in the 1996 statement: the American "occupation" of the most sacred of Islamic lands, the Arabian Peninsula. With rhetorical flourish, the statement begins: "The Arabian Peninsula has never—since God made it flat, created its deserts, and encircled it with seas—been stormed by any forces like the crusader armies spreading in it like locusts, eating its riches and wiping out its plantations." The United States is not only plundering the peninsula's riches, it is "dictating to its rulers, humiliating its people, terrorizing its neighbors, and turning its bases . . . into a spearhead through which to fight the neighboring Muslim peoples."

The second "crime" of the United States is its continued blockade and sporadic military attacks on Iraq, "despite the great devastation inflicted on the Iraqi people by the Crusader-Zionist alliance, and despite the huge number of those killed, which has exceeded one million." The statement is careful to emphasize the harm done to the Iraqi people; no mention is made of the regime of the Iraqi dictator, Saddam Hussein, which was generally reviled by militant Islamic groups as an irreligious tyranny.

The third transgression is American support for Israel and Israel's occupation of Jerusalem and repression of the Palestinians. After the 9/11 attacks, many commentators made much of the fact that support for Israel came third on this list, and that this fact signified that the Israeli-Palestinian conflict did not figure prominently in al-Qaida's motivations. We were told repeatedly that mention of Israeli occupation of Palestinian territories was nothing but a cynical ploy by bin Laden to win Muslim support. While it is true that the U.S. presence in the Arabian Peninsula seems to be al-Qaida's principal grievance, as stated explicitly both in 1996 and in 1998, it would be a mistake to discount the importance of the Israeli-Palestinian conflict. Clearly, bin Laden and his supporters seek to tap widespread Muslim hostility to U.S. policies in that conflict. But those who charge opportunism on the part of bin Laden neglect to mention that the Israeli occupation of Jerusalem figured prominently in the 1996 statement as well. Moreover, they fail to appreciate the depth of Muslim feelings on this issue. The perception that the United States provides carte blanche support to Israel as it occupies Jerusalem and large tracts of the West Bank and Gaza, that American weapons are used in the suppression of the Palestinian *intifada*, that the United States frequently shields Israel from U.N. criticism in the Security Council—all while the sanctions against Iraq remained in place for a decade after the Gulf War—sparks the rawest emotional responses. These complaints do not need to be first on the list. They require no elaboration in the 1998 declaration. They are immediately understood by the statement's intended Muslim audience. As long as the conflict in Israel and the Palestinian territories continues, militant Muslim groups worldwide will exploit this issue to attack the United States. Bin Laden admitted as much in an October 21, 2001, interview with a correspondent from the Qatar-based television network al-Jazeera. In response to the correspondent's observation that bin Laden had shifted his emphasis in the interview to Palestine rather than the American presence in Saudi Arabia, bin Laden responded, "Sometimes we find the right elements to push for one cause more than the other. Last year's blessed *intifada* helped us to push more for the Palestinian issue. This push helps the other cause. Attacking America helps the cause of Palestine and vice versa. No conflict between the two; on the contrary, one serves the other."[8]

The 1998 statement concludes that because the United States and its allies, including its so-called Muslim allies, have declared war on Islam, true Muslims have no choice but to wage a defensive jihad. Bin Laden is careful in all his statements to invoke the notion of defensive jihad, not just because self-defense is the timeworn justification for most acts of violence, but also because it provides a number of important Islamic grounds for bin Laden's particular war. In a defensive jihad, various restraints imposed on the expansionist jihad are relaxed. All able-bodied Muslims, male and female, are required as an individual obligation to rush to the defense of the Muslim victims. If some Muslims are not close to the fighting and they cannot travel to the battlefield, they are required to assist the Muslim defenders in other ways. Requirements relating to proper authority—that is, who may declare and under whose leadership the jihad may be fought—become more ambiguous. If the leaders of the Islamic state are incapable or unwilling to lead the defensive struggle, other Muslims must assume this responsibility. And finally, the normal constraints on how Muslims may fight to repulse the aggression are loosened under claims of necessity. Just how much latitude Muslim fighters have in a defensive jihad will be discussed in the next section.

If we accept the 1996 and the 1998 declarations as articulating the ideas that motivate Osama bin Laden and his supporters—and I find no reason to deny that they do—then there is nothing at all remarkable about their arguments. Like the militant Islamic groups that preceded them, they selectively quote from the Qurʾan to establish the religious basis for their defensive jihad, but they are driven by the same sort of anti-imperialism that motivates other religious and nonreligious groups in the Middle East and around the world. In other words, the driving force behind their acts of violence is far more political and mundane than it is theological or sacred.

The understanding of jihad involved here is not that characteristic of the period of Arab expansion in the seventh and eighth centuries or the Ottoman Turkish expansion of the fifteenth and sixteenth centuries, but one formed over the past two centuries as Muslims struggled to resist Western expansion. In the nineteenth and early twentieth centuries, the aggressor nations would have been identified as the British, the French, and the Russians. Since the end of World War II, the United States has increasingly occupied this position, and of course all the more so as it became the guardian of the Persian Gulf during the late 1980s and 1990s. While the United States was establishing a direct military presence in the Persian Gulf for the first time in its history, many of the men who would emerge as al-Qaida's leaders were fighting the Soviets in Afghanistan. Driving one superpower from the region, in their view, was the prelude to the battle against the second.

Members of al-Qaida may (and probably do) harbor an existential hatred for the values and culture of the West ("they hate us because they resent our freedom and envy our wealth," we were told by a number of pundits and politicians after 9/11), but that is not what drove nineteen young men to hijack and crash airplanes into buildings. Al-Qaida's recruits may view themselves as the vanguard of an ideological movement that will ultimately overturn the societies of the rich and powerful West, but their words and actions indicate they are astute enough to realize this is a remote possibility. In the minds of the 9/11 hijackers, the attack upon New York and Washington, D.C., was a continuation of the same war al-Qaida had waged in Nairobi and Dar es Salaam (where it bombed the American embassies) and in Aden (where it bombed the USS *Cole*). The hijackers died with the hope that they were helping to drive the United States out of Muslim states and thereby to weaken the Muslim governments the United States supports and which al-Qaida is determined to overthrow.

The grievances articulated by al-Qaida are hardly unique to it or in any way remarkable. The charge that Crusaders (i.e., Christians) and Zionists, in league with nominal Muslim leaders of the various Muslim states, are engaged in a campaign to weaken, humiliate, and exterminate Muslims, that they will repress by any means the legitimate demands of Muslim peoples for the establishment of an Islamic state—all of this has been heard many times before.

What is remarkable about al-Qaida is that it has declared its war against the United States directly and that it is willing to take this war to American soil. Before al-Qaida, American citizens and American interests were targeted by militant Islamic groups, but generally within Muslim countries and as a means of destabilizing the real targets, the Muslim governments the militants were battling. The 1996 declaration reversed this emphasis: "Everyone agrees that the situation cannot be rectified (the shadow cannot be straightened when its source, the rod, is not straight) unless the root of the problem is tackled. Hence it is essential to hit the main enemy who divided the *umma* into small countries and pushed it, for the last few decades, into a state of confusion."[9] "Straightening the rod" means, as the 1998 statement declared, attacking "Americans and their allies . . . in order to liberate the al-Aqsa Mosque and the holy mosque [in Mecca] from their grip, and in order for their armies to move out of all the lands of Islam, defeated and unable to threaten any Muslim."[10]

As in all propaganda, the 1996 and 1998 declarations of war against the United States and its allies contain many distortions and half-truths. The U.S. military presence in the Arabian Peninsula hardly amounts to an American occupation of the sanctuaries of Mecca and Medina. A concerted Western campaign to destroy Islam and to exterminate Muslims in a latter-day crusade is of course nonsense. Those who subscribe to this view have a hard time explaining why NATO intervened on behalf of the Muslims of Kosovo. But as in all effective propaganda, the two statements from al-Qaida identify and exploit many latent Muslim grievances. Chief among them are hostility to the perceived double standard in American dealings with Israel as compared with Muslim countries, and the support the United States lends to repressive governments throughout the Muslim world, while proclaiming its commitment to democracy and human rights. By declaring that it is willing to take on the world's greatest power in order to redress widely felt injustices, al-Qaida garners the support of many ordinary Muslims.

The Question of Means

Many Muslims share al-Qaida's stated objectives, and they accept the argument that the goals warrant the use of all means necessary to achieve them, including terrorism. But most Muslims, as polls have repeatedly shown, do not support terrorist methods even though they may sympathize with al-Qaida's goals. With respect to means, bin Laden and his supporters are indeed on the fringes of Islamic thought.

The conduct of Muslim armies has been an important concern of the jihad tradition from its very origins. In one of the first verses discussing war in self-defense, the Qur'an states, "Fight in God's cause against those who wage war against you, but do not transgress limits, for God loves not the transgressors" (2:190). The "limits" are enumerated in various statements of the Prophet and the first four caliphs. According to authoritative traditions, whenever the Prophet sent out a military force, he would instruct its commander to adhere to certain restraints, including giving fair notice of attack and sparing women and children.[11] The Prophet's immediate successors continued this practice, as is indicated by the "ten commands" of the first caliph, Abu Bakr:

Do not act treacherously; do not act disloyally; do not act neglectfully. Do not mutilate; do not kill little children or old men, or women; do not cut off the heads of the palm-trees or burn them; do not cut down the fruit trees; do not slaughter a sheep or a cow or a camel, except for food. You will pass by people who devote their lives in cloisters; leave them and their devotions alone. You will come upon people who bring you platters in which are various sorts of food; if you eat any of it, mention the name of God over it.

Clearly, then, the Qur'an and the actions of the Prophet and his successors established the principles of discrimination between combatants and noncombatants and of limited warfare. Later jurists devoted considerable attention to elaborating just who qualified as a noncombatant and what tactics were permissible against combatants. The consensus was that those who traditionally do not take part in fighting, especially women, children, the old, and the infirm, are never legitimate targets. Jihad can never be "total war," in which unnecessarily cruel or excessive means of destruction are used against the enemy.

Modern Muslim scholars have continued to develop these principles. One of the most important contributions comes from the Syrian scholar Wahba al-Zuhayli, who writes:

> Islamic law does not characterize all of the enemy population as combatants. The combatants include all those who prepare themselves for fighting, either directly or indirectly. . . . As for the civilians who are at peace and devote themselves to work that is neutral in terms of [militarily] assisting the enemy . . . none of these are termed as combatants whose blood may be shed with impunity. On this point, Islamic law and international law converge.[12]

Like the vast majority of Muslim ethicists, Zuhayli rules out the possibility of collective responsibility, that all citizens belonging to a perceived foe are somehow responsible for their state's actions. Zuhayli also echoes the overwhelming consensus of modern scholars that Islamic ethics is consistent with the basic principles of international humanitarian law, including the Geneva Convention and its related protocols, that makes the deliberate targeting of noncombatants and the terrorizing of civilian populations a war crime.[13]

In their 1996 declaration of war, bin Laden and his supporters had very little to say on how they would wage their fight. They did acknowledge that "due to the imbalance of power between our armed forces and the enemy forces, a suitable means of fighting must be adopted, i.e., using fast-moving light forces that work under complete secrecy." In addition, the statement goes to great lengths to glorify the particular type of guerrilla operation that al-Qaida was adopting: the suicide bombing.[14]

The radical break with the centuries-old jihad tradition comes at the end of the 1998 statement. In the part described as a *fatwa*, or legal edict, bin Laden and his co-signers declare, "The ruling to kill the Americans and their allies—civilians and military—is an individual duty for every Muslim who can do it in any country in which it is possible to do it."[15] Ever since this statement was released, bin Laden has been challenged by various interviewers to justify on Islamic grounds his endorsement of killing civilians. The most detailed defense by bin Laden of which I am aware came in an October 21, 2001, interview with al-Jazeera television correspondent Tayseer Alouni. The exchange is worth reproducing at some length.

> OBL: The killing of innocent civilians, as America and some intellectuals claim, is really very strange talk. Who said that our children and civilians are not innocent and that shedding their blood is justified? That it is lesser in degree? When we kill their innocents, the entire world from east to west screams at us, and America rallies its allies, agents, and the sons of its agents. Who said that our blood is not blood, but theirs is?. . . .
> Alouni: So what you are saying is that this is a type of reciprocal treatment. They kill our innocents, so we kill their innocents.
> OBL: So we kill their innocents, and I say it is permissible in law and intellectually, because those who spoke on this matter spoke from a juridical perspective.
> Alouni: What is their position?
> OBL: That it is not permissible. They spoke of evidence that the Messenger of God forbade the killing of women and children. This is true.
> Alouni: This is exactly what I'm asking about.
> OBL: However, this prohibition of the killing of children and innocents is not absolute. It is not absolute. There are other texts that restrict it.
>
> I agree that the Prophet Muhammad forbade the killing of babies and women. That is true, but this is not absolute. There is a saying, "If the infidels killed women and children on purpose, we shouldn't shy away from treating them in the same way to stop them from doing it again." The men that God helped [attack, on September 11] did not intend to kill babies; they intended to destroy the strongest military power in the world, to attack the Pentagon that houses more than 64,000 employees, a military center that houses the strength and the military intelligence.
> Alouni: How about the twin towers?
> OBL: The towers are an economic power and not a children's school. Those that were there are men that supported the biggest economic power in the world. They have to review their books. We will do as they do. If they kill our women and our innocent people, we will kill their women and their innocent people until they stop.

In his November 7, 2001, interview with Pakistani journalist Hamid Mir, bin Laden expanded on his notion of the collective responsibility, and hence the collective vulnerability, of all Americans: "The American people should remember that they pay taxes to their government, they elect their president, their government manufactures arms and gives them to Israel and Israel uses them to massacre Palestinians. The American Congress endorses all government measures and this proves that the entire America is responsible for the atrocities perpetrated against Muslims. The entire America, they elect the Congress."[16]

As for the Muslims who are killed in al-Qaida's attacks, if they are killed in non-Muslim countries, "the Islamic Shari'a says Muslims should not live in the land of the infidels for long." If they are killed in Muslim countries, al-Qaida fighters are to be excused for their deaths because when "an enemy occupies a Muslim territory and uses common people as human shields, then it is permitted to attack that enemy."[17] So, according to bin Laden's statements, in the name of retaliation, the civilians killed are either not innocents or they are collateral damage.

Throughout Islamic history, various groups have given extreme interpretations to Qur'anic verses and Prophetic traditions to justify their violent actions. Some of the most notorious include the Khawarij of the seventh and eighth centuries, the Assassins of the twelfth-century, and the Wahhabis of the nineteenth-century. Their justifications went against the weight of the jihad tradition, and they were treated as extremists by the mainstream Muslims of their times. Some observers describe al-Qaida as falling within the same pattern of disaffected, marginalized Muslim sects. There are many points of comparison: Like the Khawarij, those organized under the banner of al-Qaida have no compunction about killing indiscriminately. Like the Assassins, their fighters are trained to die in the process of killing their opponents. Like the Wahhabis, they are convinced that the Muslim societies around them are steeped in false understandings of Islam, and that they, the only true Muslims, must violently purge Muslim societies of their un-Islamic notions. Indeed, al-Qaida seems to have achieved a full amalgam of all the distinctive traits of the previous groups.

The comparison between al-Qaida and earlier extremist groups should not be taken too far, however. Certainly, it is too much of a stretch to trace a genealogy of "Islamic terrorism" that begins with the Khawarij or the Assassins and then continues through the Wahhabis to al-Qaida today. Al-Qaida's terrorism is rationalized with Islamic justifications, but it falls within a history of modern terrorism that has little to do with Islam. What is missing from the genealogy above are the historical antecedents of modern terrorism in the Middle East, which include the activities of radical Jewish groups in Palestine during the 1940s, the Arab and the European parties to the Algerian liberation struggle of the 1950s, and the Palestine Liberation Organization of the 1970s. These movements perfected such terrorist methods as bombing civilian buildings, assassinating leaders, and hijacking civilian airliners. Contemporary Muslim terrorists have their roots as much in this violent legacy inspired by European revolutionaries, anarchists, and nihilists as in earlier Muslim extremism.

But bin Laden and his supporters quote the Qur'an and not the Communist Manifesto, the prophet Muhammad and not Trotsky. It is necessary therefore to address their justifications from within the tradition they invoke. Many points could be discussed, but I will focus here on only two of the most salient issues raised by al-Qaida's methods: the justification of targeting civilians and of suicide attacks.

Bin Laden defends the targeting of civilians primarily on the basis of reciprocity. The United States and its allies are killing Muslim civilians around the world, so it is justifiable for al-Qaida to respond by attacking American civilians. In his October 21, 2001, interview, bin Laden cites two Muslim "authorities" who, he claims, provide Islamic justification for targeting civilians.[18] Neither of the men he mentions is a well-known legal scholar, however. In other statements, bin Laden has alluded only vaguely to "principles of jurisprudence" that support his position. As for the vast majority of *ʿulama* who have condemned his terrorism, bin Laden, like all extremists before him, categorically rejects their authority: "The fatwa of any official *ʿalim* [singular of *ʿulama*] has no value for me. History is full of such *ʿulama* who justify *riba* [usury], who justify the occupation of Palestine by the Jews, who justify the presence of American troops around Haramain Sharifain [the two sanctuaries of Mecca and Medina]. These people support the infidels for their personal gain. The true *ʿulama* support the jihad against America."[19] Because he claims to be waging a defensive jihad against a ruthless, unprincipled opponent, bin Laden views the normal restraints applicable to Muslim fighters as being suspended: "If inciting people to do that [defend themselves] is terrorism, and if killing those who kill our sons is terrorism, then let history witness that we are terrorists."[20]

Leaving aside the merits of bin Laden's contention that he is in fact waging a defensive jihad against an unprincipled enemy, his assertion that Islamic ethics or jurisprudence permit indiscriminate warfare is untenable. The jihad tradition cannot be interpreted as endorsing the principle that in the name of retaliation or reciprocity, any and all tactics are permissible. Muslim extremists selectively quote such Qurʾanic verses as "If then anyone transgresses the prohibition against you, transgress you likewise against him" (2:194), and "Fight the polytheists all together (*kaffatan*) as they fight you all together" (9:36) to justify their terrorism. Not only do they fail to take into account the historical circumstances surrounding these verses, they also fail to consider that both verses conclude with the line: "But know that God is with those who are mindful of God's limits (*al-muttaqin*)."

The jihad tradition relaxes restrictions on the weapons or methods of warfare in the face of military necessity, but never the principle that civilians are not to be directly targeted. This prohibition of attacks on noncombatants is defended as a rule derived from the Qurʾan and the Prophet's *hadiths*. Even bin Laden on occasion acknowledges this rule, as in his November 7, 2001, interview: "The September 11 attacks were not targeted at women and children. The real targets were America's icons of military and economic power."[21] Yet this claim is obviously disingenuous; hijacking civilian airliners and crashing them into the Twin Towers when they were known to hold thousands of civilians makes human beings and not buildings "the real targets."

So, to meet this objection, bin Laden and his supporters fall back on the notion of reciprocity. Suffice it to say in response that retaliation in kind was a pagan Arab practice (and even then one limited by notions of chivalric honor) that was forbidden by the Prophet as a fundamental part of his reform of Arab martial values. The urge to revive the practice resurfaced during the rule of Abu Bakr (632–34 C.E.). One account relates that Byzantine forces routinely decapitated Muslim prisoners, and so Muslim commanders ordered a similar execution of Byzantine prisoners. When Abu Bakr learned of the practice, he ordered its immediate cessation. The Muslim commanders then protested that they were merely answering the enemy with his own methods. To which Abu Bakr is reported to have asked, "Are the Byzantines our teachers?"[22]

Bin Laden's second justification for al-Qaida's methods is that they are "martyrdom operations." This characterization rationalizes the specific tactic now favored by Islamic militants around the world: suicide attacks. Muslim extremists certainly did not invent or perfect this technique; one needs only recall the Japanese kamikaze pilots and the Tamil Tigers, who deployed the young, individual suicide bomber with devastating effect in India and Sri Lanka. But beginning with Hezbollah's suicide attacks in Lebanon against Israeli, American, and other targets, Muslim terrorists have employed it with such frequency that it will now forever be connected in the minds of many with "jihad." Muslim groups employ this tactic because it is the most effective weapon in the arsenal of the weak. But they also justify this tactic as a form of martyrdom, as if the deliberate taking of one's life in war has always been an accepted part of the jihad tradition.

The fact is that it is not an accepted part of the jihad tradition. Suicide in general is strongly condemned in Islamic teachings, and as a result it is rare in Muslim societies.[23] The response of Muslim groups employing suicide as a tactic, and of many Muslims who support them, is that the fighter who blows himself or herself up in attacking the enemy is not committing suicide but performing an act of self-sacrifice (martyrdom) similar to that of any soldier who marches into the face of certain death. Indeed, the line between combat and suicide is often fine and easily crossed. This is especially true when soldiers of a badly outnumbered and outgunned army fight a superior force rather than retreat or surrender. Americans still celebrate as heroic such suicidal ventures as the defense of the Alamo, Pickett's charge at the battle of Gettysburg, and Custer's last stand. Similarly, Muslims commemorate many a doomed struggle, most fervently the stand against all odds by the Prophet's grandson Husayn at Karbala in 680 C.E.

But there is a distinct difference between Husayn's defense of himself and his family at Karbala and what young men and women do today with the idea that they are earning paradise through jihad. The difference has to do not only with the targets involved, as discussed above, but the very act by which innocent people are killed. The *mujahid* (one who wages jihad) goes into battle with the intention to fight and *to live*, but with the conviction that if he should die, it is because God wills it. The suicide bombers who crash airplanes or trucks packed with explosives into buildings perform their deeds with the intention *to die*, justifying their deaths as acts of self-sacrifice.

One *hadith* from the Prophet, out of the many that mention suicide, relates directly to the actions of the suicide bombers:

> There was a man who fought more bravely than all the Muslims on behalf of the Muslims in a battle in the company of the Prophet. The Prophet looked at him and said, "If anyone would like to see a man from the people of the Fire [i.e., hell], let him look at this man." On that, one of the Muslims followed him, and he was in that state [that is, fighting fiercely] until he was wounded, and then he hastened to end his life by placing his sword between his breasts [and pressed it with great force] until it came out between his shoulders. Then the man [who was watching

that person] went quickly to the Prophet and said, "I testify that you are God's Messenger!" The Prophet asked him, "Why do you say that?" He said, "You said about so-and-so, 'If anyone would like to see a man from the people of the Fire, he should look at him.' He fought more bravely than all of us on behalf of the Muslims, but I knew that he would not die as a Muslim [martyr]. So when he got wounded, he hastened to die and committed suicide."[24]

The person who pulls the trigger of an explosives belt wrapped around his or her body is committing suicide as surely as the man who falls upon his own sword.

Morality and Terrorism

Some readers may question the point of subjecting the statements and actions of terrorists to moral scrutiny. Doesn't the internal logic of terrorism itself defy any moral justification? Isn't the terrorists' goal to commit such atrocities that they demoralize their victims or induce retaliatory action that garners active support from otherwise uncommitted sympathizers? Or, as some American officials argued after 9/11, doesn't responding to the terrorists' stated grievances only legitimize their methods?

My response is threefold: First, on the intellectual level, the misappropriation of the Qur³an and *hadith* to defend terrorism must be shown for what it is: a distortion of the jihad tradition. The distortion is so complete that today Muslims and non-Muslims regularly call groups like al-Qaida "jihadis," when in fact their methods do not conform to the basic principles of jihad. The time has come for the majority of Muslims who understand jihad as a just war, in which terrorism has no place, to reclaim this concept from the extremists.

Second, on a practical level, the religious arguments of the terrorists must be answered by others from within the same tradition or else the terrorist groups will continue to attract followers. Osama bin Laden and his supporters may be completely impervious to counterarguments or moral discourse of any sort. But unless we conclude that all those who join al-Qaida or other extremist Muslim groups are pathologically homicidal or suicidal or both, there is a need to answer their ideas with other ideas. Perhaps if enough Muslims undertake this mission and sustain it with principled arguments long enough, a few young men or women who would otherwise join the ranks of the terrorists would turn away from them.[25] Even one individual so diverted would be justification enough for responding to the terrorists.

My third response is offered with the long-term fight against terrorism and America's relations with the Muslim world in mind. The support al-Qaida garners from ordinary Muslims comes from a confusion between ends and means. Because many Muslims around the world feel deeply that the world order created and dominated by the West, and the United States in particular, is inimical to their interests, they are willing to embrace any means necessary to reverse the situation—or at least to teach their alleged oppressors a lesson. Curiously, the same confusion of ends and means is apparent in the pronouncements of

American leaders who declare that because of the brutal means al-Qaida uses, it seeks to reach "maximal" goals, including the destruction of the West or the imposition of its vision of Islam all over the world. Invoking such apocalyptic ends serves quite conveniently to bolster the position of those who claim there is no point at all in addressing al-Qaida's stated grievances.

Al-Qaida's conflation of ends and means is fundamentally incompatible with the jihad tradition as it has evolved for centuries. But we turn a deaf ear to al-Qaida's arguments at our own peril. To examine and to respond to the arguments is in no way to legitimize them. Taking a close look in particular at the grievances articulated by al-Qaida is in no way tantamount to "giving in" to or "sympathizing" with the terrorists. The surest way to bolster Muslim support for the terrorists is to ignore the causes from which terrorism springs and the justifications given to rationalize it. In the end, if we are to win the war against terrorism, we must prosecute the war on all fronts: military, political, economic—and moral.

Notes

1.   For the text of this note, see http://www.fbi.gov/pressrel/pressre101/letter.htm (December 14, 2001); and http://more.abcnews.go.com/sections/world/ DailyNews/attaletter_1.html (December 14, 2001).

2.   Max Weber, "Politics as a Vocation," in *From Max Weber: Essays in Sociology,* ed. and trans. Hans H. Gerth and C. Wright Mills (New York: Oxford University Press, 1946), 78.

3.   This *hadith* is not found in any of the six canonical *hadith* collections and appears to have been introduced by Sufis in the ninth century. Over the course of Islamic history, its authenticity has been challenged by Muslim scholars eager to emphasize the military, and not purely spiritual, dimensions of jihad. Regardless of its authenticity, it is now so widely quoted by Muslims that one could argue it has become normative to Islamic tradition.

4.   "Ladenese Epistle: Declaration of War (Parts I–III)," part I, 1–2, at http://www.washingtonpost.com/ac2/wp-dyn/A4342–2001Sep21 (September 28, 2001).

5.   "Ladenese Epistle," II:2–3.

6.   Ibid. For further details on the sanctity of the Arabian Peninsula in Islamic tradition, see Sohail H. Hashmi, "Moral Communities and Political Boundaries: Islamic Perspectives," in *States, Nations, and Borders: The Ethics of Making Boundaries,* ed. Allen Buchanan and Margaret Moore (New York: Cambridge University Press, 2003), 186–94.

7.   One notable exception is Bernard Lewis's analysis, "License to Kill: Osama bin Laden's Declaration of Jihad," *Foreign Affairs* 77:6 (November/December 1998): 14–19.

8.   "Transcript of bin Laden's October Interview," 4, at http://www.cnn.com/ 2002/WORLD/asiapcf/south/02/05/binladen.transcript (November 18, 2003).

9.   "Ladenese Epistle," I:6.

10.   "Jihad against Jews and Crusaders," 2, at http://www.washingtonpost.com/
        ac2/wp-dyn/A4993-2001Sep21 (September 28, 2001).

11.   A representative sample of Prophetic statements on restrictions in fight-
        ing is available in Muhammad ibn ʿAbdallah, Khatib al-Tabrizi, *Mishkat
        al-Masabih,* trans. Mawlana Fazlul Karim (New Delhi: Islamic Book Ser-
        vice, 1988), 2:387–89.

12.   Wahba al-Zuhayli, *Athar al-harb fi al-fiqh al-Islami: Dirasa muqarana* (Damas-
        cus: Dar al-Fikr, 1981), 503.

13.   For more on contemporary Muslim views on legitimate means of waging
        war, see Muhammad Abu Zahra, *Concept of War in Islam,* trans. Muhammad
        al-Hady and Taha Omar (Cairo: Ministry of Waqf, 1961); Yadh ben Ashoor,
        Islam and International Humanitarian Law (Geneva: International Committee
        of the Red Cross, 1980); Karima Bennoune, "As-Salamu ʿAlaykum? Humani-
        tarian Law in Islamic Jurisprudence," *Michigan Journal of International Law* 15
        (Winter 1994): 605–43; and Sohail H. Hashmi, "Saving and Taking Life in
        War: Three Modern Muslim Views," in *The Islamic Ethics of Life: Abortion,
        War, and Euthanasia,* ed. Jonathan E. Brockopp (Columbia: University of
        South Carolina Press, 2003), 129–54.

14.   "Ladenese Epistle," II:4ff.

15.   "Jihad against Jews and Crusaders," 2.

16.   "Osama Claims He Has Nukes," *Dawn* (Karachi), November 10, 2001, 1, at
        http://www.dawn.com/2001/11/10/top1.htm (January 2, 2004).

17.   Ibid.

18.   The two men bin Laden mentions are Sami Zai of Pakistan and Abdullah
        bin Ohkmah al-Shehebi of Saudi Arabia. "Transcript of bin Laden's October
        Interview," 4.

19.   "Osama Claims He Has Nukes," 1.

20.   "Transcript of bin Laden's October Interview," 1.

21.   "Osama Claims He Has Nukes," 1.

22.   ʿArif Abu ʿId, *al-ʿAlaqat al-kharijiyya fi dawlat al-khilafa* (Kuwait: Dar
        al-Arqam, 1983), 222, relates this account and discusses many other issues
        relating to reciprocity in Islamic jurisprudence.

23.   See Jonathan E. Brockopp, "The 'Good Death' in Islamic Theology and Law,"
        in *The Islamic Ethics of Life: Abortion, War, and Euthanasia,* 177–93.

24.   Narrated by Bukhari, *Sahih al-Bukhari,* bk. 77 (Divine Will, *al-Qadar*),
        no. 604.

25.   Most reputable Muslim scholars condemned the 9/11 attacks as unjustifiable
        terrorism. But many of the same scholars have supported Palestinian suicide
        bombings in Israel as legitimate resistance to occupation. See Haim Malka,
        "Must Innocents Die? The Islamic Debate over Suicide Attacks," *Middle East
        Quarterly* 10:2 (Spring 2003): 19–28, at http://www.meforum.org/article/530
        (January 2, 2004). Terrorism cannot be condoned under any circumstances
        within the jihad tradition, as I have argued in this chapter. Making exceptions
        in the Palestinian case only undermines the condemnation of terrorism in
        other cases.

8 Women's Jihad before and after 9/11

miriam cooke

While I was a visiting scholar in Syria during the mid-1990s, several universities invited me to give a series of lectures on Women and War. The itinerary had been arranged and I was set to begin. On the eve of my departure from Damascus, the minister of education summoned me to her office. She announced that the trip was off.

"Why?" I asked.

"Your topic makes no sense," she replied. "Everyone knows that women have nothing to do with war. Anyhow students will not understand what you are saying."

"Well, I could change the title to Women and Peace."

But she was adamant in her refusal. She, too, was a writer, she explained, and she knew how important titles are, how carefully we choose them.

"Clearly you meant what you said. The tour will have to be postponed."

When I asked if it was in fact canceled, she shook her head. "What you need is a carefully selected, small audience who will do your topic justice," she suggested patronizingly, contradicting her earlier condemnation of the topic as senseless. This audience is yet to be found.

Why did the minister of education find my proposed lecture topic so problematic? Why was it urgent that students not be exposed to an idea that seemed so important in a society at war with its neighbor? I suspect that she understood that to imbricate women and war is a radical intervention in military discourse. It questions some foundational structures, such as men at the front, women at home. It suggests that women and war may in fact be mutually constitutive. The anxiety about women and war is redoubled when religion is thrown in the mix. What if the religion is Islam and the time some moment after September 11th, 2001?

Even before that date, jihad implicated Muslim women as well as Muslim men. In this chapter I examine the changing meanings attached to women's jihad. I explore the many ways in which Muslim women have engaged in religiously framed warfare. Since the seventh-century, the ability to be part of jihad has empowered Muslim women. Women's jihad conjoins two transgressions: (1) women in the male-specific arena of war, and (2) feminism in the realm of patriarchal Islam. When women enter forbidden space, they challenge assumptions both about male privilege and about women's appropriate place in society.

Women have not only been waging jihad for centuries, they have been waging it within the framework of a rights discourse. Women have long sought equality with men in those areas and activities that have consequences for their citizenship rights. Combat provides a vivid example: it is a duty, but more importantly it is a right because it entails civic rewards. That is why access to combat has been so carefully controlled and so insistently demanded. In general, however, women who call for women's right to participate in war are rarely advocating violence. Rather, they are drawing attention to what happens when war breaks out. Norms allow for the unprecedented but also for the unintended. War, whether real or metaphorically invoked, can provide an opportunity to stake claims that would not otherwise be tolerated or even heard. Religious language buttresses the morality of this discourse: when non-militaristic women rhetorically combine gender justice, religion, and combat, war seems less real than metaphorical. By the logic of this argument, women can associate themselves with war strategically to make the association productive.

Consider women's participation in Arab wars. In Algeria, Palestine, Lebanon, and Iraq, women generally improvised successful ways of confronting their enemies that were minimally violent.[1] The more women were present, and recognized to be present, in a space that sanctions men's violence, it seemed, the less violent that space became. The rights discourse of feminist egalitarian militarists, who link women and war in an instrumental fashion, similarly tends to gloss the violence of war.[2]

But the aftermath of 9/11 has produced an unprecedented global hyper-militarization.[3] Can one still maintain the utopian project of advancing women's rights through the discursive linking of women, war, and now Islam? The answer is not clear, the evidence ambivalent at best.

Women's Jihad in History

Many refuse the linking of women and war. "Women" are here and "war" is there, and that is how we know what is going on where. The two words are seen to be mutually exclusive. To paraphrase Cynthia Enloe, the front is where women are not.[4] There are some, like the Syrian minister of education quoted above, who find the juxtaposition of these two words threatening.

To connect feminism and Islam may be equally inflammatory. Some Muslims resist the linking of Islam with feminism because they consider the word to connote a Western ideology. Conjoining feminism with Islam today smacks of neo-colonialism. Some reject the religious component of Islamic feminism, claiming that all monotheisms, and none more so than Islam, are structured around gender inequality. They scorn the idea that Islam tolerates politics on behalf of women's rights. Even some Muslim women who are committed to gender justice subscribe to such a view.[5] Pointing to scriptural prescriptions that seem to confirm women's essential inferiority, they scoff at "apologists" who try to reclaim gender justice from the clutches of misogynist interpreters of Islamic texts.

During the late 1980s and 1990s, however, some scholars like Fatima Mernissi[6] and Amina Wadud[7] found a middle path between these camps. Their exegetical and interpretive labor with foundational scripture revealed the compatibility of Islam and feminism and reinforced the strategic effectiveness of thinking the two together. In *Women Claim Islam,* I define Islamic feminism as a "contingent, contextually determined strategic self-positioning that confirms belonging in a religious community while allowing for activism on behalf of and with other women."[8] In sum, I maintain that Muslim women can be fully loyal to Islamic norms, values, and practices while also advocating rights they aspire to share with other women, even non-Muslim women.

Women's jihad takes Islamic feminism a large step further. It sanctions Muslim women's engagement in jihad, or inner and outer struggle, because it is a central tenet of Islamic doctrine. Linking women and war, it boldly defends the compatibility of Islam and women's rights in all spheres, including combat, that most sacred of all men's domains. There is ample precedent for women's jihad. Muslim women have participated in their collective warfare since the seventh-century. Four women connected to the Prophet Muhammad still provide powerful role models.

The first is Khadija, Muhammad's employer, then his wife. She became the first Muslim, encouraging him to believe in the truth of his revelations when he feared he was losing his mind. She assured him that it was not Satan but Allah who was speaking to him through the Archangel Gabriel. She also defended him against his detractors in Mecca. Throughout the nine years between his first revelations in 610 and her death in 619, Khadija joined Muhammad in the very first jihad of Islam. This jihad was both the struggle of Muslims to strengthen and purify their inner selves and the external struggle to withstand the foes of the new religion born on the soil of the Arabian Peninsula.

Although Khadija never participated in a battle, other Muslim women did. Consider Nusayba Bint Ka'b, variously referred to as al-Najariya, al-Maziniya, and Umm 'Umara. Three years after the *hijra,* the emigration of Muhammad and his followers from Mecca to Medina in 622, Nusayba personally defended Muhammad at the famous battle of Uhud in 625. When the Muslims appeared to be losing, she is reported to have said, "I made my way over to the messenger of God, and I began to direct combat, shielding him with the sword and shooting from the bow, until the wounds I sustained overtook me."[9] References to Nusayba's bravery abound on Islamic websites, as do the Prophet's commendation of her. In his article on this woman warrior whom he calls Umm 'Umara, Hamzah Qassim quotes Muhammad as having twice extolled her bravery. Addressing her son, Muhammad said, "Your mother! Bind her wound! May Allah bless you, the people of a house! The stand of your mother is better than the stand of so-and-so." On another occasion he was heard to exclaim: "Whenever I looked to the right or left I saw her fighting in front of me."[10]

Muhammad's youngest wife, Aisha, was also a combatant, a woman waging war or jihad on behalf of Islamic ideals and values. Transmitter of the largest number of Traditions,[11] Aisha is associated with two military events that have shaped her legacy. The first was when she accompanied Muhammad on one of his military expeditions. On the return to Medina, she was inadvertently left behind and found by a young man who led her back to her husband. Tongues wagged until Muhammad received a revelation that his followers were spreading calumnies about his loyal wife; henceforth slander was considered a sin. This story reveals that it was customary for the Prophet to go to battle attended by one of his wives. The other was a battle in 656 pitting two of the Prophet's widows against each other. Aisha was on the side of two of the Prophet's companions, Zubayr bin al-Awwan and Talhah bin Ubayd Abdallah, while Umm Salamah, another wife, was with Ali bin Abi Talib, the Prophet's cousin and son-in-law. This Battle of the Camel, so named because Aisha directed the fighting from the back of a camel, culminated years of wrangling over the succession to the Prophet, and it awarded the leadership to Ali, the last of the Prophet's companions to assume caliphal powers. Twenty-four years after Muhammad's death, women were still powerful enough in early Muslim society that one of his wives oversaw a battle.

Finally, there was Muhammad's granddaughter, Zaynab Bint Ali (Sayyida Zaynab). Zaynab fought at Karbala in 680. This battle, in which her brother Husayn was killed, has become the founding moment of Shiite difference and piety. Zaynab was taken captive to the tyrant Yazid. Fearlessly, she berated him. She was the first to hold a *majlis,* or lamentation assembly, for her martyred brother Husayn. Her recognition of the significance of his killing set a precedent for a ritual that is still performed in Shiite communities all over the world.

These four women are notable because of their close link to the Prophet Muhammad and to his family, yet they are only four among the many women who took up arms in seventh-century Arabia.[12] Historian Leila Ahmed writes that some, like the Kharijites, considered jihad to be the sixth of the five central tenets of Islam, binding on women as well as men, and they were particularly proud of one of their own women warriors, Layla Bint Tarif.[13]

After the seventh-century, however, women scarcely figure in Muslim war stories. Did they disappear from the battlefield? Or was it only from the chronicles that they were erased? While there is no definitive answer, some scholars, like Ahmed, suggest that women were increasingly marginalized from the political and religious centers of Muslim affairs during the centuries following the death of Muhammad. So we do not know exactly what happened to real women who were prepared to kill and die. What we do know, however, is that authorities exhorted Muslim women not to be publicly visible, and certainly not to fight.

Yet these authorities were speaking and working against historical precedent and even scriptural injunction. It is important to note that the Qurʾan explicitly requires everyone, man or woman, free or slave, to fight for Islam should the necessity arise. In his *Risala,* or treatise on the foundations of Islamic jurisprudence, the ninth-century jurist and founder of one of the four Sunni schools of law Imam Muhammad ibn Idris al-Shafiʾi writes: "jihad, and rising up in arms in particular, is obligatory for all able-bodied (believers), exempting no one, just as prayer, pilgrimage and (payment of) alms are performed, and no person is permitted to perform the duty for another, since performance by one will not fulfill the duty for another."[14] In this articulation, warfare is on a spiritual par with prayer, pilgrimage, and payment of alms. The fact that participation in jihad bears individual rewards indicates that it is a duty that is also a right. Jihad cannot be performed on behalf of another since that substitution would deprive the one represented of rightful rewards appropriated by the one representing. The master who performs jihad for the slave would be doubly rewarded while depriving his servant of his religious right; so would the man who assumes responsibility for a woman's duty to fight for Islam.

So how did a universal duty and right become the sole preserve of men? Maher Jarrar argues that during the Crusades of the twelfth and thirteenth centuries the universal stipulation of jihad was masculinized. It was then that a genre of literature associating jihad with fighting against non-Muslims and describing heavenly rewards for martyrdom in terms of *huris*, or black-eyed paradise virgins, became an important mobilizing rhetoric.[15] Within this moral economy women were excluded from practicing jihad because they were supposed to remain out of contact with non-Muslim men, and *mujahidat* (women warriors) were sharply distinguished from *huris* (angelic women).

Even though jihad historically came to be considered a male activity, women continued to fight throughout the fifteen centuries following Muhammad's death. Consider South Asia, where Gavin Hambly has examined the phenomenon of "female Sepoys" (*urdubegis*), a practice that persisted during the Mughal period. Bibi Fatima (b. 1490) was chief *urdubegi* in the zenana, or women's quarters, of the Mughal emperor Humayun. Bibi Fatima, who had been the emperor's wet nurse, accompanied Humayun for more than twenty years on military expeditions as far as Afghanistan. Three centuries later, *urdubegis* were still in service in the nineteenth-century Hyderabadi palace of Munir al-Mulk.[16] Hambly's collection of essays about women, and especially military women, in South Asian Muslim history indicates that they were prominent during their lifetime but occluded in the collective memory of Muslims. How did that happen?

Where Have All the Women Gone?

In order to understand the occlusion of Arab women in Muslim military history, I propose looking at living examples of *mujahidat* (women warriors) and their disappearance from the record. In *Women and the War Story,* I read contemporary stories of Arab women's participation in their nations' struggles and noted their erasure in the official War Story. This War Story is the privileged narrative of male-specific activity that constructs a universe split between men and women. For this worldview to persist, women must be written out of war's space, activity, discourse, and rewards. Women must be said to be at home for it to be self-evident that whoever is at the front must be male. Women must be said to be in need of defense for men to be appointed their defenders. They must be called civilians for the men to be the combatants.

Yet women's stories describe a different reality for women in war. Their stories challenge the War Story's distortion of women's *active* presence on the battlefield into *passive* observation. The women who write their war experiences are exposing the ways in which passive meaning is attached to women's active engagement in the struggles and challenges of their communities. They write to set the record straight, to show how reality is twisted and turned so that the frame narrative of the War Story might remain intact. They write to give back to women the voices that were stolen from them. Extrapolating from these writings that celebrate women's contributions to contemporary struggles and wars and lament their disappearance in history, one can surmise that this phenomenon is not new, that women may have participated in their communities' wars throughout history, even if without consciousness of the importance of what they have done.[17]

During the twentieth century, women have become increasingly conscious of what it means for them to fight because postmodern warfare targets women as much as, if not more than, men. Innovations in arms and media technology have played a huge role in transforming the experience of war. Muslim women's significance on the battlefield was first widely acknowledged during the anti-colonial struggles of the mid-twentieth century, when women regularly fought side by side with men. During their war of independence from the French (1954–1962), Algerian women's "conscription" to the medina and the *maquis*, to both urban and rural battlefields, made new norms and behaviors acceptable for the duration.

It was during this war that the term *mujahida* gained currency. Fatima-Zohra Sai emphasizes the religious aspect of the war that was both *kifah* (fighting) and jihad. The appeal to women's participation was both military and Islamic. It was well-understood that they were struggling for the nation but also for women's full citizenship in the nation-state to come.[18] The *mujahidat* may have been aware of the significance of their participation in this jihad, but the women writers were not. Although male writers created powerful women who terrorized their male companions, the women writers remained largely unaware of the significance of women in combat. This disjuncture between the reactions of men and women intellectuals to new roles for women in a Muslim country at war may account for postbellum political and historiographical arrangements that marginalized women and erased their stories of military contributions.[19]

In the aftermath of the 1967 war, Palestinian women have invoked what is now called the "Algerian lesson." They have learned how critical it is to write the experience of participation at the time, when women can still represent themselves and assign their own meanings to their actions. In the occupied territories of Gaza and the West Bank, women resisted the Israeli soldiers with stones, burning tires, and their unarmed bodies. For twenty years their ways of fighting were effective because they disabled the Israelis who were not trained to fight civilians. Whether the Algerian lesson has been directly responsible for the increase in Arab women's writings on war is hard to prove, but it is circumstantially persuasive. Palestinian, Lebanese, Iraqi, Moroccan, Kuwaiti women are among the many women all over the world who have chosen to write about their fighting, its peculiar effectiveness in postcolonial wars, and the rewards it should entail.

For those women who do not write, the erasure of their contributions to the community's struggle persists as though it were a necessary part of the process of turning the experience of war into its narrative. To cite only one example of many, the Iraqi women who participated in the March 1991 uprising against Saddam Hussein and who were then exiled protest a double betrayal of their resistance. First, the international community allowed Saddam Hussein to attack them, and then the men denied their role in the opposition.[20]

Women writing about women warriors compel attention to women's transgressive presence. They are present today, as they have been in the past, in a space and experience programmatically said to exclude them. Women are complicating the War Story by demonstrating that war does not split space into home and front but is simultaneously present in both. Thus the distinctions between warrior and civilian, as between defender and defended, which flow from a narrowly spatial binary, become moot. The undermining of these binaries reveals that the mutual exclusivity of war and peace cannot hold except through the play of familiar signs and symbols.

The goal of these deconstructive writings is not to disable the nation, but rather to strengthen it. Women who write about women fighting are not always advocating pacifism, the stereotype of inherently peace-loving women. Rather, they are calling for more effective ways to wage a just war. A community that is oppressed or is internally oppressive demands action for change. Algerians fighting the French, like Palestinians trying to shake off the Israelis, need everyone to participate in the struggle. The continuity from colonial opposition to postcolonial resistance entails the agency of women as well as men; an effective, just war cannot be fought without *mujahidat*.

Resisting *Jahiliya*

Since the 1980s, some Muslim women have joined in a special kind of war that is more spiritual than martial. It is a jihad that opposes the evil manifestations of what Islamists are calling the current *jahiliya*, referring back to the eponymous age of ignorance and depravity that preceded Islam. Ironically, both Islamists and some Islamic feminists are invoking this *jahiliya*. Despite their diagonally opposed agendas concerning women's duties and rights, both groups have found *jahiliya* useful in their call for an end to the way things are. In this new jihad, women may be fighting with or against the men in their community.

More and more people who position themselves as Islamic feminists, whose project is to empower women within a well-understood Islam, are calling for jihad, with its double meaning of struggle with minimal violence for the improvement of the self (*al*-jihad *al-akbar*) *and* of society (*al*-jihad *al-asghar*). In apartheid South Africa of the 1980s, jihad became the rallying cry for a kind of liberation theology. It was "the Islamic paradigm of the liberation struggle . . . for freedom and justice. . . . Any Muslim who abandons the struggle in South Africa abandons Islam. Jihad in the path of God is part of the *iman* of a Muslim."[21] In 1987, the proposed introduction of Muslim personal law[22] in South Africa sparked what the activist and religious scholar Farid Esack termed "gender jihad" to describe Muslims' concurrent struggles to fight apartheid and gender oppression within the framework of a well-understood Islam. Under the banner of jihad, men and women fought together "against the dehumanization of racialism and that of gender oppression."[23]

Women's ways of fighting in late-twentieth-century wars in Muslim countries sort into three overall categories. First, there was what Frantz Fanon called "*strategie femme*" of the Algerian war of independence that described women's deployment against the French occupiers. Second, there was the "gender jihad" of the anti-apartheid movement in South Africa that was part of a national project to ensure women's full participation in the future society. And third, there was the first *intifada* in the Israeli-occupied territories that saw women and children out in the streets confronting Israeli weaponry. In each case, women were improvising ways of fighting that employed the least amount of violence necessary to impel change. Although each of these three categories is connected to a specific conflict, each became emblematic of Muslim women's ways of fighting.

Jihad does not preclude conventional fighting, *qital*, for the Qur'an does call for it.[24] In *Surat al-Baqara*, the second chapter of the Qur'an, men and women are told that sometimes they must fight with arms: "Fighting is written for you even though you hate it. But it may well be that you hate what is good for you and that you love what is bad for you. God is the one who knows and not you" (Qur'an 2:216).

This is the verse that the Saudi preacher Fatima Umar Naseef quotes in the "Right to Participate in Jihad" section of a chapter devoted to women's political rights in Islam.[25] She elaborates on the meanings attached to jihad for women. Even though some say it is "without fighting," Naseef disagrees. She is contesting a widespread attitude that is commonly found in conservative Islamist sites. They argue that while jihad is indeed enjoined on all, jihad for women means something else. One site quotes a Tradition that reports Muhammad to have said that anyone "who stays home protecting her modesty and honor will receive the rewards of jihad."[26]

Naseef rejects such interpretations and emphasizes that women are to be as active as men in defending the Muslim nation. She is unequivocal that should infidels invade *dar al-Islam*, "all inhabitants of this country should go out and fight the enemy. Indeed, it is *unlawful* for anyone to refrain from fighting." Women, children, and slaves must fight even if without their husbands', fathers', or owners' permission.[27] Careful to show that she has not exercised undue license in her reading of the Qur'an, Naseef quotes from the Egyptian Islamist scholar Sayyid Qutb, who had asserted in the 1960s that, like the women surrounding the Prophet in the seventh-century, modern Muslim women should be mobilized for jihad in cases of emergency.[28]

During the state of emergency that war creates, individuals must choose appropriate behaviors, but also appropriate authorities in their lives. In the war to advance God's reign on earth, norms are even more dispensable than they are during ordinary wars. The father is no longer the senior authority in the family, but God, and God's law supersedes that of the father when the *umma* is in danger. Naseef's advocacy of total mobilization and the resultant transgression of hierarchical norms are striking, especially when articulated by a highly respected woman scholar.

Zaynab al-Ghazali, president of the Islamist Muslim Ladies' Association, is another to call women to war. She is the model fighter whose prison memoirs, *Days from My Life,*[29] tell the story of her "days" resisting Nasser; "days" in Arabic means also "battles." Her heroines are the early *mujahidat,* especially Layla Bint Tarif and Nusayba Bint Ka'b al-Maziniyya. She calls herself a "'soldier' in the common struggle for the creation of an Islamic state."[30] This use of the term "soldier" reveals al-Ghazali's understanding of her role in the twentieth-century *jahiliya.* Soldiers for God improvise new rules of conduct that will speed the establishment of an Islamic state. This jihad is more important than any other activity, even marriage, that she often declares to be a Muslim woman's highest calling. Under the extraordinary circumstances of the current *jahiliya,* Egypt was at war with itself. Pious Muslims had to engage in a just war to eradicate the seeds of corruption. For as long as it took to fight the good fight, they would function according to the abnormal rules of war that allow for the adjustment of codes of social conduct and gender arrangements in anticipation of the utopian postbellum society.[31]

In her autobiography, Zaynab al-Ghazali (like Palestinian, Lebanese, and other Arab women warriors) is using the rhetoric of war to transform and extend the meanings attached to women's actions so that they will be accorded the civic recognition vouchsafed to male combatants. From within the Islamist movement, she cannot speak against religiously sanctioned gender norms, but rather must embrace them, while showing them to be contingent. She had written into her marriage contract that should her husband interfere in her service to God, she would divorce him. It is here that we can locate the radical move. If in exceptional times like jihad women may relate to their husbands and children as men have always related to their wives and children, and the moral order is not undone, then it may eventually be permissible for this state of affairs to continue. The good Muslima must be prepared to be a *mujahida.*

Zaynab al-Ghazali may have been an anomaly when she wrote her prison memoirs back in the late 1970s. She is no longer. Women in Islamist groups everywhere are now using her language of accommodation and resistance with no sense of contradiction. During the mid-1990s a woman Islamist leader said, "It is our duty as Muslim women to have a say in the politics of our country and the politics that shape our lives as women. Politics is not only the realm of men, as many men want to propagate. On the contrary, it has been made our primary concern throughout Islamic history since 1,500 years ago."[32] Another Islamist woman harked back to Muhammad's time when women were expected to do what the men did, saying that no man "has the right to deprive a woman of her Islamic mission. Submissiveness is only to God and not to any human being. . . . A Muslim woman should fight for her rights, even if this means in some cases divorce."[33]

The rhetoric of jihad is not restricted to Sunni women. Shiite women are also waging their own jihad. The charismatic figure for them is Muhammad's granddaughter Sayyida Zaynab, who was present at the fateful battle of Karbala in 680. She has become a symbol of resistance in defeat. Her defiant opposition to her brother's murderer, the tyrannical Yazid, epitomizes moral victory overcoming military defeat. She warns the tyrant, who has subsequently stood in for generations of unjust rulers, that he will not be able to erase the memory of the founding heroes of Islam. She is the one who "made Islam safe from the flames," to borrow the phrase used by the Hyderabadi poet Mirza Farid Beg Farid.[34]

In the imaginary of Shiite women, Zaynab is the model for women's active opposition to an unjust ruler. During the Iran-Iraq War of 1980–1988, Zaynab inspired the revolutionary women on both sides. In Iran there was even a brigade of chador-wearing, Kalashnikov-bearing women called *kommando-haye Hazrat-e Zaynab,* or "the commandos of her holiness Zaynab."[35]

Ali Shariati, the ideologue of the Islamic revolution, placed great emphasis on the role of women in the social transformation of Iran. His vision of a progressive Islam already in the 1960s included the empowerment of women within the framework of orthodox Islam. The two models for the modern, pious Iranian woman that he proposed were Fatima and Zaynab, Muhammad's daughter and granddaughter. Fatima was the ideal mother figure and Zaynab the ideal *mujahida* who was politically conscious and prepared to sacrifice herself for the true Islam.[36] Since the 1963 uprising against the shah that drove Imam Khomeini into exile, women were joining the People's Mujahidin. One of the best-known was Mother Rezai, "who came to symbolize the resistance of Iranian mothers to dictatorship and foreign domination."[37] After the revolution, women continued to fight and to insist on their superior capacity to take up arms and to sacrifice themselves for the cause of Islam.[38] Indeed, so acknowledged was women's role in the revolution that some "clerics argued that there was nothing wrong in women participating in jihad and the defense of their country," citing the precedent of Nusayba Bint Ka'b.[39]

One of these piously militant women is Marziyeh Hadidchai Dabbagh. Historian Janet Afary presents Dabbagh's life and work as an "escape from tradition through militant Islam."[40] Dabbagh was active throughout the 1970s on behalf of the Ayatollah Khomeini, even acting as his bodyguard for a while. In Europe, "she participated in hunger strikes on behalf of Iranian prisoners. . . . In Syria, she helped set up a military camp where anti-Shah combatants were trained."[41] After the success of the Iranian revolution, she became active with the Pasdaran paramilitary group. During the Iran-Iraq War, she served as a military commander, founding the women's auxiliary branch of the Basij organization that recruited young men and boys for suicide missions. For Dabbagh, "women are to be liberated from traditional life styles only to become soldiers and martyrs for the cause of Islamization."[42] Zahra Rahnavard was another to call women to change and to arms. Editor of *The Path of Zaynab* (*Rahe Zaynab*), she extolled the model of Muhammad's granddaughter to inspire women to oppose Western capitalism and to take up "arms in the name of the holy cause."[43]

Sayyida Zaynab has also inspired Iraqi Shiite women. The "heroine of Karbala" inaugurated the Husaynid Laments or *qiraʾat husayniya* that still create networks of women across time and space.[44] In her study of the life stories of women who were in some way part of the March 1991 uprising against Saddam Hussein and who were then driven out of southern Iraq through refugee camps in the Saudi desert on to European diasporic homes, anthropologist Tayba Sharif explains the role of these lamentations. They are held wherever Shiite women are in some kind of distress. They gather to share their grief in a ritual of worship and remembrance that invokes their foremother Zaynab and her grief for her brother Husayn. This ritual remembrance, which can take place as often as twice a month, focuses on Zaynab's behavior and is addressed to her. It allows for a behavior that would not otherwise be tolerated. The Iraqi government recognized the power of these religious gatherings as early as 1977 when it banned them as "backward."[45] The women, however, continued to hold these sessions in secret, thereby incurring official wrath that included raping disobedient *mullayas*.[46]

For the Iraqi women in the 1991 resistance who suffered repeated displacements, the *qiraʾat husayniya* provide a discursive frame for their own narratives of disorientation, radical fragmentation, and defiance. Resettled now in Europe and Scandinavia, these Shiite women urgently call upon Sayyida Zaynab to share pain secretly, legitimately, and appropriately. This collective remembering allows them to imagine ways of confronting tyranny.

Zaynab's twentieth-century heir in Iraq is Bint al-Huda, who was executed in 1977 for her active opposition to the brutal regime of Saddam Hussein. Her execution turned her into a martyr and invested her actions and memory with mystical significance that is politically empowering.[47] Bint al-Huda became the bridge linking a seventh-century *mujahida* with her twentieth-century descendants.

Permission for Shiite women to fight extended beyond the Iran-Iraq front. Maria Holt writes that for Shiite women in Lebanon, jihad was part of a martial motherhood. She quotes one who said, "We have first to understand where we are and where we stand before we carry arms. If we have to carry arms, then of course, we will."[48] One woman from Hezbollah was even more emphatic about women's role in war: "if the enemy enters one's country, women too may fight and therefore are liable to become martyrs."[49] It is almost as though she was foreshadowing the post-9/11 women suicide bombers inside Israel.

The Iranian Islamist women who became politically active in the 1970s and 1980s, the Iraqi participants in the March 1991 uprising, and the Lebanese Shiite activists were like Fatima Umar Naseef and Zaynab al-Ghazali in their claim that "their loyalty should first and foremost be to their husbands, children, and Islamic family values, something they themselves have not pursued either before or after the Revolution."[50] It would be too easy, wrong even, to condemn such women for insincerity and hypocrisy. Placed within the framework of their lives as strong women and committed Muslims, these statements exemplify multiple critiques. They are defending their right to belong to several communities at the same time and to criticize any who would criticize them.[51] And in so doing, they are modeling themselves on Sayyida Zaynab, who fought and transgressed seventh-century social norms.

Jihad provides the language and virtual reality of war within contemporary Muslim societies, where religious language and symbols have come to acquire such power. To argue the religious right of women to go to war was to frame the struggle for women's rights within the deeply moral language and rituals of Islam. So widespread was the appeal to jihad as a morally justified struggle that it spread to the Internet, where it became a new recruiting tool for *mujahidat*. Articles on the laudable precedence of early women fighters proliferated since the late 1990s.[52]

After 9/11

Since 9/11, however, the utopian connection between women and war and Islam has been complicated because more than ever the representation of women's association with violence is symbolizing something beyond itself. During times of crisis, women's images generally serve specific moral purposes that have little to do with the actual women portrayed. At home, women represent the nation that has to be protected. The women of the enemy may be shown to be vulnerable or armed. If armed, they demonstrate that the enemy is so aggressive that it has enlisted its most vulnerable to kill and to die. If unarmed, they may be useful targets to "soften" enemy resolve (they may be raped or carpet-bombed), or they can become political pretexts for military intervention. How does that work?

From an imperial perspective, representations of the male oppression of enemy women stand in for men's brutality, their non-conformity with universal norms of civilization, and their menace to the world. Insistence on enemy women's oppression thus justifies political and military intervention in sovereign states. This is what happened almost immediately after 9/11, when Afghan women dominated media representations of the Middle East. This was not the first time. In 1996, when the Taliban took Kabul and evacuated women from the public square, there was an international outcry. Appeals from feminist organizations to oust the misogynist regime circulated for a while and then disappeared. They were revived after 9/11, but this time the concern for the Afghan women was official, government-sponsored. In less than a month the need to save the women seemed natural; it was conjoined to the determination to "smoke out" the terrorists.[53]

Leaders in the U.S. government denounced the Taliban for their barbaric treatment of women. These victims of the Taliban added weight to arguments concerning the justification of the war on Afghanistan. In a familiar return to the gendered discourse of empire current in nineteenth-century Britain, the misogyny of the Taliban was loudly trumpeted. We had to save these women from their men and prevent them from imposing their world on ours. Laura Bush on November 17, 2001, put Afghan women on "our" side of civilization and the men beyond the pale: "Civilized people throughout the world are speaking out in horror—not only because our hearts break for the women and children in Afghanistan, but also because in Afghanistan, we see the world the terrorists would like to impose on the rest of us."[54] Concern for Afghan women soon led to state-sponsored activism on behalf of women in the Middle East in general.

I witnessed firsthand this government campaign to save Middle Eastern women. In February 2003, the State Department invited me, along with six other experts on Middle Eastern women and Islamist networks, to discuss ways to help women in the Middle East. They had identified women as key agents of change in the Middle East, the cornerstone of any kind of civil society. The State Department had already allocated $29 million to help Muslim women in the Middle East, and the deputy assistant secretary of state for Middle East affairs, Liz Cheney, was hoping for a further requisition of $125 million. She needed our help: what were the specific abuses women in the Middle East were suffering? How could the State Department and the CIA best spend this money? Because they did not want to give it to patriarchal, authoritarian governments who would surely skim off the aid these "poor women" needed, Bush administration appointees wanted to know to whom should they give it? Muslim women oppressed by their co-religionists were surely "our" collective responsibility; if we could save them we would advance universal civilization.

Did this government-down feminist support for Muslim women signal feminist solidarity across political, economic, and religious divisions? Or did it rather help the coalition of the willing make the war more palatable? By 2002, the improvement in Afghan women's lives caused by the bombs that rained down on their homes was being widely celebrated. Proof of improvement was that a few women had unveiled. Yet by late summer 2004, field report after field report stressed that far from improving their lives, the U.S.-led war on the Taliban had further degraded conditions for women. The successors to the Taliban, it turned out, were not feminists either.

While the Afghans and Iraqis dominated the headlines, the situation of the Palestinians deteriorated daily. There were house demolitions, high unemployment, humiliating searches at checkpoints, and random raids. All added fuel to an already smoldering fire. On January 26, 2002, Wafa Idris, explosives strapped to her fragile body, was the first woman suicide bomber to be deployed inside Israel. Others have followed her lead. These women consider their action to be a religious duty, a jihad. A young woman who had volunteered to become a human explosive called these bombing missions "the highest level of jihad."[55] In April 2002, Britain's *Guardian* reported that the al-Aqsa brigade had set up a special suicide unit for women.

Within the space of fifteen months, women of the Middle East had spanned the gamut of good and evil. The good were victims of an evil system. They faded into the background once their state had been crushed. They were replaced by the terrifying specter of Palestinian women perpetrating the most violent of acts.

The U.S. media stuck to black-and-white color tones in their characterization of Muslim women: they were either victims or victimizers. Whereas the victims are like us, the fighters are not. The victims are the women of Afghanistan who can be civilized, the victimizers are the women of Palestine. Then, in February 2003, images of armed Iraqi women began to appear in the U.S. media. The *New York Times* on February 9th featured a crowd of veiled women in Tikrit with their Kalashnikovs raised high; they had "assembled to demonstrate their readiness for a possible war." They looked like the Iranian women of the late 1970s and 1980s who were also wearing chadors and carrying Kalashnikovs.

These images of Iraqi women warriors and also of recruits to the al-Aqsa martyrs' brigade and to Chechen militias[56] demonstrate that the nation is totally mobilized and ready to kill. Nothing is more terrifying, dangerous, and absolutely persuasive than images of Palestinian and Iraqi veiled women in arms and calling for jihad. They deflect attention from imperial ambitions in the region. They enhance the negative image of the leader who has sunk so low that he is ready to sacrifice women. It is OK to kill such a leader and such a people.

Then, in March 2004, something changed. In commemorating the launching of a war that had failed militarily, the U.S. government tried to recuperate it morally. How? Erasing the memory of the veiled women with their submachine guns at the ready, the media started to project images of women unimaginable a year earlier. They had become emblems of democracy and women's rights *à l'americaine*. Ambassador Ellen Sauerbrey, U.S. Representative to the UN Commission on the Status of Women (CSW), reported that at its forty-eighth session, twelve women representing Iraq "spoke eloquently of their grim past and the hopeful future of their country. They were able to join us at the United States Mission to share their perspective on the problems and prospects for a democratic Iraq. Just a year ago, Saddam Hussein's torture chambers and rape rooms were in full operation. Today, Iraq is moving toward democracy and prosperity."[57] Who were these women? Had they been in Saddam's torture chambers or in his military? How were they chosen? Why did they speak? In spite of these women's voices, at the conference and perhaps also in Iraq, it was once again images of Muslim women that were used to manipulate American public opinion about a morally ambiguous war.

In the postcolonial Muslim world, women have waged greater and lesser jihads with guns and pens. They have successfully shown how women's full engagement in their society, even if it necessitates war, benefits all its members. Many have called on distinguished foremothers like Sayyida Zaynab and Nusayba Bint Ka'b to justify their engagement in the unfeminine, but until now generally non-violent, jihad to improve their society.

Since 9/11, however, we have seen a change in the representation of women's ways of fighting. They are no longer models of a different way to fight for their own and their people's rights. Some are imitating the ways men have always fought. Dressing like men, they are filming their suicide messages and becoming heroines for the next generation. When images of Palestinian and Chechen women suicide bombers are juxtaposed with images of Afghan and Iraqi women enjoying U.S. bomb–bestowed liberties, they legitimize escalation in violence and its indefinite continuation.

Judith Butler is eloquent in her condemnation of the way "feminism, as a trope, is deployed in the service of restoring the presumption of First World impermeability." [58] She is concerned with the exploitation of women's oppression not only to further neo-colonial ends but also to reassure the U.S. public about its superiority. Butler adds a sophisticated voice to the clamor to "disengage feminism from its First World presumption and to use the resources of feminist theory, and activism, to rethink the meaning of the tie, the bond, the alliance, the relation, as they are imagined and lived in the horizon of a counter-imperialist egalitarianism." [59] If feminism can indeed be disengaged from its elitist, racist presumptions and if activists and thinkers can "accept the array of sometimes incommensurable epistemological and political beliefs and modes and means of agency that bring us into activism," [60] then we can begin to counter the manipulative messages we are being fed. We may begin to understand rather than reflexively condemn some of the most ethically troubling developments in the Middle East. Whether we like what some Palestinian women are doing or not, we must remember that they represent the other side of the U.S. war for democracy in the Middle East. These women do not figure in the glowing stories the U.S. government projects of women celebrating the chance to be free of dictators and enabled to begin life anew as wannabe democrats.

Centuries of colonial rule and now decades of neo-colonial dictatorship cannot be erased. They must be acknowledged along with the role that women warriors have played to bring about significant change within their societies. These women warriors, who know that their most important rights are as citizens in a society that grants them equal access to its benefits as well as its costs, are our allies in the common struggle for a counter-imperialist egalitarian project. Their call for jihad affirms the collective good of both women and men.

Notes

1. See miriam cooke, *Women and the War Story* (Berkeley: University of California Press, 1996).
2. For an excellent discussion of these issues, see Ilene Rose Feinman, *Citizenship Rites: Feminist Soldiers and Feminist Antimilitarists* (New York: New York University Press, 2000).
3. The U.S. first attacked Afghanistan and then in the spring of 2003, the long-

sought ties between the Islamist terrorists and Iraq's Saddam Hussein drove the U.S. leadership to invade and occupy Iraq. See Richard A. Clarke, *Against All Enemies: Inside America's War on Terror* (New York: Free Press, 2004).

4. Cynthia H. Enloe, *Does Khaki Become You?: The Militarization of Women's Lives* (London: Pandora, 1988 rev. ed.).

5. Haideh Moghissi, *Feminism and Islamic Fundamentalism: The Limits of Postmodern Analysis* (London: Zed Books, 1999).

6. Fatima Mernissi, *The Veil and the Male Elite: A Feminist Interpretation of Women's Rights in Islam* (Reading, Mass.: Addison-Wesley Pub. Co., 1991).

7. Amina Wadud, *Qurʾan and Woman: Rereading the Sacred Text from a Woman's Perspective* (New York: Oxford University Press, 1999).

8. miriam cooke, *Women Claim Islam: Creating Islamic Feminism through Literature* (New York: Routledge, 2001), 59–60.

9. Ibn Hajar 4: 479 in Mohja Kahf, "Braiding the Stories: Women's Eloquence in the Early Islamic Era," in Gisela Webb, ed., *Windows of Faith: Muslim Women Scholar-Activists in North America* (Syracuse, N.Y.: Syracuse University Press, 2000), 148.

10. Hamzah Qassim, "Umm ʿUmara: The Prophet's Shield at Uhud," *Nidaʾul Islam Magazine,* Issue 22, February–March 1998, http://www.islam.org.au.

11. Traditions are the sayings and reported actions of the Prophet that, with the Qurʾan, are the primary building blocks of the Sharia or Islamic law.

12. Other famous combatants include Khawla Bint al-Azwar, who dressed as a man so that she might fight with Khalid Ibn al-Walid to save her brother Dirar (Widad El Sakkakini, *Ummahat al-muʾminin wa-banat al-Rasul* [al-Qahirah: Dar al-fikr al-Arabi, 1969]). Umm Atiyya, an Ansari from Medina, is reported to have said that she had "participated in seven battles with the Prophet (SAW)." Asma bint Yazid is said to have "killed nine Roman soldiers with a tent-pole during the battle of Yarmuk." For more on these early *mujahidat,* see Khadija Watson, "Women's Role in Jihad," *Jamaʾat ud Daʾawa,* 2003 http://jamatuddawa.org/english/articles/jihad/women.htm.

13. Leila Ahmed, *Women and Gender in Islam: Historical Roots of a Modern Debate* (New Haven, Conn.: Yale University Press, 1992).

14. Muhammad ibn Idris Shafiʾi, *Al-Imam Muhammad ibn Idris al-Shafiʾi's al-Risala fi usul al-fiqh: Treatise on the Foundations of Islamic Jurisprudence,* trans. Majid Khadduri, (Cambridge: Islamic Texts Society, 1997).

15. Maher Jarrar, "The Martyrdom of Passionate Lovers: Holy War as a Sacred Wedding," in Angelika Neuwirth, ed., *Myths, Historical Archetypes, and Symbolic Figures in Arabic Literature: Towards a New Hermeneutical Approach: Proceedings of the International Symposium in Beirut, June 25th–June 30th, 1996* (Beirut: In Kommission bei Franz Steiner Verlag, Stuttgart, 1999), 89, 97, 106.

16. Gavin Hambly, ed., *Women in the Medieval Islamic World: Power, Patronage, and Piety* (New York: St. Martin's Press, 1998), 429–467.

17. Nana Asma'u (1793–1864) wrote poetry about her father's jihad to Islamize the Nigerian people of Sokoto over whom he ruled. Her poems chronicle the occluded, but vital, educational role women played during this period of conflict. See Beverly B. Mack and Jean Boyd, *One Woman's Jihad: Nana Asma'u, Scholar and Scribe* (Bloomington: Indiana University Press, 2000), 76.

18. Fatima-Zohra Sai, "Les femmes algeriennes: citoyennes, moujahidates,

soeurs," in R. Bourquia, M. Charrad, and Nancy Elizabeth Gallagher, eds., *Femmes, culture et société au Maghreb* (Casablanca: Afrique Orient, 1996), 92.

19. cooke, *Women Claim Islam*, 118–166.

20. T. H. Al Sharif, "Resistance and Remembrance: History-telling of the Iraqi Shi'ite Arab Refugee Women and their Families in the Netherlands" (Ph.D. thesis, University of Amsterdam, 2003), 87.

21. Farid Esack, *Qur°an, Liberation and Pluralism: An Islamic Perspective of Interreligious Solidarity Against Oppression* (Oxford: Oneworld, 1997), 107.

22. Muslim personal law has been introduced, sometimes re-introduced, in places where governments recognize the multi-cultural and multi-religious makeup of the society. The demand for Muslim personal law is an anti-colonial reflex and a tool in the fight for the assertion of Muslim identity and recognition of associated rights. Muslim personal law tends to compromise women because it legislates gender-specific behavior in terms of rights and obligations that favor men and marginalize women by turning them into idealized vessels of the purity and authenticity of their community. How can women contest a political platform that is good for their people but bad for them? In *Women Claim Islam,* I have proposed that they engage in a "multiple critique."

23. Ibid., 248. On January 18, 1998, the Johannesburg *Sunday Independent* carried an obituary for the Islamic feminist activist Shamima Shaikh, using the phrase "gender jihad." *Sunday Independent,* "Warrior of the gender jihad returns to her maker after a life well lived," Shamima Shaikh Website, 2004, http://shams.za.org/sundayind.htm.

24. Several verses from Surat al-Nisa°, the fourth chapter of the Qur°an entitled "Women," are devoted to fighting with arms or *qital.*

25. Fatima Umar Naseef, *Women in Islam: A Discourse in Rights and Obligations* (New Delhi: Sterling Publishers, 1999), 152.

26. www.alsalafyoon.com/alsalafiyat/jihad.htm, accessed July 2002.

27. Naseef, *Women in Islam,* 153.

28. Ibid.

29. Zaynab al-Ghazali, *Ayyam min hayati* (Al-Qahirah: Dar al-Shuruq, 1988).

30. Valerie Hoffman, "Muslim Fundamentalists: Psychosocial Profiles," in Martin E. Marty and R. Scott Appleby, eds., *Fundamentalisms Comprehended* (Chicago: University of Chicago Press, 1995), 213.

31. In her tafsir (commentary), *Nazarat fi kitab Allah,* al-Ghazali retains a masculinist bias. For example, she remains neutral about 2:216 that Naseef had used as an argument for women's participation in jihad. She does not comment on the fact that *qital* entails bearing arms. All she says is that it is incumbent on all Muslims, without specifying gender, to protect their lands and their faith: see Zaynab al-Ghazali Jubayli, *Nazarat fi Kitab Allah* (Al-Qahirah: Dar al-Shuruq, 1994), 130.

32. Soroya Duval, "New Veils and New Voices: Islamist Women's Groups in Egypt," in Karin Ask and Marit Tjomsland, eds., *Women and Islamization: Contemporary Dimensions of Discourse on Gender Relations* (Oxford: Berg, 1998), 58.

33. Ibid., 62.

34. David Pinault, "Zaynab Bint 'Ali and the Place of the Women of the House-

holds of the First Imams in Shi'ite Devotional Literature," in Hambly, *Women in the Medieval Islamic World*, 91.

35.　Ibid., 94; see also Minou Reeves, *Female Warriors of Allah: Women and the Islamic Revolution* (New York: Dutton, 1989), 128.

36.　Reeves, *Female Warriors*, 115–129.

37.　Ibid., 101.

38.　Ibid., 173–174.

39.　Haleh Esfandiari, "The Majles and Women's Issues in the Islamic Republic of Iran," in Mahnaz Afkhami and Erika Friedl, eds., *In the Eye of the Storm: Women in Post-Revolutionary Iran* (Syracuse, N.Y.: Syracuse University Press, 1994), 68.

40.　Janet Afary, "Portraits of Two Islamist Women: Escape from Freedom or Escape from Tradition?" *Critique: Journal for Critical Studies of the Middle East*, no. 19 (Fall 2001): 65.

41.　Ibid., 68.

42.　Ibid., 71,75.

43.　See Reeves, *Female Warriors*, 22–23; see also Afary, "Portraits of Two Islamist Women."

44.　Al Sharif, "Resistance and Remembrance," 125, 140.

45.　Ibid., 48.

46.　Ibid., 49.

47.　The women used "Huda" as a code word to "undermine Baath surveillance and to advance their own cause, either for personal safety or actual government protest. . . . (Bint al-Huda) remained an important icon in the women's opposition . . . the women's movement against the regime followed in her footsteps" (Ibid., 35).

48.　Maria Holt, "Lebanese Shi'i Women and Islamism: A Response to War," in Lamia Rustum Shehadeh, ed., *Women and War in Lebanon* (Gainesville, Fla.: University Press of Florida, 1999).

49.　Ibid., 187.

50.　Afary, "Portraits of Two Islamist Women," 56.

51.　cooke, *Women Claim Islam*, 107–138.

52.　The "Women's Information Office in the Arabian Peninsula" targets young people with its online jihad training magazine. AFP, The Hindustan Times.com. http://www.hindustantimes.com/news/7242_987838,00180007.htm.

53.　For an excellent discussion of imperial feminism and Afghan women, see Zillah Eisenstein, *Against Empire: Feminisms, Racism, and the West* (London: Zed Books, 2004), 148–180.

54.　Laura Bush, "Radio Address by Mrs. Bush" (Nov. 17, 2001). The White House Website, 2004. http://www.whitehouse.gov/news/releases/2001/11/20011117.html.

55.　Gregg Zoroya, "Her decision to be a suicide bomber," *USA Today*, April 22, 2002: A.01.

56.　In October 2002, forty Chechen militants took over a Moscow theater, and eighteen of the hostage takers were discovered to be women. In late August 2004, two Chechen women hijacked Russian airplanes and blew themselves and the passengers up.

57.   Ambassador Ellen Sauerbrey, "Commission on the Status of Women (CSW) 48th Session, March 2004," *International Women's Issues Newsletter: Spring-Summer 2004,* U.S. Department of State, 2004, http://www.state.gov/g/wi/31998.htm.

58.   Judith Butler, *Precarious Life: The Powers of Mourning and Violence* (New York: Verso, 2003), 41.

59.   Ibid.

60.   Ibid., 48.

9   Who Defended the Country?

Elaine Scarry

For the past year, we have spoken unceasingly about the events of September 11,
2001. But one aspect of that day has not yet been the topic of open discussion:
the difficulty we had as a country defending ourselves. As it happened, the only
successful defense was carried out not by our professional defense apparatus but
by the passengers on Flight 93, which crashed in Pennsylvania. The purpose of
this essay is to examine that difficulty, and the one success, and ask if they suggest that something in our defense arrangements needs to be changed. Whatever the ultimate answer to that question, we at least need to ask it since defending the country is an obligation we all share.

Speed and Security

The difficulty of defense on September 11 turned in large part on the
pace of events. We need to look carefully at the time lines and timetables on
that day. But as we do, it is crucial to recall that the word "speed" did not surface
for the first time on September 11. It has been at the center of discussions of
national defense for the past fifty years. When we look to any of our literature
on the subject, we find in the foreground statements about the speed of our
weapons, of our weapons' delivery systems, and of the deliberations that will
lead to their use.

Throughout this period, the heart of our defense has been a vast missile system, all parts of which are described as going into effect in "a matter of minutes": a presidential decision must be made in "a matter of minutes"; the presidential order must be transmitted in "a matter of minutes"; the speed of the
missile launch must be carried out "in a matter of minutes"; and the missile
must reach its target in "a matter of minutes."

The matter-of-minutes claim is sometimes formally folded into the names of
our weapons (as in the Minuteman missile) and other times appears in related
banner words such as "supersonic" and "hair-trigger."[1] Thousands of miles

separating countries and continents can be contracted by "supersonic" missiles and planes that carry us there in "a matter of minutes," and thousands of miles separating countries and continents can be contracted by focusing on the distance that has to be crossed not by the weapon itself but by the hand gesture that initiates the launch—the distance of a hair.

"Speed" has occupied the foreground not only of our *descriptive* statements about our national defense but also our *normative* statements. Our military arrangements for defending the country have often been criticized for moving increasingly outside the citizenry's control. The constitutional requirement for a congressional declaration of war has not been used for any war since World War II; the Korean War, the Vietnam War, and the war in former Yugoslavia were all carried out at the direction of the president and without a congressional declaration, as were the invasions of Panama, Grenada, and Haiti.[2] Speed has repeatedly been invoked to counter ethical, legal, or constitutional objections to the way our weapons policies and arrangements have slipped further and further beyond democratic structures of self-governance.

This bypassing of the Constitution in the case of conventional wars and invasions has been licensed by the existence of nuclear weapons and by the country's formal doctrine of Presidential First Use, which permits the president, acting alone, to initiate nuclear war.[3] Since the president has genocidal injuring power at his personal disposal, obtaining Congress's permission for much lesser acts of injury (as in conventional wars) has often struck presidents as a needless bother.[4] The most frequent argument used to excuse the setting aside of the Constitution is that the pace of modern life simply does not allow time for obtaining the authorization of Congress, let alone the full citizenry. Our ancestors who designed the Constitution—so the argument goes—simply had no picture of the supersonic speed at which the country's defense would need to take place. So the congressional requirement is an anachronism. With planes and weapons traveling faster than the speed of sound, what sense does it make to have a lot of sentences we have no time to hear?

Among the many revelations that occurred on September 11 was a revelation about our capacity to act quickly. Speed—the *realpolitik* that has excused the setting aside of the law for fifty years—turns out not to have been very *real* at all. The description that follows looks at the timetables of American Airlines Flight 77—the plane that hit the Pentagon—and United Airlines Flight 93—the plane that crashed in Pennsylvania when passengers successfully disabled the hijackers' mission. Each of the two planes was a small piece of U.S. ground. Their juxtaposition indicates that a form of defense that is external to the ground that needs to be defended does not work as well as a form of defense that is internal to the ground that needs to be defended. This outcome precisely matches the arguments that were made at the time of the writing of the Constitution about why the military had to be "held within a civil frame," about why military actions, whether offensive or defensive, must be measured against the norms of civilian life, must be brought into contact with the people with whom one farms or performs shared labor, or the people with whom one raises children, or the people with whom one goes to church or a weekly play or movie. Preserving such a civil frame was needed to prevent the infantilization of the country's population by its own leaders, and because it was judged to be the only plausible way actually to defend the home ground.

When the plane that hit the Pentagon and the plane that crashed in Pennsylvania are looked at side by side, they reveal two different conceptions of national defense: one model is authoritarian, centralized, top down; the other, operating in a civil frame, is distributed and egalitarian. Should anything be inferred from the fact that the first form of defense failed and the second succeeded? This outcome obligates us to review our military structures and to consider the possibility that we need a democratic, not a top-down, form of defense. At the very least, the events of September 11 cast doubt on a key argument that, for the past fifty years, has been used to legitimize an increasingly centralized, authoritarian model of defense—namely the argument based on speed.

American Flight 77

American Airlines Flight 77 was originally scheduled to fly from Washington to Los Angeles. The plane approached the Pentagon at a speed of 500 mph.[5] It entered the outermost of the building's five rings, ring E, then cut through ring D and continued on through ring C, eventually stopping just short of ring B.[6] Two million square feet were damaged or destroyed.[7] Before September 11, the Pentagon was five corridors deep, five stories high, and five-sided in shape. Three of the Pentagon's five sides were affected (one had to be leveled and rebuilt; the other two were badly damaged by smoke and water).

The crash killed 189 people—64 on the plane, 125 working in the Pentagon. Many others were badly burned.[8] Thousands of people work in the Pentagon.[9] Two factors prevented many more people from being killed or badly burned. First, the building is stacked horizontally, not vertically like the World Trade Center towers—it is built like layers of sedimentary rock that have been turned on their side and lie flush with the ground. Second, one of the sections hit was being renovated and was therefore relatively empty of people when the plane entered.

While we continue to lament the deaths and injuries, and while we continue to find solace in the fact that the number of deaths and injuries was not higher, one key fact needs to be held on to and stated in a clear sentence: on September 11, the Pentagon could not defend the Pentagon, let alone the rest of the country.

The U.S. military had precious little time to respond on September 11 (and this fact has been accurately acknowledged by almost everyone, both inside and outside the country, who has spoken about the day). But by the standards of speed that have been used for the past fifty years to justify setting aside constitutional guarantees, the U.S. military on September 11 had a luxurious amount of time to protect the Pentagon. They had more than minutes. The pilots of the F-15s and F-16s that flew on September 11 made no mistakes, displayed no inadequacies, and showed no lack of courage—but what they tried to do now appears to have been a structural impossibility.

One hour and twenty-one minutes go by between the moment FAA controllers learn that multiple planes have been taken and the moment the Pentagon is struck. Controllers hear the hijackers on the first seized plane (American Flight 11) say "we have some planes" at 8:24 A.M., a sentence indicating that the plane from which the voice comes is not the sole plane presently imperiled. The information that "some planes" have been taken is available one hour and twenty-one minutes before the Pentagon is hit by the third seized plane at 9:45 A.M.[10]

Fifty-eight minutes go by between the attack on the first World Trade Center tower (at 8:47 A.M.) and the crash into the Pentagon (9:45 A.M.). This means that for almost one hour before the Pentagon is hit, the military knows that the hijackers have multiple planes and that those hijackers have no intention of landing those planes safely.

The crash of American Flight 77 into the Pentagon comes *fifty-five minutes* after that plane has now itself disappeared from radio contact (at 8:50 A.M.). So for fifty-five minutes, the military now knows three things:

1. the hijackers have multiple planes;
2. the hijackers—far from having any intention of landing the planes safely— intend to injure as many people on the ground as possible;[11] and
3. Flight 77 has *a chance* of being one of those planes since it has just disappeared from radio contact.

When, six minutes later, the plane loses its transponder (so that its radar image as well as its radio contact is now lost), the chance that it is one of the seized planes rises.

By the most liberal reading, then, the country had *one hour and twenty-one minutes* to begin to respond. By the most conservative reading, the country had *fifty-five minutes* to begin to respond.[12] The phrase "begin to respond" does not mean that an F-15 or F-16 could now attack the plane that would hit the Pentagon. At the one-hour-and-twenty-one-minute mark, the plane that will eventually hit the Pentagon is only four minutes into its flight and has not yet been hijacked. It means instead that a warning threshold has just been crossed and a level of readiness might therefore begin: at one hour and twenty-one minutes, fighter pilots could be placed on standby on the ground with engines running; at fifty-five minutes, fighter planes could be following the third plane, as well as any other planes that are wildly off course and out of radio contact.

One hour and twenty-one minutes and *fifty-five minutes* are each a short time—a short, short time. But . . . by the timetables we have for decades accepted as descriptive of our military weapons, by the timetables we have accepted as explanations for why we must abridge our structures of self-governance —by the intoxicating timetables of "rapid response," the proud specifications of eight minutes, twelve minutes, four minutes, one minute—the September 11 time periods of one hour and twenty-one minutes or of fifty-five minutes are very long periods indeed.

The transition from the moment Flight 77's radio is off (at 8:50 A.M.) to the moment it disappears from secondary radar (8:56 A.M.) is crucial, for it begins to confirm the inference that this is one of the hijacked planes.[13] A sequence of confirmations now follows. While the FAA controllers have been unable to reach the plane, now the airline company also discovers its inability to reach Flight 77 on a separate radio (shortly after 9 A.M.).[14] At 9:25 a passenger, Barbara Olson, places a phone call to her husband Theodore Olson in the U.S. Justice Department stating that the plane is under the control of hijackers.[15] Because the passenger is well-known to the Justice Department listener, no time need be lost assessing the honesty and accuracy of the report. This means that twenty minutes prior to the moment the Pentagon is hit, the Justice Department has direct, reliable voice confirmation of the plane's seizure.

So for *twenty minutes* prior to the hitting of the Pentagon, the military is in the position to know three things (the third of which differs decisively from what it knew at the fifty-five-minute mark):

1. the hijackers have multiple planes;
2. the hijackers intend to injure as many people as possible;
3. Flight 77 is *certainly* one of the hijacked planes. It has disappeared from radio contact, has disappeared from secondary radar, has disappeared from the company radio, and has been described to the Justice Department as "hijacked" by a passenger whose word cannot be doubted.

The steadily mounting *layers of verification* listed in number 3 continue. At 9:33 A.M., an FAA air traffic controller sees on radar a "fast-moving blip" (or "fast-moving primary target") making its way toward Washington airspace. This level of verification comes *twelve minutes* prior to the plane's crash into the Pentagon. At 9:36 A.M. an airborne C-130 sees the plane itself and identifies it as a "757 moving low and fast."[16] This further confirmation comes *nine minutes* prior to the collision. No one can suppose that in nine minutes planes could be scrambled and reach the hijacked plane (even if we have, for decades, listened dutifully to descriptions of much more complicated military acts occurring in nine minutes). But certainly the layers of alert, of scrambling, of takeoff, of tracking, could have begun one hour and twenty minutes earlier, or fifty-five minutes earlier, not nine minutes earlier. Nine minutes is presumably the time frame in which only the last act of military defense need be carried out by the fighter planes—if there is any reasonable last act to be taken, a question to which I will return.

During much of its flight, American Flight 77 was over countryside (rather than over densely populated urban areas).[17] The six successive layers of verification need to be spatially displayed so that we can begin to picture where the plane was during each of them:

- loss of radio contact (fifty-five minutes remain)
- loss of transponder (forty-nine minutes remain)

- loss of contact with the airline company (approximately thirty-six minutes remain)
- a passenger calls the Justice Department (twenty minutes remain)
- a radar image whose source is not using its official "secondary" radar is seen moving toward Washington (twelve minutes remain)
- a C-130 sights a Boeing 757 flying fast and low (nine minutes remain)

Assuming an airspeed of 500 mph, we can infer that at the time we learn that both the radio and the transponder are off (*the second layer of confirmation*), the plane would be 410 miles from Washington, with many miles of sparsely populated land beneath it.[18] By *the fourth confirmation* (Barbara Olson's phone call), it would be 166 miles from Washington. By *the sixth confirmation*, that given by the C-130, the plane destined for the Pentagon would still be 75 miles from Washington and the possibility of minimizing injury to those on the ground would be rapidly vanishing with each passing mile.

Again, the point here is not to say, "Why couldn't these airmen shoot down the plane?" Time made that extremely difficult. But much smaller units of time have been invoked to explain our battle readiness over the past fifty years and to license the centralization of injuring power rather than a decentralized and distributed authorization across the full citizenry that is, according to the U.S. Constitution, our legal right and our legal responsibility to protect. There is a second profound reason the act could not be (and ought not to have been) carried out—the problem of consent, to which I will return when we come to United Flight 93.

Let us see what actions the military undertook during this time. The country has fourteen National Guard planes responsible for defending the country. Five of those planes—two F-15s from Otis Air Force Base on Cape Cod and three F-16s from Langley in Virginia—were called into action on September 11. These five planes were not the only military planes in the air that day. Once the Pentagon was hit, the FAA ordered all aircraft to land in a beautifully choreographed landing of 4,546 planes over a period of three hours. When the FAA announced the order, 206 military planes were in U.S. airspace (most engaged in routine exercises, actions unconnected to the immediate defense of the country); ninety remained in the air after the grounding (their duties have not been entered into the public record).[19] But it is only the five National Guard planes that were called into action against the seized passenger airliners that will be described here.

The two National Guard F-15s that took off from Otis Air Force Base on Cape Cod attempted to address the events taking place in New York City. They were called into action one minute before the first World Trade Center tower was hit; by the time the second tower was hit they were seventy-one miles— eight minutes—away from Manhattan. Should they then have continued down to the Washington area? (By this time, the plane destined for the Pentagon had its radio and transponder off and was reachable by neither air controllers nor

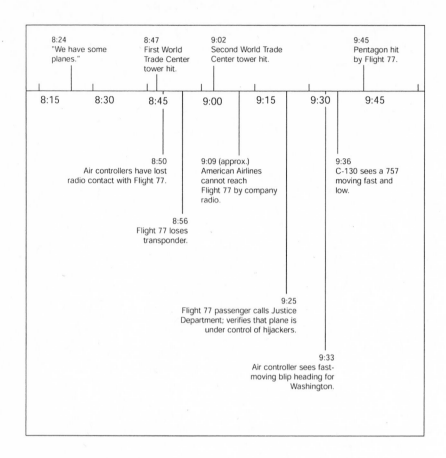

Figure 9.1. American Airlines 77
Elaine Scarry

the airline company.) The answer is no. The two F-15s needed to stay near New York City, where it was reasonable to worry that a third hijacked plane could approach. From September 11, 2001, until March 21, 2002, New York airspace was protected twenty-four hours a day by F-15s, F16s, and AWACS.

Three F-16s at Langley, Virginia, received their first order from Huntress Defense Section at 9:24 A.M. This is a late start: twenty-two minutes after the second World Trade Center tower has been hit, thirty-four minutes after the plane destined for the Pentagon has lost its radio, twenty-eight minutes after it has disappeared from secondary radar, and fifteen minutes after the airline company has failed to reach the plane on its own radio. By 9:30 A.M., the three Langley F-16s are in the air traveling at 600 mph toward New York City. Soon they are instructed to change their course and are told that Reagan National Airport is the target. They are flying at 25,000 feet.[20] The hijacked plane is flying at 7,000 feet. They reach Washington, D.C., at some unspecified time after the 9:45 collision of Flight 77 into the Pentagon. As they pass over the city, they are asked to look down and confirm that the Pentagon is on fire—confirmation that by this point civilians on the ground have already provided.

There are profoundly clear reasons why the military could not easily intercept the plane and bring it down in a rural area. But each of those reasons has counterparts in our longstanding military arrangements that should now be subjected to rigorous questioning. First, Flight 77's path was hard to track since its transponder had been turned off. Yes, that's true—and so, too, any missiles fired on the United States or its allies will surely be traveling without a transponder; their path will not be lucid; their tracking will not be easy. Second, the fact that Flight 77's radio was not working couldn't be taken as a decisive sign that it was a hijacked plane since at least eleven planes in the country had radios not working (nine of the eleven unconnected to the hijackings). Yes, that's true—and with missile defense there are likely to be not eleven but hundreds of decoys and false targets that will have to be nimbly sorted through. As difficult as it was to identify the third seized plane, it must be acknowledged that the flight had elements that made it far easier to identify than would be the enemy missiles our nation has spoken blithely about for decades. The direct voice confirmation provided by the passenger phone call to the Justice Department, most notably, will not have any counterpart on a missile attack, nor can we reasonably expect six layers of verification of any one enemy plane or missile.

A third crucial explanation for the failure to protect the Pentagon is that an F-16 cannot shoot down a passenger plane by arrogating to itself the right to decide whether the lives on board can be sacrificed to avert *the possibility* of even more lives being lost on the ground.[21] Yes, that is true—and yet for decades we have spoken about actions that directly imperil the full American citizenry (including presidential first use of nuclear weapons against a population that the president acting alone has decided is "the enemy") without ever obtaining the American citizenry's consent to those actions.

Each of these three explanations for why the attack on the Pentagon could not be easily averted raises key questions about our longstanding descriptions of the country's defense, and yet so far they do not appear to have in any way altered those descriptions. September 11 has caused the United States and its allies to adjust their timetables only in those cases where the scenario imagined closely approximates the events that occurred in the terrorist attack itself. In England, for example, "MI5 has warned Ministers that a determined terrorist attempt to fly a jet into the Sellafield nuclear plant in Cumbria could not be prevented because it is only *two minutes'* flying time from transatlantic flight paths."[22]

While two minutes' time makes it impossible to defend Cumbria against terrorists, *two minutes* is apparently plenty of time for carrying out missile defense by the United States and NATO allies. Here is a post–September 11 description of England's "Joint Rapid Reaction Force": "A new satellite communications system has been installed to allow planners in Northwood to transmit target co-ordinates to the royal Navy's nuclear submarines equipped to fire Tomahawk cruise missiles. HMS *Trafalgar* and HMS *Triumph* in the Indian Ocean both have this system. *Within minutes* of the Prime Minister giving permission to fire from Downing Street, General Reith could pass on the orders to the submarine nominated to launch the precision attack."[23] What would be the response by Western democracies if a terrorist now used chemical, biological, or even nuclear weapons? In an article describing advice to Tony Blair from his defense ministers, we learn that "one of his most trusted advisers believes that a highly effective way of preventing such an attack is to threaten states that succor the terrorists with a nuclear wipe-out, *within minutes* of such an attack, without waiting for intelligence reports, United Nations resolutions or approval from NATO."[24] Does the Bush administration have plans in place for such attack? Might it be our duty to inquire?

The plane that took the Pentagon by surprise could not be stopped despite a *one-hour-and-twenty-one-minute* warning that multiple planes had been hijacked, despite a *fifty-eight-minute* warning that the hijackers intended to maximize the number of casualties, despite a *fifty-five-minute* warning that Flight 77 might *possibly* be a hijacked flight, and despite a *twenty-minute* warning that Flight 77 was *certainly* a hijacked flight. Yet so confident are we of our ability to get information, of our power to decipher complex lines of responsibility, of the existence of evil and of the transparency of that evil, that we are still today talking about the two or three minutes to send cruise missiles and even nuclear genocide to foreign populations. This despite eleven months—475,000 minutes—in which we have been unable to determine who sent anthrax to the U.S. Senate and various centers of television communication.[25]

United Flight 93

United Airlines Flight 93 was a small piece of American territory—roughly 600 cubic meters in its overall size. It was lost to the country for approximately forty minutes when terrorists seized control. It was restored to the country when civilian passengers who became citizen-soldiers regained control of the ground—in the process losing their own lives.

The passengers on United Flight 93 were able to defend this ground for two reasons. First, they were able to identify the threat accurately because it was in their immediate sensory horizon (unlike the F-16s that hoped to intercept the plane that hit the Pentagon, the passengers on Flight 93 did not need to decipher their plane's flight path from the outside, nor make inferences and guesses about lost radio contact). The passengers were also able to get information from unimpeachable sources external to the plane; crucially, they did not rely on information from a single central authority but obtained it from a distributed array of sources, each independent of the others. Second, it was their own lives they were jeopardizing, their own lives over which they exercised authority and consent. On the twin bases of sentient knowledge and authorization, their collaborative work met the democratic standard of "informed consent."

When the U.S. Constitution was completed, it had two provisions for ensuring that decisions about war-making were distributed rather than concentrated. The first was the provision for a congressional declaration of war—an open debate in both the House and the Senate involving what would today be 535 men and women. The second was a major clause of the Bill of Rights—the Second Amendment right to bear arms—which rejected a standing executive army (an army at the personal disposal of president or king) in favor of a militia, a citizen's army distributed across all ages, geography, and social class of men.[26] Democracy, it was argued, was impossible without a distributed militia; self-governance was perceived to be logically impossible without self-defense (exactly *what* do you "self-govern" if you have ceded the governing of your own body and life to someone else?).

United Flight 93 was like a small legislative assembly or town meeting. Figure 9.2 shows the assembly structure. The residents on that ground conferred with one another, as well as with people not residing on the plane. Records from the on-board telephones show that twenty-four phone calls were made between 9:31 A.M. and 9:54 A.M.; additional calls were made from cell phones.[27] In approximately *twenty-three minutes*, the passengers were able collectively to move through the following sequence of steps:[28]

1. *Identify the location throughout the plane of all hijackers and how many people each is holding.* We know that passengers registered this information in detail because they voiced the information to people beyond the plane: Todd Beamer relayed the information to Lisa Jefferson (a Verizon customer service operator); Jeremy Glick relayed it to his wife;[29] Sandy Bradshaw to her husband; Mark Bingham to his mother; Marion Britton to a close friend; Elizabeth Wainio to her stepmother; and CeeCee Lyles to her husband.

In terms of democratic self-defense, these conversations are crucial (both at step one and at each of the seven steps listed below) to preserving the civil frame that the founders identified as so essential to military defense. The conversations enabled extraordinary events to be tested against the norms of everyday life. They were both intimate and an act of record-making: how else to explain Mark Bingham's self-identification to his mother, "This is Mark Bingham"? He both gave his mother the statement that the plane had been seized by hijackers ("You believe me, don't you?") and in effect notarized the statement by giving a verbal signature.

2. *Hear from sources outside the plane the story of World Trade Center towers.* This information was key: it informed the passengers that they would almost certainly not be making a safe landing, and it informed them that many people on the ground would also suffer death or injury from their plane.

3. *Verify by multiple sources outside the plane the World Trade Center story.* Jeremy Glick, for example, told his wife that the account of the World Trade Center attacks was circulating among the passengers. He explicitly asked her to confirm or to deny its truth: "Is it true?"

4. *Consult with each other and with friends outside the plane about the appro-*

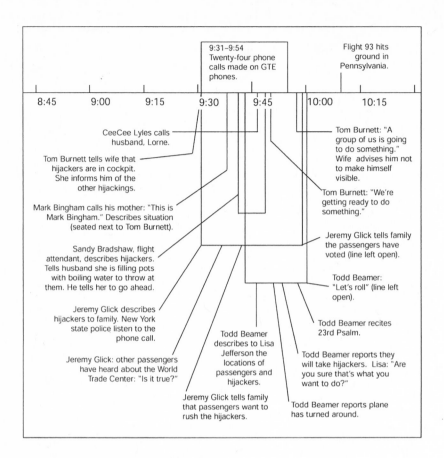

Figure 9.2. United Airlines 93
Elaine Scarry

priate action. Jeremy Glick told his family the passengers were developing a plan "to rush" the hijackers and he asked their advice. Todd Beamer told Lisa Jefferson the passengers will "take" the terrorists (she cautioned: "Are you sure that's what you want to do?"). Tom Burnett told his wife a group of passengers were "going to do something" (she urged him to lay low and not make himself visible). Sandy Bradshaw told her husband she was at that moment filling coffee pots with boiling water, which she planned to throw at the hijackers; she asked if he had a better plan (he told her she had the best plan and to go ahead).

5. *Take a vote.* Jeremy Glick described the voting process to his wife as it was under way.

6. *Prepare themselves for taking a dire action that may result in death.* CeeCee Lyles, unable to reach her husband, left on the phone a recording of herself praying, then later reached him and prayed with him; Tom Burnett asked his wife

to pray while he and others on the plane acted; Todd Beamer and Lisa Jefferson together recited the Twenty-third Psalm.

7. *Take leave of people they love.* Each of the passengers who was in conversation with a family member stated aloud his or her love for the listener; Todd Beamer asked Lisa Jefferson to convey his love to his family. The family members reciprocated: "I've got my arms around you," Elizabeth Wainio's stepmother told her.

8. *Act.*

Many passengers described the plan to enter the cockpit by force. Not every passenger assumed death was certain. Jeremy Glick left his phone off the hook, telling his wife, "Hold the phone. I'll be back." Todd Beamer also left the phone line open—either because he expected to come back, or as an act of public record-keeping. The two open lines permitted members of the Glick household and Lisa Jefferson to overhear the cries and shouts that followed, indicating that action was being taken. CeeCee Lyles, still on the phone with her husband, cried, "They're doing it! They're doing it!" Confirmation is also provided by Sandy Bradshaw's sudden final words to her husband: "Everyone's running to first class. I've got to go. Bye."[30]

The passengers on United Flight 93 could act with speed because they resided on the ground that needed to be defended. Equally important, they could make the choice—formalized in their public act of an open vote—between certain doom and uncertain (but possibly more widespread) doom. They could have hoped that the hijackers would change their planned course; they could have known that death by either avenue was certain, but one avenue would take them to their deaths in several minutes (rushing the hijackers and crashing the plane) and the other avenue would perhaps give them another half-hour or hour of life (waiting for the plane to reach its final target). They could have chosen the second; many people have chosen a delayed death when given the same choice. It is, in any event, the right of the people who themselves are going to die to make the decision, not the right of pilots in an F-16 or the person giving orders to the person in the F-16—as both civilian and military leaders have repeatedly acknowledged since September 11.

It may be worth taking note of the fact that the hijackers themselves correctly foresaw that the threat to their mission would come from the passengers ("citizen soldiers") and not from a military source external to the plane. The terrorists left behind them multiple copies of a manual, five pages in Arabic.[31] The manual is a detailed set of instructions for the hours before and after boarding the plane—"an exacting guide for achieving the unity of body and spirit necessary for success." The ritualized set of steps includes taking a mutual pledge to die; carrying out a ritual act of washing, invocation, and prayer; and dressing according to prescribed recommendations on the tightness or looseness of clothing.

The manual does not tell the terrorists what to do if an F-15 or F-16 approaches the planes they have seized.[32] It instead gives elaborate instruction on what to do if passengers offer resistance. We should not ordinarily let ourselves be schooled by terrorists. But terrorists who seek to carry out a mission success-fully have to know what the greatest threat to their mission is—and the hand-book indicates that the great obstacles were perceived to be first, the passengers, and second, the reluctance the hijackers might feel to kill any resisting passen-gers. They are instructed at length and in elaborate detail to kill any resister and to regard the killing as "a sacred drama," a death carried out to honor their par-ents. (That the hijackers would unblinkingly crash into a skyscraper, taking thousands of lives, yet balk at the idea of killing people hand-to-hand and there-fore require detailed counseling to get through it is perhaps no more surprising than the fact that we listen every day to casualty rates brought about by the military yet would not keenly kill in hand-to-hand combat.)

I have intended here to open a conversation about our general capacity for self-defense. I have compared the fate of the plane that hit the Pentagon and the plane that crashed in Pennsylvania. The military was unable to thwart the action of Flight 77 despite fifty-five minutes in which clear evidence existed that the plane might be held by terrorists, and despite twenty minutes in which clear evidence existed that the plane was certainly held by terrorists. In the same amount of time—twenty-three minutes—the passengers of Flight 93 were able to gather information, deliberate, vote, and act.[33]

September 11 involved a partial failure of defense. If ever a country has been warned that its arrangements for defense are defective, the United States has been warned. Standing quietly by while our leaders build more weapons of mass destruction and bypass more rules and more laws (and more citizens) simply continues the unconstitutional and—as we have recently learned—ineffective direction we have passively tolerated for fifty years. We share a responsibility to deliberate about these questions, as surely as the passengers on Flight 93 shared a responsibility to deliberate about how to act. The failures of our current de-fense arrangements put an obligation on all of us to review the arrangements we have made for protecting the country. "All of us" means "all of us who reside in the country," not "all of us who work at the Pentagon" or "all of us who con-vene when there is a meeting of the Joint Chiefs of Staff." What the chiefs of staff think, or what analysts at the Pentagon think, is of great interest (as are the judgments of men and women who by other avenues of expertise have thought-ful and knowledgeable assessments of security issues); it would be a benefit to the country if such people would now begin to share those views with the pub-lic. But such views can in no way pre-empt or abridge our own obligation to review matters, since the protection of the country falls to everyone whose country it is.

More particularly, September 11 called into question a key argument that has been used to legitimate the gradual shift from an egalitarian, all-citizens' mili-tary to one that is external to—independent of—civilian control: the argument from speed. The egalitarian model turned out to have the advantage of swift-ness, as well as obvious ethical advantages. This outcome has implications for three spheres of defense.

1. *Defense against aerial terrorism.* To date, the egalitarian model of defense is the only one that has worked against aerial terrorism. It worked on September 11 when passengers brought down the plane in Pennsylvania. It again worked on December 22, 2001, when passengers and crew on an American Airlines flight from Paris to Miami prevented a terrorist (now called "the shoe bomber") from blowing up the plane with plastic explosives and killing 197 people on board. Two Air Force F-15s escorted the plane to Boston and, once the plane landed, FBI officials hurried aboard, but the danger itself was averted not by the fighter jets or the FBI but by men and women inside the plane who restrained the six-foot-four-inch man using his own hair, leather belts, earphone wires, and sedatives injected by two physicians on board.

When a passenger plane is seized by a terrorist, defense from *the outside* (by a fighter jet, for example) appears to be structurally implausible from the perspective of time, and structurally impossible from the perspective of consent. The problem of time—time to identify that a plane has been seized, time to identify accurately which plane it is, time to arrive in the airspace near the seized plane—was dramatically visible in the case of the plane that hit the Pentagon, even though much more time and more layers of verification were available that day than are likely to be available in any future instance. The time difficulty was visible again on January 5, 2002, when a fifteen-year-old boy took off without authorization from Petersburg-Clearwater International Airport, crossed through the airspace of MacDill Air Force Base (the headquarters for the U.S. war in Afghanistan), and then flew into a forty-two-story Bank of America skyscraper in Tampa, hitting at the twenty-eighth floor. Two F-15 fighter jets "screamed" toward him from the south, but reached him only after he had completed his twenty-five-minute flight.[34] The time problem was visible once more on June 19, 2002, when a pilot and passenger in a Cessna 182 accidentally crossed into forbidden Washington Monument airspace, flew there for twelve miles (coming within four miles of the White House), and then crossed out again before armed F-16s from Andrews Air Force Base could reach them.

Even if the nearly insurmountable problems of time and perfect knowledge can one day be solved, how can the problem of consent be solved? There is no case in war where a soldier is authorized to kill two hundred fellow soldiers; how can an airman be authorized to kill two hundred fellow citizens? How can anyone other than the passengers themselves take their lives in order to save some number of the rest of us on the ground? During the seven months that F-15s and F-16s, armed with air-to-air missiles, flew round the clock over New York and Washington, what instructions did they have in the event that a passenger plane was seized? What instructions do they now have for their more intermittent flights?[35] Are such instructions something only high-ranking officials should be privy to, or might this be something that should be candidly discussed in public?

It seems reasonable to conclude that on September 11 the Pentagon could have been defended in one way and one way only, by the passengers on the American Airlines flight. This would have required three steps: that multiple passengers on the plane be informed about the World Trade Center towers;[36] that the passengers decide to act or instead to abstain from acting; and that, in the event they choose to act, they be numerous enough to successfully carry out their plan. As far as we know, none of these steps took place—in part because, as far as we know, there were not multiple passengers on board who knew about the World Trade Center towers. It is possible that one or more of these steps took place, even though they have not been recorded.

In stating that the egalitarian model is our best and only defense against aerial terrorism, I do not mean that passengers in any one case *must* choose to act or that—having so chosen—they will be successful. I mean only that this is the one form of defense available to us as a country, which passengers are at liberty to exercise or refrain from exercising. Measures taken by the nation that are internal to the plane (locks on cockpit door, the presence of air marshals, the cessation of the round-the-clock fighter jets over New York and Washington[37]) are compatible with this form of defense.

2. *National defense in the immediate present.* The contrast between the plane that hit the Pentagon and the plane that crashed in Pennsylvania invites consideration of the need to return to an egalitarian and democratic military not only in the specific case of aerial terrorism but in all measures we take for the nation's defense in the present year. Some may argue that we cannot generalize from one day. Can we generalize from zero days? One day is what we have. What makes this non-risky is that rather than requiring us to come up with some new system of government, all it requires is returning to, and honoring, the framework of our own laws.

Since September 11 we have witnessed many actions taken in the name of homeland defense that are independent of, or external to, civilian control. Foreign residents have been seized and placed in circumstances that violate our most basic laws; the war against Afghanistan was under way before we had even been given much explanation of its connection to the terrorists, who were all from Saudi Arabia or Lebanon or Egypt or the United Arab Emirates and not from Afghanistan; that war now seems to be over even though we don't know whether we eliminated the small circle around Osama bin Laden, for whose sake we believed we were there; we then tripped rapidly ahead to the next war, listening passively to weekly announcements about an approaching war with Iraq that had no visible connection to the events of September 11; the president's formulation of this future war sometimes seemed to include (or at least, pointedly refrained from excluding) the use of nuclear weapons and the animation of our first-use policy.[38] The decoupling of all defense from the population itself lurches between large outcomes (presidential declaration of war) and the texture of everyday life. According to the former chairman of the Federal Communications Commission, the federal agency called the National Communications Systems has "proposed that government officials be able to take over the wireless networks used by cellular telephones in the event of an emergency," thereby pre-empting the very form of defense that did work (the citizenry) and giving their tools to the form of defense that did not work (the official govern-ment).[39]

We are defending the country by ceding our own powers of self-defense to a set of managers external to ourselves. But can these powers be ceded without relinquishing the very destination toward which we were traveling together, as surely as if our ship had been seized? The destination for which we purchased tickets was a country where no one was arrested without their names being made public, a country that did not carry out wars without the authorization of Congress (and the widespread debate among the population that such a con-gressional declaration necessitates), a country that does not threaten to use weapons of mass destruction. Why are we sitting quietly in our seats?

In the short run, returning to an egalitarian model of defense means no war with a foreign country unless it has been authorized by Congress and the citizenry; no abridgment of civil liberties; no elimination of the tools that en-able citizens to protect themselves and one another (such as cell phones)—and above all, no contemplated use of nuclear weapons.

3. *National defense in the long run.* Europeans often refer to nuclear weapons as "monarchic weapons" precisely because they are wholly external to any pow-ers of consent or dissent exercised by the population. In the long run, the return to an egalitarian model of national defense will require the return to a military that uses only conventional weapons. This will involve a tremendous cost: it will almost certainly, for example, mean the return of a draft. But a draft means that a president cannot carry out a war without going through the citizenry, and going through the citizenry means that the arguments for going to war get tested tens of thousands of times before the killing starts.

Our nuclear weapons are the largest arsenal of genocidal weapons anywhere on earth. These weapons, even when not in use, deliver a death blow to our de-mocracy.[40] But even if we are willing to give up democracy to keep ourselves safe, on what basis have we come to believe that they keep us safe? Their speed? A Cessna plane (of the kind that proved impossible to intercept in Florida and Washington) travels at approximately 136 feet per second; a Boeing 757 (of the kind that proved impossible to intercept as it approached the Pentagon) travels at 684 feet per second; a missile travels at 6,400 feet per second.[41] On what have we based our confidence about intercepting incoming missiles, since the prob-lem of deciphering information and decoupling it from false decoys will (along with speed) be much higher in the case of the missile than in the cases of the planes?[42]

Nuclear weapons are an extreme form of aerial terrorism. It is with good reason that we have worked to prevent the proliferation throughout the world of nuclear weapons (as well as biological and chemical weapons of mass de-struction). But in the long run, other countries of the world will only agree to abstain from acquiring them, or to give them up in cases where they already have them, when and if the United States agrees to give them up. The process of persuading Iraq, China, North Korea, India, Pakistan, as well as our immediate allies, to give them up will commence on the day we agree to restore within our own country a democratic form of self-defense.

Notes

1. As with the matter-of-minutes vocabulary, the hair-trigger description is widely understood to apply either to the material act of firing a weapon or the mental act of deliberating. In January 2001, Peace Links asked U.S. president Clinton and Russian president Putin to take all weapons off "*hair-trigger status*," which gives "both countries *three minutes* to decide whether to launch nuclear missiles once the military tells them it thinks they have spotted an incoming missile." *South Bend Tribune*, April 29, 2001. Italics added. On "hair-trigger" arrangements throughout the last quarter of the twentieth century, see, for example, the opening chapter of Daniel Ford, *The Button: The Pentagon's Strategic Command and Control System* (New York: Simon & Schuster, 1985).

2. On the question of whether the country had a constitutional declaration of war against Iraq in the Gulf War, see Michael J. Glennon, "The Gulf War and the Constitution," *Foreign Affairs* 70 (Spring 1991): 84–101. The October 2002 "Authorization for the Use of Military Force Against Iraq" has key features which distinguish it from a congressional declaration of war.

3. Presidential First Use of Nuclear Weapons became a formal written policy in "Presidential Directive 59" during the Carter administration; it has been the country's official policy during the entire nuclear age. On Eisenhower's deliberations, for example, about using a nuclear weapon in the Taiwan Straits (1954) and again in Berlin (1959), see E. Scarry, "The Declaration of War: Constitutional and Unconstitutional Violence," in Austin Sarat and Thomas Kearns, eds., *Law's Violence*, Amherst Series in Law, Jurisprudence, and Social Thought (Ann Arbor: University of Michigan Press, 1992), 23–77.

4. For example, President George H. W. Bush boasted, "I didn't have to get permission from some old goat in the United States Congress to kick [Iraqi president] Saddam Hussein out of Kuwait" (*Washington Post*, June 21, 1992, A18).

5. On the speed of Flight 77, see note 18 below.

6. "United States Department of Defense News Briefing," *M2 Presswire* for September 17, 2001, states that it broke through the wall of corridor C, penetrating into the driveway that separates ring C from ring B (but it does not cite any damage to the B ring).

7. Angie Cannon, "The 'Other' Tragedy," *U.S. News and World Report* 131:24 (December 10, 2001), 22.

8. ABC News, September 14, 2001, described both the terrible burn injuries and the "wind of fire" spreading through the building. Angie Cannon in "The 'Other' Tragedy" gives an extended account of the injuries. Because no planes could fly into Washington, medical centers from around the country enlisted the help of marathon drivers to carry replacement skin. Two drivers from

Texas, according to Cannon, drove seventy square feet of skin to Washington in twenty-three hours and twelve minutes, stopping only for drive-through sandwiches and bathroom breaks; thirty square feet of skin arrived from Cincinnati in twelve hours; two surgeons at Washington Hospital Center, Dr. Marion Jordan and Dr. James Jeng, "worked 12- to 16-hour days" for three weeks.

9.   The figure of 23,000 is given on the Pentagon web site.

10.   Three different times have been given for the crash of Flight 77 into the Pentagon: 9:38 A.M., 9:41 A.M., and 9:45 A.M. I cite the 9:45 A.M. time because it is given by many different reporters, both as a designation of the minute the plane "pierced" the Pentagon and as the minute interviewed eyewitnesses observed the impact, beginning on September 11 and 12 (CNN broadcasts throughout the afternoon of September 11; *Facts on File* for September 11, 2001; September 12 articles in the *New York Times, Newsday, Chicago Tribune, Atlanta Journal and Constitution, International Herald Tribune, Baltimore Sun*). In the weeks and months that followed, 9:45 A.M. continued to be used in multiple reports both within any single journal (*New York Times,* September 13, 15, 16, and November 4, 2001) and across many different journals (for example, *The New Yorker,* September 23; *Boston Globe,* November 23; *CNN Live,* December 15, 2001). The early time designation of 9:38 A.M. has been introduced into the picture by the Pentagon (at first using the figure of 9:37 A.M.). On September 19, *Facts on File* noted that "the Defense Department placed [the crash] at 9:37 A.M. despite previous reports of 9:45 A.M."; and on the same day, the *New York Times* described 9:37 A.M. as the time "when the Pentagon estimates that the third hijacked jet crashed into the Pentagon." The Pentagon has had a series of commemorations, each beginning at 9:38 A.M. (starting with the three-month ceremony on December 11) and reporters have used this time in covering those events. But as the September through December publication dates listed above indicate, many journals and broadcasts have continued to use the 9:45 A.M. minute in describing the crash of the plane itself.

11.   Presumably only the first of the two World Trade Center collisions was needed for the nation to know this second piece of information, that the seized planes would not land safely. But if one wants to base this knowledge on the destruction of both World Trade Center towers (hit at 8:47 A.M. and 9:02 A.M.), then the nation had forty-three minutes in which it knew that multiple planes were involved, that Flight 77 was likely one of the planes (since it had disappeared from radar even before the second tower was hit), and that no safe landing was likely.

12.   Using the collision time of 9:38 A.M. (rather than 9:45 A.M.), the two periods would be *one hour and fourteen minutes* and *forty-eight minutes.*

13.   The times for the loss of radio contact and transponder are included in Glen Johnson's in-depth account, "Probe Reconstructs Horror," *Boston Globe,* November 23, 2001, 44–45.

14.   At this point, American Airlines lacks any clear idea of the plane's location. At 9:09 A.M., American Airlines thinks Flight 77 may have gone into the second World Trade Center tower.

15.   Barbara Olson also places a second call to the Justice Department several minutes later.

16. The timetable for both the air controllers' and pilots' sightings are given in Matthew L. Wald and Kevin Sack, "A Nation Challenged: The Tapes," *New York Times,* October 16, 2001, 1.

17. The exact flight path must by now have been precisely reconstructed, but it does not yet appear to be part of the public record. In any event, we know that the plane did not steadily circle Washington, D.C., or any other densely populated spot.

18. These mileage estimates are based on the supposition that Flight 77 was flying at the same 500 mph speed at which the World Trade Center planes were flying as they moved down the Hudson Valley at twice the legal airspeed (*New York Times,* October 16, 2001). Both air traffic controllers and the C-130 pilots described Flight 77 as "fast moving." (The *New York Times,* October 16, 2001, states that Flight 77 was moving at 500 mph when it hit the Pentagon. *U.S. News and World Report,* December 10, 2001, says the impact took place at a speed of 350 mph.)

19. See David Bond's detailed account in "Crisis at Herndon: 11 Airplanes Astray," *Aviation Week and Space Technology,* December 17, 2001, 96ff.

20. *New York Times,* October 16, 2001.

21. A retired official of the FAA said several days after the event, "There is no category of 'enemy airliners'" and added that he could recall no incident in which a military plane had ever intentionally attacked a civilian plane in the United States. (Matthew L. Wald, "After the Attacks: Sky Rules," *New York Times,* September 15, 2001, 1.) Major General Mike J. Haugen said that the crash of United Flight 93 initiated by the passengers "kept us from having to do the unthinkable . . . and that is to use your own weapons and own training against your own citizens" (*New York Times,* October 16, 2001).

22. Peter Beaumont, "Bin Laden in Plot to Bomb City: Terror Blue-print for At-tack on London," *The Observer,* December 16, 2001, 1. Italics added.

23. Tim Ripley, "Global Army Controlled from a Suburban Bunker," *The Scots-man,* October 2, 2001, 6. Italics added.

24. Chris Buckland, "Meeting Hell with Horror," *News of the World,* Septem-ber 30, 2001. Italics added.

25. The count of months and minutes here are the figures at the time this article first went to press with *Boston Review* (September 2002). As the article later went to press in book form with Beacon Press (January 2003) the count was fifteen months (648,000 minutes). As it now goes to press in *Terror, Culture, Politics* (March 2005) the count is 41 months (1,771,200 minutes). Once the book appears in print, readers can supply a fourth set of figures should the case remain unsolved.

26. For full analyses of the distributive intention of the right to bear arms, see Elaine Scarry, "War and the Social Contract: Nuclear Policy, Distribution, and the Right to Bear Arms," *University of Pennsylvania Law Review* 139 (May 1991): 1257–1316; and Akhil Reed Amar, *The Bill of Rights* (New Haven, Conn.: Yale University Press, 1998), 46–63.

27. Most of the narrative details of Flight 93 that follow here as well as in Fig-ure 2 come from two sources: "Forty Lives, One Destiny: Fighting Back in the Face of Terror," *Pittsburgh Post-Gazette,* October 28, 2001, a 6,000-word study; and "Final Words from Flight 93," *U.S. News and World Re-port* October 29, 2001, 32f, a story coauthored by Angie Cannon, Janet

Rae-Dupree, Suzie Larsen, and Cynthia Salter. The passenger and crew quotations provided in these two in-depth news stories recur (with small variations) in Jere Longman, *Among the Heroes: United Flight 93 and the Passengers and Crew Who Fought Back* (New York: HarperCollins, 2002), a book which became available after the writing of this article was complete. It contains richly textured portraits of the thirty-seven passengers and seven crew members (both their backgrounds and their actions on September 11). Although the book's purpose is to celebrate the passengers and crew of Flight 93 rather than to raise questions about U.S. defense, the preface notes that "they accomplished what security guards and military pilots and government officials could not" (p. x).

28. The overall time frame, from the moment the passengers first expressed their knowledge of the seizure at 9:31 A.M. to the moment the plane was on the ground at 10:10 A.M., is thirty-nine minutes. The reader may therefore wish to assess the sequence of steps in terms of thirty-nine rather than twenty-three minutes. I have used the twenty-three-minute frame because we only have information up through the moment the passengers collectively decided to act, not during the moments when control of the plane was wrestled over or during the time the plane fell toward the ground (the transcript of the voice recorder from the plane that would provide information about this period has so far been withheld from the public by the FBI).

29. In Jeremy Glick's case, family members used a second phone to contact the New York State Police, who then "patched in" to Jeremy Glick's phone call and listened to the ongoing descriptions of the hijacking he was giving.

30. The withholding of the plane's voice tape from the public has permitted rumors to exist that the military shot the plane down (despite consistent government statements that the military took no action). The open passenger phone lines verify that quite apart from whatever the military did or did not do, the passengers themselves did act. The fact that government officials who have heard the plane's voice tape (most notably President Bush) have publicly celebrated the courage of the passengers reinforces what the public phone lines themselves already make clear.

31. Kanan Makiya and Hassan Mneimneh, trans. and interpreters, "Manual for a 'Raid,'" in *New York Review of Books* 49:1 (January 17, 2002): 18.

32. Perhaps more accurately, they are told that such matters are beyond their own agency: "All [the United States'] . . . equipment and all their gates and all their technology do not do benefit or harm except with the permission of God." In contrast, harm from resistant passengers is not left to God but is something the manual requires the hijackers to address.

33. They left a wide margin of safety: many miles of terrain still stood between the plane and whatever target in Washington or New York was the terrorists' destination.

34. A Coast Guard plane, already in the air, got close enough to instruct him by hand signals to land, but the boy declined to follow these instructions. See Brad Smith, "Skyscraper Hit," *Tampa Tribune*, January 6, 2002, 1.

35. Repeatedly questioned about "rules of engagement" during a news briefing, Secretary of Defense Donald Rumsfeld declined to provide concrete answers: "The normal procedure is not to get into that subject in any detail" ("Federal Document Clearing House Political Transcript," September 27, 2001).

36. The events on the Pennsylvania plane clearly depended on the two-directional exchange of information between passengers and friends on the ground. There is probably a useful generalization that can be made here. Communication on planes between passengers and people on the ground should be made as easy as possible, since the most likely way passengers will get crucial information in an emergency is by being able to speak with friends or family. Emergency telephone links between passengers and government officials (FBI, FAA, Air Force, Pentagon) are much less likely to be helpful because in our present era government officials do not believe in two-directional exchanges of information with citizens.

37. Congressional testimony explaining the cessation of round-the-clock flights (Operation Noble Eagle) focused on the expense in dollars ($50 million a week), in use of airmen (11,000 airmen in comparison with 14,000 airmen for the war in Afghanistan, according to the *New York Times,* March 18, 2002), and in wear and tear on the planes, rather than on the futility of this form of defense. However, the Air Force chief of staff testified to the Senate Armed Services Committee that air marshals inside the planes themselves were a more efficient solution than the fighter jets (Gen. John P. Jumper, March 7, 2002, Senate Armed Services Committee hearing). Because General Jumper was told by Senator John Warner (R-Va) that he should give his assessment of the combat air patrols twice—first in a non-classified and then in a classified form—we do not know his full thoughts on the matter.

38. For example, President Bush's June 1, 2002, graduation speech at West Point had three features which together seemed to make it an announcement (however blurry and genial) of the possibility of a nuclear first strike: it stressed pre-emptive action; it left the form of pre-emption (ground invasion, air strike) unspecified; and it explicitly summoned nuclear weapons, rejecting as inadequate and "too late" the Cold War strategy of "massive retaliation." Transcript, Federal News Service, June 1, 2002. Although immediate news coverage did not mention the word "nuclear," the phrases "first strike" and "pre-emptive first strike" were widely used in the United States (on ABC News, for example, where Sam Donaldson asked, "When do we take these other nations out?") and internationally (headlines for the *London Daily Telegraph, The Guardian, The Independent,* and *The Herald of Glasgow* all described President Bush as warning of a "first strike," and the *Financial Times* emphasized "pre-emptive, unilateral action").

39. Reed Hundt, "A Better Network for Emergency Communications," *New York Times,* December 25, 2001. Discussions of phone use during emergencies often pose the choice of whether we want citizens or instead firemen to have phone access. But during the days following September 11, there were many reports of both citizens and firemen having difficulty completing calls. According to an article in *Government Executive* (October 2001), government executives (including financial leaders, federal executives, utility managers, and relief workers) had a 95 percent success rate in making calls during this period because they are beneficiaries of Government Emergency Telecommunication Service (GETS), which gives their calls priority over ordinary users of "AT&T, Sprint, and WorldCom."

40. For discussion of the democratic structures violated by nuclear weapons, see Elaine Scarry, "War and the Social Contract" and "Declaration of War."

41. See Paul Bracken, *Fire in the East: The Rise of Asian Military Power and the Second Nuclear Age* (New York: HarperCollins, 1999), 64.

42. On the decoy problem, see Stephen Weinberg, "Can Missile Defense Work?" *New York Review of Books* 49:2 (February 14, 2002): "The big problem, as it has been since the days of Nike X, is that any number of interceptor missiles could be used up in attacking decoys that had been sent by the attacker along with its warheads" (42); and Ted Postol, "What's Wrong with Missile Defense?" *Boston Review* 26:5 (October/November 2001): 40–45.

10 The 9/11 Commission Report: Has It Incited a Public Debate about Our Nation's Defense?

Elaine Scarry

Five years have now elapsed since September 11, 2001, and there has still been no debate about our country's defense. Of crucial importance, however, is the fact that during this passage of time there has come into our midst *The 9/11 Commission Report.* Should a public debate *someday, somehow* get underway, this formal report stands ready to be of great assistance, for it provides an excruciatingly exact, fact-laden record of the events of the day.

Of the *Report's* 566 pages, only forty-six—as it happens, the first forty-six—focus on the terrorist attacks and immediate attempts to respond to the hijackings.[1] The *Report* verifies (and supplements[2]) the already-known record of the heroic actions carried out by the passengers on Flight 93. It concludes: "We are sure that the nation owes a debt to the passengers of United 93. Their actions saved the lives of countless others, and may have saved either the Capitol or the White House from destruction."[3]

With equal starkness, the *Report* documents the failure of the formal government and military apparatus to defend the country. About Flight 93, for example, it observes: "NORAD officials have maintained that they would have intercepted and shot down United 93 [had the passengers not done so]. We are not so sure."[4] Indeed, far from being merely "unsure," the *Report* displays a set of facts which indicate that it is almost inconceivable that NORAD could have successfully intervened. The Northeast sector of NORAD—known as NEADS, or North East Air Defense Sector—only learned that Flight 93 had been hijacked four minutes after the plane had crashed.[5] At the point where the passengers stormed the cockpit (9:57 A.M.), the plane was twenty minutes from Washington. According to the Commission's calculations, Flight 93 would have arrived at the nation's capital between 10:13 and 10:23 A.M. But NEADS only received its first shoot-down order at 10:31 A.M.—eight to sixteen minutes behind the hijackers' projected Washington arrival (it is unlikely the terrorists would have spent time circling the city).[6]

The 9/11 Commission does not explicitly invite its readers to juxtapose the unsuccessful actions of the military with the successful actions of the civilian passengers; nor does it explicitly invite readers to contemplate whether our present centralized military, or instead a distributed one, would best serve the nation. However, the failures of the government and military structures are so mercilessly documented that it is hard to see how anyone would make their way through these pages without sensing the vast question looming over us.

Our formal defense apparatus on 9/11 was incapacitated by three genres of trouble, each of which follows from the highly centralized, hierarchical structures of defense. First: in a hierarchical structure, people seem to refrain from giving information to those on a level lower than, or even with, their own. The only direction in which people want to forward information is "up" the ladder. But now a second genre of trouble emerges. Attempts to forward information in an upward direction are often obstructed or resisted by that higher level of the hierarchy; for just as people do not wish *to spread* information *to* those lower than, or equal to, themselves, so they do not wish *to receive* information *from* those lower than themselves. The result of genres one and two is genre three: a stark decoupling of those at the top (and indeed at almost every other level) from any concrete contact with, or effect on, unfolding events.

The *9/11 Commission Report* provides many examples of each of the three genres. An instance of the reluctance to transmit information either laterally or downward occurred when FAA officials (both the Boston air controllers and the directors of northeast sector) failed to tell air controllers throughout the nation of the events unspooling in the northeast corridor. When, therefore, an Indianapolis air controller noticed Flight 77 disappear from radio and secondary radar, he assumed the plane had either crashed or was continuing to travel westward. Using primary radar, the air controller searched for the plane along its scheduled westward track; the idea that it had been hijacked, or that it might have turned around and be moving eastward, did not cross his mind. (The plane flew east for thirty-six minutes, eventually flying into the Pentagon.)[7]

A second instance of the interruption of lateral or downward flowing information occurred after Vice President Cheney gave a "shoot down" order. The order never reached the airborne pilots. It traveled from the vice president to the National Military Command Center to NORAD to NEAD, but was not then transmitted to the pilots. The mission commanders and senior weapons director abstained from passing this information on to the fighter pilots "because they were unsure how the pilots would, or should, proceed with this guidance."[8] A third example concerns the F-16s that were scrambled into the air at Langley Air Force Base in Virginia: although the pilots were ordered up into the air and thus themselves put at risk, no one in the military or the FAA told them that multiple plane hijackings were underway; the pilots therefore assumed the country was being attacked by Russian missiles. Combat with the Russians was an event they had elaborately trained for, but it seems probable that they could have adjusted to the new situation if any concrete, real-time information had been given to them. I myself was in Torino, Italy. Having earlier in the day completed a lecture at a physics conference on electromagnetics, I was in a plaza when a saleswoman in a Ferragamo store began crying out, and explained that planes were flying into the World Trade Towers. It was 9:30 A.M. East Coast time, 3:30 P.M. in Europe. Information was reaching me on a street in Torino, Italy that had not yet reached the pilots in the F16s.

The second genre of transmission problem—where someone attempts to direct information upstream but those upstream refuse to listen—is documented in several excruciating passages such as the following:

> At about 8:55, the controller in charge notified a New York Center manager that she believed United 175 [the second plane that would eventually crash into the World Trade Towers] had also been hijacked. The manager tried to notify the regional managers and was told that they were discussing a hijacked aircraft (presumably American 11) and refused to be disturbed.[9]

A Cleveland air controller, who was tracking Flight 93, asked the FAA Command Center in Herndon, Virginia whether anyone had yet asked the military to send a fighter aircraft. The Commission *Report* then continues:

> Cleveland [i.e., the air controller] even told the [FAA] Command Center it was prepared to contact a nearby military base to make the request. The Command Center told Cleveland that FAA personnel well above them in the chain of command had to make the decision to seek military assistance and were working on the issue.[10]

Had the Cleveland air controller contacted the nearby base, he would have done what a Boston air controller tracking Flight 11 did earlier in the day when he directly called NEADS, the North East Air Defense Sector, who in turn contacted Otis Air Force Base on Cape Cod; the Commission *Report* identifies the Boston air controller's act as bypassing many levels of protocol and formal hierarchy. (His act gave the military nine minutes before the plane hit its target, the longest lead-time of any of the four planes.)[11] Thirteen minutes after the Cleveland air controller asked the FAA Command Center to request the military to send a fighter jet, the FAA Command Center forwarded the request to FAA Headquarters:

> *FAA Headquarters:* They're pulling Jeff away to go talk about United 93.
> *Command Center:* Uh, do we want to think, uh, about scrambling aircraft?
> *FAA Headquarters:* Oh, God, I don't know.
> *Command Center:* Uh, that's a decision somebody's gonna have to make probably in the next ten minutes.
> *FAA Headquarters:* Uh, ya know everybody just left the room.[12]

Meanwhile the Flight 93 passengers—among whom information was freely circulating and who had been steadily trading information with people on the ground—were eight minutes away from storming the cockpit.

One final instance of a failed attempt to push information upstream in the hierarchy (either because the person at the higher level resists listening or is unavailable for listening) concerns Flight 77 at a moment seventeen minutes before it hit the Pentagon. This instance begins with an act of giving information laterally: passenger Barbara Olson twice called her husband, Ted Olson, to tell him

Flight 77 was under the control of hijackers. Ted Olson, the solicitor general in the Justice Department, then tried, unsuccessfully, to forward this information up the hierarchy to Attorney General John Ashcroft.[13] Since no one else yet knew that Flight 77 was hijacked or that it was approaching Washington[14] we can see the benefit that might have come had the solicitor general attempted to spread the information not only upward but laterally and downward—in fact, omnidirectionally.

The first two genres of obstructed communication—the reluctance to share information laterally or down; the intention to distribute information upward that those in the higher location are unwilling or unable to receive—lead to a third genre of trouble, the detachment of people all along the line from any ability to make useful interventions. People occupying the pinnacle of the hierarchy are shown to have carried out a repertoire of actions so detached from the actual events they appear delusional.

Video teleconferencing carried out by the FAA, the White House, and the Pentagon had no concrete effect on defense actions. Participants in the teleconference between the FAA and the Department of Defense later testified to the Commission that the teleconference "played no role in co-coordinating a response to the attacks of 9/11."[15] Inside the Pentagon, the National Military Command Center held a "significant event" teleconference that lasted eight hours and included, at various moments, the president, secretary of defense, and the vice chair of Joint Chiefs of Staff. During the first hour no one from the FAA who had any knowledge of the hijackings was present; by the time Flight 93 crashed, it had not been mentioned as a hijacked plane.[16] The *Report's* description of Vice President Cheney shows him—long after Flight 93 was down—receiving urgent information that the plane is now 80 miles from Washington . . . now 60 miles from Washington. It also shows him informing a puzzled Secretary of Defense Rumsfeld that his shoot-down order has been transmitted to pilots and they have already "taken a couple of aircraft out."[17]

The summary that has been given here of the three genres of problem that attended the official government defense is a simplification of what the *Report* shows. Included here are only the failed acts of tracking *correct* information (the four planes that were actually hijacked). Not included are the many mistakes NORAD or the FAA made in pursuing phantom planes—passenger planes unconnected with the terrorist events. Not included here either is the Commission's repeatedly expressed concern that it has been given incorrect or unverifiable information by someone at the top of the military or executive hierarchy.[18] But the brief summary shows why—should a public debate get underway about whether our current military structures can carry out the work of protecting us—the *Report* (with its relentless attempt to sort out facts and its relentless attempt to verify the truth of all statements) will be an invaluable resource.

Why—given the picture provided by the *9/11 Commission Report*—has the debate not yet begun? As mentioned at the outset, only forty-six of the *Report's* 566 pages are dedicated to the record of the country's attempt to defend itself on September 11. Much of the rest of the *Report* is dedicated to the years and months leading up to the day.[19] Included is a sometimes devastating analysis of the failures of the CIA, FBI, and other intelligence units (there are approximately sixteen such agencies[20]), as well as the failure of the Bush administration to pay attention to intelligence reports. Probably the single most astonishing moment of the Commission's public hearings—and surely the one most widely known to the public—was when Condoleezza Rice was asked if she recalled the title of the August 6, 2001, Presidential Daily Brief from the CIA. Rice calmly responded, "I believe the title was, 'Bin Laden Determined to Attack Inside the United States.'"[21]

The problem of "intelligence" (recognizing it, forwarding it to someone else, overcoming in turn the next person's resistance to recognizing it) reenacts the three genres of trouble visible on the day of 9/11 itself: the reluctance to forward information across and down, the reluctance to pay attention to information coming from below, the nearly delusional separation of those at the top from any concrete pressure or real threats. Public attention *was,* in fact, seized by the Commission hearings and the Commission *Report* (it sold 630,000 copies in the first month). But it was primarily the subject of failed "intelligence"—and the need for a re-organization of the country's intelligence—rather than the question of whether the Pentagon is properly designed to carry out the country's defense that captured national attention.

Given that the public cannot attend to everything, and given that tracking an attack before it begins is crucial to a country's defense, this may seem like a reasonable outcome. It might even be argued that if we have to choose between attending to defense matters that precede a terrorist event or instead attending to defense matters during the actual attack, it is better to concentrate on the first in the hope that we can actually prevent the attack.

But there are at least two major problems with this outcome. First, the events of 9/11 pose the large framing question of whether an executive military or instead a civilian military—a highly centralized, top down military or instead a distributed military—will provide a faster and more effective (as well as a more legal and constitutional) defense for the country. To concern ourselves with "intelligence" locates all our attention on the "executive military" side of the question: the intelligence agencies are primarily an extension of the executive branch of government. Hence we have simply missed the large framing question, and have concerned ourselves with keeping the highly centralized, topdown military and trying to improve it.

Second, what does it mean to say we have given "all our attention" to this matter, or we "have concerned ourselves" with this matter? In fact, the highly secret intelligence branches are none of our concern; the remedies and repairs put forward by the Commission are ones that have to be carried out by the government (yes, the legislature is involved, an important feature; and yes we can voice our opinions to our legislators; but other than stating an opinion, no concrete practice is required of us).

It should be observed that the concrete method of repairing the intelligence offices recommended by the Commission's report—the creation of a National Counterterrorism Center[22]—entails a heightening of centralized structures. The Commission itself has acknowledged this problem:

> The most serious disadvantage of the NCTC is the reverse of its greatest virtue. The struggle against Islamist terrorism is so important that any clear-cut centralization of authority to manage and be accountable for it may concentrate too much power in one place.[23]

But the problem of centralization, as we have seen, is not just concentration of power, but dissipation of information (and hence the crumbling of "intelligence"). If the CIA, FBI, and other intelligence agencies are an extension of the executive branch, the NCTC is the new executive branch of this extended executive branch. The disastrous failures of intelligence leading up to 9/11, and again the disastrous failures of intelligence leading up to the war in Iraq leave a *vast* space for improvement.[24] Perhaps (contrary to appearances) the newly created intelligence office will bring about improvement; it is hard to see how the record could get worse.

But even if the quality of pre-attack information within the executive branch does improve, some way must also be discovered to return to the larger framing question that moves out from the executive branch to the country as a whole. The day of 9/11 confirmed the virtues of decentralization and distribution— confirmed them not only as ethical ideals but as our best guarantee of a safe and secure nation. If the country's safety and security is of concern to us—and it is surely of concern to every one of us—then we are obligated to begin to talk about these matters openly and soon.

Notes

1. *The 9/11 Commission Report: Final Report of the National Commission on Terrorist Attacks Upon the United States* (New York: Norton, 2004). A later chapter (chapter 9, 278–323) chronicles rescue actions carried out by fire and police departments, as well as ambulances and the safety officials from particular buildings. Chapter 10 (325–38) focuses on the Bush administration response, both on 9/11 and later days.
2. The *Report* describes, and directly quotes, portions of the passengers' "sustained" assault on the cockpit that was picked up on the cockpit voice recorder. Audible on the tape are the noise of passengers storming the door, passengers' cries of continuing resolve ("Roll it!" "Into the cockpit. If we don't we'll die!") and the hijackers' decision that the moment they break through the door they will crash the plane ("Is that it? Shall we finish it off?" "No. Not yet. When they all come, we finish it off." "Is that it? I mean, shall we put it down?" "Yes, put it in it, and pull it down"). *Report*, 13, 14.
3. Ibid., 45.
4. Ibid., 45.

5. Ibid., 30. The National Military Command Center learned that it had been hijacked from their Secret Service contacts in the White House who were in turn in contact with the FAA; they learned this four minutes earlier than NORAD (by coincidence, the minute during which the plane was crashing). Ibid., 42.

6. *Report*, 28. The pilots of several F-16s from Langley were already in the air, and had been told to divert planes coming into Washington; but they still believed that the events they were being asked to address involved Russian missiles rather than hijacked passenger planes (Ibid., 45), and they had been explicitly instructed that they had no clearance to shoot ("negative—negative clearance to shoot"). Ibid., 31, 45.

7. Ibid., 25.

8. Ibid., 42. In "Who Defended the Country," I argue both that the military was unable to shoot down planes and that it ought not to shoot down passenger planes. The *9/11 Commission Report* carefully documents that the military was unable to shoot down the planes but it does not raise the question of whether or not it should be permissible to do so. It does discuss the issue of who within the government has the authority to issue the initial command. Ibid., 17, 41.

9. Ibid., 22.

10. Ibid., 28–29.

11. Ibid., 21, 38. NORAD learned of the second hijacked plane at 9:03 A.M., the same minute that the plane hit the World Trade Tower (Ibid., 23); the jet fighters from Langley were scrambled not because NORAD learned of any other hijacked plane but as backup to the Otis fighter jets which they feared would soon run out of fuel (Ibid., 24). NEADS learned Flight 77 was missing only four minutes before it crashed, and only because NEADS initiated a call to the FAA about another plane. NORAD learned Flight 93 was missing and hijacked only after the plane crash.

12. Ibid., 29.

13. Ibid., 9. If Ted Olson forwarded the information to anyone else in the Justice Department or FAA or the Department of Defense or the military, that act is not recorded in the Commission's report.

14. Recall that the Indianapolis air controller, uninformed about the World Trade Towers in New York, had been searching for Flight 77 along its projected westward course. By the time Barbara Olson is making her phone call to her husband, the air controller has learned about events in New York and has told the FAA regional center that Flight 77 is missing. But the regional center has not yet relayed that information to the FAA headquarters, and no "all points bulletin" has been issued.

15. Ibid., 36.

16. Ibid., 38.

17. Ibid., 43.

18. See, for example, the account of NORAD testimony (Ibid., 34), the vice president's statements about the time at which he received "shoot down" authorization from the president (Ibid., 40, 41).

19. A potentially grave problem with the *9/11 Commission Report* is its reliance in chapters 5 and 7 on information obtained from detainees and captured al-Qaida members. The Commission explicitly and prominently announces its

concern that it was unable to corroborate the information from these sources forwarded to it by the intelligence agencies carrying out the interrogations (Ibid., 146). But there are serious moral problems as well, given the questions about torture and possibly illegal detention that are still under review. Indeed one of the Commission's named sources, Abu Zubaydah, we know to have been tortured. See the detailed account of Zubaydah's interrogation in Gerald Posner, *Why America Slept: The Failure to Prevent 9/11* (New York: Random House, 2003), 184–94.

20.   Among them, the Defense Intelligence Agency in the Department of Defense, the "intelligence entities" of the Army, Navy, Marines, and Air Force, the Bureau of Intelligence and Research of the Department of State, the Office of Terrorism and Finance Intelligence of the Department of the Treasury (see *Report*, 407, 408).

21.   National Commission on Terrorist Attacks Upon the United States, Public Hearing, April 8, 2004. http://www.9-11commission.gov/archive/hearing9/9-11Commission_Hearing_2004-04-08.pdf, 24.

22.   *Report*, 403.

23.   Ibid., 405.

24.   For the extraordinary series of mistakes from the intelligence community about Iraq's phantom nuclear weapons, see the 589-page March 2005 Report to the President (chaired by Laurence H. Silberman and Charles S. Robb), *Commission on the Intelligence Capabilities of the United States Regarding Weapons of Mass Destruction,* http://www.wmd.gov/report/.

11 Rethinking Crisis Government

William E. Scheuerman

The dramatic expansion of executive prerogative following the 9/11 terrorist attacks has generated criticism among liberal political and legal theorists, who rightly point out that constitutionalism and the rule of law were designed for bad times as well as good. Bruce Ackerman, Ronald Dworkin, and many others have eloquently argued that Washington's legal response to September 11 has opened the door to secret detentions, the destruction of attorney-client confidentiality, frightening forms of government surveillance, and military tribunals that make a mockery of international law no less than well-worn ideas of due process.[1] Most ominous is the Bush administration's claim that it has the right to detain indefinitely U.S. citizens whom it alone designates as possible terrorists. Despite the administration's repeated emphasis on the novel character of the attacks, its response has relied disproportionately on a legal instrument harking back to a pre-liberal era in which royal prerogative determined the texture of political life: unilateral executive authority. That precisely such activities encouraged our Enlightenment predecessors to discard monarchy in the first place seems to have been lost on Republican partisans normally hostile to "big government," the administration's cheerleaders at Fox News, and millions of ordinary Americans understandably angered by the 9/11 attacks.

Unfortunately, President Bush has hardly been alone in insisting that terrorism is best fought by dramatically augmenting executive discretion. Thus far, the courts have exercised extreme caution in challenging the administration's actions.[2] An unquestioned presupposition of both Republican and Democratic lawmakers has been that the terrorist attacks call for dramatically expanding the scope of executive authority, and especially the discretionary leeway available to administrative agencies (for example, the Justice Department and FBI) allegedly best suited to the task of doing battle with terrorism. Passed with virtual unanimity by both houses of Congress, the so-called "Patriot Act" has functioned to hand over substantial but poorly defined authority to the intelligence and security apparatus. An immediate consequence is that millions of resident aliens are now denied many basic legal protections and find themselves directly subservient to federal agencies long known for their inefficiency and incompetence.[3] If we keep in mind that even some prominent liberal jurists no longer accept the view that Congress deserves a decisive role in the oversight of the federal administration, such legislative delegations of decision-making power tend inevitably to strengthen the president's legal authority to act on his own.[4]

And it is clear that the Bush administration believes it has a right to act without consultation, at home as well as abroad. How else can we explain its dismissive response to indisputable evidence that it has misled the American public about Saddam Hussein's military capacities in order to launch a pre-emptive war against Iraq?

Notwithstanding their forceful criticisms of administration policies, even liberal critics of the stampede to dismantle civil liberties fail to recognize the extent to which Washington's response to 9/11 places traditional preconceptions about crisis government in a fresh light.[5] To be sure, Democrats in Congress have criticized the president's unilateral appeal to inherent executive authority. Yet their support for the Patriot Act suggests that they have few qualms about expanding the discretionary powers of federal agencies as long as they have some say in delegating it. Nor do liberal academic critics typically challenge the assumption that the best answer to the terrorist attacks should be executive-driven and thus must entail more-or-less generous delegations of discretionary authority to the security and intelligence agencies.[6] Their chief worry is that President Bush and a cowed opposition in Congress have gone too far in doing so. Unless we challenge the well-nigh universal view that terrorism necessitates enlarging executive prerogative, however, we face the prospect of a downward spiral in which civil liberties will soon be a shadow of their former selves. Ackerman is probably correct to predict that terrorist attacks may be "a recurring part of our future" in part because "[t]he balance of technology has shifted, making it possible for a small band of zealots to wreak devastation where we least expect it."[7]

In the first section of the essay, I recall a series of assumptions about executive power with deep roots in modern political and legal theory. Those presuppositions undergird the orthodox view that expanding the scope of discretionary executive authority represents a sensible response to terrorism. Yet those presuppositions constitute a misleading starting point for those of us intent on tackling the difficult intellectual and political tasks at hand, not the least of which is to figure out how we can maintain the basic rudiments of a law-based state in a globalizing political universe. In the second section, I consider how anachronistic ideas about the temporal efficiency of the unitary executive and about the international state system, as well as the problematic traditional metaphor of the state as a body politic, haunt present-day conceptions of crisis government. In the third section, I argue that unless we challenge such ideas, we may be destined to reproduce core features of classical monarchy rightly discarded by our historical predecessors. Preliminary evidence suggests that the ongoing U.S. response to terrorism rests on a disturbing revival of monarchist conceptions of executive power.

I

What presuppositions about executive authority have guided the U.S. response to 9/11?[8] In her provocative contribution to this volume, Elaine Scarry

begins to answer this question by underlining the temporal assumptions of recent U.S. defense policy: a preoccupation with *speed* "has been at the center of
discussions of national defense for the past fifty years."[9] Yet those temporal assumptions are far broader than Scarry suggests, and their roots extend well beyond the origins of Cold War political ideology. The immediate source of the
rush since 9/11 to strengthen not only the military but the executive branch as
a whole is the presumption that the executive is best capable of rapid-fire or
high-speed action and thus should be most adept at warding off surprise attacks
like those we witnessed on 9/11. The Bush administration has expressly appealed to this traditional view to justify unilateral executive fiat.[10] What could
be more self-evident than the executive's capacity for acting swiftly and ener-
getically in a crisis? The high-speed character of executive action may be most
evident when it unleashes military force, but many other manifestations of executive power exhibit a distinctive capacity for speed as well. For precisely this
reason, the Bush administration has insisted not only on its special institutional
privileges in undertaking military activity against terrorism and its (alleged)
allies in Afghanistan and Iraq, but also on the need for far-reaching executive
discretion in the domestic context in order to ward off further attacks.

This view can lay legitimate claim to an impressive intellectual provenance.
Machiavelli points out in the *Discourses* that representative assemblies are ill-
suited to "remedying a situation which will not brook delay," arguing that the
executive is better suited to the imperatives of crisis government. While elected
representatives "have to consult with one another, and to reconcile their diverse
views takes time," a single ruler can act speedily and avoid the undue "tempo-
rizing" that necessarily plagues large assemblies.[11] The intellectual history is a
complicated one, yet a persuasive argument can be made that Machiavelli's
ready association of the executive with speed was accepted by subsequent theorists who otherwise harshly criticized the legacy of "reason of state" with which
Machiavelli's name soon was associated.[12] Montesquieu, Locke, and Hamilton
contrast the fast-paced character of executive action with the unhurried texture
of legislative politics no less categorically than Machiavelli. Following Machiavelli, they assume that popular assemblies are inherently slow-moving, whereas
the executive possesses a built-in capacity for fast-paced action.[13]

At one level, this view underlines the obvious point that deliberative exchange in any relatively numerous group, regardless of its quality, is sure to be
a slow-going affair merely because of its sequential character. Because "two
speakers at an assembly cannot be heard by everyone if they try to speak simultaneously," even a cognitively unimpressive debate in an elected body made up,
for example, of a mere fifty representatives is destined to be time-consuming.[14]
At another level, this temporal assumption expresses the considerable weight
placed by Enlightenment liberalism on rational deliberation as a source of legitimate lawmaking. The Enlightenment faith in the emancipatory potential of
human reason played a central role in liberalism's conceptualization of elected
legislatures as requiring robust—and necessarily unrushed—rational debate.[15]

The high temporal and cognitive demands placed on modern assemblies within the liberal tradition, however, simultaneously suggested their limitations as an effective instrument of crisis government. Machiavelli, Montesquieu, Locke, and Hamilton argue that the unitary character of the executive assures its superiority in situations "which will not brook delay." The fact that the executive consists, most fundamentally, of a single actor means that it can act quickly. This simple intuition also helps explain the pervasive hostility to the idea of a plural executive in modern liberal thought: Montesquieu's influential argument that a plural executive undermines the fundamental goal of executive power, namely the ability to act with dispatch, soon became a dogmatic article of faith among liberals.[16] Those who challenged the notion of a single executive—for example, the Anti-Federalists—consistently found themselves relegated to the status of obscure footnotes in the history of liberalism.[17]

In this traditional account, the temporally efficient unitary executive generates additional institutional virtues that render it especially adept at grappling with crises. A temporally inefficient plural executive lends itself to inconsistent and even incoherent state action. As Hamilton notes in refuting the Anti-Federalist case for a plural executive, "whenever two or more persons are engaged in any common enterprise or pursuit, there is always danger of difference of opinion," and such differences will probably "weaken the authority, and distract the plans and operations of those whom they divide."[18] In contrast, the "personal firmness" of the unitary executive is generally best attuned not only to the imperatives of speed but also to assuring consistency in legal implementation and the overall monitoring of state activity.[19] And what could be more desirable during an unpredictable and fast-moving crisis than making sure that all units of government operate together as parts of one coherent and harmonious whole? Even more famously, Hamilton links the unitary executive to effective democratic oversight and accountability of its activities. "The public opinion is left in suspense about the real author" of a specific action because plurality in the executive allows its members to shift blame and obscure their responsibility for political mistakes, whereas the unitary executive offers the public a genuine "opportunity of discovering with facility and clearness the misconduct of the persons they trust."[20] Not only is the unitary executive best equipped to act decisively, but its unitary character also means that the public possesses a real chance of identifying, in a temporally efficient manner, which political actor should be held responsible for a particular action. Especially during an emergency, this institutional attribute becomes particularly valuable. Members of a plural executive typically "pass the buck" when their actions have undesired consequences, requiring the public to engage in an unnecessarily time-consuming game of figuring out who is to blame for incompetent or ineffective action. Amidst the rapidly changing imperatives of the emergency situation, however, such temporally costly deliberations might easily prove extravagant and thus politically disastrous.

The conventional view of the executive as best suited to rapid-fire crisis government rests on additional unstated assumptions which continue to shape the legal response to 9/11. Why does the terrorist attack require an instantaneous response in the first place? In other words, why not a slow and deliberate answer, in which old-fashioned modes of legislative rule making, along with legally circumscribed and carefully supervised grants of authority to government agencies, predominate? Notwithstanding the obvious internal tensions in the Bush administration's rhetoric, one consistent theme since 9/11 has been that the attacks represent a direct assault on the physical integrity of the American polity, a violent invasion probably no less threatening than Pearl Harbor because it means the penetration of the territory or "body" of the American polity.[21] To be sure, such rhetoric possesses an obvious empirical plausibility in light of the murder of thousands of innocent civilians on September 11, 2001, as well as the no less self-evident view that an indispensable function of the modern state is the guarantee of basic physical security to its members. Nonetheless, neither observation provides a sufficient logical justification for the rush to augment executive discretion that we have witnessed since 9/11. Why does the task of assuring physical security necessarily require immediate executive action?

Here as well, the missing arguments can be gleaned from some of the most familiar—and therefore rarely scrutinized—dogmas of modern political thought. Recall how pervasive the metaphor of the "body politic" has been within Western political theory. The idea that political entities possess far-reaching affinities to actual corporeal (human) bodies has taken many different forms in the Western political tradition, but the crucial point here is that this metaphor probably played a pivotal role in the shaping of modern liberalism. Hobbes' description of the "artificial man" of the Leviathan is famous.[22] Yet Locke—a more obvious influence on modern liberalism—similarly employs the metaphor of a body politic at a number of crucial junctures. Locke not only describes the all-important legislative power as "the soul that gives form, life, and unity" to the political community, thereby transforming it "into one coherent body," but his influential picture of international relations as constituting part of the state of nature immediately suggests a picture of individual commonwealths as strikingly akin to the individual persons who populate Locke's state of nature before the establishment of what he calls "political society."[23] To be sure, Locke was chiefly underscoring the point that sovereign states should be seen as legal or juridical persons, and the "analogy of sovereign commonwealths in a state of nature to individual men in that state is not meant to be taken too literally."[24] Nonetheless, this analogy helps explain the conventional view that physical threats to the physical community require rapid-fire action.

During moments of crisis, high-speed executive action is necessary because the stakes are so high. Why are the stakes high? Because the political community constitutes a body politic strikingly akin to the individual human body, and as we all know, even relatively modest physical invasions of our corporeality represent violations of our physical integrity and potentially dangerous threats to our existence. By allowing others to assault us physically, we place our physical well-being and perhaps even our existence itself in alien hands. Life itself becomes precarious. Our fundamental right to self-preservation is subject to forces beyond our control. At least implicitly, certain influential strands in modern liberalism thus rely on seemingly credible preconceptions about physical self-defense to justify immediate executive action: when physically assaulted, individuals lack the luxury of debating with their peers or allies about the best conceivable response. Instead, they must move quickly to ward off immediate threats to their physical well-being, and such moments call for action rather than deliberation, dispatch instead of delay. If physical violence is imminent or already at hand, individual self-preservation can only be achieved by the imperatives of physical self-defense, where agility and swiftness are at a premium. In the political universe, the unitary executive, and not a numerous deliberative assembly, is the most likely source of such agility and swiftness.

This aspect of conventional thinking about crisis government is perhaps most noteworthy because of its implicit hostility toward pluralism and the necessary deliberative give-and-take of liberal democratic politics. In the traditional view, a dire crisis requires the body politic not only to act as a unitary whole but with one voice. After all, dangerous foes might easily take disagreement and dispute as evidence of vulnerability. As that part of the body politic outfitted with the task of swiftly responding to the physical threat at hand, the executive typically claims the authority to speak on behalf of the political community as a whole. Unfortunately, the implications of this traditional imagery of body and voice are profoundly anti-pluralistic and even anti-political; it is no accident that it derives from pre-liberal and pre-democratic sources and seems to have been particularly common in Western political thought among medieval Christian defenders of natural law–based monarchy. But the Bush administration has relied on precisely this imagery to suppress legitimate political difference and disagreement; those who challenge the president's far-right policies on a host of domestic issues fundamentally unrelated to terrorism now risk getting branded as "soft" on terrorism. As Paul Krugman noted in *The New York Times* two years after the attacks on the World Trade Center and Pentagon, Mr. Bush's advisors "saw 9/11 as an opportunity to get everything they wanted, from another round of tax cuts, to a major weakening of the Clean Air Act, to an invasion of Iraq."[25] In this spirit, Secretary of Defense Donald Rumsfeld has gone so far as to criticize opponents of the U.S. invasion of Iraq as lending aid and comfort to terrorism, despite the lack of any reliable evidence of systematic cooperation between Osama bin Laden and Saddam Hussein.

Locke is also revealing because he helps shed light on another conspicuous facet of the U.S. legal response to terrorism. Although the metaphor of physical self-defense has played a crucial role in the unresisted assertion of executive discretion since 9/11, the fact that the physical threat at hand is somehow foreign in origin has also obviously worked in the same direction. Locke not only conceives of international relations as a state of nature populated by individual corporeal persons, but he argues that the executive's foreign policy powers (in Locke's terminology, the federative power) cannot "be directed by antecedent, standing, positive laws . . . and so must necessarily be left to the prudence and wisdom of those whose hands it is in, to be managed for the public good." Far-reaching executive discretion is necessitated by "the variation of designs and interests" in foreign affairs, where the demands of diplomacy and war require swift and unhindered executive action. In Locke's account, not only the extreme case of war, but normal diplomacy as well, "admits not of plurality of governors."[26]

The Lockean vision of a body politic residing in a fundamentally lawless state of nature continues to haunt contemporary U.S. political and legal discourse. In striking accordance with this traditional notion of foreign affairs as constituting a fundamentally lawless sphere requiring scope for significant executive prerogative, U.S. courts have long been hesitant to restrict the scope of executive discretion in foreign affairs.[27] In addition, foreign affairs have been defined by courts as including not only defense and national security, but international economic policy, immigration and asylum law, and many other areas as well, meaning that the U.S. executive presently enjoys an awesome arsenal of highly discretionary legal instruments in a broad array of so-called "international" arenas.[28]

The judiciary's ingrained habit of deferring to the executive in foreign relations is undoubtedly one of the reasons the Bush administration has been so confident about its aggressive push to extend the scope of executive discretion after September 11. Describing terrorism as a foreign military threat brings obvious legal dividends to those who believe that heightened executive discretion is the best way to fight it. A legal tradition chary of restricting executive discretion in foreign affairs is sure to work to the advantage of policy makers eager for further extensions of executive prerogative in the face of what is now widely interpreted as a foreign invasion.

II

This traditional defense of executive primacy during a crisis is now implausible. Its preconditions are historically contingent and no longer readily accord with the realities of contemporary political life. Unless we discard the conventional view, we will fail to provide a satisfactory institutional response to terrorism.

The belief in the high-speed efficiency of the unitary executive rests to a significant extent on the metaphor of a single leader at the helm of state; the singular character of the executive (in contrast to the numerous legislature) purportedly allows him to act with dispatch. When first introduced into modern political thought by Machiavelli, this metaphor still possessed empirical credibility in light of the fact that rulership in many places was effectively exercised by a single leader and a relatively small group of advisors. In medieval England, for example, the king "had no standing army, no police, no large bureaucracy."[29] In early modern Europe, we still find innumerable examples of rulership in the hands of small political cliques. This simple vision of executive power was formulated for the most part before the maturation of some of the core features of the modern state. When Machiavelli or even Locke sketched out the virtues of a singular executive, modern bureaucracies, the professionalization of offi-

220   *William E. Scheuerman*

cialdom, rational systems of tax collection, and even modern forms of complex military organization remained underdeveloped.

Does the metaphor of the decisive "prince" make sense given the nature of modern executive power? At the very least, it fails to do justice to crucial components of the modern executive. The modern executive is a complex and multi-headed creature, composed of a host of (often competing) administrative and bureaucratic units, whose members are sometimes even more numerous than other branches of government. Disagreement and interest conflict are no less a part of our many-headed executive than our elected legislatures. Although the executive typically claims a predominant position in overseeing the administrative apparatus, it is noteworthy that other political institutions (notably the legislature and judiciary) sometimes successfully challenge such claims, thereby contributing to the legitimacy of the administrative apparatus but not to its temporal efficiency. Even when the executive proves victorious in the battle for control of the administration, its machinery is typically so complex that it is unlikely to follow the chief executive's commands as expeditiously as the traditional image implies. Prominent scholars of the U.S. presidency now speak of the "plural presidency," persuasively arguing that a more appropriate focus for contemporary empirical research than traditional notions of the unitary executive "is the plural nature of the presidency, its policy environment, and the demands placed upon the institution by different groups and nations."[30] In a similar vein, critics in the legal academy of the increasingly popular view that administrative agencies must be directly subject to the executive rather than Congress have expressed telling concerns about the traditional temporal portrayal of the "energetic" unitary executive.[31]

Even when the executive undertakes unilateral action, seemingly straightforward undertakings can prove enormously complex and time-consuming. The colossal difficulties faced by "Homeland Security" Chief Tom Ridge in co-ordinating the administration's domestic response to terrorism provide an obvious illustration of this point. Its failure, for example, to identify the culprits of the anthrax attacks that immediately followed 9/11 undoubtedly stem from sheer incompetence. Yet they also undoubtedly derive from the often unwieldy structure of the modern administrative state. Even if it remains true that the executive can "act first" in some areas of policy, the complexity of the modern executive means that its undertakings at times can seem even less coherent and consistent than those of deliberative legislatures.[32] Preliminary empirical support for this general claim comes from the history of executive-dominated dictatorships, which typically promise quick responses to domestic and foreign crises and thus implicitly rely on the dogma of the swift executive in order to garner popular support. More often than not, however, executive-centered dictatorship ends up mired in internal bureaucratic conflict, stymied by administrative inefficiency and incoherence.[33] Notwithstanding the claims of authoritarian ideologues, liberal democratic states committed to the procedural niceties of law making by elected parliaments and the separation of powers often evince greater temporal efficiency than their authoritarian competitors. Scarry's suggestion that egalitarian modes of political and military self-organization may in fact act faster and prove more effective than hierarchical and authoritarian ones can find substantial empirical support in the recent history of life-or-death struggles between dictatorial and liberal democratic regimes.

In a similar vein, one might legitimately wonder whether Hamilton's justly famous arguments about the popular accountability of the unitary executive obtain in light of present-day political realities. At the very least, our "plural presidency" raises tough questions for the doctrinaire view. The mind-boggling institutional complexity of the modern executive certainly makes it easier for political actors to "pass the buck" than Hamilton's argument anticipated; examples of federal agencies scrambling to blame their administrative rivals for unpopular policies are legion. The complexity of the modern administrative state also makes it difficult for the chief executive to oversee its wide-ranging activities and thereby assure their coherence and consistency. There are sometimes, then, legitimate institutional reasons why voters seem reluctant to hold the executive responsible for a particular administrative course of action. Politically precocious politicians, of course, have manipulated this genuine institutional dilemma to their personal advantage on many occasions. Moments of crisis, when many people consider it appropriate to rally around the president, provide the most obvious opportunities for such manipulation. In such situations, it may be relatively easy for chief executives to blame others for their own bad judgment and failures.[34] In any event, it is by no means self-evident that the contemporary executive lives up to the Hamiltonian promise of assuring effective accountability by allowing the public to link state action directly to particular political personalities in a timely and temporally efficient manner.[35]

Perhaps other attributes of the traditional account still buttress the intuition that the executive is best capable of high-speed action. For example, one might argue that the executive, in contrast to the legislature, is not required to undertake a demanding process of deliberative give-and-take where a multiplicity of arguments and competing interests is considered and all affected viewpoints receive a fair hearing. Whereas an elected legislature "as a collective organization takes definitive action through the legislative process, which is cumbersome, difficult to navigate, and characterized by multiple veto votes," the administrative apparatus might seem relatively well-equipped for acting with dispatch.[36] Indeed, conventional (for example, Weberian) models of administrative activity picture decision making as based on top-down command directives. In these models, administration is an efficient instrument since it minimizes the need for time-consuming deliberation during the implementation of policy. Officials need not engage in ambitious debate or worry about reaching an agreement about the aims of policy, since others have already done so for them.

Scholars of administration have not only questioned the empirical relevance of this orthodoxy to the actual workings of the contemporary state but have also pointed out that it presupposes conditions unlikely to be met. When policy goals are unclear and open-ended, or when goals are clear but bureaucratic and technical experts (as well as interested private groups) understandably disagree about the best way to achieve the goals at hand, an arduous process of consensus building will have to take place within administrative bodies. If that process is to achieve satisfying results, it too will have to be subject to the constraints of time-consuming deliberative exchange and interest mediation. Forcing administrative actors to rush their decisions is then sure to generate irrational and undesirable results no less than in the case of overhasty legislatures.[37]

The implicit presupposition that political entities constitute corporeal entities whose self-defense calls for swift action is misleading as well. Here again, we can easily see why the metaphor seemed so tenable to early modern political thinkers. Writing amidst the extreme political upheavals that plagued the European world between 1500 and 1700, they witnessed the elimination of countless political units unable to protect themselves effectively against more advanced forms of bureaucratic and military organization.[38] In much of medieval Christendom as well, where reliance on the metaphor of the body politic was ubiquitous, political life was "plagued by recurrent violence and devastation."[39] Where many political entities (for example, the city-states of sixteenth-century Italy) confronted the distinct possibility of political and legal extinction, the notion that political units should be modeled on the metaphor of a physically vulnerable body politic, against which even a seemingly modest physical assault might pave the way for profound peril, closely matched political realities.

Here as well, however, one might ask whether this metaphor meshes with the contours of our contemporary state system, in which the legal, let alone physical, elimination of competing state units is relatively rare. Compare, for example, the vast changes in the state system that took place in Machiavelli's Italy with those in twentieth-century Europe. Both regions were prone to terrible political violence, yet in some contrast, most of the states that existed on a map of Europe in 1900 still existed in the year 2000, notwithstanding the rise and decline of fascism, Nazism, and communism, as well the decisive military interventions of non-European powers (the United States). Wars obviously can be even more brutal and destructive than they were in early modern Europe. Yet even the most bloody of them no longer result in the extinction or territorial appropriation of competing states. Implicit representations of the state as fragile physical bodies, for whom physical assault can quickly become a fundamental threat to self-preservation, probably obscure crucial facets of contemporary international relations.

In a similar spirit, Brien Hallett has pointed out that we need to avoid simplistically conflating the experience of modern war with acts of physical violence. Hallett correctly observes that "in the minds of many, conceding that war often involves violent combat is tantamount to defining war as violence. Logically . . . this should not be done because it confuses the whole of war [and its many distinct facets] with one of its parts. . . . "[40] Wars are waged for political reasons, and include a complex mix of economic, cultural, and ideological elements. Because war is immediately linked to the physical violence of the battlefield, however, the metaphor of physical self-defense, along with a concomitant vision of war as consisting of life-or-death physical combat, unduly colors our political and legal ideas about war. In contrast, if we recognize that modern wars consist of a complicated set of undertakings of which physical violence is a key but hardly exclusive attribute, we can begin to challenge the metaphor of physical self-defense undergirding conventional ideas about war making. Hallett's chief concern lies in resurrecting what he describes as the lost art of formal legislative declarations of war, which increasingly play second fiddle in wars decided by an executive unbridled by traditional legislative restraints. Hallett argues persuasively that because war consists of more than direct physical violence, the traditional preference for a deliberate and reasoned legislative declaration of war, where war aims are carefully detailed, should again play a central role in guaranteeing control of war making by civilian-dominated lawmaking bodies.

Hallett's warnings are even more apt as a critical account of the risk of crude conflations of violence and terrorism. Terrorism is no less complex or multifaceted than war making. More fundamental, actual physical violence is a crucial facet of terrorism, but by no means its chief attribute. Psychological "weapons" (for example fomenting fear and hysteria) are equally pivotal. Just as modern wars involve more than physical combat and therefore leave more than enough room for deliberative legislatures to outline the goals of military action as well as its political purposes, so too should we be skeptical of the claim that terrorism is ultimately inconsistent with careful legislative rule making and the vigilant oversight of executive activities. The rush to hand over open-ended decision-making authority to the executive in the aftermath of 9/11 is by no means a necessary response to terrorism. On the contrary, it may suggest that we have already normatively caved in to the terrorists, as we rush to imitate their often autocratic structures of decision making and sacrifice our commitment to constitutionalism and the rule of law.

The traditional intuition that foreign threats call for freewheeling executive prerogative requires reconsideration as well. Despite the familiar weaknesses of the existing international legal system, picturing that system as a lawless state of nature terribly misconstrues the nature of international legal relations at least since the founding of the United Nations.[41] If executive prerogative is chiefly justified by the legal unpredictability and fast-changing character of the international arena, that justification no longer obtains. Today, recourse to anachronistic visions of international life as a lawless state of nature chiefly functions as an ideological cover for an irresponsible unilateralism in foreign policy. In addition, judicial reticence in the face of executive discretion in the "international" arena is now a recipe for destroying civil liberties and the rule of law at home. If globalization means that the domestic and foreign no longer can be neatly separated, the courts' refusal to insist on traditional rule-of-law standards whenever "foreign" issues are at stake means that Americans should ready themselves for the obliteration of basic legal protections in a vast array of policy arenas.[42]

The continuing (and potentially endless) "war on terrorism" vividly underscores the increasing difficulties of clearly distinguishing the domestic from the foreign arena. The 9/11 attacks were planned abroad by citizens of other states, but some preparations appear to have been undertaken here by legal residents of the United States. In addition, the terrorists made use of instruments—the Internet, for example, and electronic financial transactions—that have helped make national borders increasingly porous.

Washington's response no less vividly sheds light on the profound dangers at hand if we do not we reconsider our legal system's traditional deference to executive discretion in foreign affairs. Emphasizing the foreign origins of the threat, the Bush administration responded to 9/11 by immediately rounding up nearly 1,200 non-citizens, many of whom remained in jail for months even though formal charges were never leveled against them.[43] Those who were charged typically faced detention for minor immigration law violations that would otherwise have gone unpunished. The only "crime" committed by most of those rounded up is that they remain resident aliens from countries where the administration suspects terrorist activity. Appealing to traditional ideas that executive prerogative should be greatest when the country faces a foreign threat, the Bush administration has refused even to make public the names of those detained; thus far, the courts have upheld the administration's position. For its part, the Patriot Act has worked to provide little more than window dressing for an emergency legal regime now encircling resident aliens, many of whom have lived here for years, worked alongside us, paid taxes, and participated in a host of civic activities. If we keep in mind that many millions of others are intimately linked via family or personal ties to the 9.3 million directly affected by the Patriot Act, a sizable number of legal residents are now directly subject to irregular and potentially arbitrary agency decision making.

The Patriot Act thus offers a particularly disturbing illustration of how the blurring of the domestic/foreign divide might be allowed to undermine once sacrosanct legal protections. The legislation not only defines terrorism vaguely but requires only that the Attorney General declare that he has "reasonable grounds" for suspecting resident aliens of terrorism to gain equally expansive authority to determine the fate of suspects. The Patriot Act also unmasks the illusion that one can begin to strip resident aliens of basic rights without simultaneously harming the rights of citizens; under the auspices of fighting terrorism, the Patriot Act allows for secret searches of the premises and property of citizens as well as resident aliens.[44] The assault on citizens' rights is more than an example of sloppy legislative draftsmanship, however. It is a direct consequence of the growing dilemma of neatly delimiting foreign from domestic activity now characteristic of countless arenas of human endeavor, as well a failure of political and legal imagination to challenge the increasingly perilous dogma that the rule of law stops at our nation's borders.

III

Political history is filled with paradoxes. But few in U.S. history match those evident in the present juncture and, more specifically, in the Bush administration's legal response to terrorism. If the administration's answer to 9/11 is left unchallenged, it obviously bodes ill for American democracy. Indeed, it would mean that the planet's first successful experiment in liberal democracy, when faced with a suicidal attack by a handful of poorly armed rogues, was willing to embrace core features of precisely that regime-type, monarchy, which its own Enlightenment-era founders sought to relegate to the trash can of history. It would also imply that in the face of the complex pressures of globalization, the most advanced technological and economic power on earth had opted for a return to the political instruments of the pre-liberal and pre-democratic past. Neither transnational democracy nor a novel global rule of law, but instead an idiosyncratic and perhaps "post-modern" form of executive-centered rules nonetheless strikingly reminiscent of traditional royal prerogative would then constitute the decisive institutional feature of America's response to 9/11.

Why endorse this gloomy assessment of recent institutional trends? After all, does it not rest on an element of political hyperbole? Even if one is legitimately worried about the administration's aggrandizement of executive power, the United States has not altogether abandoned its basic liberal democratic normative commitments, nor have Americans jettisoned their elected representatives for a king. Americans overthrew one King George in 1776, and the possibility that their twenty-first-century successors would willingly opt for another seems remote, if not fantastic.

Of course, this rejoinder is fundamentally correct. Yet it occludes a disturbing institutional trend. Throughout Western political history, it was kings who acquired expansive legal authority to wage war and peace.[45] War making was their special prerogative, not that of the "estates" or parliament, let alone their subjects. Even those who sought to harness royal power to effective institutional and legal restraints often continued to accept the pre-eminence of royal power in the field of foreign relations. By replacing unelected monarchs with an elected executive whose foreign policy prerogatives were dramatically curtailed vis-à-vis those of its monarchical predecessors, the American and French Revolutions broke decisively with this monarchist legacy. To the extent that the executive branch continues to rely on 9/11 as a justification for outfitting the president with vast possibilities for unilateral executive prerogative, however, it is effectively reasserting a decisive form of monarchical privilege. Although it makes no use (at least no conscious use) of traditional monarchist political rhetoric, the Bush administration is now insisting that it is the rightful possessor of a key traditional royal prerogative.[46] For good reason, this claim would have worried the anti-monarchist political thinkers who helped establish our constitutional system in the first place. It should also worry us.[47]

Recall that in the distant past, kings often gained their pre-eminent political status as a result of their success as warriors. In Europe, kings were expected to lead in war because they were thought to possess charismatic or supernatural powers which supposedly made them particularly well-suited to the tasks of military leadership.[48] "English kingship began with Anglo-Saxon war-bands (*comitates*) invading and settling the British isles," with the leading warrior probably assuming the role of king.[49] The first of the Norman kings of England was, of course, the appropriately named William the Conqueror. Although the historical story is a complicated one, this is undoubtedly one of the original sources of the extensive network of decision-making prerogatives kings came to enjoy in the realm of foreign policy. As late as 1765, Blackstone attributed to the British crown a vast array of decision-making powers in foreign policy; the crown alone could name ambassadors, make treaties, enter into foreign alliances and leagues, as well as declare and subsequently wage war, since

> the king is considered . . . the generalissimo, or the first in military command, within the kingdom. The great end of society is to protect the weakness of individuals by the united strength of the community: and the principal use of government is to direct that united strength in the best and most effectual manner, to answer the end proposed. Monarchical government is allowed to be the fittest of any for this purpose: it follows therefore, from the very end of its institution, that in a monarchy military power must be trusted in the hands of a prince.[50]

Other influential early modern political thinkers who similarly sought to limit monarchical power also accepted the primacy of royal prerogative in foreign affairs. Locke famously attacked Filmer's broad reading of divine monarchical right in his *Second Treatise*. Yet his reformulation of the traditional idea of prerogative authority left the door open, especially in foreign affairs, to far-reaching royal discretion. Whereas many of Locke's fellow Whigs were already struggling to make the king's traditional authority to declare and wage war directly subject to parliamentary oversight, Locke placed the making of foreign policy squarely in royal hands.[51] Montesquieu's conception of monarchy was no less expansive. Montesquieu blamed the ancients' hostility to monarchy on their failure to understand its proper form, which he famously saw as best embodied in the British Constitution. He not only assumed that executive power was most competently exercised, as in Britain, by a monarch, but he offered an interpretation of the British system that undoubtedly exaggerated the king's actual power by the mid-eighteenth-century. Whereas the British parliament was increasingly gaining the upper hand in overseeing foreign as well as domestic affairs, Montesquieu followed Locke in arguing for the monarch's absolute supremacy in foreign policy. The principle of the separation of powers called for a powerful independent monarchy. In Montesquieu's influential theory, a stylized and somewhat anachronistic interpretation of the British crown worked adeptly to perform the requisite functions. A crucial attribute of that stylization was far-reaching royal prerogative in foreign relations.[52]

Among the American framers, this traditional view garnered support among those, like Montesquieu, susceptible to the intellectual attractions of the British monarchy.[53] But even such thinkers—most notably Alexander Hamilton— ultimately rejected executive supremacy in foreign affairs. In *The Federalist Papers*, Hamilton famously offers an interpretation of the proposed U.S. presidency in which it lacks many of the most important longstanding royal prerogatives over foreign policy making.[54] Here as well, the history is a complex one, yet there can be no question that the founders ultimately denied the president "the most vital of monarchical powers as practiced in eighteenth-century England and the paramount foreign-policy power, that of initiating war."[55] They understood that executive predominance in foreign policy opens the door to military adventurism and political recklessness: how better to extend one's own power and prestige than by perpetrating or even manufacturing foreign crises? As the framers were well aware, English history included many recent examples of the crown generating both real and fake foreign crises in order to illegitimately expand its own power and undermine political opponents.[56] As Hamilton noted at the Philadelphia convention, one of the perils of an elected executive as well was that "he would be ambitious, with the means of making creatures; and as the object of his ambition would be to prolong his power, it is probable that in case of a war, he would avail himself of the emergence, to evade or refuse a degradation from his place."[57] Thus, the framers did not conceive of the much-cited "commander-in-chief" clause as entailing the authority to declare or initiate war.

As noted earlier, the possibility of sudden attacks complicates this scenario, since the temporal dictates of the crisis situation seem to favor granting a privileged position to that institution best equipped for acting with dispatch. Therefore, "the president, for obvious reasons, could act immediately to repel sudden attacks without authorization from Congress."[58] Yet the American framers conceived of this authority in relatively narrow and clearly circumscribed terms. As soon as the immediate threat to the mortality of the body politic had been defused, the president was expected to turn to Congress for both advice and the requisite assent for any continuation of armed operations against an aggressor. It is also clear from the historical and textual record that "the framers of the Constitution, when they vested in Congress the power to declare war . . . never imagined that they were leaving it to the executive to use the military and naval forces of the United States all over the world for the purpose of actually coercing other nations, occupying their territory, and killing their soldiers, all according to his own notion of the fitness of things as long as he refrained from calling his action war or persisted in calling it peace."[59]

To be sure, President Bush is hardly the first holder of executive power in the United States to violate the original understanding of executive war-making authority. For at least a century, and perhaps longer, that original understanding has been under attack from both Democrats and Republicans.[60] The modest interpretation of executive foreign policy making advanced by the framers meshes poorly with America's imperial ambitions over the past century. It has also long been the case that the traditional presuppositions of executive-centered crisis government are anachronistic and urgently in need of reconsideration. Nonetheless, the present dangers posed by the resurgence of executive prerogative seem especially grave. As noted previously, the blurring of the domestic/international divide that has become so striking in recent decades threatens to pave the way for a massive increase in executive discretion. As it becomes ever more difficult to separate "domestic" from "foreign" affairs, it inevitably will seem to "make sense" to growing numbers of people to augment the decision-making authority of that institutional instance traditionally associated with the capacity for warding off foreign threats in an expeditious manner. The fact that the process of globalization is likely to be fraught with dangers—this is also a lesson of 9/11—offers additional reason for concern. The familiar portrayal of the executive as best suited to the decision-making imperatives of an unpredictable, rapidly changing, and often frightening international arena contains authoritarian implications in an era where virtually every facet of human existence concerns "foreign" affairs.

Many scholars have struggled to make sense of the undeniable popular appeal of monarchical rule throughout most of history. According to the political theorist Donald Hanson, "it is as if all the social imponderables, all the perturbation and anxiety involved in simple societies, hovering constantly, as they do, on the edge of hunger, violence, and war, were compensated for by the idea of stable kingship." In Hanson's interpretation, "anxiety about the endurance of social order, as well as a largely unexpressed sense of its enormous value, is the psychological truth lying behind the adulation of kings."[61] Well into modern times, "civilized" Europeans believed in the charismatic healing powers of their kings, and they flocked to see them whenever they promised to make use of those powers.[62] Even when intellectuals drew relatively complex pictures of the nexus between divinity and royalty, common people tended to treat their kings as demigods or, at the very least, representatives of divine power. At many times and in many places, the well-being of the monarch was directly identified with the fate of the political community as a whole, whose unity he alone was thought capable of ensuring. People prayed for his health and prosperity because they were deemed to be directly associated with the well-being of the community for which he served as a concrete microcosm.

To be sure, there is no reason to assume that the unchanging dictates of human nature constitute the source of such monarchist impulses. However, their ubiquity in human history cries out for a satisfactory explanation.

Americans no longer believe in either divine right or "royal touch," nor is our social order a "simple" one "hovering constantly" on the verge of hunger, violence, and war. Nonetheless, 9/11 clearly provided many millions of citizens with an uncommon sense—at least for the American context—of political fragility as well as an unsettling inkling of the potential horrors of social chaos. Is it any wonder that so many of us have looked to the executive as a beacon of stability and permanence, as countless historical predecessors once assumed that only the single person of the king could successfully preserve political and social order in a world "on the edge" of hunger, violence, and war? The fact that the present-day holder of executive power, like so many of his monarchical forefathers, has opted to take advantage of the recent crisis in order to undermine necessary legal restraints on his power should hardly surprise us either.

Notes

Many thanks to David Alexander, Andrew Arato, Bruce Altschuler, Edwin Fogelman, Steve Macedo, Terry Nardin, Daniel Sherman, and two anonymous reviewers at Indiana University Press for extensive critical comments on an earlier rendition of this essay. I am also grateful to the participants at the Princeton University Program in Law and Public Affairs Conference on Law and Terrorism held in May 2002 for a lively discussion of an earlier version of the essay, and Christopher Eisgruber and Oren Gross for an opportunity to participate.

I also would like to express my gratitude to the public employees of the city of New York, and particularly the firemen, emergency care workers, and police from my hometown of Staten Island, for helping my sister escape uninjured from the World Trade Center on September 11, 2001.

1. Bruce Ackerman, "Don't Panic," *London Review of Books* (February 7, 2002): 15–16; Ronald Dworkin, "The Threat to Patriotism," *New York Review of Books* 49:3 (February 28, 2002): 44–49. Although the Bush administration has responded to criticisms of the proposed military tribunals, those modifications fail to sufficiently guarantee basic legal protections. The tribunals will permit the admittance of hearsay, allow for no civilian review or independent judicial appeal, and permit indefinite detentions. Secretary of Defense Rumsfeld has confirmed the validity of these accusations by admitting that even accused terrorists acquitted by the military tribunals are likely to remain imprisoned. Katherine Q. Seelye, "Rumsfeld Backs Plan to Hold Captives Even if Acquitted," *New York Times*, March 29, 2002, A12. Both Amnesty International and conservatives like William Safire of the *New York Times* have denounced the final proposal. Safire, "Military Tribunals Modified," *New York Times*, March 21, 2002, A33; Katherine Q. Seelye, "Government Sets Rules for Military on War Tribunals," *New York Times*, March 21, 2002, A1. However, in June 2004 the Supreme Court dramatically challenged the president's claims to extraordinary power, insisting that those deemed enemy combatants, both in the United States and Guantanamo Bay, must be allowed to challenge their detention before a court or another "neutral decision-maker." As I write, the concrete legal consequences of this potentially landmark decision on the administration's proposed military tribunals remain to be seen. In an excellent comparative discussion of the use of such military tribunals in other national contexts, Anthony W. Pereira underscores the perils of the Bush administration's approach. "Military Justice Before and After September 11," *Constellations* 9 (2002): 477–91.

2. However, the Supreme Court's June 2004 rulings in *Rasul v. Bush, Al Odah v. United States,* and *Hamdi v. Rumsfeld* open the door to more effective judicial oversight of the executive.

3. For a detailed account of the attack on immigrants' rights, see Dworkin, "The Threat to Patriotism."

4. See the revealing article by Elena Kagan, present dean of the Yale Law School: "Presidential Administration," *Harvard Law Review* 114 (2002): 2245–2385.

5. As Clinton Rossiter observed many years ago, "in time of crisis a democratic,

constitutional government must be temporarily altered to whatever degree is necessary to overcome the peril and restore normal conditions." *Constitutional Dictatorship: Crisis Government in the Modern Democracies* 1st ed. 1948 (New Brunswick, N.J.: Transaction Publishers, 2002), 5. "Crisis government" refers to those temporary institutional alterations in the normal operations of government necessary to overcome the crisis at hand. Rossiter offers an excellent survey of how Western democracies dealt in the twentieth century with the exigencies of war, rebellion, and economic upheaval. As he points out, "crisis government is primarily and often exclusively the business of presidents and prime ministers" (12). In this essay, I challenge some of the key assumptions underlining this familiar feature of emergency or crisis government. Because of the relative ubiquity of crisis government in recent times, my argument has broader ramifications than I will be able to describe in detail here.

6.   For example, Ackerman is now calling for a "constitutional regime for a limited state of emergency," in which the executive would be given expansive— but temporary—emergency authority. Unfortunately, constitutionally based "regimes of exception" have hardly worked well as a protection for civil liberties or the rule of law. For one historical survey, see Brian Loveman, *The Constitution of Tyranny: Regimes of Exception in Spanish America* (Pittsburgh, Pa.: University of Pittsburgh Press, 1993). Andrew Arato is also sympathetic to the constitutionalization of emergency powers. See his "The Bush Tribunals and the Specter of Dictatorship," *Constellations* 9 (2002): 457–76.

7.   Ackerman, "Don't Panic," 15. The inanities of recent U.S. foreign policy certainly belong among the indirect sources of the terrorism now directed against us.

8.   To be sure, the Bush administration's model of executive powers has other sources than those described in this essay. For example, its pre 9/11 business-oriented CEO model of the all-powerful executive is probably significant as well.

9.   Elaine Scarry, "Who Defended the Country?" p. 184, this volume.

10.   "[S]peed is of the essence, administration officials say [in justifying a broad range of unilateral executive actions], arguing that even a wartime Congress would not move fast enough to help the authorities counter new terrorism threats." Robin Toner and Neil A. Lewis, "White House Push on Security Steps Bypass Congress: New Executive Orders—Administration Urges Speed in Terror Fight, But Some See Constitutional Concern," *New York Times*, November 15, 2001, A1.

11.   Machiavelli, *Discourses*, trans. L. J. Walker (Harmondsworth: Penguin, 1970), 194–95. I am referring to Machiavelli's espousal of a Roman-style constitutional dictatorship.

12.   On the Machiavellian background to modern executive power, see Harvey Mansfield, Jr., *Taming the Prince: The Ambivalence of Modern Executive Power* (New York: Free Press, 1989).

13.   Montesquieu, *The Spirit of the Laws,* ed. Anne M. Cohler (Cambridge: Cambridge University Press, 1989), 159–61 [Book XI, chap. 6]; Locke, *Second Treatise of Government,* ed. C. B. Macpherson (Indianapolis, Ind.: Hackett, 1980), 160 [paragraph 160]; "Publius" (Hamilton, Madison, and Jay), *The Federalist*

Papers, ed. Clinton Rossiter (New York: NAL, 1961), 426–27, 431–33 [Federalists 70 and 71].

14. Robert Dahl and Edward Tufte, *Size and Democracy* (Stanford, Calif.: Stanford University Press, 1973), 72.

15. Jürgen Habermas, *The Structural Transformation of the Public Sphere*, trans. Frederick Lawrence (Cambridge, Mass.: MIT Press, 1989), 57–88.

16. Montesquieu, *The Spirit of the Laws*, 161 [Book XI, chap. 6]; *Federalist Papers*, 424 [Federalist 70].

17. Yet some countries—for example Uruguay—have opted for a plural executive during some junctures in their histories. For a discussion, see Harry Kantor, "Efforts Made by Various Latin American Countries to Limit the Power of the President," in *Parliamentary Versus Presidential Government*, ed. Arend Lijphart (New York: Oxford University Press, 1992), 101–111.

18. *Federalist Papers*, 425–26 [Federalist 70].

19. *Federalist Papers*, 431 [Federalist 71].

20. *Federalist Papers*, 427–29 [Federalist 70].

21. I leave it to others to explore the gender subtext that underlies this rhetoric. The continuing influence of corporeal metaphors in the aftermath of September 11 was brought home to me during an intense political argument with a family member who repeatedly exclaimed "But our back is against the wall!" Indeed, when your "back is against the wall" during a physical assault, you may need to act swiftly and forcefully to assure self-preservation.

22. "For by Art is created that great LEVIATHAN called a COMMON-WEALTH, or STATE . . . which is but an Artificiall Man . . . and in which, the Soveraignty is an Artificiall *Soul*, as giving life and motion to the whole body." Hobbes, *Leviathan*, ed. C. B. Macpherson (Harmondsworth: Penguin, 1985), 81. There is a rich tradition of thinking about political organization in medieval English political thought in terms of a "body." See the classic study by Ernst H. Kantorowicz, *The King's Two Bodies: A Study in Medieval Political Theology* (Princeton, N.J.: Princeton University Press, 1985).

23. "It is in their *legislative* that the members of a commonwealth are united, and combined together into one coherent body. This *is the soul that gives form, life, and unity*, . . . [T]herefore, when the legislative is broken, or dissolved, dissolution and death follows . . . " Locke, *Second Treatise*, 107–108 (para. 212). On foreign relations, 76–77 (para. 145–46).

24. Richard H. Cox, *Locke on War and Peace* (Oxford: Clarendon, 1960), 147.

25. Paul Krugman, "Exploiting the Atrocity," *New York Times*, September 12, 2003, A27. For hard evidence supporting Krugman's criticisms, see Eric Lichtblau, "U.S. Uses Terror Law to Pursue Crimes from Drugs to Swindling," *New York Times*, September 28, 2002, A1. I am grateful to Edwin Fogelman for bringing the general point made in this paragraph to my attention.

26. Locke, *Second Treatise*, 146–48 (para. 108).

27. Louis Fisher, *Constitutional Conflicts between Congress and the President*, 3rd ed. (Lawrence: University of Kansas Press, 1991), 216–80; Thomas M. Franck, *Political Questions/Judicial Answers: Does The Rule of Law Apply to Foreign Affairs?* (Princeton, N.J.: Princeton University Press, 1992); Harold H. Koh, *The National Security Constitution: Sharing Power after the Iran Contra Affair* (New Haven, Conn.: Yale University Press, 1990). The claim that U.S. practice has been influenced by Locke on this point requires more documentation.

Nonetheless, there is already an impressive body of literature underscoring the Lockean background of U.S. legal and political practice in the context of crisis government. See Jules Lobel, "Emergency Power and the Decline of Liberalism," *Yale Law Journal* 98 (1989): 1385–1433.

28. I develop this point in greater depth in *Liberal Democracy and the Social Acceleration of Time* (Baltimore, Md., and London: Johns Hopkins University Press, 2004), 144–86.

29. Charles Ogilvie, *The King's Government and the Common Law, 1471–1641* (Oxford: Blackwell, 1958), 4.

30. Gary King and Lyn Ragsdale, *The Elusive Executive: Discovering Statistical Patterns in the Presidency* (Washington, D.C.: Congressional Quarterly Press, 1988), 11). As Hans J. Morgenthau noted in 1960, the institutional complexity of the modern executive, even in presidential regimes such as the American one, has rendered it "a cumbersome, slow-moving instrument of government" oftentimes "incapable of swift, decisive action and radical innovation." *The Purpose of American Politics* (New York: Alfred Knopf Publishers, 1960), 336.

31. Martin Flaherty, "The Most Dangerous Branch," *Yale Law Journal* 105 (1996): 1725–1839.

32. The quote is from Kenneth R. Mayer, *With the Stroke of a Pen: Executive Orders and Presidential Power* (Princeton, N.J.: Princeton University Press, 2001), 26, whose otherwise fine study relies on a modest restatement of the traditional association of the executive with dispatch.

33. This is one theme in Franz L. Neumann's neglected *Behemoth: The Structure and Practice of National Socialism, 1933–44* (New York: Oxford University Press, 1944). It also has been a claim implicit in debates among historians about the "polycratic" structure of the Nazi dictatorship.

34. For example, think of former President Reagan's success in disassociating himself in popular political consciousness with the flagrant criminality of the Iran-Contra affair. Perhaps President Bush is now in the process of accomplishing something similar: many of the more controversial attacks on civil liberties and the rule of law seem to be most closely linked in everyday political discourse to the figure of Attorney General John Ashcroft.

35. In addition, the Bush administration's recourse to far-reaching secrecy—also a traditional prerogative of the executive (see, for example, Hamilton in Federalist 70 [424])—raises difficult questions for effective public accountability. For a good recent discussion of the perils in the context of the administration's proposed military tribunals, see Edward J. Klaris, "Why Public and Press Have a Right to Witness Proceedings in Military Tribunals: Justice Can't Be Done in Secret," *The Nation*, June 10, 2002, 16–20. In addition, the mere fact that our political system has pursued an endless series of necessary yet slow-going investigations of executive action (Watergate, Iran-Contra) might suggest that assuring the popular accountability of the executive is more complicated and time-consuming than Hamilton's discussion in *The Federalist Papers* presaged.

36. Mayer, *With the Stroke of a Pen: Executive Orders and Presidential Power*, 26.

37. Niklas Luhmann, "Die Knappheit der Zeit und die Vordringlichkeit des Befristeten," *Politische Planung. Aufsätze zur Soziologie von Politik und Verwaltung* (Opladen, Germany: Westdeutscher Verlag, 1971), 150–56.

38. Theodore K. Rabb, *The Struggle for Stability in Early Modern Europe* (Oxford:

Oxford University Press, 1975); on European state formation, see Charles Tilly, *Coercion, Capital, and European States, AD 990–1992* (Oxford: Blackwell, 1992).

39. Donald W. Hanson, *From Kingdom to Commonwealth: The Development of Civic Consciousness in English Political Thought* (Cambridge, Mass.: Harvard University Press, 1970), 15.

40. Brien Hallett, *The Lost Art of Declaring War* (Urbana: University of Illinois Press, 1998), 99.

41. David Held, *Democracy and the Global Order: From the Modern State to Cosmopolitan Governance* (Stanford, Calif.: Stanford University Press, 1995), 73–120.

42. Scheuerman, *Liberal Democracy and the Social Acceleration of Time,* 144–86.

43. In the two years following September 11, 2001, more than 5,000 foreign citizens were detained. Only a handful were charged with crimes relating to terrorism. "Many were held initially without charges, denied access to lawyers, judged in secret and locked for months without any showing that they had committed crimes or otherwise posed any danger. More than 500 were deported for immigration violations." Daphne Eviatar, "Foreigners' Rights in the Post-9/11 Era: A Matter of Justice," *New York Times,* October 4, 2003, A15.

44. Dworkin, "The Threat to Patriotism," 44.

45. My reliance on the term "king" here merely reflects the fact the overwhelming majority of monarchs have, of course, been male, chiefly because of sexist rules governing royal succession.

46. However, President Bush's tendency to categorize (Islamic) terrorists as "evil-doers" occasionally echoes the religious imagery of traditional religiously based monarchist political rhetoric.

47. My discussion raises the broader question of the relationship of modern "presidentialism" to monarchy. Needless to say, this is a complicated matter requiring a richer discussion than I can provide here given the specific focus of this essay. Any adequate analysis of the nexus between monarchy and presidentialism would have to move beyond the Anglo-American context and ideally integrate a significant comparative perspective. For example, to understand modern French presidentialism, we would need to look closely at the experience of nineteenth-century Bonapartism, as well as at intricate debates in French political and legal thought about executive power since the French Revolution. For better or worse, my focus in this essay remains the U.S. context and its present-day pathologies.

48. The literature on this topic is vast. See, for example, Reinhard Bendix, *Kings or People: Power and the Mandate to Rule* (Berkeley: University of California Press, 1978), 25–26.

49. Bendix, *Kings or People,* 197.

50. Blackstone, *Commentaries on the Laws of England,* vol. I (Chicago: University of Chicago Press, 1979 [1765]), 254.

51. Locke, *Second Treatise,* see chapter 12, chapter 14. For a discussion, see John Dunn, *The Political Thought of John Locke: An Historical Account of the Argument of the 'Two Treatises of Government'* (Cambridge: Cambridge University Press, 1969), 148–64.

52. Montesquieu, *Spirit of the Laws,* pp. 156–68 [Book 11, chapters 6–8]. On the idealization of actual English political experience in Montesquieu and others,

see Robert Redslob, *Die Staatstheorien der französischen Nationalversammlung von 1789* (Leipzig: Veit, 1912).

53. Hamilton's sympathy for the British monarchy is most evident in his speech at the constitutional convention on June 18, 1787. For both James Madison's and Richard Yates' notes on it, see Hamilton, *Writings* (New York: Library of America, 2001), 149–66. See also the 1793 exchange about the Neutrality Act between Madison and Hamilton, where the former persuasively accuses the latter of undertaking to import royalist ideas of prerogative into the foreign policy powers of the presidency. *The Letters of Pacificus and Helvidius with the Letters of Americanus,* (Delmar: Scholars' Facsimiles, 1976), 56.

54. See, for example, Federalist 67 (407–408); Federalist 69; Federalist 74; Federalist 75.

55. Alexander DeConde, *Presidential Machismo: Executive Authority, Military Intervention, and Foreign Relations* (Boston: Northeastern University Press, 2000), 11. This general line of interpretation is endorsed by many leading contemporary scholars, although by no means the actual holders of executive power. See, for example, David Gray Adler, "The President's War-Making Power," in *Inventing the American Presidency,* ed. Thomas E. Cronin (Lawrence: University of Kansas Press, 1989), 119–54; Louis Fisher, *Presidential War Power* (Lawrence: University of Kansas Press, 1989); Koh, *The National Security Constitution,* 67–100.

56. In seventeenth-century England, the common law "conceded to the king vast powers associated with matters of war and peace, and [King] Charles had only to manufacture rumors of danger in order to exert the full force of prerogative in domestic politics." The fact that "many of the king's assertions of national emergency were bogus" was a precipitating cause in the political upheavals of the times (Hanson, *From Kingdom to Commonwealth,* 298). Also, Francis D. Wormuth, *The Royal Prerogative, 1603–49* (Ithaca, N.Y.: Cornell University Press, 1939), 79–82.

57. Hamilton, "Speech in Convention" [June 18, 1787], *Writings,* 158.

58. Adler, "The President's War-Making Power," 122.

59. John Basset Moore, cited in Adler, "The President's War-Making Power," 124.

60. DeConde, *Presidential Machismo;* Fisher, *Presidential War Power;* Koh, *The National Security Constitution;* Lobel, "Emergency Powers and the Decline of Liberalism."

61. Hanson, *From Kingdom to Commonwealth,* 71–72.

62. Marc Bloch, *The Royal Touch: Sacred Monarchy and Scrofula in England and France* (London: Routledge, 1973).

12 Human Rights and the Use of Force after September 11th, 2001

Stephen J. Toope

On the first anniversary of the attacks on September 11th, 2001, one of the most often quoted observations of the person on Main Street USA was that "everything had changed" with the grievous attacks in New York, Washington, and Pennsylvania. Consider this observation from the British newsmagazine *The Economist:*

> Eminent Americans visiting Europe recently often seem to find themselves in a state of bewilderment, almost as if they had stumbled into some sort of parallel universe. "We in America think of September 11th as an event that changed the world," says Bill Kristol, editor of the neo-conservative *Weekly Standard,* "but Europeans seem to regard it as an event that changed America."[1]

The events of September 11th did change the U.S. by opening up a yawning chasm of fear. That fear—and a consequent sense of continuing vulnerability made manifest in intermittent heightened security alerts—is felt elsewhere in the Western world, but in muted form. Despite horrific attacks in Bali, Morocco, Spain, and elsewhere, global terrorists primarily threaten the American people and their interests and, one must add, Israel.

For much of the world, then, the raw facts of September 11th did not change everything. Yet the insecurity palpably felt by many Americans, and constantly invoked by their government, serves as justification and cover for attempts by the Bush administration to promote radical normative change. Surprisingly, it is not at all clear that the administration's strident rhetoric is matched with actions designed to accomplish the legal change that is spoken of by high-ranking administration officials and by the president himself. This seeming incoherence is discussed in detail below. There can be no doubt, however, that we find ourselves in the midst of a global dialogue of the deaf wherein an American president prosecutes a "war on terror," matched with ancillary wars and threatened punishments of rogue states, while many of the U.S.'s closest allies agonize not about the terror itself but about the American response. It may not be a popular view in the heartland, but on at least one point Al Gore was exactly right in his reflections on the anniversary of the shocking attacks against the U.S.:

In the immediate aftermath of September 11th, more than a year ago, we had an enormous reservoir of good will and sympathy and shared resolve all over the world. That has been squandered in a year's time and replaced with great anxiety all around the world, not primarily about what the terrorist networks are going to do, but about what we're going to do.[2]

A dramatic expression of the failing sense of solidarity can be found in the joint statement of Jürgen Habermas and Jacques Derrida, two of Europe's most influential thinkers, calling upon European states to return to "enlightenment values" to combat American hegemony. They ridiculed the declaration of eight European leaders in support of the war on Iraq, describing it as an "oath of loyalty to Bush" and a "coup" that was subsequently denounced by "demonstrating masses in London and Rome, Madrid and Barcelona, Berlin, and Paris."[3]

As the allusion to popular demonstrations indicates, the drastic decline in empathy for the U.S. is not merely an elite phenomenon. A poll conducted in early 2003 by the Pew Global Attitudes Project showed that only 45 percent of the Germans, 43 percent of the French, 38 percent of the Spanish, and 36 percent of the Russians held favorable views of the U.S. In Muslim nations, positive views of America declined dramatically from 2001 to 2003. In 2002, some 60 percent of Indonesians professed a favorable view of the U.S. By 2003, that number had dropped to 15 percent. In 2000, 50 percent of Turks were sympathetic to America. In 2003, only 15 percent held a positive view. Less surprisingly, only 1 percent of Jordanians and Palestinians had positive feelings about the U.S. in early 2003.[4] A later poll conducted under the auspices of ten national broadcasters from around the globe, as part of an unprecedented joint project called "What the world thinks of America," confirmed these findings with only minor variations. The most intriguing result of the second poll was its finding that the growing negative views of both foes and allies of the United States were completely at variance with popular sentiment in the U.S. itself. Immediately after the formal conclusion of the Iraq War, 93 percent of Americans held favorable views of their own country, with only 5 percent expressing negative perceptions. The U.S. president was viewed positively by 70 percent of Americans, but by only 35 percent of global respondents.[5] This mid-2003 polling data suggests that while most Americans were satisfied with their government's responses to September 11th, in the rest of the world the U.S. was widely feared and mistrusted. The chasm may have widened further following the revelations from Abu Ghraib Prison.

We are presented with something of a conundrum. Many Americans believe that the events of September 11th prompted a tectonic shift in world affairs. Many traditional allies of the U.S. believe that it is primarily America that has changed. Yet September 11th and its aftermath have generated significantly changed attitudes toward the U.S. throughout the world, and dramatically among its close allies. In that sense, a great deal has changed in world politics since the autumn of 2001, but not in the way that either the U.S. administration or the governments of some key allies have framed the issue. Outside the U.S., the widespread conclusion is that Americans and their government have overreacted to the threats they face. Yet it is important to recognize that in many countries, and particularly among close allies, the events of September 11th have been used to justify normative changes that closely parallel those promoted within the U.S. itself. The war against Iraq caused a grave split between the U.S. and many traditional allies, a split that was rooted in differing normative attitudes toward the legitimate use of force in international relations. Yet on other crucial normative questions, particularly human rights, the U.S. and its allies are not so far apart.

In this chapter, I focus upon the legal reconstructions promoted since September 11th in human rights, both domestically and internationally, and in limitations on the use of force, as exemplified by the justifications offered for the Iraq War. I assess whether or not changed attitudes are mirrored by concrete legal changes that undermine the normative fabric of domestic and international orders. The legal reconstructions that we confront also raise profound ethical questions connected to the themes pursued by other authors in this volume, particularly the extent to which a confrontation with "evil" is the ultimate justification for contested political choices.[6]

Human Rights

In 2002, Michael Ignatieff wrote a provocative article in the *New York Times* addressing the question whether "the era of human rights has come and gone."[7] Although the assumption that we were ever in an "era" of human rights is doubtful, the power of human rights discourse to influence international law and politics certainly grew in the latter part of the twentieth-century. Actively promoted by the United States during the Carter administration, human rights discourse reached its apogee in the few years after the fall of the Soviet Union.[8] Since then, we have experienced dramatic growth in international criminal law addressing crimes against humanity, the expanding role of civil society in the marshalling of shame, the express linkage of human rights and good governance in international development aid, the emergence of claims that international law supports a right to democratic government, and the rise (and apparent decline) of humanitarian intervention. It is important to note that the U.S. government did not participate in all these developments, and an argument can be made that its disengagement from global human rights began a few years before September 11th. Moreover, the intellectual framework of human rights has never gone unchallenged, as revealed by the continuing discursive power of competing frameworks such as national sovereignty, cultural autonomy, market globalization, and human responsibility. Nevertheless, it is fair to say that the language of human rights has positively shaped the political evolution of post–Second World War international society, even if it has so far failed to deliver on the more extravagant transformative claims of rights theorists.

It is worth emphasizing at the outset that international human rights guarantees are not irrationally absolutist. In the International Covenant on Civil and Political Rights, for example, states are expressly permitted to limit some (but not all) rights in times of emergency.[9] The Universal Declaration of Human Rights, which arguably reflects customary law on many human rights issues, provides that "everyone has duties to the community in which alone the free and full development of his personality is possible."[10] To cast human rights in opposition to security is not accurate. In fact, the full flourishing of human rights can only take place in societies where citizens experience the peace that security brings. Nonetheless, cries for enhanced security all too often amount to claims that human rights must be restricted. Such has been the siren song of repressive regimes the world over, but the allure periodically seduces liberal democracies as well. The delicate balance between freedom and safety is easily lost, and not easily restored.

Where does the potentially liberating discourse of human rights stand today in the ghostly shadow of the World Trade Center? I agree with Michael Ignatieff that it is under threat. If the "era of human rights" is indeed drawing to a close, it is not only through the machinations of Osama bin Laden and his ilk. The need to address security concerns prompted by indiscriminate and irrational terrorism is real today, just as it was in the time of the Baader-Meinhof Gang and the Red Brigades of the 1970s. For terrorism itself is not a new phenomenon. The complicating factor in our era is the emergence of state governments that provide sanctuary for terrorist trainers and that sponsor terror systematically, thereby extending both its global reach and its destructive capacity. The scale of the attacks on September 11th was greater than any previous terrorist attack. Yet we in the North are in danger of allowing a culture of security rooted in fear to displace our laboriously constructed, and still incomplete, culture of rights. Any psychology, individual or group, that is driven by fear and a deep sense of vulnerability is likely to prompt poor judgment. We must be cognizant of that risk—and resist the errors of political and legal judgment that may be natural but are nonetheless profoundly damaging to the normative orders that guide domestic and international societies.

The outpouring of grief and solidarity from all parts of the planet after September 11th was a remarkable, almost unique, expression of the capacity for human empathy. Sadly, few of the public commentaries since then have focused on that solidarity. Instead, the changed world is depicted purely as one in which we all feel afraid and where the search for security has reoccupied its dominating status.[11]

The response is predictable but demoralizing: throw money at the security apparatus and round up the usual suspects. In the United States, Congress has showered money on the CIA while chastising it for failing miserably in its counter-terrorism mandate.[12] Meanwhile, the Bush administration has let loose a "Pentagon spending spree" that threatens to ossify the very military structures that led to failures of intelligence before September 11th and that certainly skews national priorities.[13] Similarly in Canada, large increases in the budgets of security forces have been authorized before the discipline of an operational review could target new spending appropriately.[14] In Canada and the United States, security forces have rounded up non-citizens of Arab descent or of the Muslim faith in a seemingly indiscriminate fashion. After September 11th and well into 2002, the two immigration detention centers in my own city of Montreal, which are normally half-occupied, were full to bursting with people who fit specific ethnic and religious profiles. The U.S. adopted the same approach to policing.[15] Human Rights Watch reports that after September 11th, U.S. authorities arrested more than 1,200 people, identified primarily because of their gender, religion, and ethnic background, jailed them on immigration charges, denied them rights normally enjoyed by accused persons, and held many in isolation. "The country has witnessed a persistent, deliberate and unwarranted erosion of basic rights against abusive governmental power," the report concluded.[16]

Indiscriminate repression falls into a sad but long tradition in North America. In the U.S., various anti-sedition acts dating from the eighteenth-century allowed for the deportation of "suspicious" foreigners. Catholic subversion was the subject of fevered concern from the 1830s right up to the election of John F. Kennedy. Anti-communist hysteria gripped America in 1919 and again in the 1950s.[17] Indeed, the fear of communism may be the closest historical analogy to the current fear of terrorists and their sponsors. Both Canada and the U.S. incarcerated citizens of Japanese origin during the Second World War. Canada invoked the War Measures Act to suspend many civil liberties in its own small war on terror in 1970.[18] Some evidence suggests that the pattern now repeats itself. Witness the expansive and potentially unchecked powers accorded to security forces in the Patriot Act and its Canadian equivalent, the Anti-Terrorism Act.[19] A review of the effects of the Canadian legislation undertaken by a coalition of NGOs, including the generally careful Canadian Bar Association and Amnesty International, offered the following brief summary:

> The Anti-Terrorism Act (Bill C-36) grants police expanded investigative and surveillance powers, allows for preventative detention, undermines the principle of due process by guarding certain information of "national interest" from disclosure during courtroom or other judicial proceedings and calls for the de-registration of charities accused of links with terrorist organizations. All of these changes occur on the basis of a vague, imprecise and overly expansive definition of terrorist activity.[20]

The report went on to detail other related legislative initiatives that cumulatively have "a far-reaching impact" and represent "a significant shift in the relationship between citizens and the state in Canada."[21] The Canadian government is busy amending laws related to the registration of charities, data collection by airlines, organized crime, the sharing of information by security agencies, the revocation of citizenship, and electronic surveillance, to name but a few post–September 11th initiatives. The evaluation of the NGO coalition is tough: "Each of these legislative packages is, alone, drastic and unwarranted. However, their cumulative effect represents a serious erosion of civil rights, especially with regards to due process and the right to privacy."[22]

The growing security culture is a global, not merely North American, phenomenon. Across Europe, governments are expanding police powers to detain, to wiretap, and to survey electronic communications. France now allows police to search private property without warrants; Germany has loosened regulations controlling wiretaps, the monitoring of e-mail, and access to bank records.[23] More disturbing still are the many states using the specter of terrorism to launch frontal assaults on domestic opposition and upon claimants to self-determination. Foreign governments have conveniently turned away as President Putin adopts what the *New York Times* described as "scorched-earth policies" in Chechnya.[24] China represses dissent in the Muslim Xinjian region. The pattern repeats in Egypt, Sudan, Tajikistan, Uzbekistan, and Zimbabwe.[25] Although sorely provoked by suicide bomb attacks, the current Israeli government responds by employing excessive force against the civilian population of the occupied territories. The annual human rights report of the U.S. State Department singles out many of the new-found allies in the war on terror, and in the coalition of the willing against Iraq, as egregious human rights violators. The enumerated countries include China, Egypt, Pakistan, Russia, and Saudi Arabia.[26] The contrast between America's vaunted commitment to human rights and freedom, which has become the principal public justification for the war in Iraq, and its choice of allies is striking.

One should also consider the unique situation of Taliban and al-Qaida prisoners in Guantanamo Bay—the situation that first began to break up the single-minded solidarity of U.S. allies. At first, President Bush declared that neither al-Qaida nor Taliban forces could benefit from the protections of the Geneva Conventions governing prisoners of war. After heated debate within the administration and strong international pressure, especially from the Red Cross and European allies, the decision was partly reversed, with the U.S. agreeing to apply the substantive rules of the Geneva Conventions (though formally *not* the treaties themselves) to the Taliban detainees only.[27] Al-Qaida prisoners remain outside the framework of international law.[28] Moreover, U.S. courts had initially refused to seize jurisdiction over these prisoners, who were thereby denied any opportunity to vindicate rights within U.S. domestic law.[29] This refusal meant that the administration was completely unfettered in its plan to try terrorist suspects by "military commission" rather than in federal courts, where the full panoply of due process rights would come into play. However, the one American citizen accused of fighting for the Taliban, John Walker Lindh, was speedily granted a trial in a U.S. federal court, thereby angering allies whose citizens were apparently to be denied that right.[30] In June 2004, the U.S. Supreme Court changed the legal calculus dramatically, ruling that the prisoners held at Guantanamo Bay could apply to U.S. federal courts in habeas corpus litigation, thereby requiring the federal authorities to demonstrate that the detentions are lawful and opening up Guantanamo to civilian judicial scrutiny.[31]

The controversy nonetheless persists. It is clear that the Bush administration does not know what it will do with many of the Guantanamo prisoners once intelligence-gathering sessions are over. Some prisoners have been set free, but roughly 600 men from more than forty countries were still detained in 2004.[32] Secretary of Defense Rumsfeld admitted that some prisoners might be held in Camp X-Ray indefinitely. The Pentagon's top lawyer goes further to suggest that even terror suspects who are tried *and acquitted* by military commissions may be held in indefinite preventive detention.[33] Amnesty International has warned that the hopelessness of indefinite detention gives rise to grave physical and psychological risks for the detainees, a number of whom have attempted suicide.[34] Nor is it clear how many trials will actually be held. Ruth Wedgwood, an advisor to the administration on the creation of military commissions, admitted that to build credible cases against suspects, with solid evidence, could take years.[35] On July 3rd, 2003, President Bush finally announced that six prisoners, including two Britons and an Australian, would be brought to trial before a military commission.[36] Only two weeks later, after strong pressure from the U.K. government, the Bush administration retreated. It announced that proceedings against the three nationals of close U.S. allies against Iraq would be "suspended."[37] The result of this decision may be that only citizens from developing world states will be subjected to trial by military commission.

If the military commissions were to have any credibility and legitimacy, elementary standards of due process, so fundamental to American perceptions of justice, would have to be met. Much of the public critique to which the commissions have been subjected is based upon realistic fears that due process will not be accorded to suspects. The military judges will not be independent, for they report to the president as commander in chief. It is the president or his delegate, the secretary of defense, who authorizes prosecutions. Moreover, unlike in standard courts martial within the U.S. legal system, appeals will also be heard by military judges and not by civilians. Final appeals go to the president himself. Every procedural right of the accused is "hedged with caveats" and all rights can be suspended or overridden by the commission.[38] There is no guarantee of lawyer-client confidentiality. Military lawyers are appointed by the commission, and civilians that may supplement the defense team will have no independent access to the accused. In a comparison of military tribunals employed in a range of states, *The Economist,* a magazine generally sympathetic to the Bush administration, concluded that the U.S. military commissions "are far more draconian than other terrorism courts, including apartheid-era courts in South Africa, and the so-called 'Diplock Courts' in the UK, used to try IRA suspects."[39]

The fact that the administration seems to be finding it difficult to launch the military commissions suggests that it recognizes the bind in which it has placed itself. If military commission trials are widely viewed as unfair, the U.S. would be undermining the rule of law, which is part of its very self-definition. On the other hand, full due process rights might lead to acquittals, given the difficulty of evidence gathering, and acquittals would be a public relations disaster, calling into question the entire internment policy. Anthony Lewis argues that the administration "badly fumbled justice for its captives" because it "failed to understand the power of the human rights ideal."[40] What led to this myopia when it comes to fundamental human rights values? Why is a culture of security undermining human rights in America and abroad?

There are no doubt many reasons, but let me note one, for it connects directly to the second part of this chapter. The culture of security is founded upon a Manichean posture dividing the world into forces of good and evil. Recall George Bush's powerful statement in his address to the nation just days after the attacks: "you are with us or you are with the terrorists."[41] Then, in the 2002 State of the Union address, we were told we were the targets of an "axis of evil."[42] Just a short while later a telling incident occurred in which President Bush was reported to have been outraged by the story of a North Korean museum that displays axes used to kill two American servicemen in 1976. After hearing the story, he apparently muttered to himself, "[n]o wonder I think they are evil."[43] One must ask who "they" are: the incredible North Korean regime or the North Korean people? The clearest statement of the Manichean worldview comes, not surprisingly, from former Attorney General John Ashcroft: "A calculated, malignant, devastating evil has arisen in our world. Civilization cannot afford to ignore the wrongs that have been done."[44]

If "we" are cast as wholly good and our enemies as wholly evil, ineluctable consequences flow. Most obviously, the opponent is dehumanized. Common humanity is always a casualty of war, but the absolutely evil enemy bears no consideration. The closest historical parallel may be the manner in which the Allies viewed the Japanese during the Second World War: first as an inferior race but then, after the attack on Pearl Harbor, as ruthless supermen.[45] Similarly, terrorists, once treated as the ultimate cowards, have since September 11th become dark geniuses.[46] In neither guise are they fully human. More to the point, one may extend the label "inhuman" to those states and people who support terror or who harbor terrorists. The list of the inhuman grows exponentially. This position makes political compromise almost impossible to achieve. Given that the "war" on terror is neither territorially nor temporally limited, the risks associated with demonizing the enemy are hugely amplified.

The logic of war against evil leads to the logic of regime destruction. The problem is that, try as one might, it becomes difficult to separate the regime from the people in the lead-up to war. "Iraq" is the enemy. "Iran" is the enemy. "North Korea" is the enemy. "They" are evil. To mobilize political actors in favor of the use of force, distinctions between people and state must be blurred in the popular mind. Although it is true that the United States and its allies may try to co-opt or support local opposition groups, as in Afghanistan, thereby upholding a distinction between people and state, these efforts take place on the margins of the mobilization for war. For example, during the Iraq War the U.S. popular media constantly fed the view that "the enemy" was a people either in cahoots with a dictator or so downtrodden as to be contemptible. Popular U.S. electronic media focused again and again on the Iraqi regime's propaganda as it sought to explain how Saddam could remain in power. The implicit questions were always "why don't the Iraqis get rid of Saddam, and why must the U.S. do it for them?" During the war, Fox News offered this explanation from a London-based Iraqi opposition spokesperson: "His propaganda machine to him is very important because it's a way of reaching into the minds of people so that they do not rise up against him."[47] When we later try to recapture the moral distinctions, to suggest that we are fighting not a people but a regime, that we are "liberating" the people, the damage is already done. The justification seems inauthentic, if not hypocritical. If the people we "liberate" then seem ungrateful, as in Iraq, we are not surprised. What can one expect of them? We are enmeshed in a clash of civilizations: ours (the good) against the others (the evil).[48] The laboriously constructed human rights framework linked to the United Nations system increasingly seems irrelevant at best, dangerous at worst—because it gets in the way of the battle against the forces of evil unleashed in our frightening world.

Constructing oneself as the personification of good has the further demerit of precluding critical self-assessment. In his otherwise effective speech to the nation immediately after September 11th, President Bush struck one jarring chord. In purporting to explain why these horrifying attacks took place, he said, "These people can't stand freedom. They hate our values. They hate what America stands for."[49] Although understandable in a moment of high drama, this analysis is grossly superficial. It invokes the open-ended "they" category once again. What's more, it refuses even to countenance the possibility that the good may pursue mistaken policies. As I suggested earlier, judgment is inevitably affected by fear. It is also clouded by hubris, and by its close relative in international politics, unreflective nationalism, an unpleasant strand of which seems to be growing in the United States.[50] The president's superficial analysis finds its way into the 2002 National Security Strategy as well, where one of the criteria for the designation of "rogue statehood" is that the state "reject[s] basic human values and hate[s] the United States and everything for which it stands."[51] Yet the view from outside the United States should serve to caution America about its uncritical self-description as the benign hegemon. Some Americans might be chastened to learn that in a global poll conducted for ten national broadcasters, a slight majority of respondents *disagreed* with the statement that "America is a force for good in the world." Only the British, Australians, Canadians, and Israelis viewed American influence as generally benign. Large majorities in countries as diverse as Brazil, France, Indonesia, and Russia see America as a force for whatever one wants to imagine as the opposite of good.[52]

Thoughtless invocations of the threat of evil cloud the judgment of many Western governments, particularly that of the United States. Even though the fear generated by the attacks on September 11th is more pronounced in the U.S., it does exist elsewhere, and it seems to loosen the political constraints on governments as they limit human rights. Some of the actions by U.S. allies may have been undertaken to prove commitment to the dominant power, to demonstrate solidarity.[53] But this explanation is too simple. Governments of the North should be pressed hard to explain why so many of them criticize U.S. excesses in the war on terror while adopting parallel anti-terrorist—and anti–human rights—policies. With sickening irony, the need to combat evil is being used to justify attacks upon both the international and domestic normative edifices of human rights. In the straightforward words of David Frum, a former speech-writer to President Bush and the person credited with coining the phrase "axis of evil," "In a world where there are evil governments, this is the real moral test. . . . What do evil governments do? They kill. What do good governments do? They must also kill."[54]

A sober assessment of the political and legal status of human rights after September 11th leads to the conclusion that many governments, led by the administration of the most powerful state, are using the threat of global terrorism to undermine the fragile edifice of human rights law. Attacks on hard-won human rights gains are taking place in domestic and international contexts. The two contexts are linked. Undermining domestic human rights norms in liberal democracies, as well as in authoritarian states, has the effect of further weakening international law norms, both through the degradation of customary law standards and through damaging reinterpretations of treaty law. Attacks on human rights are made possible by a media-fed climate of fear in America, which the governments of other states then use to justify repressive measures. They are also permitted by the hubris that guides the actions of the U.S. administration, a hubris that inhibits critical self-assessment and that underplays the risks to America of claims to untrammeled state power made in the name of the war on terror.

Limitations on the Use of Force

One can read the history of twentieth-century international law as primarily an attempt to limit recourse to the use of force in international relations. Sporadically but powerfully, the sentiment arose, especially in Europe, the crucible of two world wars, that war was itself an evil to be avoided at almost any cost. Efforts were made to severely curtail the grounds for war recognized in the "just war" tradition. The aim was to replace unilateral moral judgments with justificatory standards that were closer to general practice and susceptible of collective evaluation. It is worth recalling that the first principle in the Preamble of the UN Charter is that the uniting nations pledge themselves to "save succeeding generations from the scourge of war." In other words, the entire framework of post-Charter international law is predicated upon the assumption that the use of force in international relations is exceptional and subject to a heavy burden of justification. For that reason, the Charter limits the use of force to only two circumstances: self-defense, which must be reported to the Security Council, and "collective measures" authorized by the Council under Chapter VII.

More recently, states have created an international criminal law framework through treaties to address the dangers of terrorism. There are some nineteen anti-terrorism conventions, most of which focus upon terrorism directed at aircraft, or perpetrated with aircraft. However, the normative coverage is fragmented, and the treaties do not really contemplate newer forms of global, state-sponsored terrorism.[55] This framework seemed inadequate to deal with the enormity of September 11th. For that reason, the United States and many other countries concluded that the attacks on New York, Washington, and Pennsylvania could serve to engage the norms permitting the use of force. In invading Afghanistan, the U.S. chose not to request Security Council authorization under Chapter VII. The U.S. and its allies then prosecuted the second Iraq War in the explicit absence of Security Council sanctioning, having failed to convince the Council that the use of force was justified. President Bush suggested during the intense and angry debates that if the Security Council failed to act, the UN risked fading "into history as an ineffective, irrelevant debating society."[56]

The refusal of the members of the Security Council to authorize the use of force against Iraq cannot properly be cast as a failure. Indeed, the Council's unhappy deliberations over Iraq revealed the lack of consensus in international society on the utility and propriety of forceful intervention in member states. The one issue on which states could traditionally agree was the need to uphold sovereignty; any transgression of sovereignty was a potential systemic threat. Moreover, modern anti-war sentiment, epitomized by the UN Charter itself, has served to temper all arguments favoring the use of force. To justify the collective use of force therefore required the displacement of very strong normative barriers. The drafters of the Charter foresaw this difficulty and indeed constructed it intentionally. To put it another way, justification for action by the Security Council has always required a mix of normative, prudential, and political persuasion. The Iraq War is a telling case-in-point. The U.S. and its few allies against Iraq simply failed to discharge the burden of persuasion they faced in the Security Council. The fact that close neighbors of the United States, including Mexico, and economically dependent states in Africa and Latin America could not be pressured into submission signifies a remarkable failure of American diplomacy or a level of principled conduct that is rarely reached by sovereign states. Most likely, it is a combination of the two. That the Security Council was right in refusing to authorize force seems to be borne out by the inability of members of the "coalition of the willing" to discover any weapons of mass destruction in Iraq. Journalists and commentators are now asking tough questions about whether the allied governments lied about the threat used to justify the war.[57] The ill-advised comments of Deputy Secretary of Defense Wolfowitz suggesting that the invocation of weapons of mass destruction was merely the U.S. bureaucratic consensus as the pretense for war, lend credence to accusations of willful manipulation of the public.[58]

Although some media reports suggest that international lawyers are divided over the legality of the Iraq War, that assertion is misleading.[59] One could rarely find 100 percent of any professional group agreeing on a matter of professional judgment. However, in public comments, the president of the American Society of International Law suggested that at least 80 percent of international lawyers hold the invasion to be illegal. My own guess is that the figure is, if anything, understated.

One might question why it is relevant that such a broad spectrum of the international legal profession agreed on the illegality of the Iraq War. Consensus is not necessarily correctness, and the profession might simply be circling the wagons to uphold its own sense of relevance. It is beyond the scope of this essay to offer a detailed defense of the legal consensus on illegality, but a few brief observations might help to show how international lawyers contribute to the interdisciplinary dialogue on matters of international politics. Like all lawyers, international lawyers are trained to analyze with care the interrelationship of norm and fact. Legal frameworks, such as prohibitions on the use of force, are never self-applying. Norms are brought to bear in assessing specific factual situations. The quintessential lawyer's tool is analogy, analogy of a posited norm to a broader structure of norms (often called "fit"), and analogy of current facts to past circumstances where norms have been applied in a particular way. Sometimes it is relatively easy to read a new circumstance in the light of previously applied norms. At other times, the lawyer understands that she or he is pushing the parameters of past decisions in order to accommodate new facts. So at times all lawyers find themselves assessing the applicability of a relatively stable body of norms and stretching the boundaries of those norms at one and the same time. Good lawyers are never purely descriptive. Instead, lawyers are in many circumstances norm entrepreneurs; that is the essence of advocacy.[60] A good lawyer, however, will also sense intuitively when the boundaries are being strained—when either the fit of a newly posted norm within the broader framework is uncomfortable or the facts of a new situation cannot properly be analogized to past situations. These assessments are the stock-in-trade of all lawyers but especially of international lawyers, who often find themselves in situations where applicable norms are loosely articulated and where past practices are multi-directional.

A further intriguing aspect of the role of international lawyers is that the arguments of particularly distinguished lawyers can themselves contribute to the formation of binding law. Article 38 of the Statute of the International Court of Justice sets out the "sources" of law to be applied by the court and states that the writings of "the most highly qualified publicists" are a subsidiary source of law. This idea, which may seem odd to Americans who participate in the common-law tradition, is derived from the civil law of continental Europe, where "doctrine"—professorial writings—was traditionally more weighty in legal analysis than the decisions of courts. In international law, therefore, it really matters how highly qualified publicists assess a legal situation.

In assessing the legality of the war in Iraq, the vast majority of international lawyers concluded that the facts did not give rise to a proper analogy to past situations in which self-defense has been invoked to justify a use of force. They also concluded that an extension of the norms governing self-defense mooted by the U.S. administration did not comfortably "fit" with the broader normative framework. Further, they concluded that no other framework, such as "humanitarian intervention," applied to the facts at issue. Finally, they rejected the contention that the United Nations Security Council had somehow implicitly authorized the use of force against Iraq. I will now briefly set out the reasoning behind these widely shared conclusions.

In the absence of action by the Security Council, states can call upon the doctrine of self-defense to respond to terror or to the threatened use of weapons of mass destruction. What is the scope of self-defense in contemporary international law? Some have argued that with the advent of the UN Charter, self-defense is limited by Article 51 to a response to a prior armed attack.[61] There would be no right of pre-emption. This view is, in my opinion, both unrealistic and ethically unsound. No state should have to sit idly by to wait for an attack upon its population before taking action.

Customary international law admits of a right to pre-emptive self-defense that runs parallel to the rights contained in the UN Charter. Treaty and custom are complementary sources of law. Although a treaty may explicitly oust custom as between state parties, such an ouster cannot be presumed. In the case of self-defense, it cannot be said that Article 51 of the UN Charter fully occupies the field. In a leading case, the International Court of Justice concluded that self-defense exists under both the Charter and customary international law.[62] Moreover, subsequent practice can affect the interpretation of Charter provisions, as is commonly the case for the interpretation of written domestic constitutions.

The customary law right of pre-emption is not unlimited. Indeed, it is tightly and carefully circumscribed. The classic—and still controlling—definition of the customary law on pre-emptive self-defense was proposed in 1842 by no less a figure than Daniel Webster, then the U.S. secretary of state. In a delicate negotiation with the British over the legal implications of a U.S. militia raid on Canadian territory using the steamboat *Caroline,* and the British response, which was to set the ship afire and send it crashing over Niagara Falls, Webster set out the applicable rule. An attack on foreign territory can only be justified if the aggressor can "show a necessity of self-defense, instant, overwhelming, leaving no choice of means, and no moment for deliberation." He added that the pre-emptive self-defense had to be proportional to the threat.[63]

These are the legal tests for the legitimate invocation of a right to self-defense: necessity (including imminence of the threat) and proportionality. The tests were met in the initial phases of the war in Afghanistan, though there is doubt that self-defense can justify the post-war occupation of a country for an extended period of time. The invasion took place in response to an armed attack, that of September 11th, 2001—admittedly one carried out by non-state actors. But these terrorists had been actively aided and abetted by the Taliban regime. Moreover, there was credible evidence that the Taliban were providing sanctuary for the organizers of the attacks, people who continued to threaten future armed attacks on the U.S. and its interests around the world.[64] A conclusion that the U.S. could lawfully invoke self-defense to justify its invasion of Afghanistan does not preclude an argument that it would have been vastly preferable for the U.S. to work within the framework of the United Nations.[65] If there was any moment in recent world history where the U.S. could almost certainly have succeeded in marshalling the Security Council into action, it was *vis-à-vis* Afghanistan in the immediate aftermath of September 11th. Indeed, success in such an operation might well have changed the later dynamic concerning Iraq as well. One can only guess that the U.S. administration did not wish to engage in the negotiations that UN action inevitably would have required. It may have believed that its moral duty to act in the fight against evil was so clear that any negotiating would be a form of appeasement. Alternatively, U.S. war planners, perhaps recalling the difficult targeting discussions that affected the NATO Kosovo campaign, may have wished to avoid the need for any limitations upon their freedom of action.[66]

Does the doctrine of self-defense, even in its extended version encompassing a right of pre-emption, justify the war against Iraq? I believe that the answer is clear: No, it does not. In the oft-quoted National Security Strategy of September 2002, the Bush administration proposed a radical extension of the right to self-defense. It asserted a right to use force to eliminate "emerging threats" posed by "rogue states" with weapons of mass destruction.[67] President Bush had laid the groundwork for the extension of the right of self-defense in a speech delivered at Fort Drum, New York, in which he declared, "America must act against these terrible threats before they are fully formed."[68] The vast majority of the leading international lawyers in states closely allied to the U.S., and in America itself, forcefully repudiated this assertion. In Britain, the holders of the two most distinguished chairs in public international law joined a group of sixteen eminent international lawyers (including one Frenchman) in stating that "the doctrine of pre-emptive self-defense against an attack that might arise at some hypothetical future time has no basis in international law."[69] The same position was taken in media declarations by leading internationalists in Australia, Canada, and the U.S.[70] In essence, the argument is that self-defense is a limited exception to the general prohibition on the use of force. If the exception is not strictly circumscribed by the ideas of imminence and necessity, the exception will come to overwhelm the rule. Allowing a state to attack another on the basis of a unilateral assertion of a merely potential threat would lead to entirely self-serving claims of danger. Aggression would be masked as defense, reviving one of the oldest problems in the hard-fought struggle to restrict the use of war as an instrument of policy.

The administration cast the "Bush Doctrine" as "preventive" self-defense, a simple extension of the notion of pre-emptive self-defense. One would have expected that it would be front and center when President Bush sent his delegates to the United Nations to promote the waging of war against Iraq. What is striking is that over those few tense months in 2003, the United States never actually invoked the new doctrine of preventive self-defense to legally justify the use of force against Iraq.[71] Even in the letter sent by the U.S. Permanent Representative to the president of the Security Council on March 20th, 2003, justifying the invasion of Iraq, the only words that could be read as an invocation of self-defense were imprecise: the steps taken were necessary "to defend the United States and the international community from the threat posed by Iraq."[72] It is as if the phrases of the National Security Strategy were meant purely for media consumption, never intended to accomplish a real normative shift. From a prudential perspective, this decision by the U.S. administration was wise. As suggested above, the problem with preventive war is that it permits of no definable standards that could provide normative guidance or constraint upon unilateral assessments of "just" war. A historical analogy immediately comes to mind: the Cuban missile crisis. We know that during that earlier and even tenser period, the Kennedy administration explicitly refrained from invoking self-defense because it worried about an uncontrollable extension of the doctrine.[73] In November 2002, the legal advisor to the State Department seemed to argue against the position adopted in the National Security Strategy, released just two months before. In a public legal memorandum on pre-emption, he suggested that a pre-emptive use of force had to fit within the "traditional framework" of self-defense. That framework required that "a preemptive use of proportional force" could only be justified "out of necessity." Necessity further required that the threat justifying the use of force be "credible" and "imminent."[74] In a presentation to the 2004 meeting of the American Society of International Law, the legal advisor reasserted his earlier argument with greater clarity, stating directly that "Iraq was not about pre-emption."[75]

Once the U.S. administration decided not to rely upon an extended version of self-defense, the available justifications for war were highly circumscribed. Obviously, the doctrine of self-defense within Article 51 of the UN Charter was not engaged as there had been no prior armed attack by Iraq against the United States. Despite some vague statements from officials of the U.S. administration, there is no evidence whatsoever that Iraq had anything to do with the attacks on September 11th.[76] If anything, Osama bin Laden viewed Saddam's regime as an enemy, for it was resolutely secular, despite Saddam's hypocritical invocations of Allah. Nor could the United States claim pre-emptive self-defense vis-à-vis Iraq based on the practice associated with the *Caroline* incident. Prime Minister Blair's now infamous dossier on weapons of mass destruction in Iraq failed to meet the standard imposed by the concept of necessity. The dossier contained almost no revelations beyond the assertion that Iraq had illegally retained twenty ballistic missiles with a range of 650 km, and that it had tried to procure fissionable material from an African state, an assertion that was later discredited.[77] The editor of *Jane's World Armies*, hardly an unreconstructed dove, had this to say: "There is nothing new in it. Nothing that I haven't seen or heard of before. We were all expecting the evidence for war, and what we got was evidence for UN inspections."[78] The situation in Iraq in April 2003 was not demonstrably different from what it had been two or even five years before. There was no "instant, overwhelming" *necessity* for war.

By mid-2003, it had become apparent that not only did the British dossier contain little new information, it contained misleading information, so much so that the U.S. administration admitted that some of the intelligence information provided by the British had been unreliable. Even close allies of the prime minister had begun to call for a full judicial inquiry into the possible manipulation of intelligence information in the lead-up to the Iraq War.[79] The pro-war newspaper *The Telegraph* stated that the publication of the dossier was "grossly irresponsible," calling it a "PR exercise."[80] A public debate emerged pitting the U.K. government against its own security apparatus, with agents stating openly to journalists that the government had willfully misinterpreted intelligence reports to the public in order to justify going to war.[81] Though initially less intense, a similar debate developed in the United States, where security agents complained publicly that they felt pressured by the White House to doctor their analyses of both the likelihood of Saddam's possessing weapons of mass destruction and possible links between al-Qaida and Iraq.[82] It also emerged in mid-2003 that a CIA report concluding that it had "no reliable information" that Iraq was producing or stockpiling chemical weapons had been suppressed in the rush to war.[83] These revelations further undermined any claim that the Iraq War was necessary for the self-defense of members of the "coalition of the willing."

What of the requirement of proportionality in the justification for self-defense? Is "regime change" a proportional response to particular threats? On balance, I do not believe that the desire for a new and less dangerous regime can meet the proportionality requirement of pre-emptive self-defense. Usurping a people's self-determination and risking civilian casualties and mass destruction of infrastructure is not proportional to the desire to end the political discomfort and frustration felt by other states confronting an authoritarian regime. In Iraq, Saddam and his barbarous acolytes were probably deeply unpopular. Yet events after the invasion confirm that although most Iraqis were glad to see Saddam's back, they are not happy to be governed by American administrators. If there was no instant, overwhelming threat to anyone else, what was the justification for regime change?

Ex post facto, the popular justification for the war has shifted from the seemingly false threat of weapons of mass destruction to the "liberation" of the Iraqi people. President Bush began this reorientation of discourse as he announced "Operation Iraqi Freedom" on March 19th, 2003. While of course mentioning the "grave danger" and "threat" posed to others by the Iraqi regime in his speech to the nation, he placed at least equal emphasis upon liberating an oppressed people.[84] The morally attractive but practically problematic doctrine of humanitarian intervention is now widely invoked by political and some legal commentators.[85] In his weekly radio address to the nation during the hostilities, President Bush articulated the new reasons for war in stirring language. "The people of Iraq have my pledge: Our fighting forces will press on until their oppressors are gone and their whole country is free."[86] Prime Minister Blair has repeated these arguments in major public pronouncements.[87]

Again, however, one must separate the rhetoric from the legal justification. Neither the U.S. nor the U.K. invoked humanitarian intervention as the legal basis for the Iraq War. This is not surprising, for humanitarian intervention remains a controversial and at best highly exceptional justification for the use of force. Its only possible legitimate application is to forestall imminent humanitarian disasters. Such a disaster could perhaps have been foreseen at the end of the first Gulf War in 1991, but none was predicted or even suggested as a possibility by the invaders in 2003. In the most compelling recent case where humanitarian intervention was expressly, albeit retrospectively, raised as a justification for the use of force, Kosovo, the clear balance of legal opinion was that humanitarian intervention did not provide a valid justification for NATO's actions. The best that could be argued was that the air campaign over Kosovo was not legal but may have been "legitimate" because necessary.[88] Even this "necessity" may have involved less the protection of Kosovars than the need to compel President Milosevic to negotiate with NATO.

Intriguingly, neither of the oft-repeated political justifications for war, self-defense in any of its forms or humanitarian intervention, was actually put forward by the U.S. or the U.K. to legally justify the invasion of Iraq. These military powers instead relied on a highly technical, narrow, and ultimately unconvincing legal argument rooted in Security Council Resolutions of 1991 that served to authorize and, arguably, "suspend" the first Gulf War.[89] The details of the position hold little interest for present purposes. In summary, the U.K. and the U.S. asserted that the 1991 war never formally ended. A cease-fire took place, with conditions imposed upon Iraq. In failing to meet those conditions in 2003, Iraq committed a "material breach" of the cease-fire, thereby justifying a renewal of hostilities.[90] The Australian government offered the same justification, in a more detailed and clearer form.[91] I fully concur with a group of distinguished British and French international lawyers who argued that none of the UN Security Council resolutions from 1991 authorized the use of force against Iraq in 2003.[92] Even if the resolutions could be read to allow for the contingent use of force, which would require a decidedly strained approach to accepted modes of textual interpretation, invoking the contingency remained within the power of the Security Council alone and was not vested in self-appointed enforcers.[93]

By choosing to rely on a narrow legal argument rooted in the interpretation of Security Council resolutions, and to eschew even more controversial justifications for war, the U.S. and its coalition of the willing accomplished something odd. While arguing on the one hand that the Security Council had failed to act against Iraq, and that the United Nations risked irrelevancy, the entire justification for war was actually grounded in Security Council actions, albeit from 1991 rather than 2003. So the UN proved to be essential legally even as it was otherwise being ignored by the U.S. and its allies. Moreover, the U.S. fatally undermined the novel normative argument for preventive self-defense mooted in the National Security Strategy. Although the strategy is still invoked in political discourse, its legal weight is negligible when one considers the subsequent practice of the U.S. itself. For all the breathless rhetoric on CNN and Fox News about the recasting of world politics and international law in the wake of President Bush's "success" in the Iraq War, a careful analysis of the justifications for war that were actually offered up reveals that nothing much has changed.[94] The calm conclusion of the legal adviser to the Canadian Department of Foreign Affairs and International Trade in a speech in the summer of 2003 is spot on: "given the quite divergent views of governments, it seems unlikely that any of the views could be considered as representing state practice sufficient to have evolved into customary international law."[95] The National Security Strategy launched a dangerous broadside across the bow of international law, but the cannons were subsequently silenced. The ship sails on in perilous seas, but it has so far suffered minimal damage, at least as concerns the important normative framework shaping the lawful use of force in international relations.

The condition of human rights law is more worrisome. Dangerous incursions against recently constructed normative frameworks are under way under the cover of a war on terror. The most obvious casualties have taken place within states governed by repressive regimes that have committed to assist the U.S.-led anti-terrorism campaign. But incursions against human rights and civil liberties have occurred in a range of liberal democratic states as well. The attempt to create a rights-free zone in Guantanamo Bay is deeply troubling. All the modifications to domestic law justified by the war on terror can ultimately undermine hard-won international standards. They can affect both the interpretation of international human rights treaty guarantees and the evolution of parallel customary law. They also make it harder for states that have promoted human rights standards to criticize allies. Many liberal democracies are working hard to undermine their own potential influence on the evolution of human rights in world society. Yet the triumph of security over human rights is not inevitable. Signs of resistance are emerging in civil society and in academic and legal circles in America and around the globe. A petition launched at Yale Law School called into question the legality and morality of the U.S. military tribunals created to try suspected terrorists.[96] Historians are challenging the U.S. administration's monolithic construction of American values.[97] An appellate chief justice in Canada called upon all judges to uphold the rights of individuals in the face of heightened preoccupations with security. He insisted that the courts must serve as correctives "when a society is not faithful to its basic values."[98] Principled resistance by international lawyers to attempts to modify norms on the use of force seems to have had some effect in shaping the justificatory arguments of the U.S. and its allies in relation to the war on Iraq. Those people concerned with the promotion and protection of human rights must apply the same tenacious effort to limit the ill-considered and dangerous attacks on fundamental values currently taking place around the globe.

Notes

Portions of this essay are adapted from my article "Fallout from '9–11': Will a Security Culture Undermine Human Rights?" *Sasketchewan Law Review* 65, no. 2 (2002): 281–98. I thank the participants in the University of Wisconsin-Milwaukee Center for

21st Century Studies conference, as well as Jutta Brunnée, Michael Byers, and René Provost, for enlightening discussions that helped to clarify my views. This work forms part of a larger project with Jutta Brunnée funded by the Social Sciences and Humanities Research Council of Canada.

1. "Fear of america, and of being left out," *The Economist*, September 7, 2002, 43.

2. "Al Gore Attacks Bush's Iraq Policy," *Australianpolitics.com* (September 23, 2002), http://www.australianpolitics.com/news/2002/09/02–09-23.shtml (accessed June 16, 2003).

3. "Philosophizing about Europe's Rebirth," *Deutsche Welle* (March 6, 2003), trans. Nancy Isenson, http://www.dw-world.de/english/0,3367,1433_A_884292_1_A,00.html (accessed June 16, 2003).

4. "The world out there," *The Economist*, June 7, 2003, 26.

5. "What the World Thinks of America," CBC News, June 17, 2003, http://www.cbc.ca/news/america/finaldata.pdf (accessed June 18, 2003).

6. Jutta Brunnée and Stephen J. Toope, "Slouching Towards New 'Just' Wars: International Law and the Use of Force After September 11th," *Netherlands International Law Review* 51 (2004): 363; "Mr. Bush's Rash Words," *Globe and Mail*, February 1, 2002.

7. Michael Ignatieff, "Is the Human Rights Era Ending?" *New York Times*, February 5, 2002.

8. Harold Hongju Koh, "The Globalization of Freedom," 26 *Yale Journal of International Law* 305 (2001).

9. *International Covenant on Civil and Political Rights,* December 19, 1966, 999 U.N.T.S. 171, Can. T.S. 1976 No. 47, 6 I.L.M. 368 (entered into force March 23, 1976), article 4.

10. *Universal Declaration of Human Rights,* GA Res. 217 (III), UN GAOR, 3d Sess., Supp. No. 13, UN Doc. A/810 (1948), article 29.

11. Harold Hongju Koh, "The Spirit of the Laws," *Harvard International Law Journal* 43 (2002): 23.

12. "The Future of the C.I.A.," *New York Times*, February 17, 2002, sec. 4.

13. "The Pentagon Spending Spree," *New York Times*, February 6, 2002.

14. D. Leblanc, "Senate Wants $4-billion More Spent on Defense," *Globe and Mail*, March 2, 2002; J. Bronskill, "CSIS watchdog warns of potential for abuse," *National Post*, January 22, 2002.

15. J. Kahn, "Raids, Detentions and Lists Lead Muslims to Cry Persecution," *New York Times*, March 27, 2002.

16. P. Knox, "Rights Trampled in U.S., Report Says," *Globe and Mail*, August 15, 2002.

17. R. F. Worth, "A Nation Defines Itself by Its Evil Enemies," *New York Times*, February 24, 2002, sec. 4.

18. Thomas Berger, *Fragile Freedoms: Human Rights and Dissent in Canada* (Toronto: Clarke, Irwin and Co., 1981), 7.

19. Kent Roach, "The Dangers of a Charter-Proof and Crime-Based Response to Terrorism," in *The Security of Freedom: Essays on Canada's Anti-terrorism Bill,* eds. Ronald J. Daniels, Patrick Macklem, and Kent Roach (Toronto: University of Toronto Press, 2001), 131.

20. "In the Shadow of the Law: A Report by the International Civil Liberties Monitoring Group (ICLMG) in response to Justice Canada's 1st annual re-

port on the application of the *Anti-Terrorism Act* (Bill C-36)," May 14, 2003, online: http://www.cba.org/cba/News/PDF/Shadow.pdf (accessed July 21, 2003).

21. Ibid., 2.

22. Ibid., 3.

23. W. Hoge, "U.S. Terror Attacks Galvanize Europeans to Tighten Laws," *New York Times,* December 6, 2001.

24. "The Antiterror Bandwagon," *New York Times,* December 28, 2001.

25. Ignatieff, "Is the Human Rights Era Ending?"

26. T. S. Purdum, "U.S. Rights Report Criticizes Allies in Antiterror Campaign," *New York Times,* March 5, 2002.

27. P. Jarreau, "Les Etats-Unis accusés de violer le droit de la guerre," *Le Monde,* January 23, 2002; "Agency Differs with U.S. Over P.O.W.'s," *New York Times,* February 9, 2002; H. Young, "We will not tolerate the abuse of war prisoners," *Guardian,* January 17, 2002.

28. C. Lesnes, "Des prisoniers afghans bénéficieront de la convention de Genève," *Le Monde,* February 9, 2002; K. Q. Seelye, "In Shift, Bush Says Geneva Rules Fit Taliban Captives," *New York Times,* February 8, 2002.

29. *Coalition of Clergy et al. v. George Walker Bush et al.,* 189 F. Supp. 2d (C.D. Cal., 2002); J. Bravin, "Judge Won't Hear Case of Prisoners Being Held in Cuba," *Wall Street Journal,* February 22, 2002.

30. "Unjust, Unwise, Un-American," *The Economist,* July 12, 2003, 9.

31. *Rasul v. Bush,* Slip Opinion 03–334, U.S. Supreme Court (June 28, 2004) and consolidated cases.

32. Amnesty International, *Report 2004* (2004) online: http://web.amnesty.org/report2004/usa-summary-eng (United States) (accessed August 31, 2004); "U.S. mulls release of more Guantanamo Bay detainees," *Guardian,* March 10, 2003, http://www.guardian.co.uk/alqaida/story/0,12469,911513,00.html (accessed June 11, 2003).

33. K. Q. Seelye, "Pentagon Raises Idea of Indefinite Detention," *International Herald Tribune,* March 22, 2002.

34. "U.S. mulls release of more Guantanamo Bay detainees."

35. K. Q. Seelye, "Rumsfeld Lists Outcomes for Detainees Held in Cuba," *New York Times,* February 27, 2002.

36. Seelye, "Pentagon Raises Idea of Indefinite Detention."

37. "U.S. halts terror court," *Gazette* (Montreal), July 19, 2003.

38. "A necessary evil?" *The Economist,* July 12, 2003, 26.

39. Ibid.

40. Anthony Lewis, "Captives and the Law," *New York Times,* January 26, 2002.

41. "President Announces Crackdown on Terrorist Financial Network," White House news release, November 7, 2001, http://www.whitehouse.gov/news/releases/2001/11/20011107–4.html (accessed May 16, 2002).

42. D. E. Sanger, "Bush, Focusing on Terrorism, Says Secure U.S. is Top Priority; In Speech, He Calls Iraq, Iran and North Korea 'an Axis of Evil,'" *New York Times,* January 30, 2002.

43. E. Bumiller, "Damage Control," *New York Times,* sec. 1, February 24, 2002.

44. R. F. Worth, "A Nation Defines Itself by Its Evil Enemies," *New York Times,* sec. 4, February 24, 2002.

45. Ibid.

46.   R. Falk, "A Just Response," *The Nation* 273/10 (October 8, 2001): 11.

47.   "Saddam Hussein's Arsenal of Propaganda," Fox News, April 17, 2003, http://www.foxnews.com/story/0,2933,83733,00.html (accessed June 18, 2003).

48.   S. P. Huntington, "The Clash of Civilizations?" *Foreign Affairs* 72, no. 3 (1993): 22.

49.   "Bush on Finding the Terrorists," *Washington Post,* September 13, 2001, http://www.washingtonpost.com/wp-srv/nation/transcripts/bushtext2_091301.html (accessed September 20, 2001).

50.   J. Simpson, "Next up: American Triumphalism," *Globe and Mail,* April 10, 2003; Minxin Pei, "The Paradoxes of American Nationalism," *Foreign Policy,* June 2003, http://www.foreignpolicy.com/story/story.php?storyID=13631# (accessed June 18, 2003).

51.   The White House, *The National Security Strategy of the United States of America,* September 2002, http://www.whitehouse.gov/nsc/nss.pdf (accessed June 8, 2003).

52.   "What the World Thinks of America."

53.   "In the Shadow of the Law."

54.   M. Abley, "The 'evil' around us," *Gazette* (Montreal), June 11, 2003.

55.   N. Schrijver, "Responding to International Terrorism: Moving the Frontiers of International Law for 'Enduring Freedom'?" *Netherlands International Law Review* 48 (2001): 271.

56.   "Iraq: Denial and Deception," White House news release, February 31, 2003, http://www.whitehouse.gov/news/releases/2003/02/20030213-4.html (accessed June 16, 2003).

57.   "Tony Bliar?" *The Economist,* June 7, 2003, 10.

58.   "Deputy Secretary Wolfowitz Interview with Sam Tannenhaus, Vanity Fair" *DefenseLINK* (May 9, 2003), http://www.dod.gov/transcripts/2003/tr20030509-depsecdef0223.html (accessed June 13, 2003).

59.   Peter Slevin, "Legality of War Is A Matter of Debate—Many Scholars Doubt Assertion by Bush," *Washington Post,* March 18, 2003, http://www.commondreams.org/headlines03/0318-05.htm (accessed June 3, 2003).

60.   Martha Finnemore, *National Interests in International Society* (Ithaca, N.Y.: Cornell University Press, 1996), 24–28, 137–39.

61.   M. Byers, "Preemptive Self-defense: Hegemony, Equality and Strategies of Legal Change," *Journal of Political Philosophy* 11/2, (2003): 171–90, 180.

62.   *Case Concerning Military and Paramilitary Activities in and against Nicaragua (Nicaragua v. United States): Merits,* [1986] I.C.J.R. 14.

63.   R. Y. Jennings, "The Caroline and McLeod Cases," *American Journal of International Law* 32 (1938): 82–99.

64.   Thomas M. Franck, "Terrorism and the Right of Self-Defense," *American Journal of International Law* 95 (2001): 839–43.

65.   Jonathan I. Charney, "The Use of Force against Terrorism and International Law," *American Journal of International Law* 95 (2001): 835–39.

66.   House of Commons, Select Committee on Defense, "The Air Campaign: Targeting Policy," *Fourteenth Report,* October 23, 2000, http://www.parliament.the-stationery-office.co.uk/pa/cm199900/cmselect/cmdefense/347/34711.htm#a23 (accessed June 18, 2003).

67. *The National Security Strategy of the United States of America.*

68. "Remarks by President George Bush to Troops and Families of the 10th Mountain Division, Fort Drum, New York," White House news release, July 19, 2002, http://www.whitehouse.gov/news/releases/2002/07/20020719.html (accessed July 21, 2002).

69. "War would be illegal," *Guardian,* March 7, 2003, http://education.guardian.co.uk/higher/news/story/0,9830,909467,00.html (accessed March 11, 2003).

70. "Howard must not involve us in an illegal war," *The Age,* February 26, 2003, http://www.theage.com.au/articles/2003/02/25/1046064031296.html (accessed March 11, 2003); "Military Action in Iraq Without Security Council Authorization Would be Illegal" (open letter signed by thirty-one Canadian professors of international law), March 17, 2003, www.sdiq.org (accessed June 18, 2003); J. Sallot, "Legal experts say attack on Iraq is illegal," *Globe and Mail,* March 20, 2003; Slevin, "Legality of War Is A Matter of Debate."

71. J. Brunnée, "The Use of Force Against Iraq: A Legal Assessment," *Behind the Headlines* 59/4 (2002): 1.

72. John D. Negroponte, letter of the Permanent Representative of the United States of America to the United Nations to the President of the United Nations Security Council, March 20, 2003, UN Doc. S/2003/351.

73. Abram Chayes, *The Cuban Missile Crisis* (New York: Oxford University Press, 1974).

74. W. Taft IV, "Memorandum: The Legal Basis for Preemption," November 18, 2002, http://www.cfr.org/publication.php?id=5250 (accessed January 12, 2003).

75. W. Taft IV, Panel on "The Bush Administration Preemption Doctrine and the Future of World Order," American Society of International Law Annual Meeting, April 3, 2004 (notes on file with the author).

76. D. Milbank, "War in Iraq Was 'Right Decision,' Bush Says," *Washington Post,* June 10, 2003.

77. United Kingdom, "Iraq's Weapons of Mass Destruction—The assessment of the British Government," September 24, 2002, http://www.pm.gov.uk/output/Page271.asp (accessed June 16, 2003).

78. A. Freeman, "Blair's Iraq Dossier Gets Cool Reception from Allies," *Globe and Mail,* September 25, 2002.

79. "Artificial intelligence?" *The Economist,* July 12, 2003, 12.

80. J. Morley, "Blair Takes a Beating on the Weapons of Mass Destruction," *washingtonpost.com,* June 4, 2003, http://www.washingtonpost.com/ac2/wp-dyn/A11950-2003Jun4?language=printer (accessed June 6, 2003).

81. K. Sengupta and A. McSmith, "Spies threaten Blair with 'smoking gun' over Iraq," *The Independent,* June 8, 2003, http://news/independent.co.uk/uk/politics/story.jsp?story=413481 (accessed June 12, 2003).

82. W. Pincus and D. Priest, "Some Iraq Analysts Felt Pressure From Cheney Visits," *Washington Post,* June 5, 2003.

83. D. Milbank, "War in Iraq Was 'Right Decision,' Bush Says."

84. "President Bush Addresses the Nation," White House news release, March 19, 2003, http://www.whitehouse.gov/news/releases/2003/03/20030319-17.html (accessed June 16, 2003).

85. Ed Morgan, "Use of force against Iraq is legal," *National Post,* March 19, 2003.

86. The White House, "Operation Iraqi Freedom," news release, April 5, 2003, http://www.whitehouse.gov/news/releases/2003/04/20030405.html (accessed June 12, 2003).

87. Tony Blair, speech to Congress, July 18, 2003, http://www.pm.gov.uk/output/Page4220.asp (accessed July 21, 2003).

88. N. Krisch, "Legality, Morality and the Dilemma of Humanitarian Intervention After Kosovo," *European Journal of International Law* 13 (2002): 323.

89. Brunnée, "The Use of Force Against Iraq."

90. Negroponte, Letter of the Permanent Representative; "The Written Answer of the Attorney General, Lord Goldsmith, to a Parliamentary Question on the legal basis for the use of force in Iraq," March 17, 2003, http://www.britain-in-switzerland.ch/news/legal_use_of_force_doc.pdf (accessed June 16, 2003).

91. "Memorandum of Advice on the Use of Force Against Iraq, provided by the Attorney General's Department and the Department of Foreign Affairs and Trade, 18 March, 2003," http://www.pm.gov.au/iraq/displayNewsContent.cfm?refx=96 (accessed June 16, 2003).

92. "War would be illegal."

93. Brunnée, "The Use of Force Against Iraq."

94. "The Legal Arguments: Pro, con and muddled," *The Economist*, March 22, 2003, 25.

95. C. Swords, "Remarks for Luncheon Address to the Canadian Bar Association (CBA) Conference on International Law, Ottawa" (June 5, 2003), on file with the author.

96. K. Q. Seelye, "In Letter, 300 Law Professors Oppose Tribunals Plan," *New York Times*, December 8, 2001.

97. Eric Foner, "The Most Patriotic Act," *The Nation* 273, no. 10 (October 8, 2001): 13.

98. Ontario Chief Justice Roy McMurtry, quoted in S. Kari, "Don't be swayed by Sept. 11 issues, courts warned," *National Post*, January 8, 2002.

Contributors

miriam cooke is Professor of Modern Arabic Literature and Culture at Duke University. Her books include *Women and the War Story* (1997), *Hayati, My Life: A Novel* (2000), and, most recently, *Women Claim Islam: Creating Islamic Feminism through Literature* (2001).

Sohail H. Hashmi is Associate Professor of International Relations at Mount Holyoke College. His recent publications include two edited volumes: *Islamic Political Ethics: Civil Society, Pluralism, and Conflict* (2002) and *Ethics and Weapons of Mass Destruction: Religious and Secular Perspectives* (2004).

Henry Jenkins is Professor of Literature and director of the Comparative Media Studies Program at MIT. His books include *Textual Poachers: Television Fans and Participatory Culture* (1992) and, as co-editor, *From Barbie to Mortal Kombat: Gender and Computer Games* (1998). His next book, *Convergence Culture*, deals with the intersection between old and new media and will appear in 2005. His column, *The Digital Renaissance*, in *Technology Review*, explores the social and cultural dimensions of media change.

Laura Kurgan is an architect and artist whose work explores the interfaces between building, electronic media, and information technologies. She has a design practice in New York City, has taught at Princeton University, and since 2004 has been Adjunct Assistant Professor of Architecture at the Graduate School of Architecture, Planning and Preservation, Columbia University.

Susan Lurie is Associate Professor of English and Associate Dean for Graduate Studies at Rice University. She is author of *Unsettled Subjects: Restoring Feminist Politics to Poststructuralist Critique* (1997). Her current research concerns identity formation and agency in twentieth- and twenty-first-century U.S. literature and culture.

Patricia A. Morton is chair of the Art History Department and director of the Culver Center of the Arts at the University of California, Riverside. She is author of *Hybrid Modernities: Architecture and Representation at the 1931 Colonial Exposition, Paris* (2000) and of articles on Le Corbusier and the American architect Charles Moore, among others. Her current research focuses on popular culture, architecture, and the critique of good taste in the 1960s.

Terry Nardin is University of Wisconsin–Milwaukee Distinguished Professor of Political Science. He is author or editor of several books on the political theory of international relations. His most recent book is *The Philosophy of Michael Oakeshott* (2001), and, as co-editor, *Humanitarian Intervention* (2005).

Kirk Savage is Associate Professor of Art History at the University of Pittsburgh. He is author of *Standing Soldiers, Kneeling Slaves: Race, War, and Monument in Nineteenth-Century America* (1997). He is currently at work on a book about the history of monuments in Washington, D.C.

Elaine Scarry is Walter M. Cabot Professor of Aesthetics and the General Theory of Value, Department of English, Harvard University. Her books include *The Body in Pain: The Making and Unmaking of the World* (1985), *On Beauty and Being Just* (1999), and *Dreaming by the Book* (2001).

William E. Scheuerman is Professor of Political Science at the University of Minnesota, Twin Cities. He is author of several books on the fate of liberal democratic institutions in a period of rapid change, including, most recently, *Liberal Democracy and the Social Acceleration of Time* (2004).

Daniel J. Sherman is Professor of History and director of the Center for 21st Century Studies, University of Wisconsin–Milwaukee. He is author, most recently, of *The Construction of Memory in Interwar France* (1999). He is currently working on the cultural politics of primitivism in France, 1945–1975.

Stephen J. Toope is president of the Pierre Elliott Trudeau Foundation, on leave from McGill University, where he is Professor of Law and was formerly Dean of the Faculty of Law. He is author of many articles on international law and human rights, has conducted human rights seminars for government officials in Canada, Malaysia, Singapore, and Indonesia, and is chair and rapporteur of the U.N. Working Group on Enforced or Involuntary Disappearances.

Index

International Court of Justice, 247, 248
international law. *See* law, international
Iran, 174, 243
Iran-Contra affair, 233n34
Iraq, 153, 216, 243, 244, 245, 249; 1991 uprising, 171, 175; regime change, 251; sanctions against, 154. *See also* Hussein, Saddam
Islam, 150; early development of, 150–151; and feminism, 165–167; laws of war, 151
Israel-Palestinian conflict, 177–178, 241; as al-Qaida grievance, 153–154, 156, 158, 159

Jane's World Armies, 250
Jefferson, Lisa, 193–195
Jemas, Bill, 97
jihad, 6, 11; al-Qaida interpretation of, 149–150, 163; in apartheid South Africa, 172; defensive v. expansionist, 151–152; recent Muslim understandings of, 155; as obligation for Muslims, 168–169; sole preserve for men, 169; tradition of, 149–164; and women, 165–183
jingoism, 8
Junod, Tom, 61–62
Jurgens, Dan, 82
Justice Department, 188, 189, 191, 209, 214

Kakutani, Michiko, 124
Karbala, battle of (680 C.E.), 161, 168, 174
Kaseman Beckman Amsterdam Studio: Pentagon memorial, 131
Kennedy, John F., administration, 250
Khadija (wife of Muhammad), 167
Khomeini, Ruhollah, 174
Kimmelman, Michael, 131
Kirby, Jack, 81
Koolhaas, Rem, 22–23, 27; *Delirious New York*, 23

Kordey, Igor, 89–91
Kosovo: NATO intervention, 156, 249, 252
Kristol, William, 236
Krugman, Paul, 219
Kushner, Tony, 97

Laden, Osama bin, 5, 86, 149, 152, 154, 155, 157, 162, 239; alleged links to Saddam Hussein, 198, 219, 250; defending actions, 154, 158–160
Langley Air Force Base, Virginia, 189, 207
law, 3, 5, 10, 11; international, 224, 238, 244, 247, 249, 252–253; rule of, 3–4; suspension of, 10
Law and Order, 1
Layla Bint Tarif, 168, 173
Lebanon, 161, 166, 175; city of Beirut, 16
Lefebvre, Henri, 136
Levitz, Paul, 75
Lewis, Anthony, 242
liberty, 6, 10. *See also* freedom
Libeskind, Daniel, 27, 28, 116, 133
Lin, Maya, 115, 138. *See also* monuments; Vietnam Veterans Memorial
Lincoln, Abraham, 124
Lindh, John Walker, 241
Lipton, Eric, and James Glanz, 26–27, 135
literature, 5
Locke, John, 216–220; *Second Treatise*, 227
Los Angeles, 186
Los Angeles Times, 38
Lower Manhattan Development Corporation. *See* Manhattan
Lutyens, Sir Edwin, 105, 106, 108
Lydes, CeeCee, 193–195

Machiavelli, Niccolo, 216–217, 220; *Discourses*, 216
Manhattan, 9, 21, 22, 23, 25, 27; Cen-